# Reordering the World

# REORDERING THE WORLD

*Geopolitical Perspectives on the Twenty-first Century*

*edited by*

## George J. Demko
*Dartmouth College*

## and William B. Wood
*Office of the Geographer*
*U.S. Department of State*

**Westview Press**
*Boulder • San Francisco • Oxford*

William B. Wood, the Geographer for the United States Government Department of State, is the co-author of the introductory chapter and preface of this book. The views and opinions expressed there are his and do not necessarily reflect those of the U.S. Government. For the other articles in this book, he served as the co-editor on technical matters of punctuation, spelling, and the like. The content of those other chapters is the sole responsibility of their respective authors.

Published in 1994 in the United States of America by Westview Press, Inc., 5500 Central Avenue, Boulder, Colorado 80301-2877, and in the United Kingdom by Westview Press, 36 Lonsdale Road, Summertown, Oxford OX2 7EW


Library of Congress Cataloging-in-Publication Data
Reordering the world : geopolitical perspectives on the twenty-first
   century / edited by George J. Demko and William B. Wood.
      p.   cm.
   Includes bibliographical references and index.
   ISBN 0-8133-1726-6. — ISBN 0-8133-1727-4 (pbk.)
   1. Geopolitics.   2. Political geography.   3. International
relations.   I. Demko, George J., 1933–      .   II. Wood, William B.,
1956–      .
JC319.R38   1994
327.1'01—dc20                                                                94-976
                                                                                 CIP


Printed and bound in the United States of America

 The paper used in this publication meets the requirements of the American National Standard for Permanence of Paper for Printed Library Materials Z39.48-1984.

10     9     8     7     6     5     4     3     2     1

# Contents

*Preface*                                                                VII

## PART ONE
### Recurring Issues and Problems

1  Introduction: International Relations Through the Prism of
   Geography, GEORGE J. DEMKO AND WILLIAM B. WOOD          3

2  Geopolitics in the New World Era: A New Perspective on an
   Old Discipline, SAUL B. COHEN                           15

3  The Power and Politics of Maps, ALAN K. HENRIKSON       49

4  People Together, Yet Apart: Rethinking Territory, Sovereignty, and
   Identities, DAVID B. KNIGHT                             71

5  International Boundaries: Lines in the Sand (and the Sea),
   BRADFORD L. THOMAS                                      87

6  Electoral Geography and Gerrymandering: Space and Politics,
   RICHARD MORRILL                                         101

## PART TWO
### Resources, the Environment, and Population

7  Exploiting, Conserving, and Preserving Natural Resources,
   SUSAN L. CUTTER                                         123

8  Global Environmental Hazards: Political Issues in Societal Responses,
   ROGER E. KASPERSON                                      141

9  Global Ecopolitics, PHYLLIS MOFSON                      167

10 Population, Politics, and Geography: A Global Perspective,
   GEORGE J. DEMKO                                         179

11 Crossing the Line: Geopolitics of International Migration,
   WILLIAM B. WOOD                                         191

# PART THREE
## Changing International Processes and Relations

12  International Law and the Sovereign State: Challenges
    to the Status Quo, ALEXANDER B. MURPHY                          209

13  The Fourth World: Nations Versus States, BERNARD NIETSCHMANN    225

14  The United Nations and NGOs: Future Roles, CHRISTINE DRAKE      243

15  Global Hegemony Versus National Economy: The United States
    in the New World Order, JOHN AGNEW                             269

16  Maximizing Entropy? New Geopolitical Orders and the
    Internationalization of Business, STUART CORBRIDGE             281

17  Geopolitical Information and Communication in Shrinking and
    Expanding Worlds: 1900–2100, STANLEY D. BRUNN AND
    JEFFERY A. JONES                                               301


    *Selected References*                                          323
    *About the Book and Editors*                                   331
    *About the Contributors*                                       333
    *Index*                                                        335

# Preface

WHILE TEACHING a class together in the mid-1980s, we grumbled about the lack of an adequate "political geography volume" that would introduce students to major issues in the rapidly changing realm of international relations. Working in the U.S. Department of State provided us with a unique perspective on a wide range of foreign policy concerns and real-world experiences. We observed that many of the new "global issues" were inherently geographic or had significant geographic dimensions. Our careers have since diverged, but we maintain the firm belief that political geographic analyses of current international issues—now more than ever—can provide both useful insight for policy-makers and an exciting area of research and discussion for students and scholars.

This book is our attempt to meet the demands of a growing audience for political geography. It was designed to supplement and enrich rather than substitute for traditional political geography textbooks and recent theoretical approaches to geopolitics. Each chapter in our volume, however, can stand alone. The focus here is on the application of political geographic ideas, concepts, and perspectives to a broad range of current international issues: global environmental change, territorial nationalism, conflict over natural resources, population growth and migration, international organizations and laws, and new worlds of multinational economics and telecommunications. We have not attempted to be comprehensive in either the range of topics or the treatment of each subject. Instead, each chapter in this book is deliberately focused to serve as an introduction to an issue or set of related issues about which much more can and should be written.

We are very pleased that some of the geography discipline's leading and innovative scholars have joined us, using their chapters to explain their research interests to a new audience. As in all social and physical sciences, each subfield in geography has developed its own jargon and assumptions that serve as the foundation for dialogue. We asked all contributors to minimize the more abstract or technical aspects of their topics and address their chapters, as much as possible, to an audience of educated lay persons or advanced geography and nongeography students. We think they have succeeded.

The book is divided into three parts. The first covers recurring themes in political geography over the past century and how they are changing. These include such topics as geopolitical theory, boundaries, sovereignty, and nationalism. The second part addresses the linkage between societies and their environments, an old area of geographic research that has been given renewed impetus by worldwide "ecopolitics" and growing perceptions of global environmental degradation. The final part provides an overview of new arenas in geopolitical research that link transnational changes in legal, institutional, technological, and economic relationships. Some of the chapters are historical and empirical; others are future-oriented and speculative. But all are grounded in such geographic themes as the recognition of spatial patterns; the development of regions; the spatial diffusion of ideas, technology, capital, and people; and, most fundamental of all, the dynamic relationships between people and their environments.

A review of the complete set of chapters in this volume does produce some important, overarching generalizations or conclusions. First, the discipline of geography is applied here in its most varied and sophisticated sense. The "geographic" approaches employed range from the analysis of spatial relations and processes among places over the globe to the assessment of issues at various regional scales, from local to global, and they demonstrate the importance of examining societal-environmental interactions. A second significant generalization is clear: The traditional concept of state "sovereignty" is being seriously challenged by new events, processes, and relations. Relatively new and important global actors have emerged to challenge states, including intergovernmental organizations, non-governmental organizations, and even incipient suprastates. Additionally, the globalization of almost everything has altered concepts of governance and compelled scholars and others to cross disciplinary lines to understand the complexity of contemporary relations. Related to this, of course, is the impact of economic processes as a powerful set of global forces. Thus, geography and politics are joined by economics to transform "geopolitics" to "geopolinomics." And finally, new issues have arrived on our global agenda—the relative availability of weapons of mass destruction, near-instantaneous electronic communications, environmental crises, demographic pressures of many kinds, and desperately aggressive "peoples" without states, to name a few—that demand new approaches and creative management, if not solutions.

The twenty-first century will be an extraordinary time for those of us fascinated by the ways in which people organize themselves to deal with change. In the past few years, we have been on a geopolitical roller coaster: We have plunged from the euphoria of a crumbling Berlin Wall to the numbing cruelty of ethnic cleansing in the Balkans; we have risen from the pessimism of ozone depletion to the optimism of the Rio Conference on Environment and Development; and we continue to ride between the highs of the international community's growing commitment to human rights and the lows of entrenched poverty and civil war in far too many countries. This volume cannot provide any assurances of where this global roller-coaster ride will lead. It does, however, offer some insights into the workings of geopolitics, and it explains some of the vistas we may see over the twentieth-century horizon.

*George J. Demko*
*Dartmouth College*

*William B. Wood*
*U.S. Department of State*

# PART ONE

## Recurring Issues and Problems

# O N E

## Introduction:
## International Relations
## Through the Prism of Geography

GEORGE J. DEMKO & WILLIAM B. WOOD

### Political Geography—A Century of Change

THE ART AND SCIENCE of understanding and predicting spatial aspects of the shifts in political power among groups, particularly states, began in a formal sense about 100 years ago. As empires and states vied for shares of international power, generalizations about these political and military processes were enunciated by the first modern geopoliticians. The ideas of such political geographers as Rudolf Kjellen, Friedrich Ratzel, and especially Sir Halford Mackinder contributed to a growing body of generalizations that attempted to explain the complex patterns of international political relationships. As technology developed in the first half of the twentieth century—especially in the transport, communication, and military sectors—age-old constraints of space, distance, and location were radically altered. New global models evolved by geopoliticians like Nicholas John Spykman, Alfred Thayer Mahan, and Alexander de Seversky altered the roles of space and accessibility as they introduced global military strategies that were influenced by new innovations in ocean and air travel and weaponry. A major setback in the study of geopolitics, however, occurred with the adoption of selected geopolitical ideas by the Nazi regime in Germany. The Nazis justified their ruthlessly expansionist policies by distorting geopolitical theories, which cast a shadow over the discipline of political geography for several decades. A century after the first modern geopolitical theories, we again must ask whether political geography provides any insight into current international issues. The authors of the chapters in this volume answer the question with an emphatic "yes!" and verify their contention with numerous examples taken from their own research.

Many topics in today's headlines—stemming from the creation and dissolution of countries; the impact of environmental change on societies; territorial, resource, and ethnic conflicts; and spatial disparities in food production and distribution—have been long debated and analyzed by geographers. In this book, geographers of several generations address a broad range of pressing international issues. Though quite different in substance and style, each chapter demonstrates the importance of a geographical perspective and the role of geography, particularly the reinvigorated subfield of political geography, as an integrative science. This geographic approach to real-world policy-making and problem-solving, grounded in the physical and social sciences, is finally coming of age. This book is directed to the next generation of geographers who, we trust, will be at the forefront of an interdisciplinary effort toward greater international cooperation.

A few professional geographers worked in the area of geopolitics in the post–World War II period but shied away from such Nazi-tainted terminology as *geopolitics*. Political scientists and policy-makers involved in international relations did, however, gradually adopt many of the terms and approaches developed by earlier political geographers.[1] By the end of the 1980s, geography was challenged by fresh political, economic, and social paradigms, which, in turn, stimulated a renewed interest in political geography. This renaissance is detectable in many new books and research articles as well as in the plethora of conferences and symposia on political geography.

Internationally oriented research in political geography was greatly stimulated by the ending of the Cold War, the injection of radical theoretical approaches in spatial analysis, and the increasingly important role of political players other than sovereign states on the world scene. The growth of intergovernmental organizations, or IGOs (e.g., the United Nations and the Council of Europe), nongovernmental organizations, or NGOs (e.g., multinational corporations, and international environmental organizations), and integrating suprastates (e.g., the European Community) is altering the international balance of power and challenging the once unquestioned sanctity of state sovereignty in areas ranging from environmental protection to human rights. These developments call for a fresh political-geographic perspective on international relations, grounded not in ideology but in the realistic analyses of the many complex dilemmas we must better understand and try to resolve or at least manage.

One primary thesis underlies all chapters in this book—international relations are inherently geographic; that is, much of the behavior of actors in the international arena is tied to spatial relations. Both geography and political science are primarily concerned with the processes of political change—of which there is an abundance these days. The focus in this volume, however, is on the spatial processes that have dominated the thinking of political geographers from the beginning. The geographic ideas of two early theorists in modern political geography, Ratzel and Mackinder, still provide important insights into international political processes.

## Ratzel and Mackinder

The linkage between modern geography and political science originated almost a century ago, at the beginning of modern political-geographic theory. At that time, Western powers ruled vast colonial empires and had enormous influence over less powerful states and territories. In 1897, German natural scientist Friedrich Ratzel published *Politische Geographie,* in which he tried to provide a systematic framework for spatial political data. Trained in biology, he was influenced by Charles Darwin's *Origin of The Species.* In his "organic theory," Ratzel argued that a state was like an organism attached to the earth that competed with other states; to thrive, like all organisms, it needed lebensraum—living space.

The other early legend in political geography, Sir Halford Mackinder, was a member of the British Parliament who wrote "The Geographic Pivot of History" in 1904. He was interested in "political motion" and observed that the spatial distribution of strategic opportunities in the world was unequal. He also believed that technology was forcing a reevaluation of spatial concepts and, consequently, military strategies. Until the end of the nineteenth century, sea power was supreme—the sovereign who ruled the waves ruled the world—and Queen Victoria's rule of the seas allowed her to control an empire over which the sun never set. But by then, railroads were making it possible to move large armies quickly over vast land areas. Would this product of the industrial revolution shift the focus of warfare from the sea to the hinterland? Mackinder thought so and wanted his government, which had achieved glory as a sea power, to be prepared for the rise of a land-based power, notably Germany. His famous "heartland theory," written for those signing the Treaty of Versailles in 1919, claimed that the power that ruled Eastern Europe commanded the "heartland," the power commanding the heartland would rule the "world island," and, of course, the power ruling the world island would rule the world. For the time, this was an interesting insight, even if it has since been rendered obsolete by the introduction of yet more remarkable new technologies (e.g., intercontinental ballistic missiles). With the U.S.-Russian agreement on significantly reducing land-based missile arsenals—START II, concluded in December 1992—perhaps military strategy will once again focus on more conventional warfare concerns, such as those addressed by Mackinder.

The ideas of both Ratzel and Mackinder have been modified greatly by scholars who came after them, and many contemporary geographers and other social scientists have been influenced by more recent works that have employed some of Ratzel's and Mackinder's concepts. For example, George Kennan's containment theory (drafted in the late 1940s) helped define the U.S. Cold War strategy for keeping the former Soviet Union confined within the heartland. Kennan's intent was to develop a strategy to contain Soviet economic and political influence. This diplomatic focus was transformed into an active military geostrategy to keep Communism from taking over the world island—and forty-five years of battles around the rimland (Korea, Vietnam, Greece) were waged to keep it from doing so.

Similarly, Ratzel's work influenced a school of military geographers under Adolph Hitler and gave a bad name to the word *geopolitics.* Many geographers have avoided this term since it was used by German geographer General Karl von Haushofer, a nationalist who was anxious to avenge Germany's post–World War I humiliations and rebuild the German empire. His advocacy of military power to promote economic self-sufficiency was used by the Nazis as a quasi-scientific justification for territorial expansion—the logical extension of Ratzel's organic theory that the strongest state survives by capturing key resources, occupying strategic locations, and controlling larger populations that can be used as cheap industrial labor.

Despite all that has happened over the globe during the past century, we are still grappling with many of the same issues addressed by Ratzel and Mackinder—how do states evolve, survive, expand, and achieve economic and political dominance? For example, Paul Kennedy, in *The Rise and Fall of Great Powers*, essentially examines the same processes of change but on a scale that encompasses continents and several centuries of time. If anything, we have become more comfortable about thinking on a global level, but this can lead to dangerous overgeneralizations unless we first look at processes at the regional and local levels.

## Heartland Revisited

On September 12, 1990, the four World War II Allied powers signed the Treaty on the Final Settlement with Respect to Germany, thereby giving up their occupational rights 45 years after the end of the war. On October 3, 1990, the German Democratic Republic and the Federal Republic of Germany effectively united— almost 120 years after the Versailles Treaty of 1871, creating a unified Germany for the first time. Germany still grapples with the complex dilemma of being a union of two very different political and economic systems, held together by an underlying but split German nationalism. The German experience is, in some ways, a precedent for the whole of Europe as it stands poised on the edge of a bold economic and political experiment to create an integrated European Community. A new and united Europe, though still far from realized, will clearly have unprecedented global impacts, particularly in terms of international trade and migration.

In the former Soviet Union, one of the last modern empires has been disassembled. Since the fifteenth century, Moscow had been at the center of a widening circle of political centralization. But between November 1988 and December 1991, all former Soviet republics made the transition to internationally recognized sovereign states. Today, their relationships with each other and with other states, particularly in Europe, are being redefined politically and economically— a radical creation of new geographies that will keep tensions high in the region for many more years.

Recent events in the former Soviet Union and former Yugoslavia are testimony to the powerful forces of ethnic identification and raw nationalism. Until recently, however, issues such as ethnicity and nationalism were ignored by most political scientists, who were more concerned with ideological debates and abstract theories. Nationalism—although often ambiguously defined—has proven to be enduring because its appeal is more emotional than intellectual. It is strongly entwined with ideas about territory, legends of past heroics, and real or perceived injustices. If Mikhail Gorbachev had remained in power, he would have needed much more knowledge about the cultural and political geography of the old Soviet empire than about the works of Vladimir Lenin. His removal of the traditional Soviet powers of coercion unleashed long-suppressed nationalisms that still wrack the former empire. Similar nationalism-based violence—concentrated on a smaller area—has erupted in the newly fragmented and pillaged states of Bosnia and Herzegovina, where over 1.5 million people have been uprooted from their homes.

## Iraq's Drive for Lebensraum

Shifting the geographic pivot from the complex and yet fundamental changes under way in Mackinder's heartland to the military tensions in the Middle East, political geography once again comes into play. The same "geopolitik" logic that Haushofer advocated to the Nazis may be seen in Saddam Hussein's frustrated desire to ensure Iraq's position as the premier Arab power.

Iraq, just like one of Ratzel's competing organisms, attempted to assert its economic dominance by grabbing a vital resource, oil, from a weak neighbor, Kuwait. Iraq's lebensraum and control over vital oil reserves would have been considerably enhanced by taking over Kuwait, a small but strategic territory that could have improved Iraq's access to the Persian Gulf. Iraq's lack of good maritime access was considered by its leaders as a strategic Achilles' heel. After all, it spent almost a decade fighting Iran over the right to control the Shatt al-Arab waterway, which, until 1980, served as its main shipping route. Iraq also used the invasion to once again voice its self-proclaimed role as the premier nation of the beleaguered Arab masses, standing against both monarchies deemed undeserving of the oil wealth and Western, non-Moslem powers that were viewed as attempting to quash Arab nationalism. The division in the Arab realm between the haves and the have-nots represents a broader north-south schism that will likely prove far more enduring than the seventy-year-old east-west dichotomy.

Iraq—and the former Yugoslavia—are products of the division of the Ottoman Empire. Iraq was created in 1932 as a League of Nations mandate, under British supervision. Like the Iraq-Kuwait boundary, most colonial boundaries were created rather arbitrarily. The international community, however, has continually insisted that any disagreements over boundaries should be negotiated, not decided militarily. If Iraq had been allowed to unilaterally expand its territory because of an allegedly unfair boundary drawn up many decades ago, would any small country be safe? The universal condemnation of Iraq's actions may be understood better if it is remembered that an increasing number of UN members are also small states—Estonia, Latvia, Lithuania, Brunei, and even tiny San Marino. In the 1990s, the UN will probably play increasingly powerful roles in advocating the rights of its smaller and weaker states; in arbitrating boundary, territorial, and resource disputes between members; and even in intervening within states to protect persecuted or endangered groups. Regional international political organizations are also playing key roles in attempting to preserve peace and stability in disputes that were once considered bilateral. The UN's active participation in enforcing sanctions against Iraq and Serbia and the many peace-keeping forces deployed around the world testify to the expanded role of IGOs in international relations.

If Iraq had kept control of Kuwait's oil, it would have become an even more powerful oil producer; with military intimidation of other states in the region, Iraq might have been able to coerce acceptance of its policies on oil production and price-setting. It also would have gained a greater influence over poor countries such as Egypt, India, Pakistan, Sri Lanka, and the Philippines that were dependent not only upon Iraqi oil but also upon remittances from their nationals working in Iraq and Kuwait. Over 850,000 guest workers bore the brunt of political instability in the oil-based economies that brought them to the Persian Gulf and then discarded them. Displaced and unemployed gulf workers underscore the growing economic interdependence among far-flung countries brought about by oil and the powerful economic forces that direct the movements of international migrants, many of whom come from labor-surplus countries.

## New Political-Geographic Perspectives

Recent eruptions of conflict in the Middle East and tumultuous changes in Eastern Europe and the former USSR have taught us that we are all part of a closely interconnected but poorly integrated world that is undergoing rapid change. In the Middle East, the interdependence that once provided cheap oil—a major driving force in U.S. economic development over the past century—also involved the United States and other non–Middle East states deeply and quickly in a regional dispute far removed from home shores. In Eastern and Central Europe and the former Soviet Union, global economic interdependence forced political leaders to accept basic market principles to guide their economic development; many are trying to adjust quickly, despite very unpopular consequences. The proposed transition toward individual ownership of property, decentralized economic decision-making, and foreign investment is truly revolutionary. But revolutions are unpredictable and volatile.

From the perspective of political geography, today's headlines are the product of socioeconomic, ecological, and political forces and variables that have been slighted by the social sciences in the past: ethnicity, territoriality, boundaries, nationalism, natural resources, environmental quality, population growth and distribution, migration, and the growing interdependence and inequity among world regions and their economies. Geographers can make a unique contribution by focusing attention on these new challenges to national and international security.

Political geography examines how societies make decisions that affect the relationships between people and their environment, as well as the spatial patterns of human settlement. Modern political geography encompasses many theoretical perspectives—from conservative to Marxist—but political geographers, like all geographers, are involved in the fundamental quest to explain the linkages between people and evolving environments. To political geographers, the term *people* might include individuals, social institutions, and national governments, and *environment* is often redefined with each new problem. Environments might include natural ecosystems, vital resource systems (such as clean water, fertile soils, and fossil fuels), human-created features (such as cities and agricultural systems), and even decision-making milieus (cultural regions, political systems, local real estate markets, and international trade networks).

Political geography can be viewed at five general levels in which people make decisions that modify their environments. At the micro level, individuals and families must make decisions about earning and spending income, providing shelter, protecting health, and mobilizing to improve life-styles. Increasingly, geographers examine household economics for indications of broader developmental trends. At the local level, where concerns that affect a community's immediate well-being evolve, competing groups may clash over resource uses— usually involving property rights—such as decisions on where to locate a shopping center or a landfill or whether to close a factory. Local resource decisions of this type may have profound impacts on one area but be of little consequence elsewhere. Another political-geographic interest at the local level is the organization of voting districts. Gerrymandering—the manipulation of electoral district boundaries—has long been used to ensure that the wiliest political party wins the most electoral seats.

At the next level, the subnational, similar issues may link people several hundred miles apart, perhaps in a distant state. One example is the conflict among coal-producing states, coal-consuming states, and those affected by acid rain. (In some areas, the spatial scale may make this an international process—as in Europe, where states are small and numerous.) Subnational processes are also evident in the results of the 1990 U.S. census, which showed that some states gained population and some lost, thereby redistributing the number of congressional seats and affecting federal funding levels.

At the national level, competing demands among special interests, which are often concentrated in key subnational areas, complicate political activities. National governments pass and implement laws that, in many ways, define who citizens are (e.g., recent U.S. and European immigration reforms), how all residents live (a new national budget), or the relationship of a population with the physical environment (e.g., the U.S. Clean Air Act). National governments, by virtue of their recognized sovereign control over people in a defined territory, form the traditional building blocks of international relations, and thus states often become the overwhelming focus of political study.

The chapters in this book focus on the highest level in the hierarchy, the international arena, which encompasses all current sovereign states and several territories and miscellaneous spaces in between—such as the Vatican, the oceans, and Antarctica. One lesson learned over the last few years is that the number of sovereign countries in the world is not static—the world gained several new states with the breakup of the Soviet Union into independent countries and lost two through the unification of Germany and the Yemens—and more changes are likely. Although states are still the major actors in the world, IGOs and myriad NGOs are playing increasingly influential supporting roles. The chapters here are deliberately focused on issues and problems that transcend any one country or organization.

The Gulf Crisis perhaps heralded the end of traditional geopolitics and its replacement with geopolinomics, which adds economics into the old equation. Oil consumption in the world, for example, is projected to increase by about 10 percent to over 70 million barrels per day by the year 2000. The fastest growth will be in Asia, but oil imports are also predicted to rise in the United States. The Middle East has about two-thirds of the world's known reserves, and by the end of the decade, the Persian Gulf may account for about 30 percent of all oil production. The international community will have to take a very hard look at the new geopolinomics.

## A Geopolinomic World

In *The Work of Nations*, Robert Reich emphasizes the shift in the locational dimension of international economics. He speaks of "composite products," such as microprocessors with chips made in Korea, designed in California, and financed in Japan and Germany. He argues that economic locational decisions will depend on where the best and most appropriate labor is found or where the greatest returns will accrue without regard for national boundaries.[2] International financial networks and intracorporate trade and investment patterns will, to a large extent, redraw the economic map of the world. On this map, places may have less geostrategic significance than telecommunication channels.

Today's headlines touch on a broad spectrum of political-economic-geographic topics: the creation and dissolution of sovereign states, the resurgence of nationalism, the overdependence on oil, the indebtedness of states, environmental politics, the persistence of old territorial claims, and the growing role of international organizations. In whatever directions Mackinder's heartland or Ratzel's lebensraum take the international community in the next decade, a new generation of political geographers must provide some guidance through the changing geopolinomic world map.

It is already obvious that many of the international processes discussed earlier and focused upon in this volume's chapters raise questions about the *nature of sovereignty*. Once sacrosanct, the concept of a state's sovereignty—the immutability of its international boundaries—is now under serious threat. Events such as the Chernobyl nuclear disaster, the mistreatment of Kurds in Iraq, the starvation and anarchy in Somalia in 1992–1993, and the brutal human rights abuses in the former Yugoslavia are galvanizing global actors—states, IGOs, and NGOs—to reconsider whether sovereignty is, in fact, absolute. A number of triggering events, including environmental catastrophes, the development of weapons of mass destruction, human rights deprivation, and disparate humanitarian concerns, have all been identified as appropriate reasons for a state's sovereignty to be violated through some form of intervention by the world community.[3] Indeed, two recent secretaries general of the United Nations have openly questioned whether "the time of absolute and exclusive sovereignty . . . has passed."[4] Clearly, even the old rules of international behavior are being seriously challenged. And the old geopolitics must be revised to account for a remarkably dynamic set of international processes in which the rules are changing.

The new international political geography, whether it be called geopolitics or geopolinomics, may be viewed in terms of three components: the theoretical underpinnings regarding power and the control of space, the players interacting in a global system in which the spatial distribution of power is being altered, and the key geographic issues being addressed by these actors.

## Old Problems, New Theories

The requirements of an adequate theoretical framework for understanding international political relationships are infinitely more complex now than in the simpler, nonnuclear era before World War II. The early geopoliticians laid heavy emphasis on the sheer friction of distance and the buffering function of space and sparsely populated frontiers, the values of which were calculated in terms of the military technology of the time. Power relations were based on sizes of armies, earth-bound transport, and weaponry. But the technological revolutions over the ensuing hundred years have gravely complicated the variables and the tools of power. Economic and even ecological variables and technological developments are now altering our ways of assessing and measuring distance, space, power, influence, and strength.

Near-instantaneous global communications and sophisticated weapons of mass destruction—deliverable in multiple and ingenious ways—have fostered a widely held perception that the world is always on the brink of total destruction. Only recently, following the breakup of the USSR, have the hands of the nuclear doomsday clock been moved back from a position very close to the catastrophic stroke of midnight. These new variables of communication and connectivity, however, are not devoid of spatial-locational dimensions, and the roles of distance and space have not been eliminated. The rapidity of recent geopolinomic changes has led to two evolving bodies of theory: a modern elaboration and extension of the classical geopolitical concepts and an essentially new, more systems-based set of constructs. Although neither is all-encompassing, both are useful and continue to evolve and even merge. The first section of this volume is addressed, in part, to the theoretical frameworks, old and new.

## New Actors, New Roles

The gradual evolution of human organizational units occupying terrestrial space—from clans to tribes, nations, states, and empires—continues unabated but in dramatic new manifestations. In many parts of the world, the preeminence of the state dates back only to the nineteenth century. The breakup of the great empires and the gradual replacement by states is associated with European history and the formation of states like modern France and Germany. But the processes of evolution and transition have not been neat and orderly. Consequently, the variety of states is as great as are the bits and chunks of space and nations mired in interstate disputes or existing in ambiguous political realms (e.g., Antarctica, or the Gaza Strip). They include stateless nations, such as the Kurds and Palestinians, and minority populations in many states who are struggling for autonomy from the dominant ethnic group.

Since World War II, a growing number of influential actors have greatly complicated international political, economic, and spatial relations. In addition to new states, they include IGOs such as the United Nations and its many spin-off institutions and a plethora of NGOs, ranging from multinational corporations to global human rights and environmental groups. Their relationships, responsibilities, and rules of operation are not yet fully agreed upon by the expanding list of geopolitical actors, which adds confusion and friction to international relations. Changes in the stature of each actor and changing relationships among major actors, like those that altered the Cold War in 1989–1990, send reverberations through the entire international system. These processes and resultant realignments in spheres of influence are critical to an understanding of trends in international relations. Already, the much-heralded New World Order has proven to be disorderly and even tragic for the millions of victims of post–Cold War civil conflicts.

## Political Geographic Variables and Processes

The variables and processes that define political power and vulnerability have increased and become more interrelated. The forceful acquisition of territory and resources, exemplified in Kuwait and Bosnia, remains a major international dilemma. Old land boundaries continue to be a source of conflict and tension. And new maritime disputes have erupted and become complicated as states have incorporated 12-mile territorial seas and 200-mile exclusive economic zones. National claims over Antarctica, the deep seabed, and outer space threaten to prolong the process. The maldistribution of energy supply and demand, food production and consumption, and related resource issues are major stimulants of international tension and strife. Massive movements of people for economic, political, and other reasons—which often reflect significant spatial variations in population growth and concentration (the rapid growth of huge cities)—have generated other sets of international problems, policies, and polemics.

Environmental degradation is increasingly a transborder problem that exacerbates many current bilateral and multilateral disputes. At the global scale, ozone depletion continues to endanger the well-being of all, despite international agreements to curb production of chlorofluorocarbons. International efforts to limit "greenhouse gases," such as carbon dioxide, may also founder over funding and sovereignty disputes. Similarly, dangerous and deadly modern plagues—from terrorism to AIDS to illicit drugs—have forced the international community to generate policies and governance systems that must be coordinated regionally and globally in order to be effective.

Technology in its many forms and varieties has not only altered our measures of space and distance but also significantly affected economic, military, and political relationships among global actors. New technologies and their distribution and diffusion are major factors in global structural change. And a state's level of technological development is increasingly a dominant force in determining its ability to compete in the global market and circles of power. Major technologies include those revolutionizing communications and those related to new materials, space, biotechnology, and nuclear technology. The control and transfer of these technologies are heavily influenced by one set of the more recent global actors—transnational corporations.

Applied political geography—the new geopolitics or geopolinomics—is emerging rapidly and vigorously. It is a subfield that ambitiously attempts to explain the prevailing distribution of cultural influences, economic linkages, political power, and military forces as well as to better understand the processes that alter these distributions. Most political-geographic analyses employ a spatial-locational set of filters to view key players and variables in an attempt to predict regional and global events.

This volume is organized so that the reader will first acquire an understanding of the roots and recurring issues in political geography. The later chapters are divided into two broad categories: resources, the environment, and population and the ever-changing global processes and international relations. Although the authors address issues that have worldwide ramifications, they often rely on local and regional problems to illustrate their arguments. The rapidity of radical changes in the world has led the authors to emphasize political-geographic processes rather than more traditional approaches that either demand memorizing countless facts or engaging in convoluted debates over paradigms. The result, we believe, is an exciting blend of theoretical perspective and pragmatic analysis of our changing world order.

## Notes

The views expressed are those of the authors and do not necessarily reflect those of the U.S. government.

1. For an excellent survey of geopolitics from its inception to the 1980s, see George W. Hoffman, "Political Geography and International Relations," in *Earth '88: Changing Geographic Perspective,* Harm de Blij, ed. (Washington, D.C.: National Geographic Society, 1988), pp. 38–53.

2. Robert B. Reich, *The Work of Nations: Preparing Ourselves for Twenty-first Century Capitalism* (New York: Alfred A. Knopf, 1991).

3. G.M. Lyons and M. Mastanduno, *Beyond Westphalia? International Intervention, State Sovereignty, and the Future of International Society* (Hanover, N.H.: Dartmouth College, 1992).

4. UN press releases, no. 5/24111, "An Agenda for Peace" (June 17, 1992), p. 5, and no. SG/4560 (April 24, 1991).

# TWO

## Geopolitics in the New World Era: A New Perspective on an Old Discipline

SAUL B. COHEN

THE POST–WORLD WAR II era has come to a decisive end. With the bipolar global geopolitical system now only historical memory, scholars and diplomats are searching for new paradigms to anticipate the direction that the international system might take as it enters the twenty-first century. A "new" geopolitics—one offering fresh perspectives on the relationship between geography and politics—is important to the development of sound, balanced, and realistic paradigms for geopolitics offers the spatial conceptual basis for the new world map.

The outlines of this new map depend upon equilibratory forces. Many students and practitioners of world affairs viewed the end of the Cold War, Germany's reunification, the collapse of the Soviet empire, and the U.S.-led coalition victory over Iraq as harbingers of a New World Order. Such hopes were quickly dispelled. Almost immediately after these stunning events, bloody nationalistic and religious conflicts broke out in many republics of the former Soviet Union and Yugoslavia, and Saddam Hussein, still in power, ruthlessly quashed Kurdish and Shia uprisings. Expectations of a New World Order quickly turned to fears of a world in chaos.

In fact, the world is neither in order nor in chaos. It is experiencing the disturbances and short-term disequilibrium of a global geopolitical system that is entering a new stage of dynamic equilibrium. This stage is a balance that is punctuated and will also be maintained by perturbations and contradictions. The new world map now unfolding reflects this dynamic balance.

Perturbations that affect geopolitical equilibrium are constant and span the globe. Among the more salient disturbances in the recent period have been the conflicts in Bosnia-Herzegovina, Nagorno-Karabakh, Georgia, and Moldova; Islamic fundamentalism in Algeria and the Sudan; the fight to control drugs in Colombia; the flight of Haitian refugees to the United States; communal strife in Kashmir; and starvation in Somalia.

Contradictions abound in this new world era and often cause the perturbations. Even as transnationalism spurs accommodation and weakens national barriers, resurgent ethnic nationalism sparks savage local wars and uproots large minority populations. Ultimately, the excesses of war and displacement come to an end through a combination of the exhaustion of warring factions and international intervention: Witness the winding down of war in Cambodia and the localized character of the conflict in Afghanistan.

As Socialist structures crumble and the market economy begins to emerge, a Russia rich in resources and scientific and technological manpower is overwhelmed by food and energy shortages and plagued by primitive living conditions. In time, foreign capital and technology will help break the resource logjam, and a united, rejuvenated, and modernized Russia will become a surplus producer. This same Russia, freed of repressive, centralized Communist rule, has veered toward chaos and dismemberment, as regional minority interests and independent state monopolies seek to go their own ways. But the pendulum is likely to swing back toward less exaggerated decentralization as the threats of atomization and redevelopment sink in.

In the Third World, nations struggling with drought, famine, disease, fratricidal warfare, and capital investment shortages are now of less interest to the major powers that once valued them for the military bases they could provide. A diminished flow of foreign assistance to these states would mean increased human suffering and political unrest. But when disturbances in these areas reach the flash point of endangering global resource pools and markets, it is likely that international assistance programs for the less developed world will be reinvigorated. In other words, a dialectic process operates to restore balance and moderate the swings of the pendulum of contradictions.

Geopolitics underpinned the Cold War; the division of Germany; the wars in Southeast Asia, Afghanistan, and the Middle East; and the string of superpower military bases that gird the world. The old world era was influenced by the "old" geopolitics whose theoretical basis was a crude form of nationally oriented spatial determinism.

The "new" geopolitics can help foster a new world era of accommodation. Such a geopolitics is founded on the complexities of geographical phenomena and a recognition of how they contribute to the spatial and political interplay among localism, nationalism, and internationalism. A useful theory for this new geopolitics is one that conceives of the political earth as a unified system evolving in developmental stages. Such a theory provides the basis for the geopolitical assessments and conclusions that I have previously set forth and that will be further developed in this chapter.[1]

# Old and New Geopolitics

Briefly stated, geopolitics is the applied study of the relationship of geographical space to politics. Geopolitics is therefore concerned with the reciprocal impact of spatial patterns, features, and structures and political ideas, institutions, and transactions.[2] The territorial frameworks within which such interrelationships are played out vary in scale, function, range, and hierarchical level from the national, inter-transnational, and continental-regional to the provincial and local. The interaction of spatial and political processes at all these levels creates and molds the international geopolitical system.

Political geographers have a responsibility and opportunity in these extraordinary times to bring to the public arena global geopolitical perspectives that are balanced and objective, something that the old geopolitics was not. In this connection, it is noteworthy that the leading Soviet and American geopoliticians who were so instrumental in designing the Cold War strategy were not geographers and had only limited understandings of geography.

Except for its rejection of racial superiority theories, Cold War geopolitics drew much of its inspiration from the environmental and organic determination of German geopolitik. The chief exponent of geopolitik, Karl von Haushofer, provided the geographical rationale for Nazi world conquest.[3] His panregional ideas of dividing the world into three north-south, double continental regions were drawn from Arnold Guyot.[4] According to Haushofer, panregions offered global stability through a balance-of-power system. But this was only projected as a temporary stage; the ultimate goal of German geopoliticians and their Nazi masters was world dominance. Germany's seizure of the Eurasian heartland, the geographical pivot land of the world—a concept adopted by Haushofer from Halford Mackinder—would assure German command of the world island (Eurasia and Africa) and thereby the world.[5] Indeed, a new Nazi world order was the major strategic aim of geopolitik, and regional relations were central to Haushofer's doctrines (as they were to those earlier geographers upon whom he drew). However, the spatial frameworks set forward were unidimensional; they failed to take into account the differing levels of territorial frameworks that compose the world map.

In American geopolitics, geography was simplified and distorted to serve political ends. The American geopoliticians came either from the scholarly fields of international relations and history (e.g., Robert Strauz-Hupe, George Kennan, Henry Kissinger, Zbigniew Brzezinski) or from the military but not from the ranks of academic geography. For these geopoliticians, geography meant distance, size, shape, and physical features, all viewed as static phenomena. The idea of geography as spatial patterns and relations that reflect dynamic physical and human processes was completely absent.

The old geopolitics appealed to its American practitioners because it simplified the world map. The world could be divided in two without considering its underlying and changing subdivisions. This pseudoscholarly American geopolitics produced the doctrine of rigid containment and the "falling-domino" theory. It also influenced U.S. leaders to reject any strategy that would accommodate overlapping spheres of influence (as in the Middle East) or the desires of some states to remain uninvolved in the Cold War (e.g., India, which, upon achieving independence, sought to maintain its neutrality).

American geopolitics helped plunge the global system into nearly half a century of military buildups, arms transfers, and regional and local conflict. Although the strategy ultimately led to the bankruptcy of the former Soviet Union and hastened the dissolution of its empire, it also took the United States into a destructive and strategically flawed war in Vietnam and into an arms race that has undermined the U.S. economy and weakened its social fabric.

The rulers of the former USSR also espoused a crude geopolitical doctrine—heartlandic Eurasian expansionism. In the interests of geographical security, Moscow seized and annexed vast areas in Eastern Europe, expelling millions of indigenous peoples from border areas and dispersing countless numbers of ethnic minority groups within its territory. It ordered changes in the boundaries of its satellites, controlled their space militarily, and manipulated their resources and markets. Territorial expansion and oversight were considered necessary to promote the security of the Soviet homeland and to safeguard the Marxist revolution.

The end of the Cold War presents political geographers with an opportunity to promote an understanding of the holistic and dynamic nature of geopolitical processes. Such a geopolitics recognizes that spatial patterns are not containable within national boundaries. The nation-state is part of a world that is a shared arena, and the resultant geopolitical map contains nested regions with overlapping boundaries. Because the geopolitical territorial system consists of layers of interacting units, with different and often competing functions, doctrines of single or multiple great-power hegemony over the earth must be reconsidered.

In contrast to the old geopolitics that was an instrument of war, the new geopolitics can be applied to the advancement of international cooperation and peace. In an era of global accommodation, there will continue to be local wars, both formal and guerrilla, especially as the underlying ethnic, religious, and cultural forces that lead to the proliferation of national states gather momentum. But the new geopolitics focuses on the evolution of the political world as an interdependent system at varying scales—from the national and transnational to the local. It calls attention to those political areas that are either independent of or part of sovereign entities—areas that play special locational roles in linking the international system. It embraces the geopolitical study of transnational economic, social, and political forces as well as cities and the impact of changing technology on channels of movement.

By analyzing the interdependence of economic, cultural, social, and political processes within changing spatial milieus, the new geopolitics sheds light on what constitutes military-strategic considerations. For example, it challenges the Western perception that the southern continents (Sub-Sahara Africa and South

America) are fast becoming the global "quartersphere of strategic marginality" because the need for outside military bases has been so dramatically reduced. In reality, this quartersphere remains globally important in a variety of other ways: as a source of environmental warming and pollution; as the place of origin for drugs and certain diseases; as a world market with dynamic growth possibilities; as a potentially destabilizing element in world credit and commodity markets; as a source for regionally and globally disruptive migration streams; and as a locus for the massive starvation, genocidal conflicts, and human rights abuses that sorely trouble the conscience of the international community. Because a politically and economically unstable quartersphere is a cause of global instability, it warrants sustained strategic attention even though the Cold War need for military bases has passed.

## Dynamic Equilibrium and Change

A fundamental question in geopolitical analysis is whether the map reflects a system in order or disorder, in balance or imbalance. Recipes for a world order are hardly new. Immanuel Kant's "universal international state" called for a unified political mechanism to enforce the peace.[6] H.G. Wells dreamed of a New World Order based on a world state, with a common religion and education, no military, production for general use, and private enterprise controlled to serve humankind.[7] Clarence Streit called for an order based on world federalism, with a union of North Atlantic democracies as its core,[8] and Adolph Hitler sought to create a New World Order based on Nazi German hegemony.[9]

The United Nations and the League of Nations before it were attempts to fashion a world order based upon partnerships of national interests. They both failed. The league was an association of nations that lacked peace-enforcing mechanisms; its fate was sealed when the United States refused to join it. The United Nations, which does, of course, include the United States, has a two-tier structure that encompasses the Security Council and peace-keeping instruments. But the veto power held by the five permanent members of the Security Council has often undermined the ability of this international organization to take decisive action. Pushing aside this associative world system, the two superpowers created a bipolar world consisting of strategic realms and their regional subdivisions that found coexistence through a tenuous balance of shifting forces. This was not order in the commonly accepted understanding of the concept, that is, a strongly regulated, static or fixed arrangement of ranks and clusters. Rather, the Cold War balance was based on dynamic equilibrium.

Within that equilibrium, disturbances abounded. The United States and the USSR waged major wars (the former in Korea and Vietnam, the latter in Afghanistan), and their surrogates engaged in conflict in many parts of the world. Moreover, the Communist rule in Eastern Europe and the Soviet Union was only "orderly" because the centralized communist state maintained serious coercive pressure upon classes and religious and ethnic minorities.

The boundaries of the world's geostrategic realms and geopolitical regions, far from being fixed as in an orderly system, were in considerable flux during this era. Regions changed their political and economic orientations, and nations switched alliances. The balance was maintained by the superpowers' fear of mutual nuclear destruction, limiting each from overreaching in the global competition, and by the rise of other first- and second-order powers with independent interests and agendas.

The term *equilibrium* is not used here in the physical or psychophysical sense that the natural state of the organism is rest or homeostasis. Such equilibrium characterizes closed systems, it does not fit human organizations. Surely, a geopolitical system whose parts could be arranged so that their resultant force at every point is zero is both theoretically and practically impossible. Instead, *equilibrium* in the present context refers to the quality of balance between opposing influences and forces in an open system. Balance is regained after disturbance by the introduction of weights or stimuli. It is not only maintained by what Adam Smith referred to as an "invisible hand," or the rational self-interest of peoples, for in the absence of reason, excesses of war, economic greed, and environmental imbalances ultimately encounter resistance. When things go too far, there is reaction, correction, and regulation.

As systems mature, their parts multiply and draw power away from the center. In a decentralizing system, where the individual territorial units have increasing responsibility for marshaling their energies, the interaction among the components becomes self-directing. This interaction may be competitive or cooperative, but it is almost always turbulent. Without turbulence there is no change, and without change there is no progress.

A major manifestation of such change is the reorientation and realignment of political territorial units. Regrouping occurs at all levels of the geopolitical scale—from realm to region to state to national subdivisions. Such regrouping is not spatially random or independent of lines provided by nature. In fact, the world can be likened to a diamond, not a pane of glass: Its geopolitical cleavages occur along specific fault lines that are drawn from an array of optional boundaries provided by nature.[10] The relative strength of particular cores determines where and at what hierarchical scales geopolitical repartitioning takes place.

## Evolution of the Geopolitical System as a General Organismic System

Since short-term imbalance is intrinsic to dynamic equilibrium, the overriding question is whether, in the face of a world in turbulence, it is reasonable to speak of more general processes leading to a greater integration of the world system. The dissolution of the Soviet empire, Yugoslavia, and Czechoslovakia and the threat of dismemberment in Moldova, Georgia, Azerbaijan, and even Russia are disintegrative forces. Elsewhere, many other ethnic, racial, and religious divisions threaten the integrity of existing national states. These are offset, however, by larger integrative global and regional forces, including microterritories like Singapore, Hong Kong, Luxembourg, and Bermuda as well as the great powers and large regions.

Thus, in the relations between Eastern and Western Europe in the European Community or between the industrial powers of the maritime world and the various former republics of the Soviet Union, the trend is toward integration. This is also true for the North America Free Trade Agreement (NAFTA) countries and for members of the Association of Southeast Asian Nations (ASEAN) Pact. In the Middle East, one of the results of the Gulf War was to promote stronger ties among Egypt, Saudi Arabia, the Gulf States, and Syria; another is the peace negotiations between the Arab states and Israel.

All this reflects the evolution of the global system. The military equilibrium struck by superpower détente had, over four decades, been superseded by an overarching set of equilibristic forces, including multinational corporate networks, global capital flows, the specialization of industry, technological transfer and adaptation, and the rejection of Moscow's brand of Communism and one-party rule. Although these forces are viewed as global, they also often have regional clusterings. This regional impact contributes to the salience of the geopolitical region as second-order powers interact with major powers and other countries in their regional arenas. Smaller states that have become specialized centers of economic and political activity within the global network may also overshadow the regions within which they are located and draw activity from them.

In the face of all these developments, it is instructive that there has been no cataclysmic collapse and global conflagration, as posited in theories of change based upon cyclical and deterministic economic interpretations of history.[11] Immanuel Wallerstein's economic dialectics and George Modelski's long-cycle model founded on a hegemonic explanation of world political economic forces do not match current realities.[12] New regional powers have challenged and changed the bipolar and multipolar world, but they have not displaced the major powers. Rather, they have become absorbed within an evolving system. Communism and single-party rule are disappearing, with considerable disturbance to the system. But their demise has been attended by global "whimpers" rather than any "bang." The terrible bloodletting in Yugoslavia, for example, still remains a local affair, not a tinderbox for a wider Balkan war, let alone a world war.

Treating the world as a general organismic system provides insight into the relationships between political structures and their operational environments. These interactions produce the geopolitical forces that shape the system, upset it, and then lead it toward new levels of equilibrium. To understand the system's evolution, it is useful to apply a developmental approach, derived from theories advanced in sociology, biology, and psychology. The developmental principle holds that the systems evolve in predictably structured ways; that they are open to outside forces; and that hierarchy, regulation, and entropy are important characteristics.

Combining organismic concepts from Herbert Spencer,[13] the sociologist, with those of Heinz Werner,[14] the psychologist, and Ludwig von Bertalanffy,[15] the psychobiologist, provides the foundation for a spatially structured geopolitical theory. Such a theory is holistic, concerned with the order and process of interconnecting parts, and applicable at all levels of the political territorial hierarchy, from the subnational to the national to the supranational.

To adapt the developmental principle geopolitically, we hypothesize a system that progresses spatially in stages. The earliest stage is undifferentiated. Here, none of the territorial parts are interconnected, and their functions are identical. The next stage is differentiation, when parts have distinguishable characteristics but are still isolated. The highest stage is specialization and hierarchical integration. Exchange of the specialized and complementary outputs of the different territorial parts leads to an integration of the system. Hierarchical structure directs the flow of these outputs.

World War II and the end of colonialism paved the way for new world geopolitical arrangements. That era is thus a logical starting point for tracing the development of the current system. In the early postwar years, the two bipolar realms controlled by the Soviet Union and the United States were clearly differentiated from each other. Within each realm, however, the parts were relatively undifferentiated. In this era, as nations began to recover from the ravages of war, there was domination but little hierarchy within either realm. Meanwhile, both Joseph Stalin and John Foster Dulles believed that superpowers could influence all parts of their respective geostrategic arenas, without the need for any intermediaries.

That system quickly changed. Within the maritime world, specialized regional cores like Common Market Europe and Japan arose, initially as junior partners and then as friendly competitors to the United States. Europe was the first to emerge as a political and economic bloc. Within the Eurasian realm, China soon challenged the USSR for strategic parity. In time, these new power centers began to develop independent ties to other states and regions. The challenge to superpower monopoly brought new forms of hierarchy into the relations between the superpowers and their peripheries. Thus, as Albania defected from Soviet suzerainty, it looked to China for protection. And in the Caribbean, Cuba broke with the United States and turned to the USSR.

In the 1970s, a number of regionally important states also began to emerge, giving added substance to the regional structure. These states tried to impose a hierarchy of their own within their respective regions. India, for example, became dominant in South Asia, defeating Pakistan in war and casting its stamp upon Bangladesh and Sri Lanka as well as Nepal and Bhutan. Nigeria, not the United States, led the way to a resolution of the Liberian conflict, although America had been Liberia's traditional patron. Vietnam, with help from the Soviet Union, drove the Khmer Rouge from power and, for more than a decade, was dominant in Indochina.

Although hierarchy remains a major structural element of the world system, it does not follow the rigid rank order (in terms of either power or distance) that it does in the natural world. Rather, the hierarchy is flexible. States can exert influence over others without always having to defer to those in the rank above them. Albania, for example, broke away from Marshal Tito's control to reach directly to the USSR before splitting with the Soviets and turning to China. Similarly, Mexico and Venezuela have defied the United States and tried to shape an independent Central American policy in bringing peace to Nicaragua and Guatemala.

There is flexibility in hierarchy both because of the maturation of individual states and because power relations are no longer a function of sheer distance. Rapid air and sea travel and telecommunications allow ties to develop between states that are relatively far apart. Flexibility is further enhanced by the impact upon individual states of transnational corporations and international social and political organizations.

This increasingly complex and open world system can be described as a "polyocracy." The system has overlapping spheres of influence, varying degrees of hegemony and hierarchy, national components and transnational influences, interdependencies, and pockets of self-containment. It is all the more complex because its parts are at different stages of development. The continental realm is seeking to catch up with the maritime by opening itself to market forces and (with the probably temporary exception of China) political pluralism. Geopolitical regions, too, vary in attributes depending on their particular settings. And regional states play differing roles according to their spatial and economic interactions with major powers and neighbors (Figure 2.1).

## Entropy and Orders of Power

Helping to link the international system is the drive of the less mature parts to rise to levels already achieved by more mature sectors. The balance of relationships across and within the nested regional frameworks can be analyzed in terms of entropic and hierarchical conditions. This provides some guidelines for determining levels of development.

A key element in the dynamism of the system lies in shifts in power among different states and regions. Some power changes are the result of domestic developments, in either political organization, economic structures, or social patterns. Others can be attributed to external national and transnational forces. Three orders of national power—the first or major, the second or regional, and the third or subregional—affect the balance of the global system, but even lesser-order states are change agents influencing regional and global patterns (witness Angola, Afghanistan, and Ethiopia).

Entropy level indicates where a state or region fits into the various orders of power; it is also a useful measure of balance in relationships between geopolitical units. Defined in physical systems as the availability of energy to do work, entropy is always on the increase as energy becomes exhausted. Thus, a system's ability to work constantly declines. If the world were to consist of closed geopolitical units, then surely each unit would ultimately collapse.

24

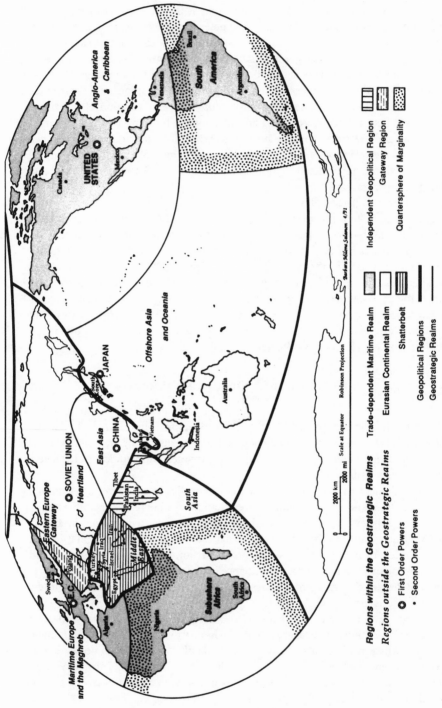

FIGURE 2.1  The world's geostrategic realms and geopolitical regions in the 1990s. SOURCE: Saul B. Cohen, "Geopolitical Change in the Post–Cold War Era," *Annals of the Association of American Geographers*, vol. 81, no. 4 (December 1991).

*Regions within the Geostrategic Realms*

*Regions outside the Geostrategic Realms*

Trade-dependent Maritime Realm

Eurasian Continental Realm

Shatterbelt

Geopolitical Regions
Geostrategic Realms

○ First Order Powers

• Second Order Powers

Independent Geopolitical Region

Gateway Region

Quartersphere of Marginality

0   2000 km
0   2000 mi   Scale at Equator   Robinson Projection

*Maritime Europe and the Maghreb*

Anglo-America & Caribbean

*Eastern Europe Gateway*

*Offshore Asia and Oceania*

*East Asia*

*Middle East*

*South Asia*

*South America*

*Subsaharan Africa*

○ SOVIET UNION   ♂ Heartland

○ CHINA

○ JAPAN

○ UNITED STATES

Canada

Mexico

Venezuela

Brazil

Argentina

Algeria

Nigeria

South Africa

Egypt

Turkey

Syria   Iraq   Iran

Israel

Pakistan

India

Tibet

Thailand

Vietnam

Indonesia

Australia

South Korea

Sweden

E.E.C.   Poland

Barbara Malome Salomon  4/91

Only hermetically sealed systems, however, behave according to this law of inevitability. This is not the case for person-environment systems. Geopolitical entities whose leaders seek to close them off from outside forces do suffer from the exhaustion of their human and natural resources and experience high levels of entropy; ultimately, however, human needs and strivings pry open the system for geopolitical entities are inherently open. They become recharged through a form of energy transport that introduces peoples, goods, and ideas as free energy. In those systems that are open to a great degree, there may be so much energy transport that the level is negative. Thus, though the Soviet Union or Albania experienced dramatic increases in entropy levels as a result of their decades-long attempts to close their systems, Singapore, in contrast, has negative entropy.

Criteria that can be used to measure entropy include: savings rates; agricultural yields; manufacturing productivity; debt repayment; percentage of research-and-development (R&D) exports; numbers of patents, scientists, and engineers and foreign scientific exchange; and reduction of fuel-energy intensity requirements. In general, based upon the criteria that have been enumerated, regions fall into four categories: (1) low entropy (Anglo-America and the Caribbean, maritime Europe and the Maghreb, offshore Asia); (2) medium entropy (heartland, Eastern Europe Middle East); (3) high entropy (East Asia, South Asia); and (4) very high entropy (Sub-Sahara Africa, South America) (Figure 2.2).

In effect, a state or region's reach or extent of influence beyond its borders is a function of the combination of its level of entropy and its military-strategic strength. The reach can be measured by external trade, capital flow, diplomatic relations, immigration and transit links, and overseas military bases. Using these measures, the United States reaches out throughout its own region and also quite strongly to five others: maritime Europe, offshore Asia, South America, Sub-Sahara Africa, and the Middle East. On the other hand, a negative flow in capital accounts, chronic budget deficits, and trade imbalance are indicative of an increase in entropic level. In terms of equilibristic relations, the United States is in balance with Europe and offshore Asia and is in overbalance with South America, Sub-Sahara Africa, and the Middle East.

The European Community dominates its region and has substantial geopolitical reach to Anglo-America, the Middle East, Sub-Sahara Africa, South America, offshore Asia, and Eastern Europe. Its entropic level is low, and it is fully capable of transporting surplus energy to Eastern Europe and the Soviet Union. Europe is in balance with Anglo-America and offshore Asia and in overbalance with its other regions of major contact.

Offshore Asia, spearheaded by Japan and its successfully industrializing neighbors, reaches to Anglo-America, the Middle East, Europe, South Asia, and East Asia. With its very low level of entropy, it is also in a position to project substantial reach to the heartland. The region is in balance with Anglo-America and Europe and overbalanced with the rest of its contact area.

The heartland is at a medium entropic level, which is rising rapidly in light of

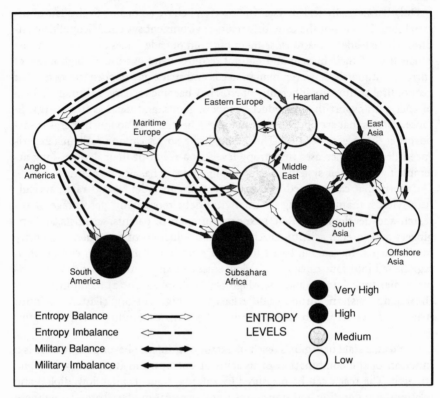

FIGURE 2.2   Geopolitical reach and balance. SOURCE: Saul B. Cohen, "Geopolitical Change in the Post–Cold War Era," *Annals of the Association of American Geographers,* vol. 81, no. 4 (December 1991).

recent economic stagnation and the collapse of the centralized Soviet political system. It reaches to East Asia, the Middle East, and Eastern Europe, and it is in balance with all these regions. China, dominant in East Asia, extends its reach to the heartland, South Asia, and to offshore Asia. It is in balance with the heartland but underbalanced with offshore Asia.

Regional or second-order powers are emerging cores within their regions. They have nodal characteristics in terms of trade and transportation as well as military influence, and they aspire to regional or subregional influence. Limited extraregional economic or political ties are also characteristic of such powers. Finally, though often overshadowed by a great power, second-order states try to avoid satellite status, sometimes by playing off one major power against the other.

Second-order states may have regional hegemonical aspirations, but such hopes are far from reality. Where regional powers are located within the same geopolitical region as major powers, they cannot mount a serious challenge.

Elsewhere, even if major powers are absent, proximate and competing second-order powers deny individual regional powers regionwide hegemony (Figure 2.1). Thus, Gamal Abdel Nasser's Egypt dominated much of the Arab part of the Middle East, but Israel, Turkey, and Iran prevented it from exercising regionwide influence, as did the great powers. Even with Soviet support, Vietnam's control of Cambodia was undermined by the Chinese backing of the Khmer Rouge. Brazil does not have the capacity to dominate the Andean states, nor could South Africa reach effectively beyond its neighbors. Only India has a dominant impact on its region. In general, then, the destiny of second-order powers is not to achieve hegemony over an entire geopolitical region. Rather, it is to exercise broad regional influence, with hegemony having practical significance only in relation to proximate states.

Third-order states influence regional events in special ways. They compete with neighboring regional powers on ideological and political grounds or in having a specialized resource base, but they lack the population, military, and general economic capacities of their second-order rivals. Saudi Arabia, Libya, Taiwan, North Korea, Malaysia, Zimbabwe, the Ivory Coast, and Hungary retain such status. Lesser-order states like the Sudan or Ecuador have impact only on their nearest neighbors, and fifth-order states like Nepal have only marginal external involvements.

Membership in the various orders is fluid. China, for example, is now only marginally a first-order power, and unless it matures by opening the system and finds genuine accommodation with a restructured and revitalized Russia, it may slip to second-order status, on a level with India. Similarly, twenty-seven states could be measured as potential second-order powers a decade ago,[16] but four of these—Saudi Arabia, Morocco, Zaire, and Cuba—have fallen from the ranking or never really attained it in the first place. The German Democratic Republic and Yugoslavia have disappeared from the map altogether. On the other hand, South Korea and Thailand have recently joined the ranks of regional powers. Third-order status is also ephemeral: Tunisia, Tanzania, Ghana, and Costa Rica have enjoyed and then lost such ranking with the waning of their ideological influence.

The combined inputs of major powers and second- and third-order states give regionalism geopolitical substance. A state that may be described as "asymmetrical" plays a special role in the regional personality. It promotes turbulence by challenging the norms of hegemonic regional structures and injecting unwelcomed energy into the system. Sometimes, this produces a dialectic response that brings change in those norms.[17] Revolutionary Cuba, democratic Israel, Titoist Yugoslavia, the market-oriented Ivory Coast of the 1970s, radical Libya, and fundamentalist Iran are examples of asymmetrical states that have had a profound impact on their respective regions. So, too, were Sandinista Nicaragua and a Romania that insisted upon conducting a foreign policy independent of the Soviet Union.

Ultimately, some of the initiatives of the asymmetrical state are grudgingly adopted by its neighbors. Kuwait could play such a role within the Arab Gulf States if frustrated forces there should overthrow the emir or convert the regime to a constitutional monarchy. Other regional "mavericks" of the future could include a revolutionary Philippines or Peru or an anti-European Morocco should the king be overthrown by the fundamentalists.

## The Global Geopolitical Structure

The *geo* in *geopolitical analysis* relates, first of all, to spatial structure. To understand geopolitical systems, we must address the spatial categories that geographers use as frameworks of analysis. The structure is hierarchical. At the highest level are two geostrategic realms—the maritime and the Eurasian continental. Realms are arenas of strategic place and movement. Their trade orientations differ: The maritime is open to specialized exchange, and the continental is inner-oriented. Below the realms are the geopolitical regions.[18] Regions are shaped by contiguity and political, cultural, military and economic interaction. They are also influenced by historical movement (Figure 2.1).

The maritime realm has a global reach. Within it are geopolitical regions that constitute the second-level geopolitical regions of the hierarchy, including Anglo-America and the Caribbean, maritime Europe and the Maghreb, offshore Asia, South America, and Sub-Sahara Africa. The Eurasian continental realm consists of two geopolitical regions: the Soviet Russian heartland and East Asia.

Most of the second-level regions are contained within the realms, but three lie outside. South Asia is an independent region. The Middle East is a shatterbelt, a zone of contention caught between the two realms. The third is the emerging gateway region of Central and Eastern Europe. This is a transitional zone that can facilitate contact and interchange between the two realms.

The third level of the hierarchy is the national state. States are hierarchically ordered, according to their power positions and functions in the world system. Gateway territories are a special category. Currently, they are components of the subnational, or fourth, level of the hierarchy. Gateways are embryonic states that can accelerate exchanges that will stimulate the evolution of larger states from which the gateways have spun off.

The world system is in a continuing process of development, becoming a seamless web as it moves toward greater specialization and integration. As national energies and transnational forces gain or lose momentum, the regional frameworks—realms, regions, states, and subnational units—change in status and in boundaries. And this, in effect, produces new parts-to-whole relationships within the system that require rebalancing.

Despite the profound changes that have taken place in the world in recent years, the basic framework remains for two geostrategic realms—the trade-dependent maritime world and the Eurasian continental world. Of the world's five major power centers, only one is now both a military and an economic colossus: the United States. Two are great military forces but relatively weak economically: Russia and China. And two are dominant economic forces without equally strong military capacities: Japan and the European Community. Because Japan and maritime Europe lack vast strategic space and are vulnerable to the military pressures of their near neighbors (China and Russia, respectively), the strategic alliance with the United States remains their strongest security card. However the North Atlantic Treaty Organization (NATO) may change, the American partnership with trade-dependent allies in the maritime realm is mutually needed.

The deteriorating economic and political fortunes of the former Soviet Union may lead some to ask whether the concept of a Eurasian geostrategic realm still has validity. Those who have heralded the triumph of liberal democracy over Communism and the collapse of the unitary governmental structure are premature in dismissing Russia from its position as a controlling state in one arena of the world that has impact upon much of the rest.[19] A revived (albeit smaller and loosely confederated) union like the Commonwealth of Independent States (CIS) under Russian leadership, ideologically compatible with its Eastern European neighbors, will remain in a position to dominate its geostrategic realm—a vast spatial arena large enough to affect the areas within its strategic-military reach. This realm is characterized by a distinct set of interrelationships expressed in terms of patterns of circulation, economic orientation, and historical, cultural, and political traditions. Place, movement, and perspective combine to shape a geostrategic realm.

In defining realms as continental and maritime, the reference encompasses not only lands and climates but also outlooks. The Eurasian continental world is more isolated, more inwardly oriented, and more heavily endowed with raw materials than its maritime counterpart. Its people have deep ties to the land. Whatever happens to the CIS, there will be a Russia and some allied or subordinate republics to occupy the Eurasian heartland. "Heartlandia" will remain a large, well-endowed, and technologically advanced power, capable of influencing events in much of the rest of the world.

China, too, belongs to the continental realm; it is not part of the maritime world as portrayed by Mackinder and Spykman in their times and Richard Nixon in his. The vast majority of Chinese live off the land, not from sea trade. Even with China's recent spurt in commerce, it only accounts for 1.5 percent of the world's imports and exports. The mountain, not the sea, holds the spiritual, mystical attraction for the Chinese. And a common border strategically links Russia and China. These states cannot turn their backs on one another; they have to find a modus vivendi. Even though the political changes in the former Soviet Union stand in sharp contrast to China's quashing of political democracy stirrings, the Chinese resistance to change must inevitably give way, especially as its opening to a market economy continues. When both continental powers are no longer trapped by competing versions of Marxist ideology and enjoy more open systems, they are likely to find more in common, including the recognition that their mutual strategic vulnerability is better served by cooperation than by conflict.

South Asia belongs to neither geostrategic realm but has a separate geopolitical region status. In their early history, especially from their Indus Valley beginnings in 3000 B.C. to Roman times, the Indians were seafaring peoples and colonizers. Since then, they have also been continentally oriented, although South Asia did become a source for special raw materials and a market for imported goods during the era of British rule. As an independent geopolitical region dominated by India, South Asia remains rurally based and largely continental. This does not minimize the growing importance to the region of overseas trade, shipping, and modern-day immigration. However, the basic orientation is inward (India's merchandise trade is only one-third that of China's)—a condition that explains the limited impact of extraregional contacts upon the geopolitical objectives of the various states of South Asia.

If trade interactions were the only criterion for defining geopolitical regions, then South America and Sub-Sahara Africa surely would not qualify as separate geopolitical regions. The trade links of their individual states are with other parts of the maritime realm, especially the United States and Europe. Moreover, the subregions of both South America and Africa are clearer political, military, and economic arenas than are their larger regions.

In rationalizing the geopolitical unity of the continent, one can argue that the weight of the eastern South American core is overwhelming. Moreover, Chile's strategic interrelationships with Argentina, the vulnerability of the Central Andean countries' transmontane rain forests and savannas to Brazil, and Colombia's ties with Venezuela inhibit western South America from gaining independent geopolitical status on a par with that of the east.

Sub-Sahara Africa's subdivisions, Southern Africa, Western and Central Africa, and East Africa are arenas of far more intense political, cultural, and military interaction as compared to the region as a whole. When the two strongest regional powers, Nigeria and South Africa, sort out their internal problems, they may, indeed, carve out two distinct geopolitical regions, with the smaller, weaker central and eastern subdivisions being included within them. This would create two geopolitical regions—the south and east lands of the Indian and South Atlantic region and the west and central lands of the mid-Atlantic region.

In contrast, intraregional flows are a major factor in linking Anglo-America and the Caribbean, maritime Europe and the Maghreb, and offshore Asia. Tourism, immigration, and petroleum flow characterize Anglo-America, and immigration and language bind the Maghreb to maritime Europe.

The two anchors of offshore Asia are Japan and Australia. I first proposed that Australia was part of a new emerging geopolitical region some thirty-five years ago.[20] This challenged the prevailing view of the time that the Australian subcontinent was geopolitically aligned with Great Britain and the United States. Today, it is clear that Australia's destiny is that of an Asian-Pacific nation. It sends 27 percent of its exports to Japan (more than it sends to the European Community and the United States combined), and half of its annual immigrants are Asian. As an exporter of raw materials like coal, iron, and gold and of processed wool, meat, and metals, Australia's main challenge is to raise its high-cost manufactures to competitive levels with its neighbors. The question now is not whether Australia *is* Asian but how it can best adjust to *being* Asian.[21]

Japan's situation as the dominant economic and political power in offshore Asia is unique because of its reluctance to exercise military pressure. The reverse is seen in South Asia, where India freely applies military options, or in East Asia, where China has been militarily involved in both Korea and IndoChina. And the Russian heartland organizes its region through economic exchange, migration of Slavs, and military force.

Although I speak of a world system, I am mindful that the system does not really span the entire globe—and perhaps it never will. Parts of the world are outside the modern economic system and do not benefit from the exchange that is so important to the developmental process. Much of Sub-Sahara Africa and South America below the Orinoco, for instance, lies outside the world economic system. The trade of these two regions accounts for only 3 percent of world exchange. Moreover, with the exception of pockets of modernity in such countries as Brazil, Argentina, and Chile and in South Africa, these regions are relatively untouched by the capital flows, technology transfer, and specialization of industry that characterizes the developed market economies (70 percent of world trade), continental Eurasia (10 percent), and South Asia (8 percent). The continents around the South Atlantic and their bordering oceans represent the quarter of the world's land and ocean areas that can be referred to as the quartersphere of strategic marginality (Figure 2.1).

Although dominated by the U.S. and European Community power centers, the quartersphere is marginal in a strategic sense. Naval and air strike forces, long-range air weapons, and satellite surveillance capabilities have minimized the significance of southern continental land bases to the maritime world. Moreover, pipelines and the Suez Canal now handle as much oil movement as the shipping routes around the Cape of Good Hope. The Panama Canal takes most of the Pacific shipping trade now oriented to the U.S. West Coast.

Economically, the quartersphere suffers from a chronic overproduction of commercial crops and minerals, competition from other parts of the world, substitutes, and changing consumer tastes. The postindustrial regions no longer regard the two southern continents as the potential storehouses of the world.

As a result of these changes, panregionalism has become an outdated concept.[22] Even though it is pursuing a massive debt-reduction program for the Third World, the United States is not likely to promote large new capital flows, business developments, or aid programs to South America, nor is Europe apt to do more than it is already doing in Sub-Sahara Africa, given its involvement with the land to its east.

The burdens of high debt, low international trade levels, overpopulation, low life expectancy, and low caloric consumption will continue to plague the two southern continents, unless the quartersphere receives much more development aid. But it will not receive substantial new help unless there is a sea change in the attitudes of the wealthy of the world. This means letting military-strategic and economic disinterest give way to humanitarian considerations and to concerns that local conflicts or the acquisition of mass weapons would negatively affect global stability.

## Shatterbelts

The concept of the *shatterbelt,* also referred to as the *crush zone* or *shatter zone,* has long been of interest to geographers. Alfred Thayer Mahan, James Fairgrieve, and Richard Hartshorne contributed pioneering studies of such regions. Mahan referred to the instability of the zone between the 30° and 40° parallels in Asia as being caught between Britain and Russia.[23] Fairgrieve referred to a crush zone of small buffer states between the sea powers of the Eurasian heartland, from Northern and Eastern Europe to the Balkans, Turkey, Iran, Afghanistan, Siam, and Korea.[24] And during World War II, Hartshorne analyzed the shatter zone of Eastern Europe from the Baltic to the Adriatic, advocating a post–World War II federation.[25]

In the operational definition used here, shatterbelts are strategically oriented regions that are politically fragmented areas of competition between the maritime and continental realms. By the end of the 1940s, two such atomized regions had emerged—the Middle East and Southeast Asia. They were not geographically coincident with previous shatterbelts because the global locus of geostrategic competition had shifted. The former Eastern and Central European shatterbelt had fallen within the Soviet strategic orbit, and the maritime and continental worlds became divided by a sharp boundary in Korea.

In discussions of the topology of the shatterbelt, it has been pointed out by Philip Kelly that other parts of the world are also characterized by high degrees of conflict and atomization.[26] It is true that wars, revolts, and coups are chronic in the Caribbean, South America, and South Asia. The distinguishing feature of the shatterbelt, however, is that it presents an equal playing field in terms of access to two or more competing powers operating from different geostrategic realms.

Thus, South Asia is not a shatterbelt. India's dominance in a divided South Asia is not seriously threatened by the United States, Russia, or China, and the loss of Soviet support did not change India's geopolitical sway over the region. Moreover, the Caribbean is under America's military-strategic and tactical sway, and the Soviet penetration of Cuba did not threaten U.S. military control of the region.

Shatterbelt areas and their boundaries are fluid. During the 1970s and 1980s, for instance, Sub-Sahara Africa became a shatterbelt, and the Soviet Union used its Cuban surrogate as well as its Eastern European satellites to provide military and technical support to Ethiopia, Angola, Namibia, and Mozambique. Furthermore, its adjoining Middle Eastern bases were important jumping-off points for Africa. The USSR also made political inroads into Guinea, Mali, Congo, and Tanzania. With the collapse of the USSR, the region has shifted back to the maritime realm (Figure 2.3).

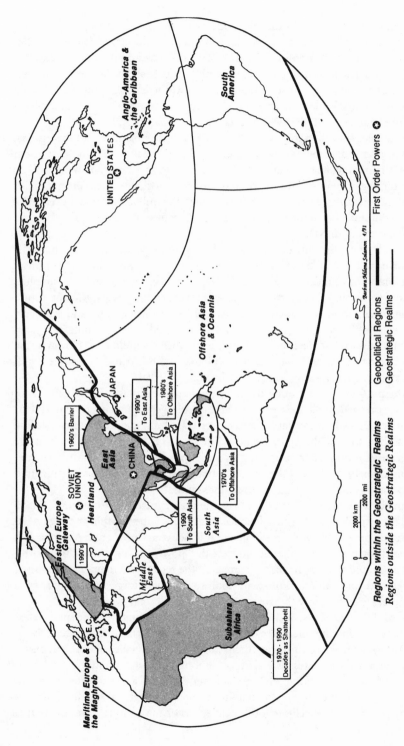

FIGURE 2.3   Major geopolitical regional changes from the end of World War II to the present. SOURCE: Saul B. Cohen, "Geopolitical Change in the Post–Cold War Era," *Annals of the Association of American Geographers*, vol. 81, no. 4 (December 1991).

Another major change in the geopolitical map is that Southeast Asia has also lost its shatterbelt status. Its insular and southern peninsular portions have become economically and politically part of offshore Asia and the maritime world. Malaysia and Thailand now enjoy considerable industrial development, and their economies are linked to those of Japan and the United States. This has followed Singapore's remarkable growth as part of the maritime realm and the realignment of Indonesia with the West and its offshore Asian neighbors.

Meanwhile, with the rapid withdrawal of Soviet support from Southeast Asia, Vietnam and Indochina as a whole are soon likely to fall within the East Asian sphere. Vietnam will have to find some accommodation with China. What will be left of the region will be an isolated and impoverished Myanmar (Burma), with almost no foreign trade or other contacts. When the military regime is eventually overthrown and the country opens itself to the world, it will probably become reoriented to South Asia.

Presently, then, the only remaining shatterbelt is the Middle East, and it, too, is in transition. The Middle East is tilting toward the maritime realm, as the former Soviet Union has suddenly ceased to be a major economic and military supplier, at least for the time being. Nonetheless, Russia remains sensitive to the future strategic orientation of the new Caucasus and Central Asian states and especially to the roles of Turkey and Iran. It cannot be expected to remain quiescent if an anti-Russian Moslem coalition arises in the northern Middle East. However, the era of broad heartlandic penetration, with bases in the Red and Arabian seas and the Eastern Mediterranean, seems to be over.

In the post–Gulf War world, the European Community is likely to exert more influence on the Middle Eastern scene and to emerge as the second major intrusive power. Indeed, European influence over Iraq, Iran, and Turkey may well be greater than that of the United States. The lead was taken by Britain and the European Community in proposing a "safe haven" for Kurds in northern Iraq and, later, for the Shiites in the south. In both instances, America was pressured to respond by supporting and adopting these initiatives.

With the United States and the EC as the major intrusive powers and Russia playing a secondary role, a new balance can be developed within the region. In fact, Russia may actually play a stabilizing role between Europe and America as it pursues its own agenda. Although shifts of the "power seesaw" should be less frequent and rapid than in the past (Figure 2.4), the region will remain a shatterbelt if the United States and the European Community fail to forge a common agenda or if Russia feels seriously threatened by events in Moslem borderlands.

The Middle East is also a shatterbelt because it is so highly fragmented internally. The region contains six regional powers—Egypt, Iran, Iraq, Israel, Syria, and Turkey—which, in turn, cast their shadows over smaller states or separate groups within those states. The alliances among these states and their subordinates are fluid, and striking a balance among the six is a complicated business. The United States and others can help in the quest for regional stability (particularly by pressing for the elimination of weapons of mass destruction, the reduc-

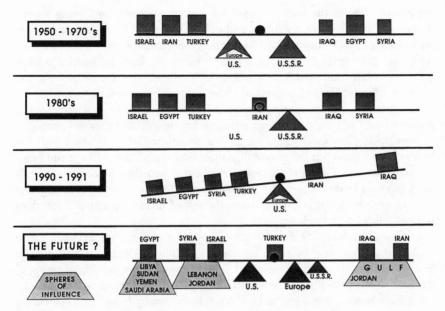

FIGURE 2.4 Equilibrium and the Middle East seesaw. SOURCE: Saul B. Cohen, "Geopolitical Change in the Post–Cold War Era," *Annals of the Association of American Geographers,* vol. 81, no. 4 (December 1991).

tion of conventional arms, and commitments to act against new regional aggressors), but outside powers cannot guarantee that turbulence will cease. The challenge, then, is to contain regional tensions and to minimize their impacts since it is not likely that they can soon be eliminated.

## Continuity of Major Core Areas

The present and previous geopolitical systems are characterized by continuity as well as change. The persistence of major power centers that lie within, are coextensive with, or overlap large states represents continuity. The Atlantic–Great Lakes United States, the Russian heartlandic industrial-agricultural triangle, the Western European–North Sea industrialized arc, the riverine plains of northeast and central China, and the central and southern Japan Inland Sea conurbations are the system's major geopolitical cores. And these cores maintain their economic and political importance in the face of ideological and economic upheavals or the geopolitical reorientation of their peripheries.

The growth and interaction of the five major power centers are a significant force for stability and continuity in the system. Maritime Europe and Japan often deter the United States from taking unilateral action, as in the Gulf War. At the same time, the hesitance of the European Community to take the lead in stopping the bloodletting in the former Yugoslavia reflects Europe's continuing dependence on American military might and political energy. The fears that offshore Asian nations harbor toward Japan in terms of its economic penetration of their region are mitigated by America's dominant military role in the Pacific. In addition, China has countered Soviet designs in Northeast and Southeast Asia, and the former Soviet Union has checked Chinese ambitions in South Asia.

The strength of these power centers is a function of their human and physical resource bases and their locational settings—and of political energies generated by overarching historically held ideals. The maritime United States, North Sea Europe, and Inland Sea Japan mobilize their total state frameworks around global exchange functions, and Russian "heartlandia" and riverine China are landward oriented in their bases and settings. Their strategic focus is on continental interior peripheries; maritime contact, though of increasing importance, does not radically change the base.

The test of the integrity and strength of a major geopolitical core is its ability to withstand the loss of substantial parts of its periphery. Thus, even without the Soviet empire and even if Ukraine and Belarus should fail to develop meaningful federative links with Russia, the Russian core persists as a world power. With its 125 million people, this industrialized triangle, extending from Saint Petersburg to Moscow to Rostov on the Don and then eastward across the Urals to the Kuznetsk Basin, also has fertile agricultural lands; rich deposits of oil and gas, iron ore, and metallic minerals; and a vast pool of scientific and technical manpower. With such resources, Russia is positioned to overcome the travails of its transition from a totalitarian Communist state to an open, democratic, and market-oriented system. Moreover, the richness of resources and space in its Siberian frontier is an unparalleled strategic reserve.

Riverine China, too, can withstand the loss of part of its periphery. This core is contained in the riverine valleys of the Yellow and Yangtse rivers and their coastal extensions, flanked by the grassy plains to the northwest and Manchuria. In contrast to the coastal south, the highly mineralized and heavily industrialized Chinese continental core, with a population of 350 million, is culturally isolated and economically self-contained. Its diversified agricultural base of grains, animals, and vegetables provides the largely rural population with an adequate livelihood. Should the southeast China coastal zone centering around Kwantung Province split off, riverine China would still be an independent colossus.

Southeast China—far different from the riverine core in dialects, culture, and orientation and suffering from overpopulation because of its limited coastal land base and narrow, interior valleys—is the maritime part of China. The overcrowded agricultural sectors cannot be supported adequately by paddy rice: Their populace seeks outlets through trade and immigration, as it has done through history. The China that is now opening itself to outside investment and the world exchange economy with such astonishing rapidity is the maritime China of the southeast, not the northern and central core. The continental core can withstand major upheaval—be it dismemberment of the People's Republic of China through defection of the south or the separation of or turmoil in Tibet, Inner Mongolia, and Sinkiang—and still remain a world power.

The American core area that once consisted of the U.S. manufacturing belt of the Northeast and Great Lakes areas, backed up by the Midwest prairie agricultural belt, has now become bimodal. California, and its southwestern extension into Arizona, has emerged as a second core of world-class standing. Moreover, southern Ontario has developed as an important extension of the Anglo-American Atlantic–Great Lakes core. Should California and the remainder of the United States–Canadian Pacific coastland break away politically to seek greater geopolitical orientation with the rest of the Pacific Rim, the Atlantic–Great Lakes core, with its 115 million people and unparalleled financial, manufacturing, research and agricultural resources, would still remain a power center of world-class proportions. This would also hold true if parts of the present periphery were lost—e.g., Alaska, Quebec, or southern Texas (the latter joining a new political configuration with northern Mexico).

Western and North Sea Europe, the economic heart of the European Community, is also a core area of such magnitude that it can withstand the shock of considerable territorial dissection. Surely, the European Community can survive without Denmark should the Danes persist in their opposition to the Maastricht Treaty. The same holds true for Ireland or other parts of the European Community that are peripheral, not core (e.g., Scotland, Iberia, southern Italy, or Greece). What makes North Sea Europe a persistent world power core is its skilled population of 175 million as well as the industries, markets, and agricultural and mineral resources of the belt that extends from midland and southeast England through the north of France, the Benelux countries, Germany, and northern Italy. Were the United Kingdom to reject European unity, the shock to the core would be comparable to the geopolitical orientation of Ukraine moving away from Russia and toward Eastern Europe. In both cases, the power of the cores would be seriously but not fatally damaged.

Because its core is so geographically compact and therefore inseparable and because its national periphery is of such limited importance, Inland Sea Japan is unique as a major core. Extending from the central and southern plains of the eastern Honshu coast (Tokyo-Yokahama, Osaka-Kobe, and Nagoya) to northern Kuyushu, this tightly packed coastal region of 80 million people contains the bulk of Japan's manpower, economy, and infrastructure. Japan has actually experienced considerable territorial expansion in modern times: Korea, Manchuria, and Taiwan were conquered and then lost in the span of half a century. However, the impact on the core was negligible.

Regarding the lands that Japan now holds, the secession of Hokkaido or Okinawa would have no geopolitical impact upon Japanese strength. In fact, Japan has gained through peaceful exchange what it failed to win in war. Its regional exchange area is the offshore Asian geopolitical region—from Australia through Southeast Asia to Taiwan, Hong Kong, and South Korea. Its major global exchange links are with the United States, but its ties to Europe and the Middle East are increasingly important. Moreover, Japan is the primary economic development partner for China and Asian Russia.

## The Gateway Concept:
## States and Regions

One of the most significant geopolitical phenomena of the past half century has been the proliferation of national states within the international system. The number of sovereign states in the world today approaches 200, which represents more than a quadrupling since 1939. Most of these states have emerged from the colonial period as subsistence-based territorial units. We can expect state proliferation to continue because there are still 30 political units in some form of dependency (colonies, dependencies, external territories) and 20 unit areas that are trust and self-governing territories, protectorates, departments, or commonwealths. Most of these are physically isolated, small islands with restricted economic bases, whose independence would not increase the world conflict probability index.

Furthermore, a considerable number of separatist or irredentist groups remain committed to military or terrorist struggles for freedom. There are over 50 such candidates for independence. For many, conflict will remain the order of the day, and these areas will then contribute to short-term global instability. Within and outside these two groupings, there are novel areas that may seek independence. These gateway states are uniquely suited to promote world peace, in keeping with the more general rise of what Richard Rosecrance calls the "trading state."[27]

The characteristics of gateway states vary in detail but not in overall context. Politically and culturally, they are distinct, historical culture hearths, with separate languages, religions, or national churches, higher degrees of education, and favorable access by sea or land to external areas. Economically, gateways tend to be more highly developed than the core areas of their host states for they are often endowed with strong entrepreneurial and trading traditions. When they are sources of migration because of overpopulation, they acquire links to overseas groups that can provide capital flows and technological know-how.

Small in area and population and frequently lying athwart key access routes, gateways are often of military value to their host states, whose security needs require defense guarantees should the gateways become independent. Although they may possess a highly specialized natural or human resource that provides an export base, they lack self-sufficiency and depend upon the host state for raw materials and a substantial market base. The models for such states have existed historically in Sheba, Tyre, and Nabataea; in the Hanseatic League and Lombard city-states; in Venice; and in Trieste and Zanzibar. Andorra, Monaco, Finland, Bahrain, and Malta are modern-day versions, as were Lebanon and Cyprus before they were dismembered.

Located mainly along the border of the world's geostrategic realms and geopolitical regions or within an integrating Europe, gateway states are optimally situated for specialized manufacturing, trade, tourism, and financial service functions, thus stimulating global economic, social, and political interaction. With independence, they will accelerate the trend of these borders being transformed from zones of conflict to zones of accommodation (Figure 2.5 and Table 2.1).

The emergence of such states can facilitate the creation of boundaries of accommodation, as foreseen by Lionel Lyde more than six decades ago.[28] Since World War II and until recently, the boundary between the two great geostrategic realms has been the world's most unstable conflict zone (from Greece to the Koreas to the Chinese-India borderland to Vietnam and Afghanistan). Now, however, war along this border zone has largely abated. Moreover, the level of conflict along geopolitical regional borders has not been higher than the world norm in recent years. This contrasts with the shatterbelt regions, which have experienced the highest intensity and frequency of war.

The addition of substantial numbers of new gateway states to the international system is in keeping with developmental theory because these will be economically specialized states that will help to link both the system as a whole and its various parts. Far from the traditional territorial unitary or federated states, whose goals included self-sufficiency and defense capacities, such states will be mini–trading states with qualified sovereignty. They will represent no military threat to their larger neighbors.

Although most gateway states are contributors to a more peaceful and stable system, a few gateways, such as Eritrea, Gaza–West Bank, or Tamil Eelam, will emerge only through bloody military conflict. But by and large, the decision to establish them will be mutually desired by the involved parties and will not mean complete secession and unqualified sovereignty, as was the case for many independent states coming out of decolonization. The conflict that will attend the emergence of most gateways will be minimal—limited by the asymmetry in strength of the opposing parties.

As the world system becomes more developed, certain portions of existing states will have to achieve flexibility in their interactions with their previous hosts. The ideal advanced general system has countless numbers of parts or hinges that can connect with each other without having to move through rigidly controlled, hierarchical pathways. The importance of having a more flexible international system within which states are linked globally, regionally, and sectorially is that this system can cope more easily with shocks as blockage points are bypassed and the system as a whole feeds on a multiplicity of nodes. In microelectronic circuitry, chips or gates permit currents to pass through arrays of transistors. Transistors are made faster by making them smaller, giving the current less distance to travel. This principle applies to the potential of gateway states to make the world system more responsive (Figure 2.6). Thus, the global linking potential of gateways stems from their ability to function as minihubs in the

40

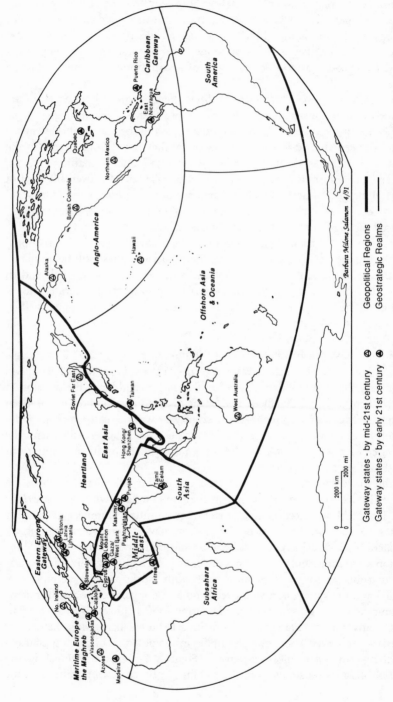

FIGURE 2.5   Prospective gateway states. SOURCE: Saul B. Cohen, "Geopolitical Change in the Post–Cold War Era," *Annals of the Association of American Geographers*, vol. 81, no. 4 (December 1991).

TABLE 2.1   *Prospective Gateway States*

| Area | Gateway states |
|---|---|
| Intergeostrategic realm orders | |
| Maritime Europe-heartland | Estonia, Latvia, Lithuania, Slovenia |
| Heartland-East Asia-offshore Asia | Russian Far East |
| Heartland–Anglo-America/Caribbean | Alaska |
| East Asia-offshore Asia | Hong Kong/Shenzhen/Kwangtung, Taiwan |
| East Asia-South Asia | Kashmir |
| | |
| Intergeopolitical regional borders | |
| Offshore Asia-Southeast Asia | West Australia |
| South Asia-Middle East | Pashtunistan, Punjab |
| Middle East-maritime Europe | Cyprus (unified) |
| Middle East-Sub-Saharan Africa | Eritrea |
| Maritime Europe–Anglo-America | Azores, Madeira |
| Anglo-America/Caribbean–South America | Puerto Rico |
| Anglo-American–offshore Asia | Hawaii |
| | |
| Intrageopolitical regions | |
| Anglo-American/Caribbean | Quebec, British Columbia, East Nicaragua, North Mexico |
| Maritime Europe/Kashmir/Maghreb | North Ireland, Vascongadas (Basque), Catalonia |
| Middle East | Gaza/West Bank, Mount Lebanon |
| South Asia | Tamil Eelam |

world system. Gateways can reach out to various first- and second-order powers, both reinforcing and helping to bridge the unique character of geopolitical regions.

Much has been written about the Baltic States and their drives for independence. The outcome of the turbulent "negotiations" (as perceived by the Lithuanians) or "discussions" (as they are termed by Soviet leadership), culminating in the collapse of the Soviet central government was international recognition of the Baltic Republics. Their development as gateway states is thus imminent. Most likely, Russia will insist upon full military control of Klaipeda (Memel), a major icefree military port with links to the Kaliningrad Russian oblast that, with Lithuanian independence, has become a Russian territorial exclave. Klaipeda's rail and road contacts with Kaliningrad and with Belarus and Moscow would have to be secured through transit rights. Elsewhere in the Baltic, Russia would want political and cultural rights guarantees for the relatively large Slavic populations in Latvia (41 percent) and Estonia (33 percent); this is only a minor problem in Lithuania where Slavs compose just 11 percent of the populace.

As with the Baltic States, Slovenia, too, has won its freedom with relatively little bloodshed—in sharp contrast to the fierce battles in Croatia and Bosnia-Herzegovina. The mild Serbian response to Slovenia's declaration of independence relates to the relatively small number of Serbs on Slovenian territory

42

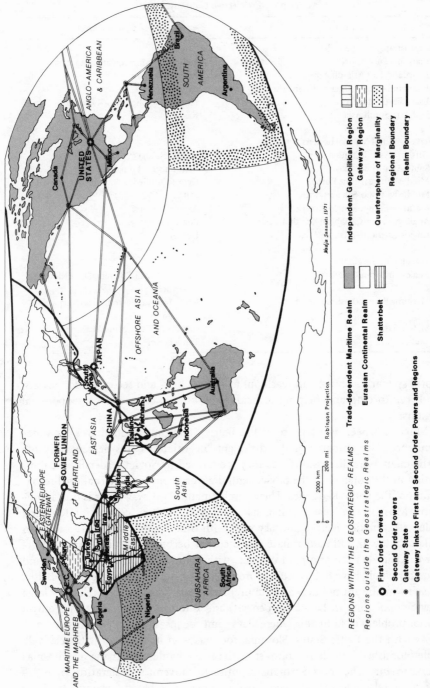

FIGURE 2.6 The gateway state network. SOURCE: Saul B. Cohen, "The World Geopolitical System, in Retrospect and Prospect," *Journal of Geography*, vol. 1 (January–February 1990).

and the physical separation between Slovenia and Serbia (Croatia lies between them).

Joining Europe is no mere slogan for the Slovenes. In contrast to the people in the eastward-oriented former Yugoslavian republics, Catholic Slovenes are culturally, historically, and geographically Central European, and they speak a south Slavic language that uses roman characters. Catholic Slovenes are also more economically advanced than the Christian orthodox Serbs. They have traditional links to Austria, Italy, and Hungary on which to promote development. Located within the southern border of the Austro-Hungarian Empire for eight centuries, the Slovenes are now prospering in an alpine valley and forested region well served with superhighways and modern housing. And they have the business and manufacturing skills to benefit from the freedom to interact with Europe on their own terms. The establishment of Yugoslavia's first stock market in Ljublijana is a reflection of Slovene entrepreneurship. Slovenia can be a prototypical gateway state. It will continue to provide markets for raw materials from Serbia, Croatia, and whatever other states emerge in the former Yugoslavia and facilitate industrial development and innovation that could be diffused to the new southern states.

Gateways may also be found among groups of peoples who have such limited defense and political foreign policy concerns that they can remain under the military umbrella of the countries to which they now belong. These gateways can evolve as microstates because they have the ability to specialize in financial services, capital flows, and tourism. Sometimes, they are the ideal place for assembling manufactured parts into finished products. And some of the gateway states, especially overpopulated areas, will have access to the capital and technical know-how of émigré populations who left crowded, agriculturally impoverished bases but retain emotional, familial ties.

Quebec is also a gateway candidate. With such status, it could focus on exploiting its advantages in human and raw materials to become a successful partner in the emerging North American free trade zone. So could a new northern Mexico state, building upon the economic vitality of its maquiladoras zone cities. Other examples are Alaska and Hawaii. Alaska, which has a very small independence party, could make its own decisions on how to exploit petroleum and where to ship it or on generating trade with the Soviet Far East. Hawaii could link the economies of Japan and the United States without being impeded by American law.

The European Community presents gateway state opportunities for European peoples who have sought independence—in particular the Basques, Catalans, and Walloons (although Waloonia may already have attained its desired status in Belgium's advanced confederal structure). These smaller groups could survive economically in a Europe without meaningful national political boundaries.

The listing of prospective gateway states in Table 2.1 does not encompass all the new states that are likely to be added to the current system. Independence forces in colonial or trust territories give impetus to the trend of national state proliferation; examples include the Kanaks of New Caledonia or ethnic minorities within existing states seeking their national freedom, like the Kurds, the Katangese in Zaire's Shaba, the Sulus in the southern Philippines, the Freitilin in East Timor, the Baluchis in Pakistan, the Shan in Burma, the Papuans in West Irian, the Nagas in India, the Afrikaaners in South Africa, and the Oromo (Galla) of Ethiopia. This proliferation has caused conflict and upheaval in much of the world since the end of World War II, as tribal and ethnic scores have been settled in the context of decolonization, and it will continue to do so.

The distinct contribution of gateways is that they can help stabilize the system because they function, above all, as links in an increasingly interdependent world. Uniquely suited to furthering peace, such novel states can help fashion what Peter Taylor has referred to as a people-centered world map.[29] Such a map is not an alternative to the state-centered map. Rather, it is a representation of a substantial number of territorial units whose goals are essentially devoted to the interests of peoples, not states; thus, it binds together states and regions.

Individuals and groups live in various categories of multiple worlds. These worlds overlap in time and in space. When they are experienced totally independently at the individual level, the person becomes dysfunctional. When they are handled in an integrated fashion, the individual enjoys harmony. The same holds true for our geopolitical lives. We live in a world system, a geopolitical region, a national state, a province or subnational state, and a locality (urban or rural). Although each of these territorially framed units has separate functions, the trend is toward greater overlapping.

Governors of various U.S. states and even mayors of big cities sign economic and cultural agreements with foreign national states that have political overtones that infringe on the prerogatives of the State Department. As the world becomes more complex, this overlapping will increase and so will the contradictions. Taylor points out that far from diminishing the importance of local forces, the enhancement of the world system will culminate in the mobilization of peoples in regions.[30]

Local forces and political power are often at odds with dominant national ideologies as well as with the restraints imposed by the world system. Reconciling these differences within national states and within geopolitical regions is the most severe challenge that a highly developed and integrated system must face. Gateway states and regions have very special roles to play in resolving these territorially based differences.

## Regions as Gateways

The most promising geopolitical mechanism for restoring the balance between the continental and maritime realms today is tied to the emergence of Central and Eastern Europe as a gateway region (Figure 2.6). Such a region could facilitate the transfer of new energies into the faltering Russian core. Extending on the west from the Oder and Neisse rivers and the Hartz and Bohemian mountains to the northern Adriatic Sea and on the east to the borders of Russia, the European gateway will be fully open to economic forces from the East and West. Its national politics and economic structures are adopting the Western European models, but it will have to find a military posture that does not challenge Russian security goals. With the exception of Greece, this region is composed of the middle tier of states between Germany and Russia whose independence and stability Mackinder felt to be crucial to Eurasian and world stability.[31]

Although demilitarization is not a viable option for the region, a form of "Finlandization" is a reasonable substitute for the breakup of the Warsaw Pact. This may occur through bilateral arrangements guaranteeing that Eastern European defense forces will oppose any attempts by Western armies to use their territories as jumping-off points against the heartland, while at the same time providing for a liaison between them and NATO (or the West European Union).

The promise of the gateway region is that it will facilitate the transfer of economic innovation from west to east and, ultimately, the reverse. As Eastern Europe (including the former East Germany) makes its painful transition to a market economy, its states should be able to exploit their low-cost, fairly well-educated labor pool and their raw material base and play a special role in serving as partners with Western transnational enterprises in developing joint agreements with Russia. Moreover, their experiences in balancing opportunities for economic growth with pressures to maintain some of the economic egalitarianism enjoyed during the past four decades should be of benefit. In the future, joint Russian–Eastern European companies may also focus on the Western market.

A gateway region has "hinges"—key states that take the lead as economic and social mediators in opening up the region in both directions. The eastern part of Germany can be such a hinge. So, potentially, can Slovenia, in terms of exchange between maritime Europe and the Balkans, and the Baltic states, in connection with northern and northwest Europe and the heartland.

Another gateway region that may emerge, although it is presently linked geopolitically to Anglo-America, is the Caribbean and Central America. It is and will remain within the security orbit of the United States, a condition that was never realistically in doubt even when the former USSR had footholds in Cuba and Nicaragua. The disappearance of the Soviet presence in the region gives greater scope for such regional powers as Mexico and Venezuela to extend their influence. At the same time, the United States, with less reason to focus on military issues, can commit more of its resources to regional development.

What makes this gateway especially important to the United States is its role as a source of immigrants. In addition, Mexico represents a major focus for "offshore" U.S. manufacturing, and the Caribbean basin as a whole has the potential for attracting Japanese and European capital via manufacturing points of entry to the U.S. market. Finally, the Caribbean's continued growth as the focus of Anglo-America's winter tourism is bright, given the demands of aging, wealthier populations in the north. On the negative side is the role of the region in drug trade. Among the hinge states in the region are Colombia, as a link to the Andean countries, and Venezuela, as an oil exporter to the United States. An independent Puerto Rico can also become a hinge gateway within the region.

## Conclusion

The world is still in its early stages of specialization and hierarchical integration, and the two geostrategic realms are sorting out the relationships of their respective internal power centers. Neither Russia nor China has yet achieved the national focus that will enable the heartland and East Asia to build a new chapter in Sino-Russian relations from the ashes of their schism. In addition, they are opening their national systems economically and, increasingly, politically. Meanwhile, the United States, the European Community, and Japan still must agree upon an allocation of global responsibilities in which the specialized military capacities of the United States are tempered by its economic parity with the other two.

At the geopolitical level, the different regions are at different stages of development, and their power and influence cannot be comparatively measured by the same criteria. They have varied attributes tied to their particular settings, including the presence or absence of major powers. The differing roles played by regional states within their regions depend on their particular qualities and thus their spatial and political-economic interactions with major powers and neighboring states. What helps link the system is the drive of the less mature parts to rise to levels already achieved by the more mature sectors.

Development means greater strength and self-confidence for the individual parts. The world system since World War II has been hegemonic, characterized by attempts to regulate from the top. In a more advanced system, the parts are more open, more capable of drawing in new energies, and more likely to find balance through self-regulation, either as the result of failure to achieve goals through war and competition or through cooperation.

In this chapter, I have set forth a global geopolitical system bound together by a series of linking and balancing mechanisms—the decrease of entropy levels for some regions, the use of gateways to strengthen the global network, or the attainment of a new strategic balance in Western Eurasia based upon offsetting economic and military inputs between the maritime and European continental realms. The system reflects not a New World Order—for order is a static, regulated, and precarious condition, subject to violent swings and upheavals—but a new stage of dynamic equilibrium. Within such a condition, change is continuing, and the system is maintained through greater self-regulation and self-fulfillment of the parts. If the aftermath of the Cold War does not mean a world free from tension and conflict, it does mean a world in which conflict is likely to be of a low level and short duration—a world in which the geography of accommodation is much more likely to attract geographers' attention than the geography of war.

## Notes

1. See the following works by Saul B. Cohen: *Geography and Politics in a World Divided,* 2d ed. (New York: Oxford University Press, 1973); "A New Map of Geopolitical Equilibrium: A Development Approach," *Political Geography Quarterly,* vol. 1, no. 3 (1982), pp. 223–242; "The World Geopolitical System, in Retrospect and Prospect," *Journal of Geography,* vol. 1 (January-February 1990), pp. 1–12; "Global Geopolitical Change in the Post–Cold War Era," *Annals of the Association of American Geographers* , vol. 81, no. 4 (December 1991), pp. 551–580.

2. Saul B. Cohen and L.D. Rosenthal, "A Geopolitical Model for Political Systems Analysis," *Geographical Review,* vol. 61, no. 1 (1971), pp. 5–31; Cohen, "Global Geopolitical Change."

3. Derwent Whittlesey, *German Strategy of World Conquest* (New York: Farrar and Rinehart, 1942); [no author] *The Economist World Atlas and Almanac* (New York: Prentice-Hall, 1989).

4. Arnold Guyot, *The Earth and Man,* trans. C.C. Felton (New York: Charles Scribner's, 1889).

5. Halford J. Mackinder, "The Geographical Pivot of History," *Geographical Journal,* vol. 23 (1904), pp. 421–444; idem, *Democratic Ideals and Reality* (New York: Henry Holt, 1919).

6. Immanuel Kant, *Perpetual Peace* (1795), trans. Lewis Beck (New York: Liberal Arts Press, 1957).

7. H.G. Wells, *Outline of History* (New York: Garden City Publishers, 1920).

8. Clarence Streit, *Union Now* (New York: Harper Brothers, 1938).

9. Adolf Hitler, *Mein Kampf* (1924), 7th ed. (Boston: Houghton Mifflin, 1943).

10. Cohen, *Geography and Politics in a World Divided.*

11. Immanuel Wallerstein, *Historical Capitalism* (London: Verso, 1983); G. Modelski, *Long Cycles in World Politics* (Seattle: University of Washington Press, 1987).

12. John O'Loughlin, "World Power Competition in Local Conflicts," in *World in Crisis?* 2d ed., R.J. Johnston and P.J. Taylor, eds. (Oxford: Basil Blackwell, 1989), pp. 289–332.

13. Herbert Spencer, "The Social Organism" (1860), in *Man Versus the State,* Donald Macrae, ed. (Baltimore: Penguin, 1969), pp. 1955–2033.

14. Heinz Werner, *Comparative Psychology of Mental Development,* rev. ed. (New York: International University Press, 1948).

15. Ludwig von Bertalanffy, *Organismic Psychology and Systems Theory* (Barre, Mass.: Clark University Press, 1966).

16. Cohen, "A New Map of Geopolitical Equilibrium," pp. 223–242.

17. Saul B. Cohen, "Asymmetrical States and Global Geopolitical Equilibrium," *SAIS Review,* vol. 4, no. 2 (1984), pp. 193–212.

18. Cohen, *Geography and Politics in a World Divided.*

19. James Atlas, "What is Fukuyama Saying?" *New York Times Magazine,* October 22, 1989, pp. 38–42, 54–55.

20. Saul B. Cohen, "Geography and Strategy: Their Interrelationships," *Naval War College Review,* vol. 10 (December 1957), pp. 1–31.

21. David Sanger, "Australia Is Striving to Be Asian, But How Asian?" *New York Times International,* August 16, 1992.

22. John O'Loughlin and Herman van der Wusten, "Political Geography of Pan-regions," *Geographical Review,* vol. 80 (1990), pp. 1–19.

23. Alfred Thayer Mahan, *The Influence of Sea Power upon History: 1660–1783* (Boston: Little, Brown, 1900).

24. James Fargrieve, *Geography and World Power* (London: University of London Press, 1915).

25. Richard Hartshorne, "The United States and 'the Shatter Zone' in Europe," in *Compass of the World,* H. Weigert and V. Stefannson, eds. (New York: Macmillan, 1944), pp. 203–214.

26. Philip Kelly, "Escalation of Regional Conflict: Testing the Shatterbelt Concept," *Political Geography Quarterly,* vol. 5, no. 2 (1986), pp. 161–180.

27. Richard Rosecrance, *Rise of the Trading State* (New York: Basic Books, 1986).

28. Lionel Lyde, *The Continent of Europe* (London: Macmillan, 1926).

29. Peter Taylor, "Tribulations of Transition," *The Professional Geographer,* vol. 44, no. 1 (1992), pp. 10–12.

30. Peter Taylor, "The World-Systems Project," in *World in Crisis?* 2d ed., R.J. Johnston and P.J. Taylor, eds. (Oxford: Basil Blackwell, 1989), pp. 333–354.

31. Mackinder, "The Geographical Pivot of History," and idem, *Democratic Ideals and Reality.*

# THREE

## The Power and Politics of Maps

ALAN K. HENRIKSON

### The World as a Map

TO APPRECIATE THE complexities of international relations, at both the academic and the professional levels, an understanding of cartography is more important than is commonly realized. "The world we have to deal with politically," Walter Lippmann wrote many decades ago, "is out of reach, out of sight, out of mind. It has to be explored, reported, and imagined." Like denizens of Plato's cave, officials who are immured inside their government bureaucracies must, for the most part, experience the events of the vast external realm indirectly. Referring to diplomats, Lippmann, who had been an adviser at the conference in 1919 that produced the Versailles Treaty, noted that "their persistent difficulty is to secure maps on which their own need, or someone else's need, has not sketched in the coast of Bohemia."[1]

Foreign policy, which comprises the spectrum from information to trade to defense and security policies, is based on diplomats' conceptions of the actual world and their own countries' situations within it. No less a political figure than Napoleon Bonaparte asserted that "the policy of a state lies in its geography."[2] In this political context, "geography" means more than topographical irregularity or climatic variation, more than distribution of mineral resources or configurations of human settlement, and even more than patterns of commerce and finance or networks of transport and communication. It signifies the almost a priori spatial frame of reference, which is usually centered on an imagined point of origin within the core area of a country from which the activities of that society are organized and proceed. The foreign thrusts as well as the domestic initiatives of a regime and nation are thus guided.

To formulate a political plan, diplomats must have a geographical conception, which requires the cartographic image of a map. In fact, actual maps, as well as mappable ideas and spatial consciousness and sensitivity ("mental maps"), are a critical variable—occasionally even the decisive factor—in the making of public

policy. Without knowledge of what is going on geographically and an actual "picture" or structured image of the developments and events taking place
at large to help organize that knowledge, it is impossible to conceive of or to effectively carry out a large-scale purpose. No military campaign, development
project, or, at a more abstract level, diplomatic strategy or information program
can be intellectually sustained or practically executed unless it is plotted spatially.
The conception, development, and implementation of policy depend on mapping in complex and interrelated ways.

Through maps and charts—through these graphic representations virtually
alone—the earth and its regions have acquired the shapes by which we know
them. Not only the outlines but also the sizes, distances, and directions of the
globe's territorial and maritime expanses are most often apprehended first
through the logical structures and vivid images of cartography. Long before they
are actually visited, the world's remote geographical areas usually are visualized,
sometimes very fancifully, in the mind's eye.

The principal sources of our world vision and much of our factual knowledge
of the earth and the happenings upon it are the terrestrial map, the nautical chart,
and, increasingly, the high-altitude aerial photograph and satellite image. Indeed,
our very concept of "world," an ideological construct that is usually more
philosophical than geographical in content, can be framed and articulated by
cartography.

Images such as the sublime "Earthrise" photograph taken from the moon
during the *Apollo 8* voyage in 1968 have transformed our sense of place and belonging. Men and women otherwise divided along lines of nationality, ideology,
race, and class could suddenly be seen as one humankind.[3] At more technical
levels of observation, too, important insights were gained into earth and its conditions. These were facilitated by the new possibilities of space-based mapping,
which used remote sensors and computers. With this advanced technology and
the development of geographic information system (GIS) software, vast areas of
the planet could be scanned at once, and masses of collected data regarding resources, habitats, and communities could readily be translated into geometri-
cally correct, flexible, and detailed cartographic forms.[4]

Maps are more than formal projections that describe the world mathemati-
cally. They are products of geographical thought that typically presents itself
visually. Maps have, first of all, a *synoptic* quality. They display conditions that
exist contemporaneously over the entire area covered, making it possible to see
everything at once—affording a general view as well as an opportunity to examine specific features more closely. The simultaneous complexity of the events
in the perceptual array of a map is perhaps cartography's dominant and most
distinguishing attribute.[5] But maps also have what has been called a *hypnotic,* or
suggestive, effect. "Cartohypnosis," as a former U.S. State Department Geographer has termed the subtle persuasiveness of maps, causes people to "accept un-
consciously and uncritically the ideas that are suggested to them by maps."[6] Finally, maps can be *emblematic,* or representative in a pictorially symbolic way of a

territory and the polity or other entity or occurrence upon it. Older maps particularly tend to be festooned with the indicia of statecraft, navigational technique, or the fruits of discovery or conquest. Map emblems have appeared in historical paintings—portraits of Napoleon, for example—as territorial symbols or geographical icons. Maps thus may be embedded in the discourse of politics and of art, just as political symbols can be embedded in the language of maps.[7]

Map representations usually (though not necessarily) are made on paper. Clay tablets were used in ancient times, and oxhide or vellum (fine-grained lambskin, kidskin, or calfskin) was employed from that point through the Middle Ages. The beautiful, large *mappa mundi* (c. 1283 A.D.) in Hereford Cathedral, for example, is drawn on leather. The mapping of exploration in the Renaissance period—the great works of Martin Waldseemüller, Gerardus Mercator, Abraham Ortelius, and Jodocus Hondius, many of which were collected in atlases—were visually spectacular.[8]

Much of the earlier cartography was ephemeral, produced for temporary or even onetime use. Religious pilgrims on journeys to holy places in Europe or the Near East, for instance, carried road maps on cloth or paper strips. North American Indians made maps on birch bark or merely drew them in the sand, indicating that they did not consider maps to be valuable in themselves but rather as merely accessories to geographic knowledge. Moreover, the heavens as well as earth can be mapped. The Pawnee apparently used star charts painted on and perforated through elkskin for orientation and probably for contemplation.[9] Indigenous American maps usually served immediate, practical needs, such as locating sites, showing directions, or tracing routes. Unlike most European and European-American maps, which emphasized boundaries, Indian maps typically were composed of small circles for villages and interconnecting lines for pathways. There were no vast rectangular frames to record property lines, land grants, or territorial claims.[10] Indeed, Native American cartography, neither legalistic in motivation nor aimed at future historical validation, probably was not even meant to last. The Indians' real maps—the timeless, cosmological ones as well as the transitory, utilitarian ones—were mostly in their heads.

Such mental or noncartographic maps should be (but rarely are) included within any consideration of mapping. "Cognitive" maps, as they sometimes are also called, are arguably the ultimate maps because they are the ones actually relied upon in making decisions regarding the environment and movement within it.[11] It can be misleading, however, to use the term *maps* for such cognitive knowledge of environmental reality unless such cognizance involves conscious spatialization. That is, there must be not merely a multitude of geographical facts in the mind but also a more or less accurate sense of the voluminousness of the world and of the places within it, in roughly correct relationship to each other. In other words, there should be not only cognitive territory but also some isomorphism, or similarity in structure, between the mental map and the physical world.[12]

The structures of mental maps can be highly complex, but they have a number of basic common features. Adapting terms from the work of planner Kevin

Lynch, who applied them only on an urban scale, one may distinguish specific constituent elements in many mental maps. These maps consist of *paths,* or the channels along which people regularly travel or imagine doing so; *edges,* or the internal and external boundaries that inhibit their movements; *districts,* or the geographical-cultural regions in which they reside or within which they might move; *nodes,* or the intersections on which their own and others' activities center; and *landmarks,* or the geographical signs they refer to for self-orientation and perhaps also for the direction of others.[13] The geographical knowledge reflected in a mental map should be capable of being transposed, in its essential elements and pattern, from the mind to a surface—that is, one should be able to actually draw or otherwise cartographically render the mental map.

What drawn or printed maps do that brain- or computer-stored geographical data bases, as such, do not is to represent clearly an *image* of the environment. Such images are useful and sometimes even necessary to communicate spatial-geographical relationships and facts to others. They may even be helpful in self-orientation, although they need not always be consciously used in this way. Even in an inattentive state, skillful behavior in space may be possible under the guidance of well-articulated schemata.[14]

Map-making (including mental map-making) and map-using (which includes map-perceiving and map-contemplating) are both visual and cognitive activities. Vision and thought—visual thinking—constitute a unified mental process.[15] It is through the lens of the map, be it cartographic and noncartographic, that we see, know, and even create the larger world.

## Map Geometry, Map Symbols, and Their Perception

The notion of a "map," in both broad and narrow senses, is essentially that of a model, a representation of a geographical area (usually) on a flat surface. Ordinarily, each point on the cartographic diagram corresponds to an actual geographical position on earth, according to a definite scale or system of projection. Map projections transform the curved, three-dimensional surface of the earth onto a two-dimensional plane. And flattening inevitably produces distortions—consider what happens to an orange peel when flattened on a table top. Hence, as an old saying warns, "All maps lie flat, therefore all flat maps lie."

In general, scale distortion increases with distance from a standard point or line. The map-maker minimizes distortion by centering the projection in or near the region to be featured by the map. The usual trade-off that has to be made in map-making is that between what is called conformality and equivalence—that is, between preserving the shapes of the earth's configurations and keeping areas everywhere equal so that there is no size variation anywhere on the map. Except for a globe, which is often made up of stretched paper map-gores, no map can be perfectly conformal *and* equivalent.

The developable, or flattenable, surfaces most commonly used for map projections are the plane, the cone, and the cylinder (Figure 3.1). Projections of the earth grid of parallels (latitude) and meridians (longitude) onto a tangent plane gives a gnomonic projection, which is especially useful in long-range aerial and other navigation. On this azimuthal map, the earth's shapes become highly distorted as the distance along the radiating azimuths from the center of projection (point of tangency) increases. All great-circle, or shortest-distance, routes, however, can be represented conveniently as straight lines.

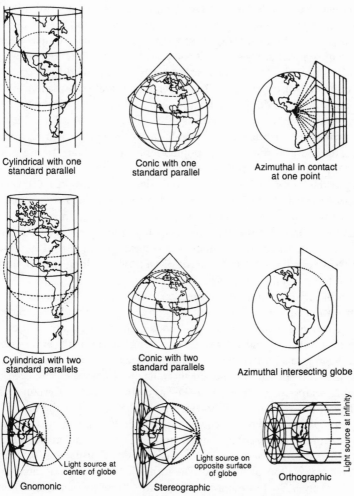

Cylindrical with one standard parallel

Conic with one standard parallel

Azimuthal in contact at one point

Cylindrical with two standard parallels

Conic with two standard parallels

Azimuthal intersecting globe

Gnomonic — Light source at center of globe

Stereographic — Light source on opposite surface of globe

Orthographic — Light source at infinity

FIGURE 3.1 Geometrical properties of various cylindrical, conic, and azimuthal projections. SOURCE: Norman J.W. Thrower, *Maps and Man: An Examination of Cartography in Relation to Culture and Civilization* (Englewood Cliffs, N.J.: Prentice-Hall, 1972). Reprinted by permission.

Projections onto a cone produce maps on which many elements—shapes, distances, angles—are true but only along the line of tangency, or standard parallel. Away from that line, distortion develops. Conic maps have been used for showing areas of vast east-west extent, such as the territory of the former USSR.

Projections upon a cylinder, often favored for world maps such as Gerardus Mercator's famous conformal projection, are not faithful to area. High above and far below the line of tangency at the equator, the sizes of lands and seas become greatly exaggerated. The classic illustration of the Mercator map's faults is the island of Greenland, which is actually about the same size as Saudi Arabia but appears larger than South America (see Figure 3.2). The wonderful utility of the Mercator projection lies in the realm of maritime navigation because, since a line between any two points on it gives true direction, a sailor's compass course can easily be drawn as a straight line. If such a compass route (rhumb-line or loxodrome) lies near the equator or nearly on a meridian, the difference between it and the shortest-distance, great-circle route is comparatively small. As most shipping occurs in the middle latitudes, the advantages and benefits of the Mercator projection are therefore considerable.[16]

To show the distribution of elements upon the earth, such as mineral resources, agricultural products, or population, it is necessary to use equal-area maps. One equal-area map that presents the earth without rounding or interrupting is the so-called Peters projection (Figure 3.2), advocated during recent decades by German historian Arno Peters.[17] Such is the distortion of continental outlines and political boundaries on this rectangularly framed map, however, that Arthur Robinson, a senior academic cartographer interested in the "look" as well as the technical qualities of maps, has remarked that, on the Peters map, "the landmasses are somewhat reminiscent of wet, ragged, long, winter underwear hung out to dry on the Arctic circle."[18]

The principle of geometrical projection is not the only factor that influences the perception of maps. The orientation of the map—that is, the direction in which the earth is turned on a map—also is a powerful determinant of the way the world is imagined and studied. Seeing "north" traditionally at the top of global maps can lead an uncritical map-viewer to assume, without realizing the subtle effects of this convention, that northern territories, peoples, and even cultures are higher—superior qualitatively as well as cartographically. Certain societies—early Egypt, for example—did not invariably place north at the top; for Egyptians, perhaps even today, the course of the Nile River suggested a downward, south-to-north cartographic flow. In medieval Christian maps, which were highly schematic, the East, or Asian, part where "Eden" or paradise was fancied to be located was on top, at the head. The form of these maps was circular—an O partitioned by a T—representing the world's three principal waterways, the Tanais (Don) and Nile rivers across and the Mediterranean downward (Figure 3.3). Jerusalem, the "navel" in this figurative world body, was usually placed at the center of these T-in-O designs. The large thirteenth-century map in Hereford Cathedral was a culmination of this tradition.[19]

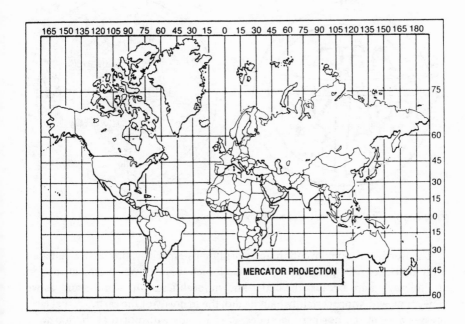

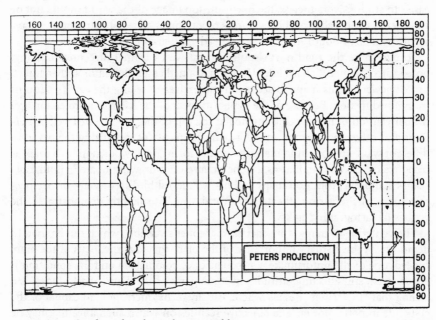

FIGURE 3.2 Conformal and equal-area world maps.

FIGURE 3.3   The Asia-oriented medieval world view.

The north-on-top convention, for world maps especially, probably originated with Greek scientist-geographer Claudius Ptolemy. North was placed at the top in Ptolemy's maps because the better-known localities of the world—and, as we now know with more certainty than he did, the majority of the earth's actual land areas—were in the northern latitudes. World maps with north at the top were easier to study.[20] Nonetheless, the north-on-top image of the world should not be considered unalterable, as the producers of a popular series of "turnabout" maps, with Australia or South America at the head, cartographically point out.[21]

To overcome the rigid north-south or east-west cardinal-direction thinking, noted cartographer Richard Edes Harrison, trained as an illustrator and architect, urged viewers of his maps to accustom themselves to seeing the earth's patterns from *any* direction. Because of the hypnotic effect of the Mercator projection and the convention of north being situated at the top of the page, he believed, Americans and others had compromised a critical capacity of visualizing the world in different ways. He sought to make the earth's forms, in any position on a map, as recognizable and as familiar as a french curve on a drawing board.[22] Both Harrison's standard-projection maps and his wonderful bird's-eye-view, or perspective, maps of the various theaters of World War II brilliantly demonstrated the virtues of cartographic agility.[23]

The centering of maps is another cartographer's variable, which can be used to demonstrate the primary importance of the place that is at the focus of the map. Indeed, one of the unfortunate consequences of colonialism and the condition it engendered, still affecting attitudes in some parts of the Third World today, is a feeling that "the center" lies elsewhere, usually in the metropolitan capital of the erstwhile imperial power. The objective realities on which such a feeling may be grounded and the sensation of peripheralness itself cannot be altered, of course, simply by shifting or reducing the graphic frame of the map. Nonetheless, it is noteworthy that one of the first steps of a newly independent country often is to commission a national atlas, to print stamps with a map of the country's outline on them, and to otherwise use the emblem of the map to assert the country's new identity in a new setting—reflecting a new pride of place.[24]

Alternatively, the centering of maps can also be used to demonstrate "encirclement," suggesting vulnerability, weakness, and uncertainty. Before and during World War I, Imperial Germany proclaimed its fear of *Einkreisung*, that is, of being encircled by hostile powers intent upon choking off its access, limiting its opportunities, and blighting its future. The German Imperial Fleet, for example, was said to be "bottled up" by the British Royal Navy. A generation later, propagandists in Nazi Germany complained of the same discriminated-against geographic condition. By force of arms, especially naval but also aerial and land-based arms, the German war machine sought to break through the enclosing circle of Allied power. Some of the Third Reich's maps illustrated this *Durchbruch*, or breakout, attempt.[25]

The U.S.-led Western policy of "containing" the Soviet Union and its presumed effect on the Russians is roughly analogous, even in the encircled party's tendentious use of maps. During the U.S.-Soviet summit meeting off Malta in December 1989, for example, Soviet leader Mikhail Gorbachev handed President George Bush a blue-and-white map allegedly showing the Soviet Union's encirclement by U.S. bases as well as American aircraft carriers and battleships. Prepared by Marshal Sergei Akhromeyev, this map was designed to underscore the Soviet General Staff's contention that U.S. vessels armed with submarine-launched cruise missiles (SLCMs) posed an especially serious threat to the USSR. For a moment, according to a detailed account of this episode, President Bush was at a loss for words. President Gorbachev then said tartly: "I notice that you seem to have no response." Bush, in response, pointed out to Gorbachev that the Soviet landmass was shown on the map as a giant, white, empty space, with no indication of the vast military complex that U.S. forces were intended to deter. "Maybe you'd like me to fill in the blanks on this," he said. "I'll get the CIA to do a map of how things look to us. Then we'll compare and see whose is more accurate."[26]

Besides geometry, which, as noted, includes issues not only of projection but also of perspective, coverage, and centering, it is symbolization that determines the nature and the effectiveness of a map. Apart from the basic question of selecting map features—that is, the thematic content of a map and the characteristics of earth that are to be observed and described—*symbolization* refers to the kind of graphic indicators used. In a comprehensive listing of map symbols produced by cartographer Mark Monmonier, symbols are representative markings that may vary in size, shape, graytone value, texture or surface pattern, orientation or direction, and hue or color attribute. Shape, texture, and hue are effective in showing qualitative differences, as among land uses or dominant religions, he notes. For quantitative differences, size is more suited to showing variation in amount or count, whereas graytone is better for portraying variations in rate or intensity. The symbols that vary in orientation are most useful for "representing winds, migration streams, troop movements, and other directional occurrences."[27]

The most obviously dynamic map symbols are the oriented, or directional, ones, such as the concentric circles and arrows drawn on German maps to indicate the pressures of Einkreisung constraint and the counterforces of a Durchbruch strategy. Even the contrasting of colors and the juxtaposition of filled and voided areas, as in the Soviet map that was designed to show the Western encirclement of continental Russia, stimulate interest. Many studies have been made on the psychological effects of variations of color and other symbols on maps.[28]

Propaganda maps, many of which are patently purposive and "readable," are not the only ones that can have an energizing effect on a viewer. Because of the systemic variations and unique elements in them, nearly all maps are dynamic to some degree. As cognitive psychologist and art theorist Rudolf Arnheim maintains, the shapes and colors of cartography have an "animating" quality. What meets the eyes first and foremost when looking at a map, he explains, are not the measurable phenomena represented by dimensions, distances, or the geometry of shapes on the map but "the expressive qualities" carried by the stimulus data. Studying a map can actually make the viewer feel the underlying spatial forces of the map structure "as pushes and pulls in his own nervous system."[29] Indeed, it is the "look" of maps that is decisive: If a map does not engage the mind of the active viewer and create a reciprocal exchange of the map-maker's ideas and information and the viewer's understanding and interests, it does not succeed in achieving its purpose as a map. It is, in that case, not a map but rather an inert collection of lines, dots, and blank spaces, perhaps mixed with color.

The processes of map-perception can never be completely analyzed by purely scientific measurement of the interchange between map and viewer. The geometrical and symbolic elements of maps must combine to communicate concepts and images, which must be perceived as wholes, as mentally integrated *sets* of sensations and induced feelings. The whole-forming qualities, or *Gestaltqualitäten*, of maps are grasped by the unifying intuition, rather than simply through an accumulation of stimulus-response reactions.[30]

## Power, Politics, and Policy

Maps are purposeful and persuasive, sometimes explicitly and nearly always implicitly. "Every map is someone's way of getting you to look at the world his or her way," proposes Lucy Fellowes, cocurator of the Cooper-Hewitt National Museum of Design exhibition entitled "The Power of Maps." Part of the reason why maps are so effective, further suggests Denis Wood, the other cocurator of the exhibit, is "the impression they manage to convey that they are precisely above such interest. They are convincing because the interest they serve is masked."[31]

The patronage of maps repays thought.[32] Cartography, as Brian Harley, a sociologically inclined historian of mapping, points out, was always "the science of princes." In the Moslem world, the caliphs and then the sultans were known to have sponsored map-making, as did the Mughal emperors of India and the rulers of China. In early modern Europe, absolute monarchs lent their patronage to cartography. Beginning in the eighteenth century, when national topographic surveys began, state sponsorship increasingly took over, favoring the policies and interests of elites.[33]

The map is almost the perfect representation of the state. It evenly covers the territory of a country.[34] And it hierarchically organizes it, with the capital—Paris, London, Berlin, or Washington, D.C.—symbolically at the center, and provinces, counties, *Länder* (German provinces), or states on the periphery marked down, through the use of symbols, as inferior orders of government.[35] Beneath these, there are still-lower orders of civic organization. The existence of some social and cultural realities—ethnic clusters or religious centers, for example—might not be recognized on state-sponsored maps at all.

Some of the "silences" on maps, as Harley calls the blank spaces on them, are "silences of uniformity," of standardization. Others are more specifically intended, the result of deliberate exclusion, willful ignorance, or even actual repression. The removal or the alteration of place names—the named locations of conquered peoples or minority groups, for instance—creates eloquent "toponymic silences."[36] The state projection of geometrical designs throughout a country in the form of straight-line jurisdictional boundaries, transnational highways, and preserves of one kind or another—thus establishing "order upon the land"—can also produce what might be termed *geographical silences,* or the structural subordination of the natural landforms that shape human communities. In Harley's characterization, cartography, like politics itself, was and remains today "a teleological discourse, reifying power, reinforcing the *status quo,* and freezing social interaction within charted lines."[37]

The teleological thrust or natural purposefulness of state-centered cartography also extends into the external realm. Exploration into unknown parts, and the cartographic recording thereof, was sponsored by Portugal's Prince Henry the Navigator and by subsequent monarchs or presidents of other countries, including Spain, France, Great Britain, the Netherlands, and the United States. American expansion, no less than that of European empires, was preceded by mapmaking and geographical imagining. President George Washington himself was a surveyor. His fellow Virginian Thomas Jefferson became a continentwide and global plotter: His Lewis and Clark Expedition (1803–1806) measured the width of the continent and opened it to the course of Manifest Destiny, aimed at establishing an empire on the Pacific.[38]

When the United States attained a broad position on the Pacific slope after its military victory over Mexico in the 1846–1848 war, it was placed at the center of world maps for the first time.[39] Other factors influencing this Americentric cartographic adjustment were Lieutenant Charles Wilkes's U.S. Exploring Expedition into the Pacific (1838–1842), the discovery of gold in California (1848), the restoration of the Union with the North's military success in the Civil War (1865), and the American purchase of Alaska from Russia (1867). The U.S. victory in the Spanish-American War of 1898 confirmed the centrality of the United States in the world order. On American-produced world maps, such as the "Map of the World on the Mercator Projection" shown in S. Augustus Mitchell's *New General Atlas* and subsequent works, the whole global frame shifted—the world moved![40]

In U.S. foreign policy at that time, it was not, in truth, the world as a whole but rather the "Western Hemisphere"—a cartographer's convention before it became a geopolitical concept—that seemed appropriate for American concerns. The 1823 Monroe Doctrine had postulated that the European and American hemispheres were "essentially different" systems. It seemed, therefore, that the future of the New World ought to proceed independently, in clear political separation from that of the Old World.[41] The cartographic template for the "two spheres" in international politics was the European split-hemisphere *mappemonde* dating from the Renaissance era (Figure 3.4).[42]

Since the nineteenth century until at least World War II, the notion of "hemisphere defense" was the touchstone of American thinking on national security. This was in part a subtle consequence of a prevailing mental picture of the United States as being located in a separate hemisphere or at the center of the world, shielded by two vast oceans. This cartographic logic either removed the Eastern

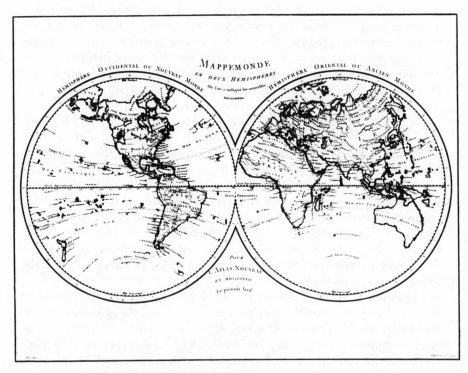

FIGURE 3.4   *Mappemonde* in two hemispheres.

Hemisphere from any contact with the New World altogether or split the mighty Eurasian landmass in two. The Europeans' Far East ended up on the far west of American world maps. Efforts to dehypnotize American popular thinking by demonstrating graphically, through a series of alternatively centered maps, that the Western Hemisphere idea is arbitrary and that hemispheres could be defined that would cover all of Europe and indeed most of the rest of the globe (including the United States) probably had little effect in themselves (Figure 3.5).[43] Only the Japanese attack on Pearl Harbor, launched far across the Pacific, and the conversion of the Atlantic Ocean by U.S. Navy forces into an "American lake" joining America and Europe would disabuse the country of the notion of continental or hemispheric impregnability and safety.[44]

Despite the post–World War II alliances between the United States and Western Europe as well as Japan, the concept of "this hemisphere" as a relevant policy idea continues to exert an intellectual and emotional force in America. President Bush's Enterprise for the Americas Initiative of June 1990 (which was based upon President Ronald Reagan's North American Accord proposal of November 1979, favoring Canadian-U.S.-Mexican cooperation) is a recent case in point. The role of geographical imagery in engendering a sense of North American or even pan-American diplomatic coordination and comity can be crucial. Whether the successfully negotiated North American Free Trade Agreement (NAFTA) succeeds in fostering a sense of North American community may depend partly on whether the Canadian, American, and Mexican peoples have a strong enough and a sufficiently shared mental map of North America as a unified entity.[45] The use of actual cartography to define and describe that landmass, which for three centuries after Columbus had no political dividing lines and whose natural geological-economic "grain" runs mainly north and south, could enhance NAFTA's chances of larger success, beyond a mutual sharing of markets.[46] The same proposition—the indispensability of a vibrant geographical concept and an image of their common region—may also govern the outcome of

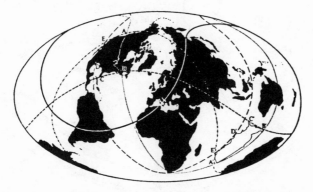

FIGURE 3.5  The sum of all hemispheres containing all of the United States.

future economic discussions between North American and South American countries.[47]

From the experience of World War II, an entirely different and cartographically novel image of the future international relations of the United States developed. This was the notion of an "Arctic Mediterranean" space—which synoptically gathered all the lands, seas, and air spaces around the Arctic Circle and outward from it in every direction—in a New World Order of peace, friendship, and commerce, particularly by means of aviation. The base map for this alternative image, often touted as a replacement for the equator-based Mercator projection, was the North Pole–centered global chart, such as the widely reproduced azimuthal equidistant world map prepared by Richard Edes Harrison (Figure 3.6).

Harrison's map, rotated 90° in order to situate Europe (with the prime meridian running through Greenwich, England) rather than the continent of North America upon the vertical axis, or spine, of the world body, was used in designing

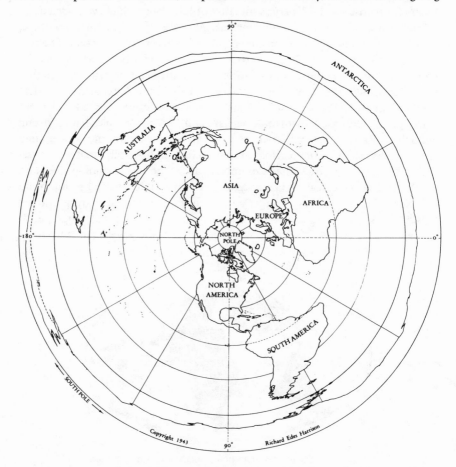

FIGURE 3.6  Azimuthal equidistant world map centered on the North Pole.

the map emblem of the new United Nations. This symbol of pacific universalism, which expressed Americans' postwar hopes if not their realistic expectations, was officially described as follows: "A map of the world representing an azimuthal equidistant projection centered on the North Pole, inscribed in a wreath consisting of crossed conventionalized branches of the olive tree; in gold on a field of smoke blue with all water areas in white."[48] No political boundaries are indicated on it. Today, with the military-strategic barriers between East and West overcome, that idealistic map image can perhaps become relevant in a practical sense.[49]

Polar projections increasingly have been used to demonstrate the oneness of the world in more scientific ways as well. Satellite imagery, often produced by spacecraft that repeatedly circle the earth in polar orbits, is synoptic enough to be capable of revealing global, systemic patterns. The visual emergence of the ozone hole over Antarctica in the late 1980s is a case in point. The actual picture of the hole, shown in the striking false colors of the widely publicized satellite imagery, contributed powerfully to international recognition of the problem and to public support for a negotiated solution.[50] So, too, did graphically presented information regarding ozone depletion over the more heavily populated higher latitudes of the Northern Hemisphere. The September 1987 Montreal Protocol on Substances That Deplete the Ozone Layer benefited from this widespread awareness, even if it did not directly result from it, as some have asserted.[51] The influence of "ecospectral mapping" from space will continue. When maps are linked to GIS models of environmental processes like ozone depletion or the greenhouse effect, they can serve as crystal balls.[52]

For addressing contemporary international issues of economic and social concern, the more conventional, equal-area maps are most frequently used. Distributional data are best displayed on such projections for with them, accurate spatial and statistical comparisons can be made. Today, the technical virtues of equal-area maps are not the only features valued for their use in the comparative analysis of data regarding issues such as population growth, mineral allocation, or the world distribution of hunger or disease.[53] The emblematic and therefore political quality of the equal-area projection has also contributed to its popularity.

In a veritable battle of the maps, the controversial Peters projection has been pitted against the Mercator projection as the preferred symbol for world order— "a map for our day"—in the twenty-first century.[54] Arno Peters himself has charged that it is always the countries of the Third World, often ex-colonial states, that are "disadvantaged on Mercator's map."[55] His cartographic correction of the alleged Eurocentric bias of Mercator's projection is a map that not only shows countries in correct size relation to each other (at the cost of considerable and needless distortion of shape) but also puts the equator back in the middle of the map (as the modified versions of the Mercator conformal map commonly used today do not). The consequence of these simple changes is to make South America, Africa, and Australia larger and more visually prominent (see Figure 3.2).[56]

The Peters map has been enthusiastically adopted by church groups, development institutes, various national governments, and even certain international organizations on the basis of an apparent belief that cartographic equivalence will militate in favor of social and cultural equality, economic equity, and political equilibrium.[57]

## Conclusion

The notion of objectivity in cartography is an aspiration for the map-maker and a presumption for the map-viewer. At the same time, objectivity is an impossible ideal. Not even the globe, which permits us to see the world as round but not all at once in its entirety, is a perfect map. There is no single framework that will satisfy every criterion of map-making (notably conformality and equivalence), but there are many map concepts and designs that do suffice for particular purposes. The Robinson projection, which is an attempt to circumvent some of the more overt political criticisms of other projections, is described by its maker, Arthur Robinson, as an attempt to "create a portrait," albeit an inaccurate one, of the earth. For Robinson, the "artistic" approach came first, which was followed by "the mathematical formula" to produce the visual effect he liked. John Garver, chief cartographer of the National Geographic Society (which, in 1988, replaced the Van der Grinten projection with Robinson's projection for its new world map), judged Robinson's map as "the best balance available between geography and aesthetics" (Figure 3.7).[58]

Cartography is a combination of science and art, of the objective and the subjective in human thought and activity. Like the world itself, the map is both an object and an idea, a material entity and a mental construct. Map-making and map-viewing are both, therefore, influenced and informed by biases, some obvious and others subliminal. However, a basic knowledge of how maps are planned and how they may be intended, that is, the politics of mapping, enables a map-reader to gain the faculty of graphic literacy and thereby an awareness of the power of maps.

## Notes

1. Walter Lippmann, *Public Opinion* (New York: Harcourt, Brace, 1922), pp. 16, 29. Lippmann's reference to "Bohemia" probably was literary as well. In Shakespeare's comedy *The Winter's Tale*, one of the stage settings is Bohemia, identified incongruously as "A desert Country near the Sea" (act 3, scene 3).

2. Yves Lacoste, "Geopolitics and Foreign Policy," *SAIS Review*, vol. 4, no. 2 (Summer-Fall 1984), p. 213.

3. President Lyndon B. Johnson sent copies of the *Apollo* photograph to all the world's heads of state, including Ho Chi Minh. See Walter A. McDougall, *The Heavens and the Earth: A Political History of the Space Age* (New York: Basic Books, 1985), p. 412.

## ROBINSON PROJECTION

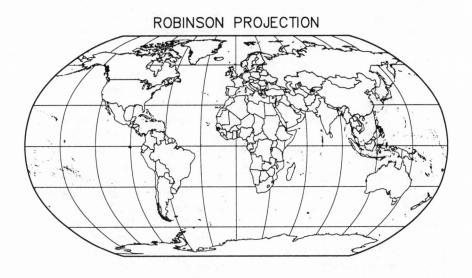

## VAN DER GRINTEN PROJECTION

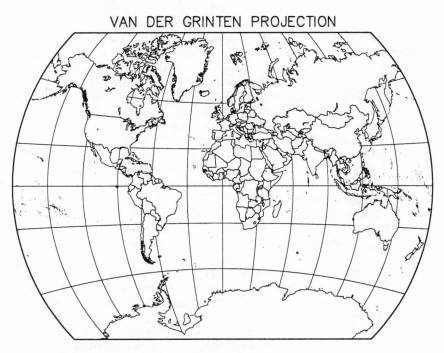

FIGURE 3.7   A new shape for the world.

4. For an extraordinary example of the translation of satellite imagery into finished cartography, juxtaposing computer maps and photographs with conventional thematic maps of the same areas, see *Images of the World: An Atlas of Satellite Imagery and Maps* (Chicago: Rand McNally, 1983). The geographic information system "revolution" is well reported by David Bjerklie, in "The Electronic Transformation of Maps," *Technology Review,* vol. 92, no. 3 (April 1989), pp. 54–63.

5. Arthur H. Robinson and Barbara Bartz Petchenik, *The Nature of Maps: Essays Toward Understanding Maps and Mapping* (Chicago: University of Chicago Press, 1976), p. x.

6. S.W. Boggs, "Cartohypnosis," *The Department of State Bulletin,* vol. 15, no. 390 (December 22, 1946), pp. 1119–1125. Maps can also be used, as Boggs points out, to "dehypnotize people."

7. J.B. Harley, "Maps, Knowledge, and Power," in *The Iconography of Landscape: Essays on the Symbolic Representation, Design and Use of Past Environments,* Denis Cosgrove and Stephen Daniels, eds. (Cambridge: Cambridge University Press, 1987), pp. 277–312.

8. For informative historical surveys of cartography, see Lloyd A. Brown, *The Story of Maps* (New York: Dover Publications, 1977), Norman J.W. Thrower, *Maps and Man: An Examination of Cartography in Relation to Culture and Civilization* (Englewood Cliffs, N.J.: Prentice-Hall, 1972), and John Noble Wilford, *The Mapmakers: The Story of the Great Pioneers in Cartography from Antiquity to the Space Age* (New York: Vintage Books, 1982).

9. A Pawnee star chart, from the Field Museum of Natural History in Chicago, was included in the "Power of Maps" exhibition at the Cooper-Hewitt National Museum of Design, Smithsonian Institution, held in New York City from October 6, 1992, to March 7, 1993.

10. On this characteristic of Indian mapping, see Gregory H. Nobles, "Straight Lines and Stability: Mapping the Political Order of the Anglo-American Frontier," *The Journal of American History,* vol. 80, no. 1 (June 1993), pp. 26–27. Contrast this with John Mitchell's 1775 "Map of the British and French Dominions in North America with the Roads, Distances, Limits, and Extent of the Settlements." A third edition of this map, consulted during the 1783 Paris negotiations to establish the boundaries of an independent United States, is generally regarded as the most important map in American history; see Seymour I. Schwartz and Ralph E. Ehrenberg, *The Mapping of America* (New York: Harry N. Abrams, 1980), p. 164.

11. Phillip C. Muehrcke, with the assistance of Juliana O. Muehrcke, *Map Use: Reading, Analysis, and Interpretation* (Madison, Wis.: JP Publications, 1978), p. 2.

12. Robinson and Petchenik, *The Nature of Maps,* pp. 4–5.

13. For an elaboration with examples from around the world, see Alan K. Henrikson, "Mental Maps," in *Explaining the History of American Foreign Relations,* Michael J. Hogan and Thomas G. Paterson, eds. (Cambridge: Cambridge University Press, 1991), pp. 177–178.

14. This important point is made by Yi-Fu Tuan, in "Images and Mental Maps," *Annals of the Association of American Geographers,* vol. 65, no. 2 (June 1975), pp. 205–213.

15. This is persuasively demonstrated by Rudolf Arnheim, in *Visual Thinking* (Berkeley: University of California Press, 1969).

16. Among many possible expert discussions of the principles of map projection, see the brief corrective analysis by Mark Monmonier, *How to Lie with Maps* (Chicago: University of Chicago Press, 1991), pp. 8–18, and the more technical treatment by David Greenhood, *Mapping* (Chicago: University of Chicago Press, 1964), especially chap. 6.

17. Arno Peters, *The Europe-centred Character of Our Geographical View of the World and Its Correction* (Munich-Solln: Universum Verlag, 1979).

18. Arthur H. Robinson, "Arno Peters and His New Cartography," *The American Cartographer*, vol. 12, no. 2 (1985), p. 104. Robinson points out that the Peters projection—a cylindrical, equal-area map with standard parallels at 45° from the chosen central great circle—was one of three cylindrical-projection variants proposed by Edinburgh clergyman-cartographer James Gall in 1885.

19. W.R. Tobler, "Medieval Distortions: The Projections of Ancient Maps," *Annals of the Association of American Geographers*, vol. 56, no. 2 (June 1966), pp. 351–360, is a rare effort to consider the technical properties of the Hereford map and other premodern cartography.

20. Brown, *The Story of Maps*, p. 71; see also the Ptolemaic world map on p. 55.

21. Among the realizations that can be gained from viewing such reversed-image maps is the striking fact that South America lies almost entirely east of Florida—and much farther from Asia and closer to Africa than is generally assumed.

22. See Richard Edes Harrison's essay "The Geographical Sense" in his *Look at the World: The FORTUNE Atlas for World Strategy* (New York: Alfred A. Knopf, 1944), pp. 10–12, and his remarkable maps themselves.

23. The influence of his work is discussed in Alan K. Henrikson, "The Map as an 'Idea': The Role of Cartographic Imagery During the Second World War," *The American Cartographer*, vol. 2, no. 1 (April 1975), pp. 19–53. Harrison's maps were used, for example, to illustrate *General Marshall's Report: The Winning of the War in Europe and the Pacific* (New York: Simon and Schuster, 1945).

24. Monmonier, *How to Lie with Maps*, pp. 89–94. The surprising variety of projections and other technical characteristics of philatelic cartography is shown in a paper by Donald T. Clark, c. 1983, "The Round Earth on Flat Paper: An Essay on Map Projections on Map Stamps."

25. Giselher Wirsing et al., *Der Krieg 1939/41 in Karten* (München: Verlag Knorr & Hirth, 1942).

26. Michael R. Beschloss and Strobe Talbott, *At the Highest Levels: The Inside Story of the End of the Cold War* (Boston: Little, Brown, 1993), pp. 162–163. Cf. the similar arguments of an earlier Soviet leader, Leonid Brezhnev, in Henrikson, "Mental Maps," pp. 182–184.

27. Monmonier, *How to Lie with Maps*, pp. 19–20, 24n.

28. Ibid., Chapter 10, "Color: Attraction and Distraction." Monmonier emphasizes that the "decorative" role of color—in television cartography, for example—can easily interfere with its "functional" role.

29. Rudolf Arnheim, "The Perception of Maps," *The American Cartographer*, vol. 3, no. 1 (April 1976), p. 6.

30. The term is that of Christian von Ehrenfels. See Wolfgang Köhler, *Gestalt Psychology* (New York: Mentor Books, 1947), pp. 102–105.

31. Diane M. Bolz, "'Follow me . . . I am the earth in the palm of your hand,'" *Smithsonian*, vol. 23, no. 11 (February 1993), pp. 112–117; the words in the title are those of aviator-author Beryl Markham. See also Denis Wood, *The Power of Maps* (New York: Guilford Press, 1992).

32. That the federal government is, by far, the preeminent patron of map-making in the United States is implicitly demonstrated in Ralph E. Ehrenberg, *Scholars' Guide to*

*Washington, D.C., for Cartography and Remote Sensing Imagery (Maps, Charts, Aerial Photographs, Satellite Images, Cartographic Literature and Geographic Information Systems)* (Washington, D.C.: Woodrow Wilson International Center for Scholars, Smithsonian Institution Press, 1987).

33. Harley, "Maps, Knowledge, and Power," p. 281.

34. A story by Jorge Luis Borges imagines a map, produced by a government's college of cartographers, that is physically coextensive with the country! See Jorge Luis Borges, "Of Exactitude in Science," excerpted in Nobles, "Straight Lines and Stability," p. 9. For the expression of geography in prose and poetry, see also Jorge Luis Borges, in collaboration with María Kodama, *Atlas* (New York: E.P. Dutton, 1985).

35. On the iconographic setting of Washington, D.C., in national and international context, see Alan K. Henrikson, "'A Small, Cozy Town, Global in Scope': Washington, D.C.," *Ekistics: The Science and Study of Human Settlements,* vol. 50, no. 299 (March-April 1983), pp. 123–145, 149.

36. J.B. Harley, "Silences and Secrecy: The Hidden Agenda of Cartography in Early Modern Europe," *Imago Mundi,* vol. 40 (1988), pp. 65, 66.

37. Harley, "Maps, Knowledge, and Power," pp. 302–303.

38. On Jefferson, see William H. Goetzmann, *New Lands, New Men: America and the Second Great Age of Discovery* (New York: Viking, 1986), pp. 110–118. Meriwether Lewis and William Clark's "Map of Part of the Continent of North America" (1809) is reproduced on p. 116. On westward movement and the role of mapping, see also idem, *Army Exploration of the American West, 1803–1863* (New Haven: Yale University Press, 1957), and *Exploration and Empire: The Explorer and the Scientist in the Winning of the American West* (New York: Alfred A. Knopf, 1967). On Americans' geographical orientation toward the Pacific more generally, see Norman A. Graebner, *Empire on the Pacific: A Study in American Continental Expansion* (New York: Ronald Press, 1955), and Frederick Merk, *Manifest Destiny and Mission in American History: A Reinterpretation* (New York: Vintage Books, 1963).

39. Among the earliest U.S.-centered world maps were David H. Burr's "The World, on Mercator's Projection," published by J. Haven in Boston in 1850, and "Colton's New Illustrated Map of the World on Mercator's Projection," published by J. Colton in New York in 1851. Curiously, an even earlier German map placed North and South America at the world's center. See "PLANIGLOB in Mercators Projection: Zugleich als KARTE v. AUSTRALIEN," map 2.b, in Adolf Stieler, *Schul-Atlas* (Gotha, Germany: Justus Perthes, 1841). This information was obtained courtesy of John A. Wolter and Richard W. Stephenson in the Geography and Map Division of the Library of Commerce.

40. On this theme of U.S. power and cartographic centrality, see Alan K. Henrikson, "America's Changing Place in the World: From 'Periphery' to 'Centre'?" in *Centre and Periphery: Spatial Variation in Politics,* Jean Gottmann, ed. (Beverly Hills, Calif.: Sage Publications, 1980), pp. 79–80, 95n; the Mitchell *Atlas* world map is compactly reproduced on p. 80.

41. The standard historical interpretation is Dexter Perkins, *A History of the Monroe Doctrine,* rev. ed. (Boston: Houghton Mifflin, 1963).

42. The use of the double-hemisphere world map increased in popularity after such a map appeared in Mercator's *Atlas Sive Cosmographicae* (Duisburg, Germany, 1595). The usual projection for double-hemisphere maps is the orthographic, which shows half the earth as if viewed from an infinite distance (see Figure 3.1).

43. S.W. Boggs, "This Hemisphere," *The Department of State Bulletin,* vol. 12, no. 306 (May 6, 1945), pp. 845–850.

44. Henrikson, "The Map as an 'Idea,'" pp. 19–20, 28–33; Arthur P. Whitaker, *The Western Hemisphere Idea: Its Rise and Decline* (Ithaca: Cornell University Press, 1954).

45. On the genesis and the diplomacy of NAFTA, see Alan K. Henrikson, "A North American Community: 'From the Yukon to the Yucatan,'" in *The Diplomatic Record, 1991–1992*, Hans Binnendijk and Mary Locke, eds. (Boulder: Westview Press, 1993), pp. 69–95.

46. Robert M. Lunny, *Early Maps of North America* (Newark: New Jersey Historical Society, 1961). One of these older maps of North America before political partitioning occurred was used to publicize "The North American Concept: A Symposium on Issues That Affect Canada, the United States, and Mexico, and How They Are Internationally Managed," sponsored by the Center for the Study of Foreign Affairs, Foreign Service Institute, U.S. Department of State, April 15, 1987.

47. As early as 1941, economist Eugene Staley, in "The Myth of Continents," *Foreign Affairs*, vol. 19, no. 3 (April 1941), pp. 481–494, attacked the tendency toward regionally based economic groups by pointing out that, in terms of cost-distance, cities in the United States were sometimes "closer" to cities in Europe or even in Asia than they were to each other.

48. Henrikson, "The Map as an 'Idea,'" p. 45, 53n.

49. Alan K. Henrikson, "'Wings for Peace': Open Skies and Transpolar Civil Aviation," in *Vulnerable Arctic: Need for an Alternative Orientation*, Jyrki Käkönen, ed. (Tampere, Finland: Tampere Peace Research Institute, 1992), pp. 107–143.

50. One example is the map of ozone levels in the Southern Hemisphere based on data from the total ozone mapping spectrometer (TOMS) on board the National Aeronautics and Space Administration's *Nimbus 7* satellite. See Richard S. Stolarski, "The Antarctic Ozone Hole," *Scientific American*, vol. 258, no. 1 (January 1988), pp. 30–36, and map on p. 31.

51. Richard Elliot Benedick, *Ozone Diplomacy: New Directions in Safeguarding the Planet* (Cambridge, Mass.: Harvard University Press, 1991), pp. 18–20, 110–111.

52. Bjerklie, "The Electronic Transformation of Mapping," p. 61.

53. A classic study of the maldistribution of food in the world is Josué de Castro, *The Geography of Hunger* (Boston: Little, Brown, 1952). A recent work emphasizing the spatial misallocation of public-health efforts is Peter Gould, *The Slow Plague: A Geography of the AIDS Pandemic* (Cambridge, Mass.: Blackwell, 1993).

54. Scott Minerbrook, "'Mental Maps': The Politics of Cartography," *U.S. News & World Report*, vol. 110, no. 14 (April 15, 1991), p. 60.

55. Peters, *The Europe-centred Character of Our Geographical View of the World and Its Correction*, p. 7.

56. Peters's projection (which may have been original with him, though it is basically the Gall projection of 1885) is only one of a variety of equal-area projections that preserve correct size relationships, almost any one of which portrays the equatorial countries with more faithful shapes. Peters's projection, his faulty conceptual basis for it, and his fallacious claims for it have drawn sharp criticism from professional cartographers around the world. See, for example, Arthur H. Robinson, "Arno Peters and His New Cartography," *The American Cartographer*, vol. 12, no. 2 (October 1985), p. 104; Miklos Pinther, "The View of Our World," [United Nations] *Secretariat News*, vol. 40, no. 2 (January 31, 1985), pp. 5–7; John Loxton, "The Peters Phenomenon," *The Cartographic Journal*, vol. 22, no. 2 (December 1985), pp. 106–108; The Board of the German Cartographical Society, "The So-called Peters Projection," *The Cartographic Journal*, vol. 22, no. 2 (December 1985), pp.

108–110; and Phil Porter and Phil Voxland, "Distortion in Maps: The Peters Projection and Other Devilments," *Focus,* vol. 36, no. 2 (Summer 1986), pp. 22–30.

57. One of the first prominent uses of the Peters map was on the front cover of the report of the Independent Commission on International Development Issues, chaired by Willy Brandt, the Social Democratic former West German chancellor; see his *North-South: A Program for Survival* (Cambridge, Mass.: MIT Press, 1980). On this map, an awkward curved line is drawn, crossing the equator, to try to differentiate the "North" from the "South" more clearly than the Peters projection itself can do. Australia, which by virtue of its very name is southern, is delineated as being within the "North."

58. Bruce Van Voorst, "The New Shape of the World," *Time,* vol. 132, no. 19 (November 7, 1988), p. 127; John Noble Wilford, "The Impossible Quest for the Perfect Map," *New York Times,* October 25, 1988. The Robinson map is based on an ellipse, with the lines of longitude curving toward the poles; the latitude lines are straight. His standard parallels are 38° north and 38° south. Only at these latitudes are size and shape relationships accurate, as on a globe.

# FOUR

## People Together, Yet Apart: Rethinking Territory, Sovereignty, and Identities

### DAVID B. KNIGHT

HUMAN *communities* are not discernible by the human eye from an earth-orbiting spacecraft, but many features, some of human origin, can be seen. A person on board a spacecraft can identify major features (such as Madagascar, South Asia, the Iberian Peninsula, Australia, and perhaps New Zealand) and may reflect on the thought that millions of people live "down there." Whatever can be seen will not, in itself, reveal *who* lives below nor anything about the nature of their communities and socioeconomic or political organizations. Some straight lines on the land (due to sharply contrasting vegetation types on one side as compared to the other or significant breaks in land-use patterns) may suggest the existence of political boundaries (as across parts of western Canada and the United States). But otherwise, it is not possible to discern from space much partitioning on the earth's surface nor, especially, the means by which people form communities and relate to and structure political territory. As the cliché goes, "spaceship earth" suggests oneness. Once on the surface, however, the reality is otherwise in numerous respects (which is just fine for a geographer, who is naturally interested in the "world" of differences).

Imagine the satellite descending: At what moment would one see discrete settlements that might, just might, suggest more clearly how people and their territories are divided? In stating this, an important assumption is made—that is, that such divisions actually do exist. The late Boyd C. Shafer concluded that humankind is more alike than not, yet he spent his lifetime studying what keeps people both together and yet apart, namely, nationalism.[1] This chapter considers this thought from a political-geographic perspective.

## Basic Attributes of the State

The basis of international society today is the territorial partitioning of the earth's surface into States and the application or denial of sovereignty and some related attributes to the resulting territorial units, all of which are set within an international system of States.[2] There has never been a fixed number of States; instead, there have been periods of reasonable stability and other periods when the number of States has changed markedly. Four periods of change stand out in this century: the years immediately following World War I, with their significant impact on the map of Europe; the period during and following World War II; the 1960s era, featuring a decolonization drive in various parts of the Third World, most notably Africa; and, beginning in 1989 and continuing to the present, the period of the disintegration of the former USSR and its satellite States in "Eastern" Europe (including Czechoslovakia), plus political-territorial and other changes in Yugoslavia, various parts of Africa, and Asia.

Some common criteria must be met before a State can be said to exist, although the particular reasons why States exist vary quite markedly. The criteria for Statehood are: a particular defined territory; a permanent resident population; a constituted effective government; formal and real independence; sovereignty; recognition by other States in the international system of States; the expectation of permanence; the capacity to enter into relations with other States; a State apparatus; a circulation system; an organized economy; and various "fictional parts" of States, such as the official residences of foreign diplomatic envoys.[3] Of these numerous criteria, territory, population (especially when considered from the perspective of group identities), and sovereignty are fundamental, and so they form the focus of this chapter. (Other criteria are, of course, important in the overall scheme of things.)

The concepts considered in this chapter are human constructs: They are not givens. They are linked, each one to the others, in myriad changing ways; hence, it is somewhat artificial to separate them. Even so, it is useful to separately identify some largely legal dimensions at the outset, before reconsidering them in a more conceptual and interrelated manner and in conjunction with some additional concepts.

## Three Key Criteria

### *Territory*

From the perspective of international political geography—and international law—any State needs a particular defined territory that is not shared with other States (although other States or minorities in other States may covet part or all of the territory). This territory must also have limits that are more or less clearly defined (even if some of the boundaries may be unexplained or in contention). Territorial exclusivity pertains to the particular land area; its offshore waters and portions of rivers and lakes along or through which international boundaries exist; airspace above the areal limits of the territory (although the height of control in such airspace is contingent upon means for controlling entry into that space); and obviously, subterranean areas (including the resources therein) and the rivers, lakes, and other features that are internal to the territory. The essential component is land, to which all other attributes are ancillary. Robert Oppenheim pithily sums up the essential importance of territory: "A State without territory is not possible."[4]

When a territory is delimited and organized as a State, there is a juxtaposition between jurisdiction and territory; the territory becomes infused with a legal function, a function that coincides with the existence of the State within the international system of States. Further, the State's territory provides both the base and the frame for the exercise of power at Statewide and lesser (sub-State) scales. Indeed, as Sack observed, "the State is reified by placing it in space."[5]

A State's territory, in terms of acquisition, size, and shape, may vary from place to place and, sometimes, through time.[6] Competing claims to territory are often the basis for conflict, and though international society has recently reached new levels of understanding and cooperation, there is still no reason to believe that conflicts over territory have necessarily ceased. In fact, boundary disputes—varyingly at the (greater or lesser) margins of territory—continue to be the major reason for conflict,[7] with all sorts of reasons cited for the territorial claims being advanced.[8] Most conflict over territory is based on historical claims (some of which are quite dubious).

With respect to historical claims, a problem remains—namely, how far back in time can contemporary claims be based? Consider, for instance, Israel's biblically based claim to Palestine and Indonesia's "precolonial" claim to East Timor. These cases raise related issues stemming from the fact that almost all of the earth is now claimed by existing States. Thus, any expansion of current States and the creation of new States will necessarily involve the territories of existing States. This clearly means that the territorial integrity of some existing States will someday be threatened. Since territorial integrity is believed to be a fundamental quality of Statehood, violent reaction can be expected by threatened States, although recent experience has demonstrated that violence need not always occur.

Territory is *the* critical quality for Statehood. It is a legal concept, and yet it is also much more. Territory without people is meaningless for, as noted earlier, without people there is no territory—it is a human construct. Territory alone does not constitute Statehood; but Statehood, first and foremost, is tied to territory. Territory is at once the territorial frame for certain types of human societies and the substance upon which they live, and it is also the essential basis for international organization as currently structured.

## Population

For a State to exist, there must be a permanent resident population. The government speaks and acts (or claims to speak and act) on behalf of the total population of the State. The term *population* is neutral; other, more emotive terms are often used to describe a State's population. Primacy is given to those who automatically acquire nationality (through birth) and to those to whom nationality is otherwise granted. Nationality is dependent upon Statehood for without Statehood, nationality would not exist. It is generally accepted that the population of a State will thus have a sense of nationhood but also that, as a nation, it will use its nationalism in the search for national stability and security.

Nationality with respect to individuals refers to the quality of being a member or "subject" of a specific State. Each State is free to decide who its nationals will be and how nationality may be granted or rescinded. Some States automatically withdraw nationality if, for instance, an individual acquires a new nationality elsewhere by naturalization or marriage. If the withdrawal of someone's nationality is based on political grounds, then it will likely be condemned internationally for such an act is commonly considered of doubtful validity in international law. Of course, nationality can be "returned" by governmental or legal action—as was the case of some now-famous exiles from the former USSR. In contrast, some States hold that nationality can never be "lost"; hence, for instance, we hear the slogan "once British, always British."

*People* is another word often used to refer to a State's population. This word has international legal meaning: The UN Charter and numerous other legal instruments state that "all people" have the right to self-determination. However, when the term is used in that sense, a question arises: Does the use of the word *people* refer only to *all* of the people of a State, regardless of whether or not they all relate to and identify with the national identity and the national government? Some scholars hold that the word *people* can also refer to *parts* of the national population in *parts* of the State. The latter people, as a minority (e.g., some Quebeckers within Canada) or even as a dominated majority (e.g., black South Africans), may have primary allegiance to a sub-State "national" identity (or identities) that separates them from the remainder of the existing State's population. Despite the very gradual acceptance by some States of the term *people* to refer to certain sub-State groups, the word is primarily used as a reference to the whole people of a State, not to minorities within it. Indeed, under international law, the population of the *total* State is considered paramount over *parts* of either the population or the territory within.

This is not to suggest that international law ignores other measures of humanness. For instance, there is international legal recognition of certain minorities—as individuals and as collectives—within States through such human rights instruments as the UN Covenant of Civil and Political Rights; the UN Covenant of Economic, Social and Cultural Rights; and the Helsinki Final Act.[9] But—and here I raise an important point about perception and self-definition—some such minorities (specifically, many indigenous peoples in various States) do not see themselves as mere minorities for they know they are people and thus are due international recognition.

It should be clear that the mention of a State's permanent population or people raises questions pertaining to how group identities are defined and how they relate to the State. Group identities have religious, political, cultural, historical, and psychological bases. For our purposes, it will be enough to refer to *group territorial identities,* a term that encompasses such other terms as *tribe, ethnicity, ethnonationalism, nation, nationalism, mininationalism, sub-State nationalism,* and so on, all of which are used in the literature.[10] All these identifiers ultimately refer to a group's distinct character, which sets it apart from others. This character may also have a reasonably observable territorial dimension—being dominantly or primarily located in a particular portion of a State (as with Scots in the northern part of the United Kingdom, the Basques in Euskadi in northern Spain, and the Sikhs in the Punjab in India) or referring to a nation that claims the whole State ("Americans" in the United States).

Although the ideal of achieving a good areal fit between nation and State leads some nations to seek the creation of their particular nation-States, the reality is that the concept of the nation-State is questionable; thus, the term is of limited value.[11] Regrettably, the term *nation-State* is used by political geographers and others when what is meant is either *nation* separately or, more generally, *State.* The word *nation* is too often carelessly and incorrectly used to refer to *States.* Also, the term *nation* is all too often used when the more accurate term *national society* would be nearer to the truth.

Some States give shelter to refugees. The latter, by definition, are homeless and are said to be Stateless; they lack both national and international identity. This harsh reality and the hesitation of States to fully support the right to a nationality mean that most refugees will continue to lack nationality due to their forced removal from their respective homelands, their States of birth. In contrast to refugees who have been forced to leave their homes due to war, famine, natural catastrophes, and so on, there are individuals who may have left their States under duress but who are not seen to have given up their nationality. Political exiles, for example, may manage to win recognition, loyalty, and support for their causes among people and even governments in other States.[12]

## Sovereignty

In the past hundred years, sovereignty as a legal presumption has come to apply only to territories formally constituted, accepted, and recognized as States by other States in the international system of States. Sovereignty, or the unqualified competence that States prima facia possess, implies competency to control the territory and its contents and also relationships with other States through the totality of powers that States, under international law, have and may use. Sovereignty once was equated with the monarch or with a group of people who exercised rulership, but it now pertains to an impersonal and legal prescription. Today, it is the State that wields sovereignty, and the exercise of a State's authority over its territory implies that sovereignty is complete and exclusive. A sovereign State is under no obligation to accept people, goods, and ideas from other States, and it may restrict or otherwise control all that is within the territory.

As mentioned, sovereignty also implies recognition by other States, and recognition, in turn, implies that each State respects the rights of other States. The term *recognition,* as used here, refers to the recognition of the entity, the State, not necessarily the government. A government can be rejected by other States—perhaps with sanctions imposed against the State because of that government's actions—or a government may fall even as the State continues to exist. Thus, for example, when Lebanon was in tatters in the 1980s and there was no effective government, the State was still said to exist. However, for a *new* State to be given recognition, a constituted and (reasonably) effective government must exist (as with the new States that emerged from the recently failed USSR), and there must be at least the promise of permanence.

Sovereignty becomes legal fiction if a State loses effective control of its territory (perhaps by being occupied by another State) and will be discarded by other States if it becomes clear that there is no prospect for that sovereignty to be regained. Finally, sovereignty cannot reside in a government in exile for sovereignty, under international law, implies actual "possession of, and control over, a territory."[13]

## Elaborations and Complications

With these thoughts in mind, it is instructive to reconsider the three basic concepts—territory, identity, and sovereignty—from a more conceptual perspective and to discuss them with an awareness of how they relate to each other and to some additional concepts.

### *Territory*

Human societies create territory out of meaningless space for they partition space and use it for their betterment. Thus, the delimited territory is special for the people concerned, particularly when it is acknowledged as being sovereign territory within the confines of an independent State. A given territory is, by definition, separate from the territories of others, not only physically but, by and large, also ideologically for the people involved will have a territorial ideology that reflects their understanding of themselves in relation to their own territory and that helps guide, if not necessarily govern, the relations their State will have with other States.[14]

A delimited State-territory is, of course, but a particular type of region on the world's political map; any State covers only a particular portion of the surface of the earth. As with all regions that pertain to human social organization, a State's territory is a social construct.[15] The areal dimensions of territory also clearly are not givens for it is people who decide where the bounds of territory should be, if the boundaries should be changed, or if they should be left alone once they are agreed upon. After all, "territory is not; it becomes, for territory itself is passive, and it is human beliefs and actions that give territory meaning."[16] The bounds of territory can simply be delimited (i.e., agreed to, perhaps by treaty, and thus generally written in some fashion), but they may also be demarcated (i.e., physically marked on the land).

Territory is real in the sense that it can be seen, felt, (perhaps) smelled, walked on, flown over, manipulated, and thus altered. In this physical sense, it is quite concrete for it has substance, can be measured, and can be changed (as with the building of new highways, the spread of towns, or the changing of the land tenure system). The internal characteristics of the territory will therefore change with the passage of time as the society and its economy develop. The external dimensions of the territory may be altered too, but for this to happen, there must be a change in the territory's relationship with one or more other territories.

But territory is more than just a physical and measurable entity. It is also something of the mind because people impute meaning to and gain meaning from territory. Indeed, many people fully believe in the landscape of "their" territory as a living entity that is filled with meaning. Such beliefs are psychologically and culturally based and therefore exist, at one key level, simply as parts of the "geographies of the mind." But since people's cultural ecology and spatial patterning (as in agricultural and settlement systems) can be powerfully influenced by their beliefs, it is, in turn, often possible to "read" those beliefs from the landscape. They can be inferred from the creation of landmarks (personal ones and, of significance here, major ones like monuments and shrines that may have "national" significance); from the naming of places;[17] from the "sacredness" invoked with respect to both specific parts or the generalized "national" whole of the territory;[18] and so on. The territory and the nation are celebrated as providers of security via the singing of a national anthem and the acknowledgment of a national flag. Above all, since the territory "is the very basis on which national existence rests, *true* citizens will be prepared to give their lives" in defense of "the 'sacred soil.'"[19]

Territory, at one and the same time, will serve the State both as the locus of an inwardness, apart from international links, and as the basis for linking with people and territories elsewhere. Political geographer Jean Gottmann has suggested that a State's territory—as "the model compartment of space resulting from partitioning, diversification, and organization"—offers a people dichotomous options: security (to look inward and preserve the integrity of the society against outside forces) and opportunity (from which to reach out to other societies). It is useful to think of these competing options as being at opposite ends of a continuum and to be aware that a State may tend more toward one end of the continuum than the other in its trade and foreign policies and actions. However, a change of emphasis from one of these options to the other may occur—for example, when, after a period of stressing opportunity by means of open international trade, a State takes a more isolationist stance and imposes tariff barriers to "protect" home producers and markets. Clearly, from this perspective, involving opportunity versus security, the concept of territory implies the possibility for conflict.

Territory may also form the basis for conflict in a different sense, as when competing claims are made with respect to a particular territory. Such claims need not involve two States because competing claims can exist within a State's own territory. Consider the following definition of *territory:* "space to which identity is attached by a distinctive group who hold or covet that territory and who desire to have full control over it for the group's benefit."[20] This is a provocative definition in that it links territory with people (who have distinct group identities) and the desire for control—that is, self-control by the people who inhabit the territory. Obviously, from a political-geographic perspective, territory cannot be considered without reference to the concepts of identity and control. Attention must therefore be placed on whether people with distinct identities have control of themselves within their own territories.

Although a government will normally represent the majority of the people within the State, there are many situations in which this does not occur. Some examples include: Fiji (where a racial or "traditional" minority claims to speak for the whole people of the State when, in fact, it does not); South Africa and Guatemala (where minorities still rule); China (where power and authority are maintained by a minority through the threat and use of force); and, of quite different types, Israel-Palestine (where the Jewish minority, despite notable attempts to effect peace and so permit change, continues to prevent the meaningful expression of self-determination for the Arab majority in the occupied territories) and East Timor (where the people in an illegally invaded territory have suffered dreadful persecution and death even as the world turns a blind eye—in contrast to the dramatic military response by some of the world's States to Iraq's invasion of Kuwait). At a minimum, the minorities (or minority-dominated majorities) may seek appropriate and adequate recognition. But who is to decide what "appropriate and adequate recognition" means? Most such peoples want to gain at least the right to live their lives peacefully, without what they perceive to be the destructive power of the State taking and damaging their land and resources or otherwise influencing their lives. These thoughts prompt us to again consider the degree to which a State's population can be regarded as having some linking "national" identity.

It may be that the total population of a State draws meaning and strength from a collective sense of self as a nation. But nationhood is not a necessary attribute of Statehood. Even so, the people of the State (especially those born therein), who may, indeed, see themselves as forming a nation, will draw strength from "their" territory. As Shafer noted, "In diverse ways [the people will] love it and oppose any diminution of its size."[21] They may have a nationalism that has a real or created historical basis and is tied to the territory occupied by the State—and, perhaps, coveted territory in another State's control. A nationalist ideology will be formulated to interpret the occupation and control of the territory, both in the past and as a plan for the future. The ideology is based, in part, on a distinctively created "iconography" that reflects the set of symbols that the people of the State believe in and with which they identify.

The "Janus-like quality, [of] looking both ways to the past and the future, is equally relevant for States which seek to create and reinforce a sense of nationhood, and for nationalisms that oppose existing States in their attempt to carve out autonomous identities."[22] This observation refers to the many instances when some inhabitants of certain States have a *sub*-State "national" identity, that is, an identity that pertains to only part of the total population of the State within but part of the total territory, who may seek to have that identity more fully or totally recognized within the State and perhaps even internationally.[23] If the latter is desired, they may have to resort to secession, with a portion of the population in one part of the State breaking off to become a "nation" in its own new State, thereby creating a new nationality. But secession presents a threat to the international system because it represents a challenge to an international order based on the concept of the sovereign State.

As noted, the territorial integrity of States is commonly held to be more important than any minority claims coming from within a territory that advocates self-determination. Thus, for instance, the Aland Islanders' request for secession from Finland in the 1920s was rejected because, in the words of some League of Nations representatives, "to concede to minorities, either of language or religion, or to any fraction of a population the right of withdrawing from the community to which they belong, because it is their wish or their good pleasure, would be to destroy order and stability within States and to inaugurate anarchy in international life; it would be to uphold a theory incompatible with the very idea of the State as a territorial and political unity."[24] Even though this conservative stance was known during World War I and II and the interwar period, many secessionist movements existed in the British and French empires, the Arab world, Central America, and the Philippines; they also appeared where they were least expected, namely, in France, Britain, Belgium, and Spain. World War II put a temporary cap on such movements, as attention was focused on conflicts in Europe and East and Southeast Asia. But after the war, the quest for self-determination became a dominant force in the Third World, with colonized peoples seeking the removal of control by alien Europeans. Demands for decolonization and independence were more or less met by the end of the 1960s, without significantly altering the colonially derived boundaries of existing territories. Over eighty new States were created in the 1960s and early 1970s, generally with the blessing of the United Nations. Today, all of the major former colonies have achieved independence, although many continue to experience nagging unresolved problems of decolonization (e.g., in parts of Southwest, South, Southeast, and East Asia, the Pacific, and Africa and in many European-settled States where indigenous peoples were displaced—the United States, New Zealand, Canada, Australia, and Russia).

Demands for self-determination continue in a context that would often involve secession from existing States, including some States in Africa and Asia that obtained independence only recently. But under international law as it is generally understood today, self-determination can be granted but once to a people within any territory because self-determination has been restricted by two dominating, overriding principles—sovereignty and territorial integrity. Whereas it was legitimate for a whole "people" (defined by being located in territories delimited by European-imposed decrees) who were subjected to overseas colonial rule to seek self-determination—by the application of the so-called salt-water theory—it was not legitimate for people who formed a minority within a national territory to seek self-determination, whether on their own initiative or with help from any outside power, for that would "dismember or impair" the existing State. In short, international law remained grounded in the belief that the population of the total national territory was paramount over parts of the population or a territory within it. Any departure from this required the free choice of the majority of the total population of the State from which the new State was to be carved, not just the sub-State minority that sought separation.

The rationale for the stances of the UN, the Organization of African Unity, and other international bodies is easy to understand: These bodies are made up of States, and their memberships are hesitant to permit parts of their respective territories to be hived off to create other States. To fail to speak out on this would be to invite or justify attacks on the territorial integrity of the existing member States. This is why States declared that self-determination could be applied only once to any territory, that is, when independence from the colonial power was achieved. Of course, exceptions to this (as in Bangladesh and, more recently, in Eritrea) have been permitted by the international community, which has claimed that the resulting secessions were due to unusual circumstances (i.e., excessive human rights abuses in one case and a remaining postcolonial element in another) and thus were not to be regarded as setting a precedent.

Although the UN position reflects a desire for territorial stability, the formal application of the right to self-determination in all colonial territories sometimes created absurd situations, as in some tiny island States. Self-determination has not always been granted to the peoples within certain previously decolonized territories, such as in Goa (India) and West Irian and East Timor (Indonesia). Any rights to self-determination by the peoples of those territories were taken from them by the "invading" States.

A different challenge to the territorial integrity of existing States outside a colonial setting occurred recently when the USSR disintegrated and some of its constituent territories and the former Eastern European States declared independence. New States have been created both from territories that were well defined within the former State and from a splitting of territory, as with the recent creation of the Slovak and Czech republics out of Czechoslovakia and the splitting of Slovenia from Yugoslavia. Most of these changes happened with remarkably little violence; in other cases, there have been bitter conflicts, as in Azerbaijan and Armenia, where there is, as yet, no clear territorial solution to a difficult situation. And the atrocities in parts of the former Yugoslavia stand as grim reminders that the link between identity and territory can have disastrous consequences.

## Identity

Self-determination necessarily involves issues of identity for it is the people in a particular territory who express the desire for self-determination and, possibly, secession and the creation of a new State. This leads to the issue of how the population is to be defined. Many people give primacy of belonging to some sub-State group, however defined and measured. Thus, for instance, some people within the province of Quebec in Canada recognize their sub-State regional identity as having primacy, that is, as a Quebeçois identity. A population *subset* not having any allegiance to what is otherwise a national identity is problematic in any State. The issue is contentious all around the globe because there is a lack of homogeneity in almost all States, with perhaps Portugal and Iceland being the most clearly defined exceptions since they each have a fair fit between a homogeneous population and the State territory. In that sense, they are perhaps the only—or the best—examples of the concept of the nation-State. Most States, in contrast, have plural societies, with minorities.

The minorities or national minorities problem of the 1920s and 1930s was replaced after World War II with the demands of various sub-State groups for recognition. The term *ethnic* came into vogue in the 1950s and especially the 1960s to describe increasing numbers of sub-State groups that sought either some degree of self-government—not always apart from existing States—or, in the extreme, secession and the creation of new States. The "ethnic kick" of the postwar years may have been, in part, a reaction against Statewide modernization processes under way in many States, which, it was believed, would help to create and strengthen *national* identities and override all other (sub-State) identities. Modernization did not necessarily bring about the expected areal fit between a nation and its State, however, and even today, a very weak sense of nation exists in most former colonial territories. In the latter States (e.g., the Sudan, Nigeria, India, and Sri Lanka), certain sub-State allegiances remain very strong, and wars continue to be fought over who has the ultimate right of control. Even in Western Europe, sub-State regionalisms are considerable and growing in vitality. Some sub-State groups demand the devolution of power from the center; others call for secession and back their demands with violent acts. Interestingly, some demands for self-determination and secession are not based in an ethnic or national identity but rather in a strong regionalism within parts of existing states. Examples include the incipient independence movements in western Canada and western Australia, fostered by people of varied European heritage who seem more driven by alienation from the geopolitical center of their respective States than by their regional sense of self.

The phrase *group territorial identity* has frequently been suggested to encompass a whole variety of regional, ethnic, tribal, and national identities.[25] The term is flexible and can be applied to any level in the hierarchy of attachments to territory, from a small group to a parochial localism to a broader (but still sub-State) regionalism to a nationalism (which may, of course, also be sub-State in areal focus), and even to an internationalism. The most potentially divisive level in this hierarchy of attachments is the political-territorial identity of the sub-State group, which, as a regionalism within the State, is an expression of self-determination. The use of the word *political* here implies that the group's sense of identification has taken on a political dimension. A group political-territorial identity can provide a threat to the State if its regionally based concerns become a sectionalism whereby political concerns are considered more important than those that pertain to the whole State. If a sectionalism is potent and if accommodation cannot be reached between it and the existing State, then the sub-State group political-territorial identity may seek and possibly achieve secession. If it is successful in achieving secession and if it is granted recognition by other States, then sovereignty could be said to have been achieved by applying self-determination according to the wishes of the people involved. At that point, the group political-territorial identity would cease to be a regionalism, however, for it would have become a new territorial identity pertaining to a differently defined, smaller territorial frame—the new State. If international recognition were granted, it would be granted to the State, not to the people, because it is the State that would be accepted into the international system of States, not the territorially encompassed identity as such or those who claim to speak on its behalf.

Without doubt, one key group territorial identity in today's world is the nation. How is a nation defined? At one level, it is simply a territorially based community of human beings who have like attributes, such as language and religion, with accepted societal structures, a common (real or imagined) history, and so on. More provocatively, a British scholar has declared that "any territorial community, the members of which are conscious of themselves *as* members of a community, and wish to maintain the identity of their community, is a nation."[26] But to permit all groups to define themselves would or could create anarchy.

A we-they dichotomy is confronted with all group identities, especially in nations. Inherent in the definition of *nation* is the idea of separation from other nations. This dichotomy, as an essential dilemma inherent in the concept of territory, also applies to a group's concept of its self. Consider how this may have an impact on a sub-State regionalism, which can be defined as a sub-State nationalism—as with Ukrainians in the former USSR. There is a danger—for the State—if inwardness can lead to an uncritical, self-congratulatory self-glorification of the nation, which, in turn, may lead to a blinkered, petty, narrow nationalism, with broader associations being ignored. In ignoring the value of broader associations, the sub-State nationalism may determine that the only means for providing a secure place for the distinctive identity is through the creation of a separate sovereign State.

Clearly, tension will exist between those who attach priority to belonging to the total community within an existing State structure and those who attach priority to belonging to a sub-State regional group that desires self-determination via secession. Those who identify with the broader existing State—like the Canadian federalists or Scots in the United Kingdom—can charge that it is always easier, in the short term, to live in a universe that conforms exactly to every aspect of one's personality. However, federalists (and also nationalists who seek to counter the secession movements of regional groups within unitary States) believe that the challenge of coexisting obliges each community within a State that has a plural society to continually extend and surpass itself; in so doing, each group can then seek and achieve goals that would never be attainable for each community taken separately. Federalists in Canada, like nationalists in other federal and unitary States, have a notion of oneness that pertains to the whole territorial unit, however well or poorly understood, and to all people who live within the State. The challenge for those who believe in the nation or at least in a national identity is to get people within the State who have a different sense of self to accept the merit of unity with diversity. This challenge presents grave difficulties within numerous States in many parts of the world, where demands for separation and autonomy or secession and independence are considerable. But there are instances where the challenge is not only being met but it is also being linked to new inter-State definitions of *self,* as in Western Europe. Interestingly, there are people in the latter area who are willing to extend their sense of self to a transnational entity, to a Europeanwide level of attachment even as their respective States fumble toward a united European Community. As they proceed, a new appreciation is developing for the limitations of sovereignty because creation of a "new Europe," if it is fully formed, will mean that certain functions will be granted to an extra-State administration that would never have been entertained in the past. However, many Europeans, who conceive of themselves first as nationals (Germans, Belgians, etc.), do not want to see the sovereignty of their States undermined by handing over a critical mass of State functions and powers to EC bodies that have no clear legitimacy. The issue is perhaps toughest for Germans who are concurrently being asked to expand their sense of what it means to be German within the recently reconstructed State.

East Germany was relinked to West Germany following the fall of the Berlin Wall and the collapse of the Communist regime. Those events and related processes elsewhere in Eastern Europe (what is, once again, Central Europe) and in the former USSR led Lithuanians, Ukrainians, Slovenes, and others to claim self-determination and receive international recognition. At the same time, however, other peoples (including a number of groups within Russia) have been denied Statehood, even though they have a clear territorial base. The issue of double standards applies elsewhere, too. Why, for example, were the Kuwaitis and not the East Timorese aided internationally when their territories were invaded, even though self-determination was clearly called for in the case of East Timor and though its "denial" was used as a pretext for retaliation in the case of Kuwait? It should be clear that when one deals with the political geography of self-determination, so clearly linked to issues of identity and territory, important philosophical and moral issues must be faced. We live in exciting and yet difficult times, as old notions of separateness and sovereignty are being challenged and debated.

## Sovereignty

The previous section identified changes in the concept of sovereignty, most notably the new extra-State linkages in Western Europe. To some politicians in certain States in Western Europe, the thought of "giving up" to a European Community decision-making process that pertains to matters within a State (including such mundane concerns as the fat content of sausages and whether double-decker buses are acceptable) is tantamount to giving up sovereignty. Other politicians, however, see the old, rigid notions of sovereignty as impediments to be overcome and are not threatened by a uniting Europe. Either way, people in Europe are actively dealing with new and freer concepts of sovereignty. But tension will continue between people who stress security at the local (now State) level and those who desire opportunity within an expanded European Community.

The concept of sovereignty is increasingly under attack from other sources, too. Therefore, it is being rethought due to such varied events and processes as:

- international human rights demands that cut against the notion that States are free to treat the people within their boundaries in ways the States' regimes think fit;
- the often invidious ways the capitalist world economy operates without due regard for the views and decisions of the political leaders of the States;
- a new legal or moral persuasiveness internationally about environmental matters that challenges the rights of States to develop resources within their territories as they wish without consideration for what others think and expect—as with the decimation of "national" forests and, not so incidentally, the indigenous peoples who inhabit some of those forests;
- sudden and isolated bombing of a State's territory without a declaration of war;
- UN troop involvements within a State's territory, with or without the approval of the State's government;
- the declaration by a neighboring State or the UN that part of a State's territory is to be treated as a "no-fly" or "security" zone, despite the protests of the State in question;
- violent attacks against people and property within a State's territory by terrorists who may or may not be acting on behalf of or with the support of the governments of States in other parts of the globe.

Several of the points noted here involve acts and decisions that transgress the sovereignty and territorial integrity of States. The latter, it should be remembered, have unchallenged core notions of Statehood and the underlying bases for international society.

The notion of a State's territory and its population being protected by virtue of sovereignty and territorial integrity is now increasingly passé, and yet, in so many ways, it is still the sovereign governments that make rules and regulations for people within their territories. The tension between old and new notions of sovereignty clearly promise that interesting times lie ahead.

## Toward New Understanding

This chapter has touched on many concepts and processes that grow from a consideration of three essential characteristics of Statehood, namely, territory, population, and sovereignty. All three can be considered in terms of their legal character, but they become more interesting and challenging once they are approached from a more conceptual stance. These characteristics of Statehood thus can be seen to be dynamic and subject to change—undoubtedly because they always remain human constructs. They are not fixed, although they sometimes have been thought to be, especially by those who have wished to use their substance to justify a particular State's actions. As the political geography of the late twentieth and early twenty-first centuries is considered, it is important to adopt a conceptual perspective to gain an understanding of how the world's "one people" is organized in changing yet still divided ways.

## Notes

1. B. C. Shafer, *Faces of Nationalism* (New York: Harcourt, Brace, Jovanovich, 1972).

2. Throughout this chapter, *the State* (big S) refers to a sovereign, independent, self-governed territorial organization; *a state* (small s) is but a sub-State territorial unit. Thus, e.g., Michigan is a state within the United States, the latter being the State.

3. D.B. Knight, "Statehood: A Politico-Geographic and Legal Perspective," *GeoJournal*, vol. 28, no. 3 (1992), pp. 311–318; M.I. Glassner, *Political Geography* (New York: Wiley, 1993).

4. L. Oppenheim, *International Law*, vol. 1, 8th ed. (London: Longman, 1955), p. 451.

5. R.D. Sack, *Conceptions of Space in Social Thought: A Geographic Perspective* (Minneapolis: University of Minnesota Press, 1980), p. 178.

6. See Glassner, *Political Geography*, pp. 61–71.

7. A.J. Day, ed., *Border and Territorial Disputes*, 2d ed. (London: Longman, 1987).

8. A.F. Burghardt, "The Bases of Territorial Claims," *Geographical Review*, vol. 63 (April 1973), pp. 225–245; A.B. Murphy, "Historical Justifications for Territorial Claims," *Annals of the Association of American Geographers*, vol. 80, no. 4 (December 1990), pp. 531–548; idem, "Territorial Ideology and International Conflict: The Legacy of Prior Political Formations," in *The Political Geography of Conflict and Peace*, N. Kliot and S. Waterman, eds. (London: Belhaven, 1991), pp. 126–141.

9. J. Crawford, ed., *The Rights of Peoples* (Oxford: Clarendon Press, 1988).

10. D.B. Knight, "People and Territory or Territory and People: Thoughts on Post-Colonial Self-Determination," *International Political Science Review*, vol. 6, no. 6 (November-December 1985), pp. 249–250.

11. M.W. Mikesell, "The Myth of the Nation State," *Journal of Geography*, vol. 82 (1983), pp. 257–260.

12. Y. Shain, *The Frontier of Loyalty: Political Exiles in the Age of the Nation-State* (Middletown, Conn.: Wesleyan University Press, 1989).

13. A. Cassesse, *International Law in a Divided World* (Oxford: Clarendon Press, 1986), p. 78.

14. J. Anderson, "Nationalist Ideology and Territory," in R.J. Johnston, D.B. Knight, and E. Kofman, eds., *Nationalism, Self-Determination and Political Geography* (London: Croom Helm, 1988), pp. 18–39.

15. C.H. Williams and A.D. Smith, "The National Construction of Social Space," *Progress in Human Geography*, vol. 7 (September 1983), pp. 502–518; A.B. Murphy, "Regions as Social Constructs," *Progress in Human Geography*, vol. 15 (1991), pp. 22–35.

16. D.B. Knight, "Identity and Territory: Geographical Perspectives on Nationalism and Regionalism," *Annals of the Association of American Geographers*, vol. 72 (1982), p. 517.

17. W. Zelinsky, *Nation into State: The Shifting Symbolic Foundations of American Nationalism* (Chapel Hill: University of North Carolina Press, 1989); S. Cohen and N. Kliot,

"Place-Names in Israel's Ideological Struggle over the Administered Territories," *Annals of the Association of American Geographers*, vol. 82 (1992), pp. 681–695.

18. Y.-F. Tuan, *Space and Place* (Minneapolis: University of Minnesota Press, 1977), pp. 149–160; B.C. Lane, *Landscapes of the Sacred* (Mahwah, N.J.: Paulus, 1988).

19. J. Gottmann, *The Significance of Territory* (Charlottesville: University Press of Virginia, 1973), p. 15, emphasis added.

20. See Knight, "Identity and Territory," p. 526.

21. See Shafer, *Faces of Nationalism*, p. 17.

22. R.J. Johnston, D.B. Knight, and E. Kofman, "Nationalism, Self-Determination and Political Geography: An Introduction," in R.J. Johnston, D.B. Knight, and E. Kofman, eds., *Nationalism, Self-Determination and Political Geography* (London: Croom Helm, 1988), p. 3.

23. See Knight, "Identity and Territory," p. 16; M.W. Mikesell and A.B. Murphy, "A Framework for Comparative Study of Minority-Group Aspirations," *Annals of the Association of American Geographers*, vol. 81 (1991), pp. 581–604.

24. J. Crawford, *The Creation of States in International Law* (Oxford: Clarendon, 1979), p. 86.

25. See Knight, "Identity and Territory," p. 16.

26. A. Cobban, *National Self-Determination* (Oxford: Oxford University Press, 1945), p. 48.

# FIVE

## International Boundaries: Lines in the Sand (and the Sea)

BRADFORD L. THOMAS

*Plus ça change, plus c'est la même chose.*

—Old adage

The WORLD POLITICAL MAP might well be likened to a giant mosaic depicting the world's geopolitical structure, with each of the individual pieces representing a separate state and the lines of mortar dividing them representing international boundaries.[1] To those of us accustomed to this mosaic, the recent breakups of the Soviet Union and Yugoslavia seem to have introduced a phase of unprecedented change—a shattering of some of the pieces and a recementing of the shards with new lines of mortar, as it were.

Yet the geopolitical structure of the world has gone through other major upheavals and not so long ago. Between 1946 and 1986, ninety-five new states joined the world community, emerging from former dependencies in Africa, Asia, Oceania, and the Caribbean. In 1960 alone, seventeen new African states were added. Most of these were broken out of once larger and continuous pieces of the world mosaic, such as French West Africa. The breakup of the Soviet Union can be viewed as simply the most recent phase in the postcolonial independence process.

### A Dynamic Mosaic

Notwithstanding temporary surges in the numbers of states as empires have broken up, the geopolitical mosaic in postcolonial African and Asian areas, once formed, has been fairly stable. The Latin American mosaic (with rare exceptions) for the most part has been stable since the beginning of the twentieth century. Geopolitical instability, in turn, has not been limited to former colonial areas. The mosaic of Europe, though stable from 1946 to 1990, had earlier gone through some wrenching changes—in states after 1919 and in their boundaries after 1945 (Figure 5.1). These

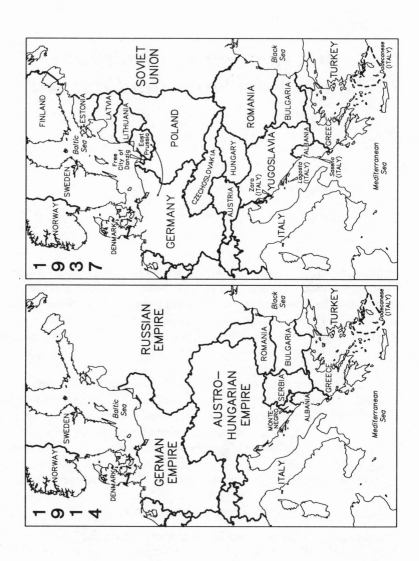

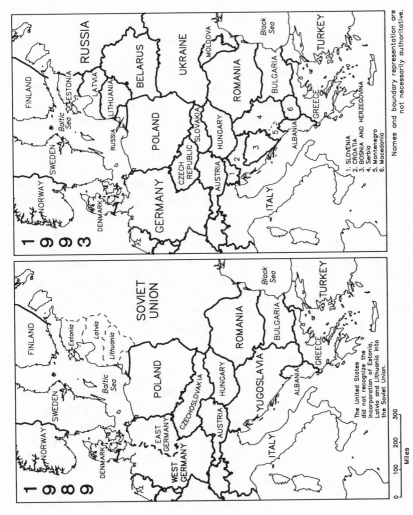

FIGURE 5.1  Europe at four stages through the twentieth century, showing the dynamic nature of the geopolitical mosaic over time.

alterations only continued a trend of periodic territorial adjustments between European states or empires throughout the nineteenth century as well as throughout history. Major adjustments were also made in the territory of the United States and its neighbors during the nineteenth century.

International boundaries were regarded by European scholars during the nineteenth and early twentieth centuries as fluid and changing phenomena, a concept clearly stemming from and supported by the incessant ebb and flow of the territorial expansion and contraction of states during that period. This aspect of international boundaries clearly lives on in the numerous disputes over boundaries that persist to this day. German political geographer Friedrich Ratzel regarded the state as a dynamic organism, of which the border zone was the epidermis that expanded as the state grew.[2] By contrast, however, the states of Latin America generally followed early on the principle of *uti possidetis juris,* or respect for the boundaries in place upon independence, though some conflicts did arise.[3]

After World War II, a trend developed in Europe, Africa, and Asia toward the preservation of existing international boundaries. In 1964, the member states of the Organization of African Unity (OAU), in spite of having inherited the arbitrarily drawn boundaries of colonial powers that split ethnic and tribal groups into different states, issued a landmark resolution at Cairo pledging respect for "the borders existing on their achievement of independence."[4] This action doubtless was taken in recognition of the utter chaos that would ensue in attempting to alter the boundaries. In Asia, newly independent states have often based their claim to national territory on decrees of a colonial government: Even Iraq's claim to Kuwait, as noted earlier, was based on its status in the Ottoman Empire.

In 1975, in the Helsinki Final Act, the Conference on Security and Cooperation in Europe (CSCE) called for the inviolability of international boundaries. And with some notable and unfortunate exceptions (such as the territorial struggle between Armenia and Azerbaijan), this principle has governed national policies throughout Europe and the area of the former Soviet Union ever since. It tempered a great many of the reemergent ethnic and territorial disputes that accompanied the disintegration of Communism in Eastern Europe and, subsequently, the dissolution of the Soviet Union. A notable example is Hungary's official denial of any claim on the Transylvania region of Romania, where a major Hungarian population lives.

The principle of the inviolability of existing boundaries has been extended to former internal administrative boundaries that have become international through the breakup of nation-states. Thus, republic boundaries in the former Soviet Union, in the northern area of the former Yugoslavia, and in the former Czechoslovakia have become international when component republics have attained independence.

Nonetheless, there have been some violent departures from the principle of respect for existing boundaries in recent times. In Africa, despite the Cairo resolution, boundaries were violated when Ethiopia and Somalia fought a war in 1978 over Somalia's portion of the Ogaden region, when Libya occupied part of the Aozou Strip of Chad, and when Morocco occupied Western Sahara in 1975. In Asia, the war between Iraq and Iran and Iraq's later attempt to absorb Kuwait provide other examples. In the Transcaucasus region of the former Soviet Union, Armenia and Azerbaijan fight over the Armenian enclave of Nagorno-Karabakh (Figure 5.2). In the Balkans, ethnic Serbs and Croatians in Bosnia and Herzegovina and Serbs in Croatia are attempting to carve off autonomous states.

The disassembling of some states in Eastern Europe contrasts with the preparations made by twelve Western European states toward forming a larger political union. The lack of change in the European geopolitical mosaic over the last fifty years has perhaps lulled us into an illusion of stability that has made the disintegration of familiar states all the more exceptional and unsettling. In a longer view of history, however, the apparent stability of international boundaries would seem to be more the exception than the rule.

FIGURE 5.2   Azerbaijan, showing the ethnically Armenian autonomous oblast of Nagorno-Karabakh, currently the object of armed conflict between Armenia and Azerbaijan.

# Lines in the Sand

Turning from the changing pieces of the geopolitical mosaic to the mortar that binds them together, one encounters the idea of an international boundary. All the breaking and remaking of the mosaic around the world has taken place under the basic principle of a single bounding line of cement between the pieces—the sanctity of sovereignty as defined by international boundaries. We assume that a finite line marks the limit of territorial jurisdiction of each state that is formed. Adherence to this assumption has gradually grown through time and space as new states have joined the international community.

The idea of circumscribing the territory of a state with a finite line developed with the growth of nationalism and the concurrent evolution of the nation-state as a political organism.[5] These concepts, in turn, developed principally in Europe and were exported around the world with the expansion of colonial empires. They were not originally part of cultures like those in Asia or Africa over which the Europeans gained hegemony,[6] but they are practiced there now because non-European areas, in gaining their independence from European powers, have had to adopt the nation-state concept. Boundaries are essential to the administration of the state power and control that is vested in a national government.

Asian states in the past were based more upon control over people than over territory.[7] Though the center of the state could be easily identified, the periphery was amorphous and ill defined. In many cases, the sovereign's power radiated outward from the people over which he held absolute control to reach peoples or states that recognized his suzerainty—a looser and more distant form of control that often consisted principally of the payment of tribute by the subjects. Some of the peripheral peoples or states recognized and paid tribute to two suzerains. The Asian "state" or, more properly, empire was thus more a phenomenon of gradation than of finite limits.

The loosely defined traditional nature of the Asian state also characterized the Ottoman Empire. The legacy of this ambiguity was evident recently in Iraq's claiming of Kuwait because Kuwait had been under Ottoman suzerainty between the 1870s and 1918 and was a part of the Ottoman province (*wilayet*) of Basrah, which subsequently became part of Iraq. In 1899, however, Kuwait became a protectorate of Great Britain, an arrangement that ultimately led to its independence as a separate country in 1961. Kuwait's history testifies to the different levels of political control and allegiance that were traditional in the Arab cultural milieu.[8]

A loose delimitation of national territory does not work well in a modern world that requires administration of populations and resources. Where such delimitation has persisted, the lack of finite boundaries has been an impediment to the development of frontier area resources, such as oil and gas, that are often vital to raising the economic levels of the countries involved. Even in southern Arabia, where undefined boundaries in vast desert regions have been common, some of the countries are now busy trying to define their boundaries precisely through agreements and demarcate them on the ground (Figure 5.3).

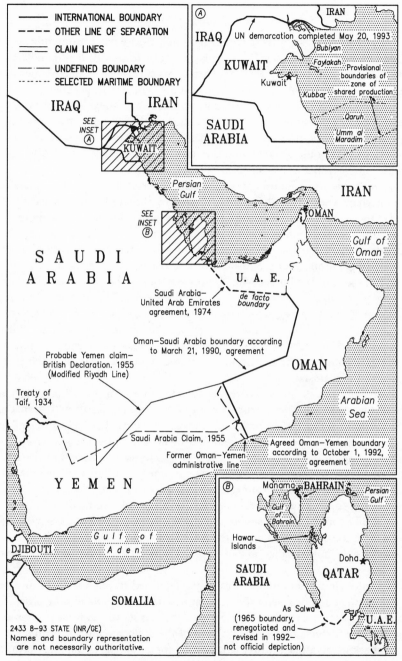

FIGURE 5.3 The Arabian peninsula, showing international boundaries in several stages of evolution. Note the lack of an agreed boundary and the conflicting claims between Saudi Arabia and Yemen over most of their frontier. Determination of this boundary is now the subject of talks between the two nations.

## Concepts

The term *boundary* signifies the finite and often precise *line* surrounding and de-fining the territory of a state. In popular parlance, the words *border* and *frontier* are often used as synonyms, but these two terms have other, distinctive meanings. A border can mean both a boundary, as just defined, and the general zone within which the boundary lies—an *areal* concept. Sometimes, the phrase *border dispute* refers not to a disagreement over the location of the boundary but to a conflict over border functions between governments or groups of people on either side of an undisputed boundary line. And the term *borderlands* is often used to distin-guish more clearly the areal concept of a border.

A *frontier* is also an areal concept, usually referring to a more loosely defined and perhaps wider zone than that indicated by the word *border*. It usually sig-nifies the territory leading up to a boundary on both sides of that boundary, sometimes representing a zone of gradation from one state to another in either jurisdiction or cultural attributes. The idea of a frontier may be translated into legal applications of diminished jurisdiction, as with the *Zona Fronteriza* of Mexico, south of the border with the United States, where Mexican citizens are not required to pay duty on goods purchased in the United States.[9] Frontier zones may be set up as geopolitical entities of greater local autonomy for ethnic groups that extend beyond the boundary of the national territory, as with the autonomous North-West Frontier Province in present-day Pakistan that had been established by the British on the border between what was then British India and Afghanistan.

A frontier can be an area between two states where a precise boundary has never been defined. This is true of most of the area between Saudi Arabia and Yemen. In such regions, where local cultures have not traditionally observed pre-cise boundaries, disputes have arisen over ownership of oil and gas resources. A frontier can also be the amorphous region that forms the margin of the settled and developed territory of a nation, as in the American frontier of the nineteenth century. This notion of a frontier often carried with it the concept of a steadily expanding edge of national development and control. Although such frontiers may still be found in some land areas (e.g., the Amazon Basin), the newest fron-tiers of national expansion are in the sea, where many coastal states have set out zones of maritime jurisdiction within which they exploit resources in and under the sea.

An international boundary is usually established through a treaty or agree-ment between the two states that it separates. The treaty may simply provide an *allocation* of territory in principle between the two states, but it more often con-tains a *delimitation,* that is, a description of the boundary alignment in a text or by a marking on a map. It may also provide for a boundary commission to exe-cute a *demarcation,* which is the precise location of the alignment in the field and the marking of it with pillars. The commission customarily is given authority to make minor adjustments in location for realities on the ground. Not every boundary that is agreed upon and honored between states is demarcated; many boundaries, for reasons of history or geography, remain delimited but not demarcated (for example, the boundary between Iraq and Kuwait prior to 1993).

A boundary agreement does not come into force until it has been ratified by each government and the instruments of ratification have been exchanged. Ratification may follow the agreement quickly or take a few years. States may elect to honor the boundary in the interim, even though the agreement is technically not in force. Sometimes, temporary or provisional lines are established between two states pending the negotiation of a final treaty, the ratification of an agreement, or some other political process. Other lines of national separation like this are often referred to as de facto, as opposed to de jure (or legal) boundaries.

## Lines in the Sea

This idea of a single, finite line bounding national territory has been considerably diluted in recent times in coastal states. As these states increasingly turn their attention to capturing the resources in and under the sea, maritime boundaries are drawn to mark off which parts of the sea or seabed pertain to which coastal state. In earlier times, the shoreline of a coastal country and a narrow band of controllable water just off it marked the edge of national jurisdiction. Now, however, maritime limits are drawn to establish a set of zones of progressively diminishing jurisdiction moving seaward from the shore.

The expansion of the jurisdictions of coastal states into the oceanic realm in the post–World War II era might also be seen as lending new dimensions to the definition of national territory. Despite the clear limitation of state jurisdiction in "exclusive economic zones" (EEZs) to resource exploration and exploitation, there is a growing tendency, albeit *totally without legal justification,* to perceive the EEZ as an extension of the national territory. The territorial sea, not the EEZ, is the limit of full sovereignty, and it represents the true "edge" of a state's territory. Maritime areas seaward of the territorial sea might be more properly termed *maritory.*

The 1982 United Nations Convention on the Law of the Sea (LOS Convention) set the territorial sea limit at no further than 12 nautical miles from a state's legal baseline.[10] About three-fourths of the world's coastal states (including the United States) now claim the maximum allowed 12-mile territorial sea.[11] Gradually, countries that have previously claimed territorial seas of different breadths are adjusting those claims to conform to the 12-nautical-mile standard. A surge of EEZ declarations has also followed the LOS Convention. That convention, however, set a limit for the breadth of an EEZ at 200 nautical miles, and no allowances for greater seaward extensions of national jurisdiction by the UN are foreseen. States will continue to initiate claims to EEZs, but the magnitude of the maritime reach of the sovereign state is probably entering a period of stasis.

## Sea Frontier Concepts

The term *maritime boundary* refers, in general, to the limits of the maritime zones established off the shores of coastal states for administration and resource exploitation. The rules governing these zones have been codified in the LOS Convention and in an earlier convention in 1958. In addition to separating one zone from another, these limits separate the maritime jurisdictions of neighboring states, whether adjacent along the same coast or facing one another across a body of water. In spite of this function, they are not, in a strict sense, *international boundaries*. The closest to an international boundary would be the limit of the *territorial sea*, which marks the edge of the sovereignty of a state, with the caveat that innocent passage of all foreign vessels through the territorial sea be allowed.

The baseline from which the territorial sea is measured seaward is usually the mean low water mark of the shoreline. A state may employ straight baselines along the coast in certain geographical situations specified in the LOS Convention, such as across deep indentations in the coastline or between fringing islands. Inland from these baselines is a regime of *internal waters* in which the sovereignty of the state is no different than it is on land (except that allowance for innocent passage is still required if such waters had not been enclosed before) (Figure 5.4).

Archipelagic states such as Indonesia and the Philippines are entitled to enclose the waters within their islands as *archipelagic waters* by establishing a set of archipelagic straight baselines connecting the outer edges of the outermost islands. Archipelagic sea-lane passage, a new concept in which all ships are allowed to pass in their normal mode, applies to sea-lanes that are generally used for international traffic. Innocent passage is still allowed in other parts of archipelagic waters.

Seaward from the territorial sea, a state may claim a *contiguous zone* not to exceed 12 nautical miles, the purpose of which is to allow the state to prevent or punish infringement of its customs, fiscal, or sanitary laws pertaining to the territorial sea. Beyond the territorial sea and its contiguous zone are several varying kinds of maritime jurisdiction over resource exploration and exploitation. The broadest is the EEZ in which a state controls both the resources of the seabed and the water column above it. The outer limit established for EEZs by the LOS Convention is 200 nautical miles. Although no other state can explore or exploit the resources of the EEZ without the express permission of the coastal state, this zone is, in all other respects, high seas, beyond the control or jurisdiction of the coastal state.

In other resource exploitation zones beyond the territorial sea, the jurisdiction of the coastal state is more restricted, limited to fishing in the *fishing zone* and to seabed resources (usually petrochemical) in the *continental shelf*. The fishing zone may be of any breadth up to 200 nautical miles; the outer edge of the continental shelf is where the submerged prolongation of the landmass drops down to the deep ocean floor. This drop-off may occur beyond 200 nautical miles, in

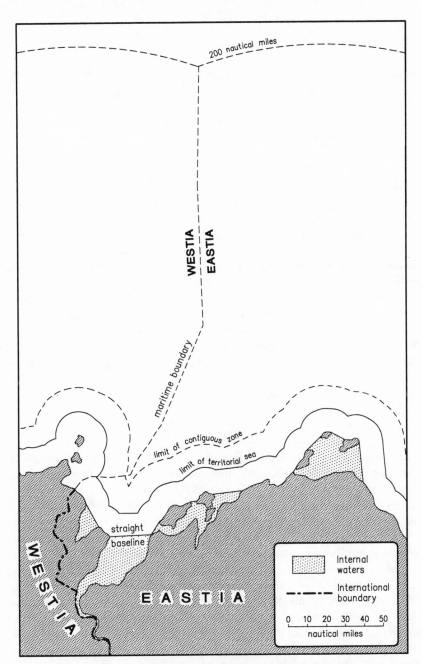

FIGURE 5.4  Diagram illustrating the concept of maritime limits. The 200-nautical-mile line could be the outer limit of a continental shelf, a fishing zone, or an exclusive economic zone (EEZ), depending on the law of the coastal nation. Where fewer than 400 nautical miles separates coastal nations facing each other across an enclosed sea, a mutually agreeable maritime boundary must be negotiated. Where straight baselines are used to connect the outer islands of an insular nation, they are called archipelagic straight baselines, and the internal waters created by them are called archipelagic waters.

which case a coastal country can claim a continental shelf up to 350 nautical miles if submarine topography so indicates. If a state's physical continental shelf does not extend to 200 nautical miles, the LOS Convention allows the state to claim that breadth for continental shelf jurisdiction.[12]

## The Airspace Dimension

In addition to being a line on the earth's surface, an international boundary is also a two-dimensional plane that extends from that surface both to the center of the globe and to the top of the atmosphere. Projection of the boundary downward determines rights to subterranean mineral or hydrocarbon deposits in the frontier area. Projection upward creates airspace above each state that is also presumably inviolable. The world's states have developed a cooperative system for civilian airliners to use in serving international passenger and traffic routes. Serious problems do arise, however, when states refuse permission to enter or even transit that space. Unauthorized entry into a state's declared sovereign airspace had tragic consequences in 1983 when Soviet fighters shot down a Korean airliner that was alleged by Soviet military authorities to have intruded into their airspace. And the U.S. bombing of Libya in retaliation for its sponsorship of terrorism was complicated by airspace transit denials that required the U.S. planes to fly a more circuitous route through the Strait of Gibraltar.

## Conclusion

The world's geopolitical mosaic continues its historical pattern of shifting and changing. The source of the older changes—the conquering of one state by another—may be phasing out, if the Helsinki Final Act and the response of the international community to Iraq's takeover of Kuwait are any indication. Yet states continue to split or merge, and new states are still being created.

Through the continuing changes of the geopolitical mosaic, the concept of separate and discrete pieces, separated by single bounding lines, may be going through subtle changes, especially among the coastal states intent upon capturing the resources of the marine environment lying off their shores. There, instead of a simple, sharp termination of a state's jurisdiction, we see an outward gradation of zones of diminishing jurisdiction. The brightly colored coastal pieces of the mosaic do not end abruptly but essentially fade away through a broader zone.

Finally, it should be noted that international boundaries have a myriad of political and economic functions, ranging from immigration control to financial flow filters to customs controls. At the same time, there is a tendency among the world's states, through bilateral trade agreements or multilateral federations, to eliminate or reduce the number of these functions. The current effort by members of the European Community to eliminate among themselves such boundary functions as labor and capital flow and controls on the movement of people is the most prominent and advanced of several examples. In addition, pressures from vastly increased flows of refugees and economic migrants have caused some of these states to stiffen their immigration controls. To the extent that states do choose to shed some of their traditional border functions, we could see a blurring of finite land boundaries similar to that in the gradations of different sea boundaries. Indeed, the time may come when the analogy of a mosaic becomes inappropriate altogether.

## Notes

The views expressed are those of the author and do not necessarily reflect those of the U.S. government.

1. See E.J. Soja, *The Political Organization of Space*, Commission on College Geography Research Paper no. 8 (Washington, D.C.: Association of American Geographers, 1971), p. 9. In this chapter, the term *state* is used to indicate a sovereign and independent geopolitical unit. It is considered synonymous with the terms *country, nation-state, sovereign state,* or *independent state*.

2. See, for example, J.R.V. Prescott, *Political Frontiers and Boundaries* (London: Allen & Unwin, 1987), pp. 8–9.

3. Ian Brownlie, *African Boundaries: A Legal and Diplomatic Encyclopaedia* (Berkeley and Los Angeles: University of California Press, 1979), p. 12.

4. Ibid., p. 11.

5. Alexander B. Murphy, "Historical Justifications for Territorial Claims," *Annals of the Association of American Geographers,* vol. 80 (December 1990), pp. 531–548.

6. See Soja, *The Political Organization of Space,* pp. 9–11. See also S. Whittemore Boggs, *International Boundaries: A Study of Boundary Functions and Problems* (New York: Columbia University Press, 1940), pp. 6–9.

7. R.D. Hill, "Fishing in Troubled Waters: Some Thoughts on Territorial Claims in the South China Sea," in *Fishing in Troubled Waters: Proceedings of an Academic Conference on Territorial Claims in the South China Sea* (Hong Kong: University of Hong Kong, Centre of Asian Studies, 1991), pp. 2–3.

8. Richard Schofield, *Kuwait and Iraq: Historical Claims and Territorial Disputes* (London: Royal Institute of International Affairs, 1991), pp. 14–18.

9. See also Boggs, *International Boundaries,* pp. 101–105.

10. *The Law of the Sea: United Nations Convention on the Law of the Sea* (New York: United Nations Secretariat, 1983). A nautical mile is equivalent to 1.15 statute miles or 1,852 meters.

11. Robert W. Smith, "The State Practice of National Maritime Claims and the Law of the Sea" (Paper presented to the conference on "State Practice and the 1982 Law of the Sea Convention," Cascais, Portugal, 1990), p. 16. The LOS Convention will enter into force one year after the sixtieth instrument of ratification is deposited with the United Nations. As of this writing, fifty-six states have submitted ratifications.

12. Article 76 of the LOS Convention defines the continental shelf in detail. See *The Law of the Sea*.

# SIX

## Electoral Geography and Gerrymandering: Space and Politics

### RICHARD MORRILL

FOR THOSE SOCIETIES in which elected representatives have meaningful power and are elected from districts, the geographic design of districts is itself a major element of the balance of power. This chapter briefly reviews how manipulation of the layout of electoral districts has been used to influence the distribution of power. Geographers are interested in territorial behavior—how and why people organize themselves on the landscape, as they do through electoral districts.

The emphasis here is on the U.S. experience, but the principles, if not the details, are universally applicable. A short historical review of the idea of territorial representation, from the battle over malapportionment to racial discrimination to gerrymandering, follows. This is supplemented by a discussion of criteria for and methods of redistricting. The chapter then concludes with a review of recent trends and critical issues, particularly the sacrifice of geographic integrity in redistricting efforts.

## International Variation in Electoral Systems

The U.S. system of election by plurality or "winner take all" within individual districts of constituencies is characteristic of relatively few countries—Canada, the United Kingdom, Australia, New Zealand, South Africa, Chile, Japan, and France; the system diffused from Britain to many of its former colonies (the United States imposed on Japan its postwar constitution). The Australian senate employs the "alternate-vote" system to correct somewhat for the electoral bias prevalent in the other systems that developed from British roots. France requires a double ballot or runoff election to ensure that the winner obtains a majority.

Japan elects 511 diet members from 124 districts; since each voter gets only one vote, some of the bias can be overcome.

Most countries, however, follow various forms of proportional representation to ensure that parties receive seats in proportion to their share of popular votes (over some minimum threshold). Ireland employs a quite complex system called the "single transferable vote." Germany uses a rather simple and ingenious system called "additional member"; each voter votes twice, first in a constituency such as those in the United States and United Kingdom and then for a party with a state (Länder). The latter are used to "top up" or achieve proportional representation overall, clearly reducing the incentive to gerrymander. Nevertheless, territorial manipulation may be useful to protect individual incumbents or provide representation for particular places.

The large majority of countries in northern and southern Europe, Latin America, and Asia employ various forms of a "list" for proportional representation. Voters usually do not vote for individuals but for party slates within large multi-member districts, which are, in fact, usually traditional administrative areas. The extreme cases of proportional representation are in Israel and the Netherlands, where the entire nation is one constituency. In countries with proportional representation, electoral districts may be unimportant, but change in the definitions of administrative territories, like the boundaries of major cities, may become quite important since this greatly influences the variation in partisan control and the election of important regional figures (e.g., governors and mayors).

Although proportional representation is often advocated by members of the Left (the British Labour party, for example) on grounds that their supporters are more concentrated in large cities, the Democrats in the United States are ironically vastly benefited by the individual district system. This is because they are able to dominate many districts with very small voter turnouts, which would be submerged by areawide Republican majorities.

There are unusual examples of electoral systems in which representation may be granted to groups other than bounded, territorial districts or political parties. The system used at the end of the Soviet period in Russia, for example, granted a third of all seats in the People's Congress of Deputies to special-interest groups. Thus, a third of the members were elected from a set of organizations that included the labor unions, the Academy of Sciences, and the All-Union Geographical Society.

## Malapportionment, Racial Discrimination, and Gerrymandering: The Constitutional Road

Today, the electoral district is quite ephemeral. But prior to this century, it did not differ from the basic political subdivisions of countries. Thus, each English borough was entitled to two seats in the Commons. The English and Scandinavian idea that representation was territorial and not determined strictly according to "who you were" was fundamental: After all, representation might have been accorded based on social position, interest group, or occupation. Most democratic societies adopted a territorial basis for representation to reflect the actual regional structure that had evolved historically—based on the landed aristocracy, the rise of cities and exchange, and cultural variation. Over time, concerns arose because all the traditional units no longer had an approximately equal stake in the nation. As the franchise extended to all adult males and as the population became more urban, the issue of the fairness of the system of districts arose.

The manipulation of territory for political ends is hardly a new phenomenon. Complaints about gross inequality in population were already being lodged in eighteenth-century Britain against the "rotten" boroughs. Malapportionment, or the inequality in the population size of districts, has been of concern for centuries, and gerrymandering, or the manipulation of the boundaries and compositions of districts for partisan purposes, has been an issue almost as long.

Many states chose to maintain representation from traditional territories by means of proportional representation: A province receives seats in relation to its share of the national population, and within the area, parties receive seats in relation to their share of the total vote. The U.S. Senate (and soon the Canadian senate) continues pure representation by territory—two senators per state. But in Britain and most of its former colonies, the lower-house members are elected from single-member, winner-take-all districts, and there has been a gradual acceptance of the principle of somewhat equal population per district. Over time, it has been more and more difficult to create districts that are reflective of any traditional administrative or cultural areas.

## The United States

The U.S. Constitution provides for the allocation of representatives among states and guarantees that each state will also have a representative system of government. Indeed, the very existence and continuity of the census are based on the constitutional mandate to reapportion seats in the House of Representatives among the states. If the number of seats remained the same and the population of the states changed, then so did the allotment of seats, thereby requiring redistricting within those states. Even so, virtually until the 1970s and except in the very largest cities, it was customary and possible for both congressional and state legislative districts to be composed of whole counties or cities.

Gross levels of malapportionment within states and the prevalence of gerrymandering were routinely criticized throughout the nineteenth and twentieth centuries in the United States. But as recently as 1946, in *Colgrove v. Green,* the U.S. Supreme Court dismissed a complaint that a Chicago congressional district with 915,000 people was treated unfairly compared to a rural one with 112,000. Most states had long ignored their own constitutional requirements for redistricting and routinely overrepresented rural areas; one-third of the states maintained the "little federal" scheme, with state senates having one voter per county, regardless of population size.

## The Reapportionment Revolution

By 1960, the underrepresentation of urban areas had become extreme. In 1962, in *Baker* v. *Carr,* the Supreme Court established the general principle of population equality among congressional districts, and in 1964, it introduced the phrase *one man, one vote* in striking down Georgia's congressional plan featuring an Atlanta district of 824,000 and a rural district of 272,000. In the same year, in *Reynolds* v. *Sims,* the Court extended the principle of substantial population equality to both houses of the state legislatures, arguing that the vote is given to humans, not trees. By 1970, the principle had been extended to all representative bodies, including county commissioners, city councils, and school districts. And by 1975, via a long series of court cases, all fifty states had redistricted both their congressional and their legislative districts. As a result, malapportionment effectively ceased to be a major issue.

However, gerrymandering—the purposeful drawing of districts to benefit some and restrict others—remained. The major aims of such discrimination are related to issues of political parties, race or ethnicity, incumbent members, and kind of territory (e.g., urban versus rural). Many are surprised to learn that, except for gerrymandering against a racial or ethnic minority, the practice remains not only legal but normal and widespread. The term *gerrymander* immortalizes Governor Elbridge Gerry of Massachusetts, who signed into law a districting designed to maximize the election of Republican-Democrats over Federalists. A classic example of gerrymandering is shown in Figure 6.1, where the layout of districts was blatantly designed to prevent the election of a black congressman after federal marshals had begun to register blacks to vote. In Illinois, New York, and Ohio, among other states, gerrymandering long maintained a Republican domination of the legislatures, despite statewide Democratic majorities. Ironically, in recent years, Democrats used the same techniques to try to maintain dominance in the face of statewide Republican majorities.

**Racial Gerrymandering.** Even after districts became more equal in population and as blacks began to register and vote, legislatures tried to minimize black representation. In 1966, the Supreme Court held that states could not draw districts with the intent of minimizing the possibility of blacks being elected. After the Voting Rights Act of 1968, the courts gradually became more and more restrictive, not only striking down plans with any appearance of discrimination but virtually requiring what is called "affirmative gerrymandering" to enhance the chances of minority candidates being elected. Interestingly, in June 1993, the Supreme Court ruled that such "gerrymandered districts" may violate the rights of white voters, casting some doubt on the validity of gerrymandering, at least in extreme cases. Under the Voting Rights Act (VRA), the protected groups are racial and linguistic minorities—the latter primarily people of Hispanic origin. The Court has also disallowed the use of multimember districts if the purpose or intent is to dilute minority representation.

FIGURE 6.1   The original gerrymander (from the *Boston Gazette,* March 26, 1812).
SOURCE: Richard Morrill, "Political Redistricting and Geographic Theory,"
*Resource Publication in Geography* (Washington, D.C.: AAG, 1981).

Within the last few years, there have been several cases aimed at partisan political gerrymandering. *Bandemer* v. *Davis* (1986) concerned an obvious Republican gerrymander of the Indiana legislature, relying on multimember urban districts to dilute Democratic chances. *Badham* v. *Eu* (1989) dealt with the even more blatant and quite effective Democratic gerrymander of the congressional districts of California. Nevertheless, in both cases, the Supreme Court held that the other party could conceivably have won despite the gerrymandering, and thus it decided that there was no constitutional issue of electoral fairness—that is, some individuals' votes were not made less "effective."

## Criteria for and Methods of Redistricting

The purpose of voting is to enable people to express their will with respect to issues of collective choice.[1] One may vote directly on issues, or one may vote indirectly—via supporting a party that expresses a program with which one agrees, via a representative who shares a sense of belonging to a territory and reflects its interest, or via a representative who shares a racial or linguistic heritage that may have been historically suppressed. The goal of districting is to make possible the meaningful participation of voters in electing individuals who provide representation on such bases as party, place, and perhaps race: A voter must feel that his or her vote matters.

Districting can be done well or done poorly. If done poorly, it can create a sense of disenfranchisement and futility. Characteristics of poor-quality districting are:

1. malapportionment;
2. fragmentation of the territorial base of a party so that it cannot, over time, win seats in proportion to its popular appeal;
3. overconcentration of a party's adherents so that the party's strength is wasted and it cannot win seats in proportion to its popular appeal;
4. manipulation of territory to unfairly advantage or disadvantage incumbents of particular parties;
5. fragmentation of the territorial base of a racial or linguistic minority;
6. overconcentration of a racial or linguistic minority;
7. unnecessary fragmentation or division of a territory with which people identify or of districts with which voters traditionally identify;
8. a very high proportion of very safe seats so that voters, in general, feel that there is no possibility of change; and
9. a very high proportion of highly competitive seats so that representatives are not in office long enough to gain experience or commitment.

Characteristics 2 through 9 are all forms of gerrymandering with respect to party, race, language, or meaningful territory. Preelection evidence of poor districting can be gleaned from an analysis of prior election returns and maps. Outcome evidence of the effectiveness of gerrymandering can be obtained from information on who runs or retires, from turnout, and from electoral returns.

# Criteria for Districting

## *Constitutional Criteria*

**Equal Population.** The degree of population equality in the United States depends on the level of jurisdiction. Thus, U.S. congressional districts must be well within 1 percent—that is, about 5,000 people (plus or minus)—for the 1990s redistrictings. Legislatures, county commissioners, and the like are given much greater latitude, often plus or minus 10 percent, especially if the states are small and the population per district is small. States with large populations per district, like California, tend to require fairly strict equality. Population experts argue that extreme population equality—often carried to within a few persons—is absurd, given the uncertainty of the census count, the likelihood of an undercount, and the rapid change in population during the years between censuses. In practice, a decision on population equality may give the courts a backhand excuse to strike down a grossly gerrymandered plan (like the New Jersey congressional plan in 1981) without ruling on the gerrymander as such. The United States appears to be far more extreme regarding the criterion of equal population than other countries, including Canada and the United Kingdom, where traditional arguments prevail that rural areas have a greater need for representation.

**Racial Fairness.** The 14th and 15th Amendments to the Constitution, and the Voting Rights Acts of 1965, 1968, and 1982 have created a strong requirement for equal representation or fairness for racial and linguistic minorities. The VRA lays out criteria defining racial discrimination and the procedure for a judicial review of districting plans, taking into account any history of discrimination, minority access to candidate selection, other forms of discrimination in the region, and the composition and design of districts.

With modern computers and programs, plans with equal populations are very easy to create, and the main basis for judicial complaint is discrimination against racial or linguistic minorities. In effect, a criterion has evolved that requires that the redistricting entity—usually a legislature or other governing body but at times courts or special commissions—maximize the number of districts that would permit the likely election of a minority. This usually means that districts must be drawn to have at least a 50-percent voting-age population; for Hispanics in most areas and for blacks in many areas, this also means a 60- to 65-percent majority of the total population. To achieve this, gerrymandering or the stringing together of appropriate territory is expected and encouraged, at least until the June 1993 Supreme Court ruling on racial gerrymandering.

## *Other Criteria*

One may be surprised that equal population and racial fairness are the only major criteria. Although some state constitutions add other criteria, their weight is inconsequential in comparison.

**Compactness.** Geographers know not to expect too much from a compactness criterion: After all, one can discriminate and maintain appearances! Rather, compactness is an operational aid in avoiding discriminatory gerrymandering. It is preferable to irregularity simply because compact territories make for easier communication and internal cohesion when human settlement is clustered. What is of concern in this regard are egregious irregularities that reveal an intent to discriminate.

Much work has been done on developing measures of compactness, yet the courts have not been impressed. The better measures are based on population distribution rather than external boundaries—for example, the proportion of population inside or outside the district within a polygon enclosing a number of districts.

**Respect for the Integrity of Political Units.** This criterion is and should be an important one. Local governments are vital, legal, and familiar communities of interest. In much of the country, counties have traditionally been a basis of representation and the building blocks for larger districts, and they represent a simple barrier to extreme gerrymandering for racial, partisan, or geographic purposes. The courts generally agree that this is a criterion of wider purpose than compactness and deserves higher priority.

**Community of Interest.** This is the least well defined but the most geographic criterion, in the sense that a major concern of geography is to identify the territories with which citizens identify. The idea of community of interest overlaps with both racial and partisan identity and with political jurisdictions. Communities are revealed through patterns of work, of residence, and of social, religious, and political participation. On a broad scale, there is divergence of identity between an urban core, suburbs, and rural and small-town areas because they are different jurisdictions, have different needs, and attract people with different values. There are also regions defined by a small city and its hinterland. Within a metropolis, broad similarities in age, class, and political leaning exist.

**Why Does Community of Interest Matter?** Community of interest matters because, as stated earlier, one of the three bases of representation is territories—not as arbitrary aggregations of geography or space for the purpose of conducting elections but as meaningful entities that have legitimate collective interests arising from the identification of citizens with real places and areas. Since it is the people of real places who pay taxes to support national and local activities, it is only reasonable that they should develop a sense of common interest as to how the money is spent. Indeed, it was a profound sense that territorial interests (i.e., those of cities) were not being fairly represented that led to the reapportionment revolution in the first place. Although we may vote in a highly partisan manner, the elected representative stands for the district. This is the very essence of our federal-territorial system of governance, and this is why the United States does not have proportional representation. It is also why gerrymandering matters.

**District Stability.** If it is true that voters develop a sense of cohesion over time, then the district becomes "real," as exemplified by organizations, meetings, and the like. A defensive case can be made for minimizing the number of voters who would have to be shifted to another district and whose customary allegiance would be disrupted. But this has the simultaneous effect of protecting incumbents, and it may decrease both the number of competitive seats and the responsiveness of the system to swings in voter sentiment. Also, if an existing set of districts were unusually bad, there would be no virtue in preserving its imperfections.

**Electoral Fairness.** The principle of electoral fairness reflects the idea of a "level playing field"—that, over a set of districts and over a period of time, the number of seats won will be in proportion to the share of votes. It is not possible to totally avoid discriminatory packing and splitting of partisan concentrations because of the geographic concentrations of partisan strength. But the point is that the parties should be treated symmetrically in the redistricting process—that one party should not be disproportionately favored or hurt. Whether such discrimination occurs can be measured on the basis of registration data or returns from recent elections. Obviously, the parties use such data as tools to gerrymander effectively.

Why is this criterion important, despite the Supreme Court's indifference? Why should parties be entitled to protection? Answers to such questions cut to the very core of the theory of representative democracy—a theory based on dual premises: the will of the majority and respect for the rights of the minority. Fairness implies that majority parties should win legislative majorities and that minority parties should nevertheless win seats in proportion to their numbers. It is not the parties but the view of voters that matters. Voters choose representatives and therefore parties in order to entrust them with governing. In a winner-take-all system, the voters accept the reality that the other party may win. But the very ideas of fairness and will of the majority insist that, over the long run, there will be an equitable correspondence between the share of votes received and the number of seats won. Otherwise, the frustrated minority voters can only conclude that they are effectively disenfranchised.

How blatant and destructive to the other party or area does gerrymandering have to be before a sense of fairness tells us that it should be invalidated? The presence of some electoral bias—that is, the difference between the share of votes and seats—is not enough since some disparity may be the result of the natural distribution of partisan strength (i.e., there may be relatively "safe" areas for one or the other party). Rather, a linked set of indicators is needed: electoral bias, the presence before the election of a discriminatory opportunity for election, asymmetry in the distribution of partisan majorities, splitting and packing or incumbent discrimination, irregularity and breakup of communities of interest and of political units, a process that excludes the minority party, and lack of competitiveness.

Partisan gerrymandering is not always successful, and its effects can be transient. This occurs when the perpetrators have overreached, when they have been overconfident about a supposed voter realignment, and when they have riskily tried to maximize their number of seats with smaller margins while packing the other party. If adroitly done, gerrymandering can be successful and lasting; if this were not true, gerrymandering would not have been so common a practice over the generations and the subject of continuing debate and litigation.

**Balance of Safe and Competitive Seats.** This is a difficult and controversial criterion. The idea is that each party should have a similar share of fairly safe seats (e.g., seats won by over 60 percent of the vote) and of competitive seats and that, overall, probably no more than two-thirds of seats will be safe. Given the 95- to 99-percent reelection success of congressional incumbents in the United States, some have proposed a higher proportion of competitive seats or even a limitation on the number of terms. Those who argue for more competitive seats believe this will result in greater elasticity or responsiveness to swings in voter sentiment; those who want to keep safe seats believe this will foster continuity of leadership, accumulation of experience, and balance between legislative and executive power.

## Methods of Gerrymandering and Redistricting

There are four useful techniques for gerrymandering, or manipulating territory for unequal power: (1) packing or wasting the opposition, (2) splitting or diluting the opposition, (3) differential treatment of incumbents, and (4) selective use of multimember districts.

If the minority—be it a political party, a racial or ethnic group, or an urban or rural territory—is much smaller than the majority, then a degree of "affirmative gerrymandering" or manipulation may be practiced in order to even approach parity of votes and seats.

Packing, illustrated in Figure 6.2(a), is simply a matter of overconcentrating the minority so that their votes are "wasted": They win too few seats by too large margins. Thus, ghetto blacks in Chicago or New York were given a 90-percent black district in 1991, when their numbers were sufficient to elect two or more representatives.

Packing occurs when it is impossible to deny the other party some degree of representation. Beyond that core or where minority concentrations are not so large, additional or even any representation at all can be denied by the practice of diluting the minority vote. This is illustrated in Figure 6.2(b), where a concentration large enough to elect one representative is split among several districts, each with a majority for the gerrymandering party. This technique was used by

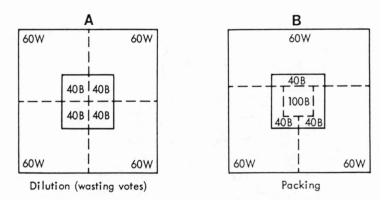

FIGURE 6.2   Racial gerrymandering. SOURCE: Richard Morrill,
"Political Redistricting and Geographic Theory," *Resource Publication
in Geography* (Washington, D.C.: AAG, 1981).

the Mississippi legislature to prevent the election of a black representative, despite the fact that blacks constituted 39 percent of the state population. After
court litigation, the Mississippi districts were redrawn in 1991, resulting in the
election of the first rural black representative since the Reconstruction period
after the Civil War. (See Figure 6.3.)

Because of the great value of incumbency, discriminatory treatment can be
very effective. The idea here is to place members of the same party in the same
redrawn district, while creating open districts without incumbents but with a
majority of voters for the gerrymandering party. In the famous Burton redistricting of California congressional districts after 1980, all three of these techniques
were used. As a result, Democrats received six more seats than their share of
the votes would warrant; half of these could be attributed to discrimination
against Republican incumbents, and half resulted from a mixture of packing and
dilution.

The fourth technique is to create multimember districts with a moderate but
safe margin for the gerrymandering party. This is well illustrated by the equally
famous post-1980 Republican Indiana legislative redistricting (Figure 6.4), in
which the large Democratic vote in greater Indianapolis was submerged by yet a
larger Republican vote in the suburbs. It is a sad commentary on the role of race
in the United States that the gerrymandering was probably made possible only by
the collusion of some Democrats who feared black control of the Indianapolis
Democratic establishment: Recall that the so-called good-government merger of
Indianapolis and Marion County was, in fact, a scheme to secure Republican
control of Indianapolis and to prevent possible election of a black mayor.

Does gerrymandering work? The examples I have cited show that it does. In an
evaluation of all the congressional districting of the 1980s, electoral bias or difference between seats won and votes received were compared for states that had

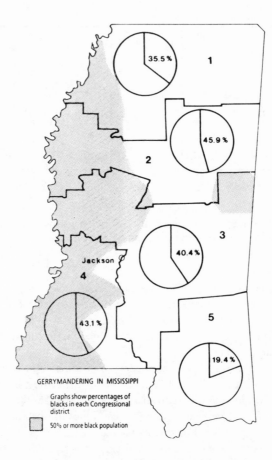

FIGURE 6.3 Gerrymandering of congressional
seats in Mississippi. As Mississippi blacks became
registered, congressional districts were shifted
from a north/south to an east/west pattern,
preventing any district from having a black
majority population. SOURCE: Richard Morrill,
"Political Redistricting and Geographic Theory,"
*Resource Publication in Geography* (Washington,
D.C.: AAG, 1981).

partisan, bipartisan, or court or commission redistricting (and that also adhered
to other criteria, such as communities of interest, compactness, and integrity of
political units). States with intentional or "strong" partisan redistricting stood
out as having quite successfully raised the share of seats 11 percent above the share
of votes. Competitiveness was very low and in the worst cases—California, New
Jersey, Indiana, Pennsylvania, and Massachusetts—political units and commu-

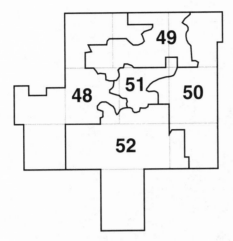

FIGURE 6.4   Multi-member districts
around Indianapolis–Marion County.
SOURCE: Richard Morrill, "Political
Redistricting and Geographic Theory,"
*Resource Publication in Geography*
(Washington, D.C.: AAG, 1981).

nities of interest were routinely split by the use of classic gerrymandering irregularities (see Figure 6.5). States with bipartisan redistricting—that is, a split in
power between the legislature and governor or between houses of the legislature—
had low electoral bias but also low competitiveness since incumbent protection
loomed so large. Commission and court redistricting were, on average, superior
to partisan or bipartisan redistricting across all the measures, especially in terms
of increasing competitiveness. The size of states mattered independently; in general, the smaller the states, the better the redistricting, perhaps because there is
less room for manipulation. Closely balanced states were worse than "one-party"
states perhaps because each party is tempted to employ drastic measures to
maintain or enhance its fragile power. In less balanced states, gerrymandering
was more often employed with respect to ideological or urban-versus-rural interests, rather than strictly partisan ones.

## Redistricting Techniques and Models

An important consequence of the reapportionment revolution was the development of redistricting technology. The greater need to redistrict also coincided
with the revolution in computers, computer software, and computer graphics.
In the 1960s, political scientists, geographers, and others had already begun
to develop relevant models. The two major approaches might be called the
accounting-graphics models and the optimizing models. The first began with a

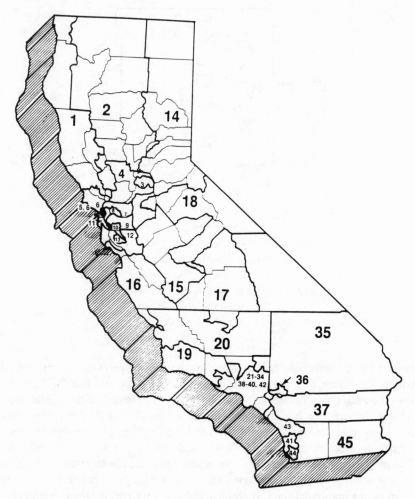

FIGURE 6.5   California congressional districts, 1980. California had the most infamous gerrymanders. SOURCE: *Congressional Districts, 1980* (Washington, D.C.: Congressional Quarterly, Inc., 1980).

simple technology of assigning subunits, like census tracts or precincts, to districts and calculating their population and political profiles. This has since evolved to a high level of sophistication: In the 1990s redistricting, a number of national firms provided graphics-redistricting software packages that permitted the user to select pieces of territory on the screen and obtain instant district profiles and then trade bits of territory among districts to refine district sets. This capacity is immensely popular with politicians as well as with all interest groups. The full technology was only available in the 1990s round of redistricting since it was based on the Census Bureau's completion of the TIGER (topologically integrated geographic encoding and references) files of census geography at the block level for the entire United States, to which population and political data could be attached.

Optimizing models were developed in the late 1960s and 1970s. These are of the location-allocation type in which the objective function is to minimize total travel (distance) of voters to hypothetical centers of districts, subject to some constraints-equal population and territorial integrity. This type is a size-constrained, optimum location model. An example is the LAP (location allocation programs) algorithm developed by Bryan Massam and Michael Goodchild. Since the objective function assures compactness, such models would seem ideal for redistricting; indeed, they work quite well and have been used by commissions in Iowa and Connecticut. They are not, however, popular with political redistrictors: These individuals do not view compactness as particularly important, and the models are unable to incorporate political criteria directly. Where one party is more concentrated than the other, compactness can result in electoral bias against the more concentrated party. Thus, a simple compactness criterion will tend to pack Democrats unfairly in northern cities and Republicans unfairly in southern cities. Also, if communities are more linear than circular, as along a river valley or in a sector of a city, the model may be too simple, and it may violate their integrity. A simple model places too much weight on compactness and not enough on race, community, or political fairness. As a result, these models are more likely to be used to develop a set of alternative "first-cut" configurations, which are subsequently refined politically. Clearly, to the extent that racial sensitivity requires affirmative gerrymandering, the traditional models are inadequate. However, it is possible to modify such models (for example, to minimize "social" distance, rather than geographic distance) and therefore to incorporate race, class, and political allegiance. Some experiments along these lines are reported elsewhere.[2]

## Recent Developments and Continuing Issues

In the United States, the recent round of massive redistricting of congressional and legislative districts has been completed. The task was accomplished rather quickly due to the availability of the census returns and the TIGER geography file and due to the prior preparation of legislatures, interest groups, and specialized redistricting consultants. Four related issues deserve further discussion: the matter of undercount and census adjustment, the advantages and disadvantages of computer technology, the question of partisan gerrymandering, and the problem of geographic integrity and racial affirmative gerrymandering.

### Census Undercount and Adjustment

**No Census Is Complete.** In a country as large, diverse, and individualistic as the United States, it is astounding that some 97 to 98 percent of the population was counted in the most recent census. Nevertheless, the 2 to 3 percent who were not counted were not evenly distributed geographically. The undercount was greatest in areas of racial and ethnic minorities (especially Native Americans, blacks, and Hispanics) and in inner-city poverty areas with transient populations. An undercount of 10 percent or more may have occurred in such areas. On the other hand, there was probably an overcount in some other areas, especially of the elderly or where college students were counted both at home and at school. The result was a shift in political power from the poorer and weaker to the richer and stronger, from the largest cities like Los Angeles and New York to suburban and rural, small-town regions. The magnitude and geographic concentration of the undercount were sufficient to imply the reallocation of several congressional seats among the states and similar redistribution within some states.

Although Census Bureau statisticians and demographers demonstrated that they could adjust the counts to be more accurate at higher levels of geography—states, counties, and cities—they could not do so at the level of the block, which is critical to the contemporary redistricting process. Because of both these technical issues and the obvious politics of those who would benefit from adjustment, the Bush administration decided not to adjust the census.

**Advantages and Disadvantages of Computer Technology.** In two consulting exercises for Illinois and for California, I had the opportunity to work with the most sophisticated graphics techniques for redistricting. On the positive side, these techniques make it possible to develop and experiment with alternatives with amazing speed, and many citizens groups (for example, racial minorities) are now able to develop their own plans or to evaluate the plans of others. On the negative side, the techniques have made redistricting an exercise in micro-adjustment and territorial adjustment or reconciling many special interests at the margin, so that it becomes difficult to make plans that have reasonable macro-level validity that mean anything to the residents. They also encourage users to push the equal-population requirement past the point of absurdity, shifting blocks about to get mathematical precision, regardless of what this does to people and places.

**Partisan Gerrymandering.** The 1990s round of redistricting has not yet been evaluated adequately, but early evidence suggests that the magnitude and severity of gerrymandering, for both partisan and territorial discrimination, is undiminished. In general, this means a further erosion of the principles of community, of interest, or of geographic integrity toward a purely functionalist view of electoral districts. Although it is also true that consistent partisan allegiance is probably becoming ever weaker and that the efforts at gerrymandering are thus really an exercise in political futility, this does not address the erosion of the meaningfulness of districts to voters.

**Affirmative Gerrymandering and Geographic Integrity.** The most dramatic development of the last few years has been the rise of affirmative gerrymandering for racial and linguistic minority representation. The Voting Rights Act requires that redistrictors aim at achieving proportionality, that is, a share of seats approaching the minority's share of the population. Almost all involved in the process interpret this to mean maximizing the number of districts with more than a 50-percent voting-age population, however much gerrymandering is required, on grounds that it is never possible to reach proportionality. The maximum number of black and Hispanic, other racial, or general minority districts must be carved out first, after which the remaining districts can be delineated. As a result, in about half of all states with large minority populations, a majority of all districts will probably be determined by the single criterion of race or ethnicity (and population) and any other sense of community or political unity integrity will be sacrificed. Again, as noted earlier, this will certainly be affected by the 1993 Supreme Court ruling.

This development creates a dilemma for the geographer who is concerned with racial discrimination but also dedicated to the meaningfulness of electoral districts. For example, a consultant prepared a plan for Chicago that was astounding for its irregularity but that created eighteen minority districts. It was argued that the correct proportional share was only fifteen and that the plan was obviously designed to destroy the nonminority Democratic establishment in King County. This argument was overruled, and the courts accepted the more-than-proportional plan. A similar story unfolded in California, where a plan had been prepared that went far toward maximizing the number of minority districts. This plan, however, did not go far enough for the minority group leaders as well as the courts. Although it is important to recognize the significance of long-term discrimination, it should be noted that we are risking a fundamental shift from the historical territorial basis of representation toward a pluralist idea of representation first because of racial or Hispanic identity. Perhaps later on other ethnic or social group lines will emerge. The need to gerrymander for racial purposes effectively undermines arguments to avoid gerrymandering for political or other reasons. Racial gerrymandering could be avoided only if residential integration existed. But the racial basis for representation and power places a premium on maintaining racial segregation.

The issue of race-conscious districting remains in the forefront. The ill-fated nomination of Lani Guinier for a post in the attorney general's office revealed the ambivalence felt even within the racial minority communities regarding a strategy of racial exclusiveness; Guinier argued for fewer gerrymandered multiperson districts with transferable voting. In June, the Supreme Court ruled, in *Shaw v. Reno*, that the North Carolina congressional districting, which resulted in the election of two blacks to Congress, was, in effect, a deliberate segregation by race (see Figure 6.6); the case was remanded to the district court.

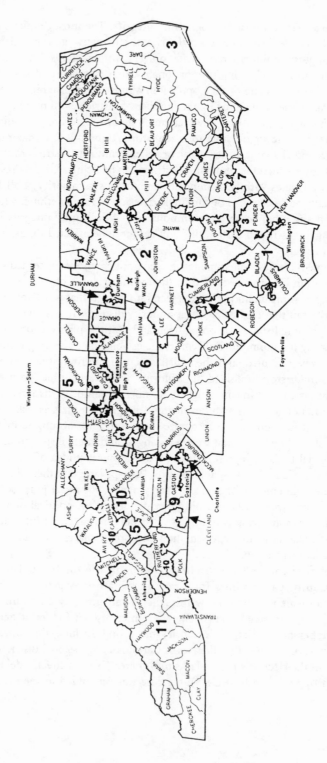

FIGURE 6.6  North Carolina congressional districts, 1990. The North Carolina districts reflect the age of affirmative gerrymandering and led to the case of *Shaw v. Reno*. SOURCE: *Congressional Districts, 1990* (Washington, D.C.: Congressional Quarterly, Inc., 1990).

# Conclusion

Electoral districts are ephemeral, and in the years ahead, it will be increasingly difficult for American citizens to describe their legislative or congressional districts. Yet electoral districts profoundly affect the distribution of political power. To the extent that they do not *fairly* represent territories, political parties, or racial and ethnic communities, the structure of districts can help some and hurt others. Although malapportionment is no longer a problem, gerrymandering remains a prominent tool for discrimination, most commonly used by one political party against the other or, in some areas, to discriminate against urban or rural territory or more liberal or conservative populations. Meanwhile, the requirement of racial fairness has led to the use of affirmative gerrymandering to maximize minority-group representation. All this has had the effect of diluting the historical significance of electoral districts, representing communities with identifiable interests.

## Notes

1. Robert Dixon, *Democratic Representation: Reapportionment in Law and Politics* (New York: Oxford, 1968).
2. Richard Morrill, "Making Redistricting Models More Flexible and Realistic," *Operational Geographer*, vol. 9, no. 1 (April 1991), pp. 2–10.

# PART TWO

---

## Resources, the Environment, and Population

# SEVEN

## Exploiting, Conserving, and Preserving Natural Resources

SUSAN L. CUTTER

*"In March 1987, I decided to run for president . . . campaign analysts had been correct; the issue of the global environment would not help me get elected president."*[1]

*"By the end of nature I do not mean the end of the world. The rain will still fall and the sun shine, although differently than before. When I say 'nature,' I mean a certain set of human ideas about the world and our place in it. . . . More and more frequently . . . our sense of nature as eternal and separate is washed away, and we will see all too clearly what we have done."*[2]

ENVIRONMENTAL DEGRADATION becomes an international, political, and geographic issue when it undermines a state's resource base and compromises its national security. Local resource issues can rapidly assume global significance as societies grapple with how best to use and sustain their cache of relatively scarce natural resources in relation to other countries. Disputes over natural resources, for example, often mar diplomatic relations. In fact, wars over resource disputes may be the rule rather than the exception in years to come, as countries attempt to reduce internal and external threats to their environmental security.

This chapter examines the international system of natural resource production and use. Natural resources are not evenly distributed on, below, or above the earth's surface. Some places are rich in highly valued natural resources, and other places are seemingly poor, leading to uneven access to these basic building blocks of economic systems. Some resources are owned by a sovereign state; others are transnational in their distribution and must be shared. Still others are global and part of the earth's "common heritage." The use and management of these various types of resources are functions of political ideology, technology, and market forces, which, in turn, influence the type and rate of resource consumption. Variations in political ideology and economic affluence among countries and differences in access to technology and markets often lead to confrontations over the management of natural resources. These clashes over resources can occur at the local or national level, but disputes over transnational resources and the global commons are becoming increasingly frequent.

## Diversity in Nature

Even before any human intervention occurs, there are fundamental inequities in natural resource distribution. Land areas vary greatly from country to country, as does the amount of arable land capable of supporting cultivated agriculture. Only 11 percent of the world's land is currently in cropland production, and this, too, is unevenly distributed (see Table 7.1). The rest of the land is either too dry, too cold, too wet, or too mountainous or it has poor soils or is already severely degraded. Only 6 percent of Africa, for example, is arable, around 0.3 hectares per person (less than 1 acre). The largest percent of arable land is in Europe, a region with a long tradition of intensive agricultural production on a very small land base. Although additional land can become productive through inputs such as water (irrigation), fertilizers, pesticides, and more drought- and pest-resistant crop varieties, there is still a finite amount of arable land. Perhaps more to the point, the economic cost and potential environmental problems increase as farmers are forced to use more marginal land (i.e., lands poorly suited for growing crops). Human population pressures, overgrazing, and the unsustainability of modern agricultural practices, which rely heavily on intensive fertilizer and pesticide inputs, are placing enormous burdens on land resources, especially in Asia and Africa. Though overall agricultural outputs have increased worldwide since the 1970s, regional production trends are quite different. In Africa, for ex-

TABLE 7.1    *Arable Land*

|  | Percent of World's Land | Percent of World's Cropland | Percent of Region's Arable Land | Percent of World's Population | Per Capita Cropland (hectare per person) |
|---|---|---|---|---|---|
| Africa | 22.6 | 12.6 | .2 | 12.1 | .29 |
| North and Central America | 16.3 | 18.5 | 12.8 | .1 | .64 |
| South America | 13.4 | 9.6 | 8.0 | 5.6 | .48 |
| Asia | 20.8 | 30.8 | 16.6 | 58.8 | .15 |
| Europe | 3.6 | 9.5 | 29.7 | 9.4 | .27 |
| CIS | 17.0 | 15.7 | 10.4 | 5.5 | .80 |
| Oceania | 6.4 | 3.3 | 5.9 | 0.5 | 1.90 |

SOURCE: World Resources Institute, *World Resources 1992–93* (New York: Oxford University Press, 1992).

ample, per capita agricultural production was stagnant during the 1980s, with a slight decline near the end of the decade. Despite the global increases, nearly 1 billion people are still undernourished and go hungry every day.[3]

Water resources are also highly variable—bountiful in some regions and during some seasons, scarce in others. Societies routinely manipulate the supply and quality of freshwater resources. Dams and diversions capture, store, and channel freshwater for a variety of local, regional, and national needs—irrigation, power generation, industry, and domestic consumption. Because rivers can flow and aquifers can permeate through several countries, the potential for international disputes over their use is increased, especially when the water resources become scarce through natural variability or short-term droughts or through industrial or agricultural contamination. Even when water is plentiful in supply, industrial and agricultural pollution may reduce the availability of drinking water from both freshwater and groundwater sources. The lack of safe drinking water is especially acute in the overcrowded urban slums and squatter settlements in developing countries, where diseases such as cholera and dysentery sporadically reach epidemic proportions. The lack of safe drinking water also affects many rural areas of the developing world.

Mineral and energy resources vary because of continental quirks in geology. Australia, Canada, Chile, China, Cuba, the former Soviet Union, South Africa, and the United States have the largest reserves of nonfuel mineral resources (Figure 7.1). South Africa alone has 11 percent of the world's fifteen most important mineral reserves and a virtual monopoly on chromium and manganese (Table 7.2). Fuel resources derived from minerals (coal, petroleum, natural gas, uranium) are also spatially concentrated in North America, China, the former Soviet Union, and the Middle East (Figure 7.2).

## Uneven Access: Territorial Ownership Versus the Global Commons

Natural resources exist independently from human activity and are variable regardless of whether or not we choose to use them. Only when society finds some utility in some of the world's "neutral stuff" is a value given to the resource. Individual states have internationally recognized "rights" to natural resources that are part of their sovereign territory. This national control allows unlimited governmental access to these resources, which can then be sold to private corporations or developed by state-owned resource utilities such as PEMEX (the Mexican national oil company) or Hydro-Quebec (the provincial developer of hydroelectric resources in Canada).

Some resources, such as freshwater lakes and rivers, transcend political or territorial boundaries, necessitating shared access. These transnational resources often require cooperative agreements between neighboring countries. Rivers, for example, flow through many states and also provide territorial boundaries for

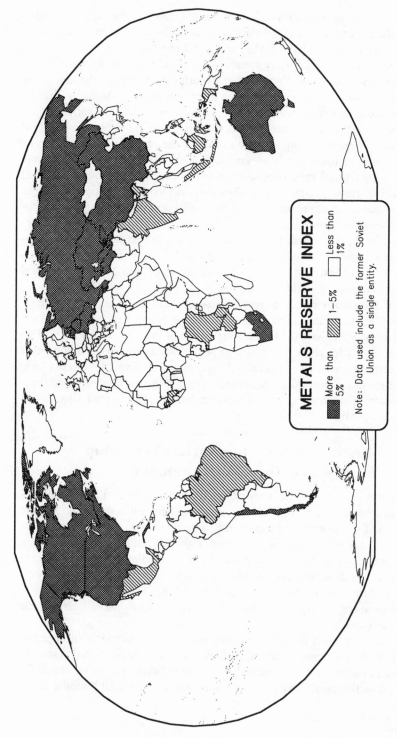

FIGURE 7.1   Metals reserve index 1990. The metals reserve index is the mean global share of fifteen minerals (copper, lead, tin, zinc, iron ore, manganese, nickel, chromium, cobalt, molybdenum, tungsten, vanadium, bauxite, titanium, and lithium) for each country. It provides a comparative measure of the location of the world's mineral powers. The percentages reflect that country's overall share of the world's known reserves.

TABLE 7.2   *Major Mineral-producing Countries*

| | Country | Percent of World Reserves | Percent of World Production in 1991 |
|---|---|---|---|
| Bauxite | Guinea | 26.0 | 16 |
| | Australia | 20.6 | 38 |
| | Brazil | 13.0 | 8 |
| Chromium | South Africa | 70.5 | 35 |
| | Zimbabwe | 10.4 | – |
| | Russia/CIS | 9.5 | 30 |
| Cobalt | Zaire | 41.1 | 50 |
| | Cuba | 31.4 | – |
| | Zambia | 10.9 | 21 |
| Copper | Chile | 26.5 | 20 |
| | United States | 17.1 | 18 |
| | Russia/CIS | 11.5 | 7 |
| Iron ore | Russia/CIS | 36.4 | 24 |
| | Australia | 15.8 | 13 |
| | Brazil | 10.1 | 17 |
| Lead | Australia | 19.9 | 16 |
| | United States | 15.6 | 14 |
| | Russia/CIS | 12.8 | 13 |
| Manganese | South Africa | 45.4 | 38 |
| | Russia/CIS | 36.3 | – |
| | Gabon | 6.5 | – |
| | China | 3.2 | 14 |
| Molybdenum | United States | 49.2 | 54 |
| | Chile | 20.5 | 13 |
| | China | 9.0 | – |
| Nickel | Cuba | 37.3 | 4 |
| | Canada | 16.7 | 21 |
| | Russia/CIS | 13.6 | 27 |
| Tin | China | 25.3 | 19 |
| | Brazil | 20.2 | 15 |
| | Malaysia | 18.5 | 13 |
| Tungsten | China | 44.7 | 52 |
| | Russia/CIS | 11.9 | 21 |
| | Canada | 11.1 | – |
| Zinc | Canada | 14.6 | 16 |
| | United States | 13.9 | 7 |
| | Australia | 13.2 | 14 |

SOURCE: World Resources Institute, *World Resources 1992–93* (New York: Oxford University Press, 1992); J.E. Young, "Mining the Earth," *Worldwatch Paper 109* (Washington, D.C.: Worldwatch Institute).

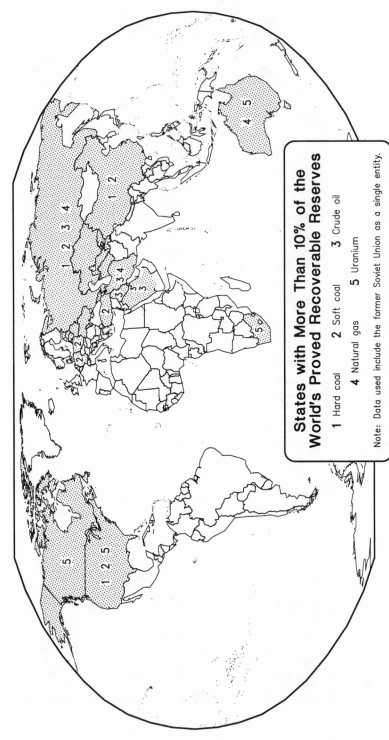

FIGURE 7.2   Energy reserves. Countries with greater than 10 percent of the world's proved recoverable reserves for coal, oil, natural gas, and uranium are highlighted.

some (such as the Rio Grande between the United States and Mexico). Diverting or reducing the flow of water upstream has considerable impact on downstream users. Dams like Turkey's new Ataturk Dam near the headwaters of the Euphrates, which is to be used for hydroelectric power and irrigation schemes, may have considerable impact on the downstream users like Syria and Iraq, who fear a decline in water quality and quantity. Under a 1987 agreement, Turkey is to supply Syria and Iraq with a certain amount of flow, but there is no guarantee that Turkey will abide by this agreement should relationships between the countries sour as a result of Syrian support for Kurdish insurgents in eastern Turkey. Similar water-flow problems exist along the Colorado River and create a source of tension between the United States (the upstream user) and Mexico (the downstream user) and between California and Arizona.[4]

National boundaries are permeable to most environmental contaminants since pollution transported by air or water recognizes no nationality. The degradation of freshwater resources by pollution is a good example. Contamination of the Rhine from the 1986 Sandoz chemical spill in (upstream) Basel, Switzerland, affected not only Swiss residents but also residents in all those countries downstream (Germany, France, and the Netherlands). Transboundary industrial pollution has helped to strengthen the role of regional political alliances, such as the European Community, in regulating environmental quality issues. It has also fostered cooperation between environmental non-governmental organizations (NGOs), who are increasingly adopting an international outlook.[5]

There are other resources, however, where ownership is less clear, such as the atmosphere, biotic resources in the deep oceans (like whales or fish), or minerals in Antarctica. These common-property resources are extraterritorial and have been exploited by private individuals, corporations, or governments for their own profit because they have the technical and economic means to do so.[6] Since the exploiters are not held responsible for the resource, they have no vested interest in safeguarding it. This conflict between ownership, unequal access, and management responsibility is one of the underlying causes of the exploitation of the global commons. Common-property dilemmas are often solved by institutional arrangements, such as trade sanctions, multilateral treaties, or privatization. A variety of international treaties are now aimed at managing resources as part of the global commons (Table 7.3). Protection regimes such as the Conference on the International Trade in Endangered Species (CITES) and the International Whaling Commission have facilitated the recovery of certain commons. Yet some argue that these protection regimes can create an entirely new set of tragedies, especially for developing countries.[7]

The current debate surrounding greenhouse gas emissions is a good example of common-property dilemmas. The implementation of the Climate Change Treaty—including emissions limits for greenhouse gases and a carbon tax if voluntary reductions prove ineffective—represents an attempt at managing the most common property resource of all, the atmosphere. Because of the global impact of local and national resource-use policies, there is a growing recognition of the pressing need for international cooperation in protecting the planet. United Nations agencies as well as international non-governmental agencies have played key roles in fostering multilateral treaties on resource use, illustrating the salience of global environmental politics.[8]

TABLE 7.3   *Major Global Treaties on Natural Resources and Environmental Protection*

|  | *Date* | *Resource Protected* | *Number of Participating States[a]* |
|---|---|---|---|
| Antarctic Treaty | 1959/1980 | environment and marine resources | 40 |
| Nuclear Test Ban | 1963 | atmospheric protection from radioactive fallout | 122 |
| Ramsar | 1971 | wetlands, waterfowl habitat | 61 |
| World Heritage | 1972 | natural heritages | 108 |
| Ocean Dumping | 1972 | marine protection from dumping | 72 |
| CITES | 1973 | endangered species | 109 |
| MARPOL | 1978 | marine protection from oil spills/pollution | 85 |
| Long-Range Transboundary Air Pollution, Europe (LRTAP) | 1979 | regional atmospheric protection from transboundary industrial pollution | 32 |
| Migratory Species | 1979 | wild animals | 46 |
| Law of the Sea | 1982 | access to common-property marine resources | 137 |
| Ozone Layer | 1985 | ozone layer protection | 68 |
| Montreal Protocols | 1987 | atmospheric protection and CFC ban | 69 |
| Basel Convention | 1989 | protect land and water by restricting transboundary movement of hazardous waste | 52 |
| Bamako Convention, Africa | 1991 | transboundary hazardous waste movements | 17 |
| Climate Treaty | 1992 | reduction of atmospheric greenhouse emissions | 160 |
| Biodiversity | 1992 | protection of biotic resources, especially tropical rain forests | 150 |

[a]Participating countries are either contractors or signatories to the agreements.
SOURCE: World Resources Institute, *World Resources 1992–93* (New York: Oxford University Press, 1992).

## Controlling Interests

Technological innovations and economic motives provide access to resources, but ultimately, it is political regimes that determine how resources are exploited, conserved, or preserved. *Exploitation* is the complete or maximum use of a resource for immediate societal gain or individual profit. *Conservation* is the attempt to balance current resource use with longer-term availability through efficient, prudent, and ecologically sound management. Finally, *preservation* is the nonuse of a resource—an insurance policy that guarantees full protection of the resource, leaving it unimpaired for future generations.[9] These strategies are employed by individuals, private corporations, and governments, and they vary according to changes in technological and economic conditions as well as political regimes.

## Political Economy

Natural resources provide the raw materials for industrialization and economic development. The type and pace of development are determined by the political ideology of the ruling elites and a number of other factors. In capitalist–free market theory, resources are allocated in the marketplace where the producer and consumer (through the imperfectly understood principles of supply and demand) determine how much of a resource is used and at what price. The producer can be an individual entrepreneur, a private corporation, a multinational corporation (MNC), or a state.

In Socialist theory and the remaining Socialist systems, resources have no intrinsic value. Their value is derived from the labor that is used to produce them. The desirability of economic development and resource consumption reflects the goals and values of the people (embodied in the state apparatus), not those of special interests or elites. Instead of using the "free market" as the exchange between producers and consumers, there is centralized economic management and distribution of resources by state-controlled producers.

Underlying both systems is a technocentric ideology—the mastery of and domination over nature.[10] Nature is viewed as a means to support increased material and economic growth. Domination and mastery over nature are achieved through science and technological innovations that not only improve our ability to exploit resources but also allow us to do so more quickly. Technocentrists feel that there are ample supplies of key resources and that scientific and technical advancements will alleviate potential resource problems, including dwindling supplies, without any decline in economic prosperity.

This worldview results in an exploitative approach toward resources, in which they have only one purpose—to serve humans.[11] Some argue that the ideology originates in Judeo-Christian theology; other scholars give more complex explanations for these exploitive attitudes.[12] They argue that "Western" societal processes—industrialization, urbanization, gender domination, capitalism, and scientism—provided cultural tools to dominate nature. Yet capitalist societies are not the only ones to exploit and degrade resources. Examples of the Socialist-Communist system's inability to handle the social costs of industrialization (rapid resource depletion and environmental degradation) can be seen throughout Eastern and Central Europe and in many of the republics in the former Soviet Union.[13] Regardless of how it is implemented (whether through capitalism or socialism), technocentrism has become the dominant perspective on natural-resource use since the industrial revolution.

Over the last thirty years, there has been a fundamental shift in attitudes about nature, moving toward a more ecocentric vision—living in harmony with nature. The accelerating pace of global environmental change and its impact on the human condition has led us to reconsider our basic relationship with nature and our role in transforming the earth.[14] Increasingly, the earth is viewed as a closed system with a finite supply of resources—the "spaceship earth" concept. Ecocentrism advocates preservation and strict resource conservation. Economic growth is tempered by resource stewardship to provide the basic needs of society but not the excesses of unbridled consumerism. Environmental protection and economic growth become inseparable, with the latter tempered by environmental responsibility and social justice. Ecocentrism, the underlying principle of sustainable development and resource use, is not antiscience or antitechnology; rather, it emphasizes small-scale, appropriate technology to provide for basic needs.

Often, these environmental ideologies are taken up by special-interest groups who try to influence resource decision-making. Environmental activism or "green rage"—be it expressed through local grass-roots movements (Green Belt, Chipko), environmental organizations (Earth First!, Greenpeace), or formal political parties (Germany's *die Grunen*)—takes an aggressive ecocentric stance in the protection of the environment. In contrast, multinational corporations and some governments often cling to technocentric ideologies that form the basis for their management decisions. Governmental environmental agencies and more mainstream NGOs stand somewhere in between, arguing for both stewardship of resources and sustainable development of society—a pragmatic, conservationist view.

## Technological Change

Technology, the tool used to exploit resources, has, of course, changed dramatically during the past 2,000 years. By becoming more complex and powerful, technology has enabled modern societies to exploit resources more quickly and efficiently than ever before.[15] Technological innovations like the steel plow and barbed wire helped transform the vast prairies and grasslands in the U.S. Great Plains into one of the most productive agricultural regions in the world. Much earlier, the fifteenth- and sixteenth-century voyages of exploration and discovery—made possible by technological breakthroughs in shipbuilding, mapping, and navigation—profoundly altered the global patterns of food resources through "ecological imperialism" (the introduction of many species of plants and animals from the New World to the Old World and vice versa).

But technological change and innovation have a price, often in the form of unanticipated consequences on social, economic, and environmental systems.[16] The mass production of goods, for example, leads to mass inputs of raw materials, which may require a global search for new raw materials that results in their rapid exploitation. What begins as a solution to a particular scarcity issue at a specific time in a particular locale often leads to greater resource destruction over larger areas and longer time periods.

Energy resources provide a good example. Currently, the world uses in one year the equivalent amount of fossil fuel energy that it took nature 1 million years to produce. In Europe after 1750, traditional fuel sources (firewood, animal and plant waste, charcoal) were rapidly replaced by coal as the industrial revolution progressed. In the 1880s, Welsh anthracite coal was shipped worldwide on steamships until supplies dwindled. The need for additional reserves of coal resulted in the transfer of mining technologies and operations to distant lands. Lower-grade coals were also mined at greater depths, and surface deposits were strip-mined. The rapid exploitation of coal for fuel industrialization led to severe environmental degradation in many of the great coal-bearing and coal-burning regions in the world: the former Soviet Union, China, Australia, Western and Central Europe, and the eastern United States.

Although the first commercial oil well in the United States was drilled in 1859, oil did not become a competitor with coal as a primary fuel until the internal combustion engine was invented. After that, however, oil use rose exponentially, replacing coal as the primary fuel for heating and transportation by the middle of this century. Today, plastics, synthetic fibers, pesticides and fertilizers, chemicals, and a host of other consumer products are all manufactured from petroleum and its derivatives. Indeed, we are so totally dependent on oil—from the clothes we wear to the food we eat—that some observers refer to the latter half of this century as the era of the "hydrocarbon society."[17] Many developments in international relations over the past fifty years have been based on the worldwide demand for and supply of oil.

Another technological innovation in energy production is the fission process. First used to generate electricity in 1957, fission reactors made uranium a valued resource. Nuclear power currently accounts for only 2 percent of the world's total energy production and 17 percent of its electricity output. But in several European countries, it is the primary source of electricity, including France (75 percent), Belgium (60 percent), and Hungary (51 percent). Nuclear energy is a relatively "clean" fuel; it does not contribute to acid rain nor does it increase the amount of greenhouse gases emitted into the atmosphere. However, a failure in this technology, as the Chernobyl meltdown aptly illustrated, can cause catastrophic environmental destruction at both the regional and global level.

# Market Imperfections

Even if countries have the desire and ability to exploit resources, they may be unwilling to do so because it is unprofitable for them, especially within a free-market economic system.[18] As the commodity becomes more (or less) in demand, the price will change, which, in turn, will affect future demand. A deposit of deep seabed manganese may be too expensive to exploit today, but if technology allows cheaper exploitation, if new demands arise for its use, or if prices rise substantially, it may become profitable to mine manganese nodules in the future.

Scarcity affects supply, demand, and price relationships. If a natural resource becomes scarce while its demand remains constant, its value will increase. There are two types of scarcity—absolute and relative. Absolute scarcity occurs when supplies of a finite resource (minerals and fossil fuels) are insufficient to meet current as well as projected future demands. Relative scarcity occurs when there are short-term variations in supply as a result of natural hazards (frosts, floods, droughts) or the intentional manipulations of the market by resource producers.

Unfair competition exists in global markets based on the preferential trading policies of states or resource monopolies (cartels) that band together to gain an economic advantage by reducing production to keep prices artificially high. For example, between 1975 and 1981, the price of a barrel of oil rose from $13 to $35, largely because of the influence of the Organization of Petroleum Exporting Countries (OPEC). This thirteen-member cartel (consisting of Algeria, Ecuador, Gabon, Indonesia, Iran, Iraq, Kuwait, Libya, Nigeria, Qatar, Saudi Arabia, the United Arab Emirates, and Venezuela) controlled around one-third of the world's oil production during the 1980s. To reduce the influence of OPEC, many countries increased domestic production and reduced demand through greater efficiency, thereby improving their position on the supply-and-demand pendulum. The result is that oil prices now hover around $19 per barrel.

Oil dominates energy and economic markets, creating a "world order of oil." It strains the economies of both industrialized and developing countries who increasingly rely on imported sources and thus depend on the international marketplace to purchase their oil. Moreover, the fluctuating price of oil can cripple the national economies of both exporting and importing states. When oil prices are low, exporters (many of whom are single-commodity countries) suffer, and tensions between rich and poor producers over production quotas intensify (as they have within OPEC). When prices are high, importing countries suffer as their foreign debt increases and inflation accelerates at home. During the next two decades, the geopolitics of oil will focus more specifically on the Middle East, a region with 75 percent of the world's proven reserves of oil.

Another factor in global markets is the role played by MNCs, private corporations that operate in several countries simultaneously. These corporations have the ability to shift production and marketing activities from one country to another, depending on where profits are greatest. Some MNCs (Shell, du Pont) are large enough to control and manipulate markets at the national level, if not globally. For example, around 70 percent of the world's grain surplus between 1987 and 1989 was produced by only five countries—the United States (39 percent), France (11 percent), Canada (9 percent), Australia (6 percent), and Argentina (4 percent).[19] A handful of private, family-dominated companies, transnational in their operations, dominate global trading in foodstuffs.[20] Collectively known as the grain merchants, they are primarily based in the United States and France and include the firms of Cargill, Continental, and Louis Dreyfus.

The economic diversification of MNCs and their ability to move commodities and money internationally limit the regulatory controls of individual governments. With a few exceptions, MNCs are the masters of the markets and the purveyors of technology to exploit natural resources and then deliver them to consumers. In seeking new resource reserves or to continue exploiting existing ones, MNCs must pay countries for access in the form of production rights or extraction fees. All too often, however, the prices are extremely low. The state consequently feels exploited but often lacks the technology to extract the resource itself. Internal political struggles and nationalistic fervor in many developing countries have fostered anti-MNC sentiment. The MNCs, viewed as a threat to national security, may then be seized by the host government. Iran's nationalization of Anglo-Iranian Oil (the forerunner to British Petroleum) in the 1950s and Chile's seizure of American copper companies during Salvador Allende's regime in the early 1970s are good examples. The internal political struggles of these states affect global markets, where matters of national security often collide with free-market competition and trade.

## Affluence

Affluence is perhaps the greatest controlling factor in resource consumption as well as a harbinger for political confrontations over its use. The imbalance between the largest consuming nations and population size is a measure of this affluence. The United States, with 5 percent of the world's population, consumes most of the world's resources. For many resources (arable land, timber, water), the United States is self-sufficient—it produces what it consumes. Japan, on the other hand, is relatively resource poor and must import most of the natural resources that fuel its affluence. For example, both the United States and Japan are the top consumers of many of the world's major minerals (Table 7.4); these resources are the essential building blocks of industrialized economies. The United States has considerable mineral reserves (copper, lead, tin, zinc, iron ore), but Japan's are extremely limited. Both countries rely (to differing degrees) on mineral imports to drive their industrial economies. In addition, the United States consumes 25 percent of the world's energy. Japan, which imports 90 percent of its energy supply, is much more efficient in energy use, consuming only 5 percent of the world's supply with about 2 percent of the world's population.

TABLE 7.4    U.S. and Japanese Consumption of Mineral Resources in 1990
(percent of world's total)

|                  | United States | Japan |
|------------------|:-------------:|:-----:|
| Aluminum/bauxite | 24.3          | 13.5  |
| Cadmium          | 15.0          | 23.2  |
| Copper           | 19.9          | 14.6  |
| Iron ore         | 7.9           | 11.6  |
| Lead             | 23.2          | 7.5   |
| Nickel           | 14.8          | 18.9  |
| Tin              | 16.0          | 15.2  |
| Zinc             | 14.2          | 11.7  |

SOURCE: World Resources Institute, World Resources 1992–93 (New York: Oxford University Press, 1992).

# Confronting Inequities:
# Armed Conflicts and Peaceful Compromises

Variations in ideology, technology, and economic capability, coupled with the unequal distribution of resources, set the stage for political confrontations over resources at the local, regional, and global scale. Regional inequities in wealth and resources within nations can precipitate civil unrest and fuel separatist feelings. The Nigerian Civil War (1967–1970) is a good example. The eastern region of Nigeria, rich in mineral resources (especially oil), was also the most developed and heavily populated by Ibos. When it declared its independence (renaming itself Biafra), a civil war escalated into an international issue as the central Nigerian government implemented a naval embargo to prevent oil exports. Moreover, since Shell and British Petroleum produced 85 percent of Nigeria's oil, the civil strife became a national security concern for the United Kingdom. France and the United States also had strategic interests in the region as well.

As societies have evolved, many have exhausted their own territorial (in situ) natural resources. Either at the state or village levels, perceived carrying capacities have been exceeded either by swift increases in population or by the rapid exploitation of resources and the subsequent degradation of the environment. The quest for land and the resources it contains has always been a motivating factor in national territorial expansions, as Ratzel suggested (see Chapter 1). To achieve economic and political dominance and internal environmental security, states have tried to expand their territory or their zones of influence. Some have resorted to military threats and actions to ensure their access to an adequate supply of natural resources.

A number of examples illustrate the transnational politics of resource control. The Iberian conquest of the Americas, for instance, was prompted by a need to find more resources, especially gold, to replenish the Spanish treasury after its war with the Moors; the Spanish were much less excited about the scientific joy in discovering the "New World." World Wars I and II were partially caused by population pressures in Central Europe, providing a justification for German territorial expansion in the quest for more living space. Japan's expansionist tendencies in Southeast Asia were partially motivated by its own lack of indigenous natural resources.[21] Similarly, the Falklands-Malvinas War between Argentina and Great Britain was nominally fought over access to marine resources within the 200-mile exclusive economic zone (EEZ) that surrounds the islands. Domestic Argentine politics and national pride also played a major role in the armed conflict. More recently, the 1991 Persian Gulf War was partially fought over access to oil, one of the most important natural resources now influencing international relations. There are many more examples of armed conflicts between states over natural resources (Table 7.5).

Unrestricted access to natural resources continues to be an important element in foreign policy. For example, international disputes over water resources can mar bilateral relations between countries, often requiring regional intervention in the dispute.[22] Hydropolitics and unresolved water disputes could prompt the next regional-scale armed conflicts in Africa (control of the Nile), South Asia (dry-season flow in the Ganges), or the Middle East (reduced water flow and salinization in the Euphrates, Tigris, or Jordan rivers).[23] The latter case is perhaps the most worrisome since water, not oil, is the most precious resource in the region.

Peaceful methods for resolving transnational resource conflicts are being tried by more and more countries who see the need to develop multilateral environmental alliances to ensure resource availability. One method to protect ecosystems is to create national parks around them. Globally, there are close to 7,000 areas covering 650 million hectares that are protected as national parks.[24] Ecuador is the international leader, with 14 protected areas covering 38 percent of its

TABLE 7.5   *Selected Twentieth-Century Transnational Armed Conflicts over Natural Resources*

|  | Countries/Conflict | Resource in Dispute |
|---|---|---|
| 1932–1935 | Paraguay-Bolivia (Chaco War) | oil |
| 1967 | Arab States–Israel (Six-Day War) | water |
| 1969 | El Salvador–Honduras (Soccer War) | arable land |
| 1972–1973 | Iceland–United Kingdom (Cod War) | fish |
| 1974 | China-Vietnam (Spratley Islands Dispute) | oil |
| 1982 | United Kingdom–Argentina (Falkland-Malvinas War) | fish, oil |
| 1991 | Iraq–United Nations Coalition (Persian Gulf War) | oil |

SOURCE: A.H. Westing, ed. *Global Resources and International Conflict: Environmental Factors in Strategic Policy and Action* (New York: Oxford Univ. Press, 1986).

national territory. However, many fragile ecosystems straddle political boundaries, and bilateral and multilateral cooperation is needed to ensure the protection of these cross-border ecosystems. In 1988, six Central American countries banded together to establish a series of "peace parks." These parks are designed to preserve the region's disappearing rain forests—belatedly recognized as a precious global resource—and to promote sustainable development. In 1989, there were 68 border parks involving 66 countries.[25]

## The End of Nature or a New Beginning?

The politics of natural resources are undergoing unprecedented changes as we near the end of the twentieth century. Bill McKibben's apocalyptic vision of the "end of nature" reflects the political realities of the 1980s—economic growth regardless of environmental cost. Yet the political winds shifted during the late 1980s and early 1990s, for several reasons. First, a sharp degradation of critical world resources was observed and measured, such as the expanding hole in the ozone layer. Second, the relative overconsumption and affluence of the few wealthy nations was widely publicized and criticized by developing countries for exacerbating the twin worldwide problems of resource use and environmental degradation. Continual degradation of the soil, water, and marine resources promises, ultimately, to reduce food production. Pollution in areas such as the former USSR has become so severe as to produce measurable effects on human bodies and the ability to bear healthy children. Ozone depletion, global climate change, and reductions in biodiversity increasingly threaten the basic life-support system of our species, and these threats are political realities in many parts of the world.

The rate of resource use, the scale of environmental degradation, and the looming exhaustibility of many of our most important resources are forcing governments to reevaluate their basic assumptions about economic growth and planetary stability. Many countries have realized that economic prosperity is inextricably linked to environmental health. Even the industrialized Group of Seven (G7) nations (the United States, Canada, the United Kingdom, Japan, Germany, France, and Italy) have publicly acknowledged the importance of environmental issues in economic growth and global security. And though international security and the global economy continue to dominate foreign relations, the international system of resource production and use is becoming the third issue of importance.[26]

## Conclusion

Environmental issues are at the center of many of the world's most pressing problems, but environmental protection strategies alone will not solve them. This became quite clear during the 1992 Earth Summit meetings in Rio de Janeiro, attended by 170 national delegations. "Sustainable development" became the rallying cry for many participants who viewed that as the only viable path states could take to ensure their own survival and environmental security. With sustainable development, resources are managed to provide for the needs of the present generation without compromising the ability of future generations to meet their own needs.[27] The implementation of sustainable development ideals, however, remains largely untested (see Chapter 9).

Within the United States, the public has slowly recognized the links between economic and environmental survival. Ideas about resource conservation that were viewed as radical a few years earlier (such as higher taxes for gasoline or consumption taxes on material goods) are no longer dismissed, mostly because they make economic sense. After his frustrated bid for election in the 1987 presidential contest, Al Gore became vice president of the United States five years later, providing a national voice for the view of sustainability and a balance between human wants and environmental stewardship—a vision that underscores the integration of local, national, and international policy.[28]

Future economic development will be tempered by environmental responsibility. Issues of poverty, land tenure, population, health, and women's status will be increasingly linked to global environmental improvements and environmental security. East-west tensions already have been replaced by strains in north-south relations, and they will intensify. The implementation of sustainable practices will mean dramatic changes in the quality of life for millions of people, both rich and poor. But the changes will not come easily and they may result in altered political regimes, civil unrest, and realignments in foreign relations, all of which will further affect exploitation, conservation, and preservation of natural resources in the decades ahead.

## Notes

1. Al Gore, *Earth in the Balance: Ecology and the Human Spirit* (Boston: Houghton Mifflin, 1992), pp. 8–9.

2. Bill McKibben, *The End of Nature* (New York: Random House, 1989), p. 8.

3. World Resources Institute, *World Resources 1992–93* (New York: Oxford University Press, 1992).

4. M. Reisner, *Cadillac Desert: The American West and Its Disappearing Water* (New York: Viking/Penguin, 1986).

5. L.K. Caldwell, "Globalizing Environmentalism: Threshold of a New Phase in International Relations," in R. Dunlap and A.G. Mertig, eds., *American Environmentalism: The US Environmental Movement 1970–1990* (Philadelphia: Taylor and Francis, 1992).

6. G. Hardin, "The Tragedy of the Commons," *Science*, vol. 162 (1968), pp. 1243–1248.

7. B.J. McCay and J.M. Acheson, eds., *The Question of the Commons* (Tucson: University of Arizona Press, 1987).

8. G. Porter and J.W. Brown, *Global Environmental Politics* (Boulder: Westview Press, 1991); see Chapter 9.

9. S.L. Cutter, H.L. Renwick, and W.H. Renwick, *Exploitation, Conservation, Preservation: A Geographic Perspective on Natural Resource Use,* 2d ed. (New York: John Wiley & Sons, 1991).

10. T. O'Riordan, *Environmentalism* (London: Pion, 1976); D. Pepper, *The Roots of Modern Environmentalism* (London: Croom Helm, 1986).

11. L. White, Jr., "The Historical Roots of Our Environmental Crisis," *Science,* vol. 155 (1967), pp. 1203–1207.

12. L.W. Moncreif, "The Cultural Basis of Our Environmental Crisis," *Science,* vol. 1709 (1970), pp. 508–512; C.J. Glacken, *Traces on the Rhodian Shore: Nature and Culture in Western Thought from Ancient Times to the End of the Eighteenth Century* (Berkeley: University of California Press, 1967); C. Merchant, *The Death of Nature: Women, Ecology, and the Scientific Revolution* (San Francisco: Harper and Row, 1980); C. Merchant, *Ecological Revolutions: Nature, Gender, and Science in New England* (Chapel Hill: University of North Carolina Press, 1989).

13. M. Feshbach and A. Friendly, Jr., *Ecocide in the USSR: Health and Nature Under Siege* (New York: Basic Books, 1992).

14. R. Carson, *Silent Spring* (Boston: Houghton Mifflin, 1962); W.L. Thomas, *Man's Role in Changing the Face of the Earth* (Chicago: University of Chicago Press, 1956); B.L. Turner II, W.C. Clark, R.W. Kates, J.F. Richards, J.T. Mathews, and W.B. Meyer, eds., *The Earth as Transformed by Human Action* (Cambridge: Cambridge University Press, 1990).

15. D.R. Headrick, "Technological Change," in B.L. Turner II, W.C. Clark, R.W. Kates, J.F. Richards, J.T. Mathews, and W.B. Meyer, eds., *The Earth as Transformed by Human Action* (Cambridge: Cambridge University Press, 1990), pp. 55–67.

16. L. Winner, *The Whale and the Reactor: A Search for Limits in an Age of High Technology* (Chicago: University of Chicago Press, 1986).

17. D. Yergin, *The Prize: The Epic Quest for Oil, Money, and Power* (New York: Simon and Schuster, 1991).

18. J. Rees, *Natural Resources: Allocation, Economics, and Policy* (London: Methuen, 1990).

19. World Resources Institute, *World Resources 1992–93.*

20. D. Morgan, *Merchants of Grain* (New York: Penguin, 1979).

21. A.H. Westing, ed., *Global Resources and International Conflict: Environmental Factors in Strategic Policy and Action* (New York: Oxford University Press, 1986).

22. M. Renner, "National Security: The Economic and Environmental Dimensions," *Worldwatch Paper 89* (Washington, D.C.: Worldwatch Institute, 1989).

23. S. Postel, *Last Oasis: Facing Water Scarcity* (New York: Norton, 1992).

24. World Resources Institute, *World Resources 1992–93.*

25. Renner, "National Security."

26. Porter and Brown, *Global Environmental Politics.*

27. World Commission on Environment and Development, *Our Common Future* (New York: Oxford University Press, 1987).

28. Gore, *Earth in the Balance.*

# EIGHT

---

# Global Environmental Hazards: Political Issues in Societal Responses

### ROGER E. KASPERSON

AS THE TWENTIETH CENTURY draws to a close, a new class of environmental hazards confronts the global community. Actually, George Perkins Marsh anticipated their appearance over 100 years ago in detailing the extensive alteration of the earth by humans.[1] More recently, concern has centered on the types and magnitudes of environmental change for which humans are responsible, particularly the recognition that the extent of human perturbations is now exceeding the range of natural fluctuations. Moreover, the life-support systems of the earth may be affected. Many of these changes came as surprises (e.g., the hole in the Antarctica stratospheric ozone); others have long been apparent, but their consequences have been newly assessed (e.g., global warming). The World Commission on Environment and Development and the Earth Summit in 1992 have been important in creating a new global agenda for environmental action.[2]

## The Nature of Global Environmental Hazards

Clarity is needed in order to understand the meaning of the terms *global environmental change* and *hazards*. Much of the current debate about hazards focuses on greenhouse warming as the ultimate threat to the global environmental system. The type of change represented by climate change is defined as *systemic* in that such a change at any locale can affect the environment anywhere else or even the global system itself.[3] Climate change, stratospheric ozone depletion, and biodiversity in particular have commanded much of the attention of the world's scientific and policy communities. But there is a second type, here termed *cumulative environmental change*, that may well eclipse systemic changes in both long-term and (certainly) short-term consequences. This type of change refers to the accumulation of regional and localized impacts that are distributed widely throughout the world. Such changes, involving forest, grasslands, and wetlands conversion as well as biogeochemical flows that remain below the global scale in their movement, represent most of the severe environmental problems currently confronting human (and particularly developing) societies. Table 8.1 summarizes these two types of change.

Both systemic and cumulative environmental changes pose distinct challenges in terms of appropriate societal responses. Systemic global environmental change involves difficulties that, although present in other types of hazards (e.g., acid deposition or low-level toxins in aquatic systems), are complex and entail new levels of analytic difficulty. Cumulative global environmental change often lies beyond the pale of existing data bases, and its human consequences are embedded in local cultures, religion, and indigenous knowledge systems.

*Assessment,* as used in this chapter, refers to the identification, measurement, and characterization of threats to human beings and what they value.[4] This chapter explores the distinctive characteristics of global environmental hazards and the major difficulties in coping with and resolving them.

The sources and effects of both systemic and cumulative global environmental hazards are very different and often unmeasured, and they accumulate over long periods of time. Almost all human activities modify the environment in some way, and over long enough spans, they significantly degrade ecosystems. The enormous variety of land-use changes causes global change in many ways—by disturbing carbon storage, nutrient cycles, the hydrologic cycle, atmospheric concentrations, and the reflection of solar energy from the earth's surface.[5] Spe-

TABLE 8.1    *Types of Global Environmental Change*

|  | *Characteristic* | *Example* |
|---|---|---|
| SYSTEMIC | Direct impact on globally functioning system | Industrial and land-use emissions of greenhouse gases |
|  |  | Industrial and consumer emissions of ozone-depleting gases |
|  |  | Land cover changes in albedo |
| CUMULATIVE | Impact through worldwide distribution of change | Groundwater pollution and depletion |
|  |  | Species depletion/genetic alteration (biodiversity) |
|  | Impact through magnitude of change (share of global resource) | Deforestation |
|  |  | Industrial toxic pollutants |
|  |  | Soil depletion on prime agricultural lands |

SOURCE: B.L. Turner et al., "Two Types of Global Environmental Change: Definitional and Spatial-scale Issues in Their Human Dimensions," *Global Environmental Change: Human Policy Dimensions,* vol. 1, no. 1 (December 1990), pp. 14–22.

cific information concerning human activities is very meager, and the impacts of such activities are apparent only over the long term. Furthermore, many of the interactions in environmental processes and cycles are often poorly understood and unmeasured. Characterizing the hazards, therefore, is intrinsically difficult because they are *elusive,* imperceptibly altering global life-support systems and the basic conditions of human welfare, or *hidden,* in that they are obscured by ideology, competing priorities, marginality, and cultural bias.[6]

Global environmental change is among the least clearly understood hazards because it involves "hazard bundles" resulting from interactions among fundamental human processes, public policies, economic activities, and encounters with nature and technology. Just as the human threat from hazardous waste sites is the result of synergism among hundreds of unknown chemicals, global environmental hazards are *interactive phenomena,* involving human processes and environmental processes as well as environmental changes and both human and nonhuman harm. The U.S. Environmental Protection Agency's (EPA's) recent self-assessment of its "unfinished business" after twenty years of existence explicitly recognizes that risk generation is embedded in fundamental economic processes and state policies.[7] The agency recognizes that progress in reducing environmental risks requires intervention into the economy, the state role in agriculture and industry, the process of technology development and deployment, and all the associated political ramifications.

Even where causality is clear, the relationship between cause and effect may be nonlinear or even chaotic. Certainly, research has resulted in a clearer understanding of environmental processes and the driving forces of change, as well as an awareness of the limits of our understanding of the environment and of the character of human-induced change. The traits of such change are largely unknown. The increase in carbon dioxide concentrations recorded at the Mauna Loa Station is rather consistent, but the reaction of ecosystems, climatic processes, and other systems may exhibit thresholds and sharp perturbations, nonlinear responses, or even chaotic behavior. The rate, magnitude, and timing of change, the interconnections among biophysical and social processes, and the spatial distribution of effects involve uncertainties and often result in vigorous scientific disagreement. The development of anticipatory assessment strategies, such as the Famine Early-Warning System (FEWS) supported by the United Nations Environment Programme, is an example of appropriate response to such issues. Most current monitoring systems were not created with a warning purpose in mind; rather, they provide information on the changing "noise" level in the environment. Effective early-warning systems are needed to address three related issues: (1) the existence of irreversible changes; (2) the possibility of overshoots, flip-flops, and other discontinuities in ecological, physical, and socioeconomic systems; and (3) the effectiveness of proposed management approaches in avoiding or minimizing the possibility of irreversible trends or discontinuities.

Vulnerability is a shadowy concept in global environmental change. Past hazard studies are quite definitive in demonstrating that the consequences of environmental change and the extent of associated human harm and disruption are uneven across regions, countries at different levels of development, social groups, and generations.[8] Diana Liverman notes that vulnerability arises from diverse sources, including social relations, technology, biophysical conditions, economic relations, and demography. This vulnerability has different forms and magnitudes at national, regional, local, and household scales. Yet vulnerability is often neglected in assessment studies, as proven by the ongoing debate over greenhouse warming. Sensitive biophysical systems and vulnerable social groups often fail to coincide, thereby complicating analysis. The social sciences have generally failed to develop a robust theory of vulnerability or to relate it to environmental change. This limited state of understanding complicates assessments of global environmental change and its distributional effects.

A further challenge to creating an accurate knowledge base for global environmental hazards is, as William Clark states, their simultaneous local *and* global character.[9] Indeed, both the human and environmental processes of change and their impacts are both scale- and place-specific. Recognition of this fact has been evident in Russian studies of environmental change that have related human-induced perturbations to the evolutionary dynamics of particular landscapes. Analyses at different spatial scales and at different places reveal particular "faces" of environmental transformation and societal impacts, but they also focus attention on the interactive processes that link different scale levels. Such linkages provide key insights into the structure of hazard causation. The long traditions in geography of studying the "hazardousness" of place[10] and cultural ecological studies of small-scale areas[11] attest to the multitude of ways in which humans transform the earth and by which cultural values shape hazard experience. It is also apparent that the regional (or meso) scale offers a powerful entry point for connecting the global and local scales. Since environmental degradation is often "exported" from one region to another, studies must take account of spatial linkages and interactions, and the failure of concepts such as "carrying capacity" to do so limits their usefulness. Effective response systems and institutions require political coordination of institutions and interventions at several scales or the creation of new international regimes,[12] and credible analyses must be multilayered and spatially structured. William Wood's recent notion of an "ecopolitical hierarchy" suggests several key dimensions that must be considered.[13]

Although global environmental hazards will be prioritized according to some imperfect scientific and political scale of importance, each hazard problem is, in fact, part of a broader process of environmental transformation. Each hazard is one element in a constantly changing societal risk portfolio or syndrome. The extraction of a global hazard from the fabric of competing hazards that make up the total risk at particular places and in particular societies is dangerous. Robert Smith, for example, argues that developing countries pass through a "risk transition" in which the historically high "traditional" risks associated with rural poverty (e.g., infectious diseases) decrease with economic development (although at different rates in different regions, places, or groups), and industrialization, agri-

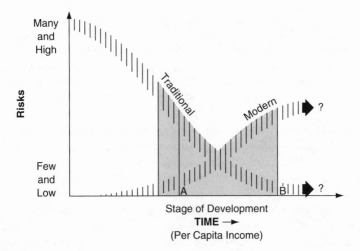

FIGURE 8.1   Risk transition. Risk transition denotes the period when traditional risks decline during a development process while modern risks are rising. The shaded area is risk overlap, when the community has significant risks of both kinds, with resulting possibilities for interaction. SOURCE: Adapted from K. R. Smith, "The Risk Transition," *International Environmental Affairs*, vol. 2, no. 3 (1990).

cultural changes, and urbanization increase the number and severity of "modern" hazards (Figure 8.1).[14] Society's risk portfolio thus changes its internal composition and may even decline in aggregate, and some social groups and regions may become even more vulnerable. Also, at a particular time (e.g., Stage A in Figure 8.1), traditional risks may still be significant while new and unfamiliar risks are developing. The new risks may be additive and may interact with existing risks to produce greater risk syndromes, thereby confounding familiar political means of coping and complicating the assessment task.

This shifting, overlapping, and interacting portfolio of risk produces new risk situations. Both types of global environmental change constitute a part of a dynamic societal risk portfolio. Smith identifies five types of interactions that societies in such transitions must face:[15]

- *Risk mimicry:* Morbidity and mortality may be attributed to familiar risks but may actually be due to modern or synergistic risks (e.g., lung cancer deaths are attributed to acute lung disease).

- *Risk competition:* Abnormally high or low risks from one disease may actually be an indication of a change in the risk from another disease.

- *Risk synergism:* Exposure to one hazardous agent causes increased immunity or susceptibility to other hazardous agents in the future. Traditional intestinal diseases due to poor water quality, for example, can increase susceptibility to waterborne and airborne industrial pollutants.

- *Risk layering:* The migration of people may concentrate risk in one region while diluting it in another. In rural-to-urban migration in developing countries, for example, migrants are usually healthier than the people left behind in rural villages.

- *Risk displacement:* Societal interventions to control traditional risks may actually create or enlarge modern risks (e.g., the use of pesticides to control malaria). Such displacements often also involve risk shifts in time, place, or social groups.

Problems of such complexity are only partially understandable. Much of the current discussion of climate change assumes that improving our scientific understanding, creating more complex models, constructing faster computers, and a more assiduous search of historical experience will help scientists unlock the truth. Well-conceived and properly mounted assessment programs are believed to whittle back uncertainties so that well-founded public policy choices will become evident. This optimism reflects a dangerous hubris about the human capacity to comprehend the universe, predict the future, and create the requisite knowledge through the application of science. Such optimism is clearly not based on hazard analysis experience: Assessments of complex problems and technologies in which scientific questions and sociopolitical and moral issues mingle have revealed that as assessors narrow some uncertainties, they often uncover new ones.[16] Global environmental problems, particularly systemic ones, certainly appear to be more complex than the most perplexing of what Ward Edwards and Detlof Von Winterfeldt[17] call "technological mysteries" and Alvin Weinberg[18] calls "transscientific problems."

Understanding past, ongoing, and future environmental changes clearly requires diverse ways of knowing. When combined with other knowledge systems, formal hazard analysis has a potentially important role. The concept of hazard— of threats to people and what they value—is explicitly interdisciplinary and particularly well adapted to joint inquiry by both natural and life sciences and the social sciences and humanities. The focus on threats and their potential consequences provides immediate power for informing policy and societal response. Since the origin of hazard analysis lay in the systematic appraisal of highly complex problems involving large uncertainties associated with human interactions with nature and technology, hazards research has established a knowledge base and methodological capability well suited to addressing issues of global environmental change. Therefore, the World Commission on Environment and Development singled out the establishment of a Global Risk Assessment Programme as a particularly urgent priority.[19] It outlined the specific contributions of global risk analysis as:

- identifying critical threats to the survival, security, or well-being of all or a majority of people, globally or regionally;

- assessing the causes and likely human, economic, and ecological consequences of those threats and reporting regularly and publicly on their findings;

- providing authoritative advice and proposals on what should or must be done to avoid, reduce, or, if possible, adapt to those threats; and

- providing an additional source of advice and support to governments and intergovernmental organizations for the implementation of programs and policies designed to address such threats.[20]

The effectiveness of risk analysis, however, will also require a keen appreciation of its limits. The use of science and scientifically based assessment in creating an adequate knowledge base for coping with global environmental change can generate illusions or overconfidence. Scientific analysis, as Timothy O'Riordan and Steve Rayner contend, moves along pathways that inevitably distort the character of the phenomenon under study.[21] The disaggregation, modeling, scenario construction, and generation of prediction that make risk analysis so powerful are also its nemesis—they strip away the essential interconnections by which the phenomenon can ultimately be understood holistically. Thus, the biospheric wholeness in physical and social processes that Vernadsky or the Gaian enthusiasts seek cannot be achieved by the customary process of decomposition, analysis, and reintegration. O'Riordan and Rayner introduce the metaphor of global environmental change as *specter,* that "shadowy and elusive phenomenon" whose indistinctness challenges management response.[22]

Silvio Funtowicz and Jerome Ravetz argue that a new sort of scientific inquiry is emerging to deal with the most difficult of assessment problems, those that combine "high systems uncertainty" (as described earlier) with "high decision stakes" (Figure 8.2).[23] When both systems uncertainty and decision stakes are

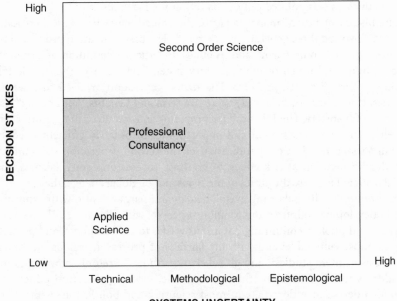

FIGURE 8.2 Three kinds of science. SOURCE: Silvio Funtowicz and Jerome Ravetz, EUR 12803 EN (Ispra, Italy: Joint Research Centre of the European Communities, 1990), p. 13.

low, solving traditional problems works.[24] When either factor reaches a medium level, then the "professional consultant's" skill and judgment become necessary. But in cases of the outermost region (Figure 8.2), such as those characteristic of global environmental change, traditional science becomes totally inadequate, and a new type of science—"second-order" or "post-normal" science—is necessary. This new science will require not only new types of expertise but also a new conception of the objects, methods, and social functions of the material world and the interactions of this world with structures of power and authority. Accordingly, each of the three types of hazard problems requires a different type of knowledge and a different type of science.

If hazard analysis is to enrich the knowledge base for decision-making, it cannot be divorced from moral and ethical questions. Both science and risk assessment have become highly secularized, isolated from the moral purposes that they once served. Calls to distinguish sharply between risk assessment (the scientific job) and risk management (the value-setting job) illustrate this division (e.g., U.S. National Research Council in 1983).[25] Of course, all of the truly difficult hazard problems, including the global environmental change problems in the outer region of Funtowicz and Ravetz's schema, are laden with basic value issues— whether humans will survive and, if so, with what kind of existence, whether the future can be ensured, whether harmony or disharmony with nature will prevail, and whether existing humans are responsible to distant peoples, generations, and species. The planetary crisis is thus both a scientific and a spiritual crisis. It seems clear that scientific progress must go hand in hand with the creation of a new global ethics, as was pointed out extensively at the Earth Summit.[26]

The history of hazard management in the United States has, as Robert Kates suggests, involved three generations of ethics.[27] The first generation proceeded on the principle of "do no harm," and its ethics underlie the definition of corporate responsibility and much of the regulatory system enacted over the decade following the first Earth Day in 1970. The second generation involved cost-benefit analysis. It weighed (or balanced) aggregate risks and benefits, "optimizing" risk reduction for society. The EPA's call for programs and resources that accord more closely with expert assessment and opportunities in order to efficiently reduce overall societal risk is a clear indication of the second-generation risk ethics.[28] The third generation of risk ethics, by contrast, focuses on equity, fairness, and social justice. These are the ethics of the 1990s and of global change; they are concerned not only with balancing overall benefit and harm but also with exporting risk to developing countries and to unborn people; with allocating risks between workers and publics, commiting hazardous wastes to the biosphere, and protecting the most vulnerable; and with the fairness of process as well as outcomes. Hazard assessment studies[29] and global change studies[30] are only now beginning to address third-generation ethics. Meanwhile, second-generation ethics and second-order science dominate in most scientific and political assessments of global change.

A final social issue concerning the knowledge base needed to address global environmental hazards is, Who is creating the knowledge and for what ends? *How* the world community learns about global change may be as important as the degree of understanding achieved. Little is known about the distribution of scientific knowledge within and among the different states in the global community or among political elites, scientists, policy-makers, and policies. It is clear, however, that much of the formal knowledge is being created by Western scientists as part of the Intergovernmental Panel on Climate Change program, the International Geosphere-Biosphere Program (IGBP), and other large efforts. Oran Young's study of how scientists and their knowledge affect decision-making in international resource regimes suggests that the creation of science plays a key role in at least four different policy-making contexts—agenda-setting, regime formation, social choice, and compliance.[31] The degree of influence that scientific knowledge has on state behavior and international policy-making institutions depends on such factors as the degree of scientific consensus or disagreement, the degree of the conflict for their proposals by powerful interest groups, and the mainstream ideology of the state.

Peter Haas's study on the politics of environmental cooperation in the Mediterranean Sea underlines the significant impact that scientific consensus can have on achieving political agreement on regional action plans.[32] Decision-makers' reliance on "epistemic communities" (experts and knowledge-based groups) to reduce uncertainty while protecting their own autonomy extensively shaped governmental learning and the development of new state objectives. The "empirical-analytical" knowledge of the scientist influences, in varying degree, the responses of governments to global environmental hazards. Effective tools are needed for individual nations to cope with their own perceptions of the problem and to shape regional or global responses. Thus far, little attention has been paid to the political implications and financial feasibility of various assessment methods with which developing countries can tackle issues like climate change. How the environmental monitoring programs of states and international institutions (such as the United Nations Environmental Programme [UNEP] and the Food and Agriculture Organization [FAO]) are designed, financed, and implemented and how greater international access to the information is created will help determine the degree of self-reliance and autonomy achievable by various countries. The Haas study provides insight into ameliorating problems of cooperation between lesser and more developed countries, such as those in the Mediterranean Sea. Through wise planning by the United Nations Environment Programme, an equal distribution of laboratories ensured developing countries of access to resources for indigenous research and for dealing more effectively with regional marine pollution. Such a process focused on equity helped minimize pressure from economically dominant countries via the intervention of UNEP's planning secretariat. It also suggests the importance of distributional issues in social access to knowledge and, therefore, the capability to act on issues of national and global environmental change.

These knowledge-base issues suggest that both the causes and potential political responses to such changes are deeply embedded in the human driving forces that create these hazards. The goals of the global economy and international finance system typically conflict with environmental values, and global patterns of inequality between developed and developing society are growing, rather than narrowing. State systems associated with traditional notions of military security and armaments systems bias the global consumption of resources. International institutions are only now beginning to understand how development and market economies may internalize environmental values, and material conceptions of human well-being dominate most of the world's vision of desirable futures. Meanwhile, corrupt and inept governments in many parts of the Third World siphon off the limited social investments that do occur. It is these global driving forces, pervasive inequalities, and power structures that must change if global environmental hazards are ultimately to be confronted and ameliorated.

## A Model of Societal Response

The natural and life sciences effectively used a so-called wire diagram to support the International Geosphere-Biosphere Program. Harold Jacobson argues that the social sciences need the counterpart of the "general circulation model" used in climate change studies to help structure research questions and to interrelate emerging research findings.[33] Toward this end and given the limits of science and modeling, Figure 8.3 displays such a model.

This model is specifically designed to mesh with a model of biogeophysical processes. The underlying "driving forces" identified in the model correspond to those broadly identified in previous analyses of the human dimensions of global environmental change,[34] namely, population growth, industrial ecology, land-use change, global political economy, and societal values. The starting point for analyzing societal responses is, therefore, the "driving forces" component on the left side of the diagram.

It is a process model, intended to show cyclical processes and feedback loops. Scale and time are obviously important factors, but it is not feasible to represent them graphically in this diagram. Therefore, to use this model appropriately, it is necessary to conceptualize different scales and changing conditions through time using multiple iterations of the model. Furthermore, relationships among different scales need to be explicitly considered in applying the model. Separate iterations can also be run for various social groups or for a higher level of aggregation as "society."

The basic structure of the model purposely shows that failures to address environmental degradation at various points in the system eventually feed back to the driving forces, as does the whole societal response system. In other words, responses either mitigate or aggravate the effects of the driving forces. To call explicit attention to the role of political and economic power as constraints on the response system, a "political influence and resources" component, largely shaped by the driving forces, feeds back into all major components of the response system. Each major section of the model is, needless to say, a gross simplification of very complex processes. An example for the "social amplification and attenuation"

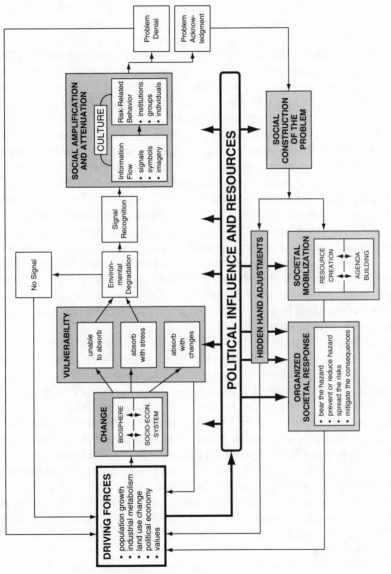

FIGURE 8.3   Societal response to environmental change.

component is provided. The discussion that follows depicts major issues and processes that require attention in analyzing political responses to global environmental change.

In more detailed discussions, human driving forces feed into the "proximate" causes of environmental change. In this model, driving forces directly cause changes in both the biospheric and the socioeconomic systems, which also feed into each other. The potential risk of environmental change is related not only to the forces of change but also to the degree of vulnerability of the biosphere and the socioeconomic system. The varying degrees of vulnerability are, in this model, arbitrarily divided into three outcomes: Highly vulnerable systems are unable to absorb changes and degradation results; less vulnerable systems may absorb changes for a time, until some threshold level is reached in the environmental or socioeconomic system, and then serious degradation occurs; a highly resilient system is able to absorb changes. All instances of absorption of change are themselves agents of change; that is, the system that absorbs new stresses is not homeostatic but dynamic. Some absorption may occur through spontaneous or even unconscious adjustments (and become "invisible-hand" responses); these also feed back into the driving forces, either as mitigating or aggravating influences.

Degradation is accompanied by events and effects that are potential "signals" to society. Such signals occur with or without societal recognition. If there is no recognition, there is no signal—at least not to the societal response system—and the problem feeds back into the driving forces (perhaps as positive feedback, thereby enlarging the forces of degradation). If the degradation is recognized, whether by individual farmers, the media, or government officials, then a signal is sent to the response system.

Once the signal is received that a change poses a threat, society proceeds at risk. This may occur at any scale and with varying degrees of formality. This process is the "social amplification or attenuation" of risk by which society gauges whether a problem exists and, if so, how serious the problem is. Key elements in the processing of risk include information flow, communication channels through which information is exchanged, perceptions influenced or shared, and risk-related responses undertaken. Information is construed in this model very broadly and includes mass or popular information, traditional knowledge, scientific knowledge, and propaganda. Also included is information disseminated by interest groups or power factions for the purpose of molding societal opinion. Based on this information, individuals and groups will respond to the risk according to their cultural biases and values. The direct physical attributes of the risk interact with social processes in ways that enlarge or attenuate the consequences for society.

Eventually, some sort of societal assessment (formal or ad hoc) is made as to whether action or attention (i.e., response) is required. Two outcomes are possible—problem denial or problem acknowledgment. Problem denial feeds back positively to the driving forces. Problem acknowledgment, by contrast, leads to actions in the response system to assess and (perhaps) reduce the risk.

When social acknowledgment of the problem occurs, it is structured into an "issue." Political ideology and cultural values are major factors influencing this stage. The power structure directly influences this process, of course, and particular values or ideologies will probably be dominant in a given society or set of constituencies. If the problem is constructed as one of concern only to those directly involved with the production process (the manager closest to the environmental source), adjustments will be largely those of the "invisible-hand" type and thus incremental and ad hoc in nature. If, however, the problem is determined to require concerted and mobilized social action, political processes are activated.

Societal mobilization must occur to set the terms of debate, to generate support, to influence opinion, and to allocate the problem to appropriate institutions. Agenda-building and resource-creation are major activities in societal mobilization. Actions loop back into information processes at this point.

The next step is the activation of organized societal response—some kind of action to deal with the problem. There are many different ways to characterize societal responses; this model centers on the overall risk strategy employed. Such strategies typically include bearing the risk, risk prevention or reduction, risk spreading, adaptation, and consequence mitigation. One can add structural changes—those responses that seek to directly address the basic nature of the driving forces. Technology development; the redistribution of land, wealth, and power; and a massive reorientation of social and economic priorities are responses with substantial ability to address global environmental change. Other important responses in this category include enhanced status for women, family planning, debt cancellation, appropriate aid, land reform, support for the traditional rural sector, and inclusion of environmental (and social) costs in national accounting systems. Among the risk response strategies, *avoidance* involves evading the problem or exposure to it (migration from degraded areas); *consequence mitigation* is an attempt to ameliorate impacts (as through medical programs or food relief); *bearing the risk* means deciding to absorb the stress caused by the degradation (although the deciders and the bearers are often not the same people); *risk-spreading* refers to strategies, such as insurance, that reallocate the risk over larger populations without changing the risk itself; and *adaptation* entails strategies by which society changes itself in order to reduce the impacts of the risk.

The whole complex of organized societal response is strongly influenced by the *political system* and the influence emanating from the driving forces. The responses feed directly back into the driving forces, as agents of either mitigation or aggravation.

## Selected Sociopolitical Issues

The model suggests, at least implicitly, a large number of points meriting special attention as society responds to environmental change. To illustrate this, one may select an issue such as vulnerability for more detailed discussion.

## "Neglected" Vulnerabilities

The concept of *vulnerability,* defined as "the capacity to be wounded by a given insult," is a central although incompletely developed concept in analyses of environmental change. It is clear, as Figure 8.4 suggests, that the impacts of environmental stress depend, in part, on the characteristics of the change—magnitude, spatial extent, and exposure—and partially on the vulnerability of the regions, ecosystems, people, and social organizations. Early research identified differences in the impacts of natural hazards in developing and developed countries, noting that the former experienced higher losses of life and lower property losses than developed states,[35] a pattern more recently confirmed by research associated with the International Decade for Natural Disaster Reduction.[36]

The impacts of global change, then, will reflect the distribution of environmental change and the sensitivity of the biophysical regions and social groups. Impact magnitude will depend on the *extent* of environmental change— decreased length of the growing season or number of hectares inundated by increased flooding or rise in the sea level—and on the ongoing processes and factors contributing to a group's or a region's ability to benefit or be harmed (i.e., its vulnerability). The serious nature of threats potentially posed by climate change verify that vulnerability is a pressing concern. Three broad categories of factors and processes are important in determining the vulnerability of impacted populations: *ecosystem sensitivity, economic sensitivity,* and *social structure sensitivity.*

*Ecosystems sensitivity* addresses the spatial shifts as well as the regional changes accompanying environmental change. Much of the research on the impacts of climate change has focused on this ecosystem dimension of impact. General circulation models (GCMs), for example, predict different levels of climate warming across latitudes. In some areas, warming may increase the growing season; in others it may require a change in cropping or farming practices. Other analyses focus on the *rate* of climate change and the *ability* of species to adapt.[37] Thus, predictions of sea-level rise emphasize the vulnerability of island states and coastal regions and populations. Depending on the sensitivity of the ecosystem, relatively small environmental changes may have tremendous impacts, a finding

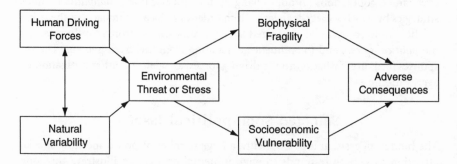

FIGURE 8.4   Interaction between environmental hazard and vulnerability.

well established in the literature on climate impacts.[38] Marginality in ecosystems suggests that the greatest impacts may arise outside the areas experiencing the greatest quantitative climate change.

Liverman points out that the most vulnerable people are often believed to live in the most biophysically vulnerable areas.[39] Research on natural hazards, however, demonstrates that natural disasters take a much higher toll on life in developing regions (and losses associated with property damage, as suggested by Hurricane Andrew in 1992, are higher in developed countries) and that socio-economic factors play a critical role in determining the impacts of a natural event.[40] Recent studies suggest that global warming may be accompanied by an increase in the number and severity of extreme events like droughts and hurricanes. Identification of the social and economic dimensions of vulnerability is essential in identifying the most vulnerable populations and guiding policy and decision-making.

The *vulnerability of the economic system* is a key issue in impacts. The economic marginality of an activity in relation to first- and higher-order impacts of change that cascade through the economic system is important. Economic marginality describes a situation in which the returns to an economic activity barely exceed the costs. Thus, a group may have sufficient resources through several extreme years, but prolonged stress may reduce those economic reserves and significantly increase vulnerability. The importance of assets and a knowledge of the probability and magnitude of events are important to small-scale farmers in order to cope with climatic variability in drought-prone areas. Uncertain changes in environmental patterns render them more vulnerable.

*Social structure sensitivity* is concerned with the response *capabilities* of particular social groups, and it includes the impact of class and gender on access to societal resources as well as the nature of social institutions. Political economy perspectives stress the importance of social divisions (e.g., class) in accounting for differential access to resources and assets and differences in the magnitude of impacts. Variation among states is another critical factor in the international context of global change and response. Those with adequate access to resources and information benefit from the global economy, whereas others struggle to survive.

The nature of social and economic institutions also contributes to vulnerability. The infrastructure of social institutions and resource-management practice pervasively shapes the breadth and depth of the response capability. Vulnerability results from the growth of technological specialization, homogeneity, and centralization (and the related loss of diversity, multiplicity, and redundancy). Whether institutions are highly adaptive or more narrowly prepared only to respond to a limited set of opportunities, the potential to benefit largely depends on the ability to identify and react to opportunities. Increasing the reliance on management systems to reduce the variability of an ecosystem may erode the overall resilience of the ecosystem and its associated social and economic system.[41] In the context of global climate change and the potential shifts in the availability of water, the ability of the legal system to adjust to changes in the resource

base obviously affects the magnitude of potential disruptions; the legal and institutional rigidity of water-resource management in the western United States is an
excellent example. Similarly, the ability of social institutions to provide warnings,
diagnoses, insurance, and planning support is key to shaping successful societal
coping responses.

## Failures in Alerting Systems

Society employs many means to alert itself to potential environmental and social
hazards. *Monitoring* implies an active and systematic search for information or
signals. *Alerting* refers to the warning function associated with risk communication. Such monitoring and alerting functions are critical in identifying social
problems and initiating societal responses. Richard Rappaport[42] points out that
the perception of a hazard begins with the first sense of danger and *changes with
increased information.* Identification of risks is closely tied to social perceptions,
and it occurs in a variety of public arenas—television, movies, the mass media,
social action groups, and the research community. Monitoring and alerting functions arise according to principles of cultural and political selection, including
agenda competition among problems, cultural preoccupations, and political
biases.

Global environmental change poses distinct challenges to societal monitoring
and alerting practices. As already noted, a high degree of scientific and political
uncertainty pervades such issues. And because past experiences may be unreliable guides to future interpretation and response, societal alerting and assessment systems must be more anticipatory.

Alerting occurs in a wide array of institutions, roles, and contexts. Knowledge
of change does not always arise from direct monitoring of the environment but
rather from monitoring a related societal process. Often, the motivation for
monitoring derives from other societal goals, such as health promotion, economic growth and development, or policy effects. Additionally, institutions and
groups experience change in different ways or via different information or cues.
The mountain-dwellers of Nepal, for example, learn of environmental change
through increased mudslides, hazards, declining crop yields, and the growing
scarcity of fuelwoods, whereas the government learns about them through accounts of local crises trickling up from remote areas or through reports of the
failure of development or aid programs.[43]

Many elements of society are potential sources of alerts. These might include
daily checks on the weather or the level of a river in midsummer, the conduct of
formal science, the activities of citizen groups watching and reporting on issues
of concern to them, and the scrutiny of events by the media. From this diverse
array of perspectives and capabilities emerges a complicated web of interactions—scientists monitoring atmospheric composition, journalists looking
over the shoulders of scientists and the government, and individuals searching
for information directly through their own experiences and indirectly through
interaction in social and information networks.

The Famine Early-Warning System is an active system at the international level that suggests what is possible in terms of integrated physical-social alerting systems on global environmental change. It selects both ecological and social indicators of prefamine conditions, based on research linking indicators of vulnerability to famine impacts. These indicators include agrometeorological measures of rainfall, pest damage, flooding, growing conditions, animal carrying capacity, brushfire damage, social measures (including the level of food reserves), existing food stress, contribution of cash crops, changes in cereal price behavior, food production trends, health and nutritional data, and conflict or civil disruption. At the same time, as the severity of the 1992 famine in Somalia indicates, there are limits to what even an early warning can provide in the face of more general political disintegration.

The complex array of societal efforts to collect information about the environment provides some level of awareness of the unfolding environmental hazards. Such systems comprise diverse mechanisms (official and unofficial) and a blend of knowledge, ignorance, and bias. How to design the alerting function and thereby increase the resilience of society to surprises is an issue that requires both greater understanding and more integration with particular political cultures.

## *Social Amplification and Attenuation*

The model of societal response suggests that society has recognized the signals emerging from environmental change and that the threat has been identified, with social institutions and groups then processing the risk. How this social processing occurs can amplify or attenuate the risk signal and shape the interpretation of risk and the ways by which society will respond to it. The notion of risk amplification and attenuation is based on the recognition that psychological, social, institutional, and cultural processes can heighten or reduce perceptions of risk and shape behavior.[44]

Behavioral responses, in turn, generate secondary social-economic consequences, which extend far beyond direct harms to human health or the environment. They include significant indirect impacts, such as liability, insurance costs, loss of confidence in institutions, stigmatization, or alienation from the political system (Figure 8.5).

Such secondary effects (in the case of risk amplification) may trigger demands for additional institutional responses and intervention or, conversely (in the case of risk attenuation), place impediments in the path of necessary protective actions. In our usage, amplification includes both intensifying and attenuating signals about risk. Thus, alleged "overreactions" of people and organizations receive the same attention as alleged "downplaying."

In this review, environmental risks are seen partly as objective threats of harm to people and partly as a product of culture and social experience. Hence, hazardous events are "real": They involve transformations of the physical environment but also perturbations in social and value structures. Such changes and events remain limited in the social context unless they are observed by human

158

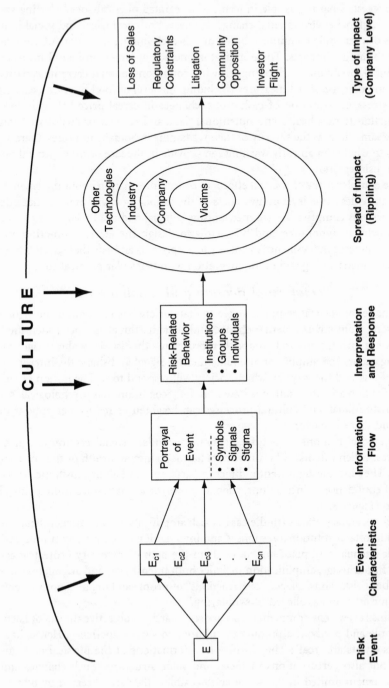

FIGURE 8.5  Model of societal response to risk.

Risk Event

Event Characteristics

Information Flow

Interpretation and Response

Spread of Impact (Rippling)

Type of Impact (Company Level)

CULTURE

E

$E_{c1}$
$E_{c2}$
$E_{c3}$
$...$
$E_{cn}$

Portrayal of Event
• Symbols
• Signals
• Stigma

Risk-Related Behavior
• Institutions
• Groups
• Individuals

Other Technologies
Industry
Company
Victims

Loss of Sales
Regulatory Constraints
Litigation
Community Opposition
Investor Flight

beings and communicated to others.[45] The consequences of this communication and other social interactions may lead to other physical transformations, such as changes in technologies, methods of land cultivation, or the composition of water, soil, and air. The experience of risk is, therefore, both an experience of physical harm and the result of culture and social processes by which individuals or groups acquire or create interpretations of hazards. These interpretations provide rules to select, order, and explain signals from the physical world. Additionally, each cultural or social group selects certain risks and selects out other risks as not meriting immediate concern.

Once conceived, the amplification process starts with either a process or a physical change—an event or a report on environmental or technological events, releases, exposures, or consequences. Some groups and individuals actively monitor the experiential world, searching for hazard events related to their agenda of concern. Individuals or groups select specific characteristics of these events and interpret them according to their perceptions and mental schemes. They also communicate these interpretations to other individuals and groups and receive interpretations in return. Social groups and individuals process the information, place it in on their agenda of concerns, and may feel compelled to respond. Some may change their previously held beliefs, gain additional knowledge and insights, and be motivated to take action; others may use the opportunity to compose new interpretations to send to the original sources or other interested parties; still others may find the added information confirms long-held views of the world and its order.

The individuals, groups, or institutions that collect information about risks communicate with others and, through behavioral responses, act as *amplification stations*. It is obvious that social groups or institutions can amplify or attenuate signals only by working in social aggregates and participating in social processes. But individuals in groups and institutions do not act or react merely in their roles as private persons; rather, they respond according to the role specified by their positions. Amplification may, therefore, differ among individuals in their roles as private citizens and in their roles as employees or members of social groups and organizations.

Role-related considerations and membership in social groups shape the selection of information that the individual regards as significant. Thus, interpretations or signals that are inconsistent with previous beliefs or that contradict the person's values are often ignored or attenuated. They are intensified if the opposite is true. Individuals act also as members of cultural groups and larger social units that codetermine the dynamics and social processing of risk. In this framework, these larger social units are *social stations of amplification*. Individuals in their roles as members or employees of social groups or institutions not only follow their personal values and interpretative patterns, they also perceive risk information and construct the risk "problem" according to cultural biases and the rules of their organization or group.[46] Cultural biases and role-specific factors are internalized and reinforced through education and training, identification with the goals and functions of institutions, beliefs in the importance and justification of social outcomes, and both rewards (promotions, salary increases, symbolic honors) and punishments (demotions, salary cuts, disgrace). Meanwhile, conflicts between personal convictions and institutional obligations evoke psychological stress, potentially leading to alienation.

The information flow depicting the risk and the associated behavioral responses by individual and social amplification stations generates secondary effects that extend beyond the people directly affected by the original hazard event or report. Secondary impacts include such effects as:

- enduring mental perceptions, images, and attitudes (e.g., antitechnology attitudes, alienation from physical environment, social apathy, or distrust of risk-management institutions);
- impacts on the local or regional economy (e.g., reduced business sales, declines in residential property values, and drops in tourism);
- political and social pressure (e.g., political demands or changes in political climate and culture);
- social disorder (e.g., protests, riots, sabotage, and terrorism);
- changes in risk monitoring and regulation;
- increased liability and insurance costs;
- repercussions on other technologies (e.g., lower levels of public acceptance) and on social institutions (e.g., erosion of public trust).

Secondary impacts are, in turn, perceived by social groups and individuals so that additional stages of amplification may occur and produce higher-order impacts. Impacts may thereby spread or "ripple" to other parties, distant locations, or future generations. Each order of impact will not only disseminate social and political impacts but may also trigger (in risk amplification) or hinder (in risk attenuation) positive changes for risk reduction. The concept of social amplification of risk is hence dynamic, taking into account the continuing learning and social interactions that result from social experience with risk.

The analogy of dropping a stone into a pond (see Figure 8.4) illustrates the spread of higher-order impacts associated with the social amplification of risk. The ripples spread outward, initially encompassing the first group to be notified, then touching the next higher institutional level (a company or an agency), and, in more extreme cases, reaching other parts of the industry or other social arenas with similar problems. This rippling of impacts is an important element of risk amplification since it suggests that the processes can extend (in risk amplification) or constrain (in risk attenuation) the temporal and geographical scale of impacts.

## *Equity and Societal Response*

As the political system responds to environmental threats, difficult equity problems arise and must be assessed and addressed. As risk issues intermingle with value considerations, equity problems often become the dominant factor shaping the broad patterns of societal response. There are many types of equity problems—geographical equity, cumulative geographical equity, intergenerational equity, and social equity—all involving "outcome" or "end state" considerations. *Procedural equity* focuses on the processes employed.

The primary concern in *geographical equity* is the geographical pattern of benefits and eventual harms associated with a particular set of human activities. Thus, the global pattern of carbon dioxide and other greenhouse gas emissions could, in principle, be compared with the pattern of harmful and beneficial impacts that would ultimately occur. In simple cases, these empirical patterns can then be used as a basis for making inferences about the obligations and responsibilities (if any) that beneficiaries have for those harmed and the adequacy of legal structures and institutional mechanisms for meeting these responsibilities.

Assessing the geographical attributes of impacts associated with global environmental change is extraordinarily challenging. Only the broadest types of patterns resulting from climate warming are readily apparent—subtropical monsoonal rain belts may be wetter, growing seasons at high latitudes longer, springtimes in high and middle latitudes drier, and extreme heat waves more common.[47] Generally, there is widespread agreement that, because of the poor spatial resolution of global climate models, the prediction of impacts (and thus the extent of hazard) from global warming at scales smaller than continental regions is unreliable now and is likely to remain so for one or more decades into the future. Thus, the question of discerning who the winners and losers will be is a major stumbling block to the development of international societal responses or governance.

What is quite well known, however, is the geographical pattern of past and current *beneficiaries* from the burning of fossil fuel. Gross predictions as to how these may change over the next several decades under differing assumptions are also possible. So the past and current beneficiaries driving potential global warming are known at least grossly, and they are strongly concentrated in developed countries—information that may be useful in allocating responsibilities. What can be said about future impacts is that substantial economic dislocation (depending on rates of change) is likely to occur from the pattern of global environmental change. The loss of options for potentially impacted regions can also be inferred. So, although future impacts cannot be precisely determined, some indication of future hazard can be estimated. The most compelling arguments involve the need to respond to spatially ambiguous future hazards through spatially clear beneficiaries.

Equity, however, cannot be assessed solely within a particular regime or policy area. Climate warming cannot be divorced from other types of environmental change and past inequities involved in the global interactions of peoples, nations, and economies. Indeed, "cumulative" global change, with the greatest impact on the planetary environment and developing societies, is receiving the least attention.

This broader view of inequity is called *cumulative geographical equity.* Inequities that correlate with other inequities suffered by disadvantaged societies or marginal groups are particularly pernicious because their effects are likely to be multiplicative, not simply additive. Previous inequities are also certain to increase the vulnerability of some groups to global environmental change. Thus, it is not surprising that developing countries object vehemently to admonitions from developed countries to reduce future fossil fuel emissions for the well-being of the global environment. Cumulative geographical inequities, in short, may be expected to form the core of many debates over global environmental policy. Those inequities also may be highly relevant to the sequencing of management intervention—that is, to concerns about which messes should be cleaned up first.

For *intergenerational equity,* some empirical realities are clearer. There is a widespread belief that, if present emission trends for greenhouse gases continue, some degree of global warming will occur during the next century. Although substantial disagreement exists as to the precise effects that such warming will have on natural ecosystems, water supplies, agriculture, and the sea level, enough indication of the potential for significant global harm exists to support international efforts to find solutions. Because two-thirds of the world's population lives in low-lying coastal areas, for example, a sea-level rise of even 0.5 to 1.5 meters would have major effects. In some areas, such as Bangladesh (where half the population lives at elevations below 5 meters), the impact would be catastrophic. Although the impacts of global climate change and their precise distribution will continue to be debated, assigning responsibility for the global impacts is easier for the causal mechanisms are at least generally understood.

*Social equity* provides another "cut" through the world population to contrast with equity analyses that focus on the nation-state. It is essential to assess the distribution of impacts according to wealth, social class, or stage of development. Natural disasters continue to take a disproportionate and growing toll in developing countries, a fact that helped to stimulate the 1987 UN General Assembly designation of the 1990s as the International Decade for Natural Disaster Reduction. Similarly, the links between world poverty and the incidence of famine and hunger have been widely noted. Many other hazards have remained "hidden" from the public view, eliciting neither media attention nor institutional response.[48]

Finally, there is the *procedural equity* of the processes that have created global environmental problems and by which they may be resolved. This differs from the other equity analyses described earlier, each of which addresses the distributions of problem causation and projected outcomes. Here, the concern is with the adequacy and appropriateness of the decision processes leading to stratospheric ozone disruption, carbon dioxide emissions, global deforestation, and the development of a research agenda and other response efforts. The issue appears straightforward: Unlike other regimes or policy areas, equity has not been part of the considerations involved in decision-making so that self-interest has externalized damage and the burden placed on other places, groups, and generations. The adverse impacts on the global environment have only recently been recognized, and the state or the corporation has been the focal point. International institutional mechanisms for incorporating equity, meanwhile, have generally been unavailable or undeveloped in any event. The absence of procedural equity is one of the few unambiguous attributes of global environmental change problems.

Each of these empirical analyses of distributions provides one "face" of environmental change and a challenge to societies, scientists, and governments. The risks associated with impact distributions depend, ultimately, not only on the distributional attributes outlined thus far but also on the vulnerability and resiliency of the ecosystems, populations, and sociopolitical systems.

## Looking to the Future

In this chapter, I have suggested major issues that must be confronted if society is to deal adequately with the array of environmental changes that threaten global well-being. As the millennium approaches, it is abundantly clear that the past is an imperfect guide to the future. Because accumulated and growing environmental stress is likely to be a principal source of international instability and conflict during the coming decades, the burden on society to identify and anticipate such changes in advance of their impact has grown enormously. At the same time, it has become clear that the international political economy and existing governance arrangements are deeply implicated as sources of the problems. The changing role of the state and the growing power of non-governmental organizations and scientific networks point to the possibility of major changes in the structure of international regimes addressing environmental problems. Such regimes must overcome the continuing divergence between the rapid pace of environmental change and the much slower rate of societal response if the planetary environment is to be sustained.

### Notes

1. George Perkins Marsh, *Man and Nature; or, Physical Geography as Modified by Human Action* (New York: Charles Scribner, 1864).

2. World Commission on Environment and Development, *Our Common Future* (Oxford: Oxford University Press, 1987).

3. B.L. Turner II, R.E. Kasperson, W.B. Meyer, K.M. Dow, D. Golding, J.X. Kasperson, R.C. Mitchell, and S.J. Ratick, "Two Types of Global Environmental Change: Definitional and Spatial-scale Issues in Their Human Dimensions," *Global Environmental Change: Human and Policy Dimensions*, vol. 1, no. 1 (December 1990), pp. 14–22.

4. James K. Mitchell, "Human Dimensions of Environmental Hazards: Complexity, Disparity, and the Search for Guidance," in *Nothing to Fear: Risks and Hazards in American Society*, Andrew Kirby, ed. (Tucson: University of Arizona Press, 1990).

5. T. Malone, "Mission to Planet Earth: Integrating Studies of Global Change," *Environment*, vol. 28, no. 8 (October 1986), pp. 6–11, 39–42.

6. Roger E. Kasperson and Jeanne X. Kasperson, "Hidden Hazards," in *Acceptable Evidence: Science and Values in Hazard Management,* D.C. Mayo and R. Hollander, eds. (New York: Oxford University Press, 1991), pp. 9–28.

7. U.S. Environmental Protection Agency, *Unfinished Business: A Comparative Assessment of Environmental Problems* (Washington, D.C.: EPA, 1987); idem, *Reducing Risk* (Washington, D.C.: EPA, 1990).

8. A. Baird, P. O'Keefe, K. Westgate, and B. Wisner, *Towards an Explanation of Disaster Proneness* (Bradford, England: University of Bradford, Disaster Research Unit, Occasional Paper no. 11, 1975); Ian Burton, Robert Kates, and Gilbert White, *The Environment as Hazard,* 2nd ed. (New York: Guilford Press, 1993); Paul Susman, P. O'Keefe, and B. Wisner, "Global Disasters, A Radical Interpretation," in *Interpretations of Calamity from the Viewpoint of Human Ecology,* K. Hewitt, ed. (Boston: Allen and Unwin, 1983), pp. 263–283; Roger E. Kasperson, ed., *Equity Issues in Radioactive Waste Management* (Cambridge, Mass.: Oelgeschlager, Gunn, and Hain, 1983); Diana M. Liverman, "Vulnerability to Global Environmental Change," in *Understanding Global Environmental Change: The Contributions of Risk Analysis and Management,* R.E. Kasperson, K. Dow, D. Golding, and J.X. Kasperson, eds. (Worcester, Mass.: Clark University, Earth Transformed Program, 1990), pp. 27–44.

9. William C. Clark, "Towards Useful Assessments of Global Environmental Risks," in *Understanding Global Environmental Change: The Contributions of Risk Analysis and Management,* R.E. Kasperson, K. Dow, D. Golding, and J.X. Kasperson, eds. (Worcester, Mass.: Clark University, Earth Transformed Program, 1990), pp. 5–22.

10. K. Hewitt and I. Burton, *The Hazardousness of Place: A Regional Ecology of Damaging Events,* University of Toronto, Department of Geography Research Publication no. 6 (Toronto: University of Toronto, 1971).

11. Piers Blaikie and Harold Brookfield, *Land Degradation and Society* (London: Methuen, 1987); also see Turner et al., "Two Types of Global Environmental Change."

12. O. Young, *International Cooperation* (Ithaca: Cornell University Press, 1989).

13. William B. Wood, "Tropical Deforestation: Balancing Regional Development Demands and Global Environmental Concerns," *Global Environmental Change,* vol. 1 (December 1990), pp. 23–41.

14. K.R. Smith, "The Risk Transition," *International Environmental Affairs,* vol. 2, no. 3 (Summer 1990), p. 230.

15. Ibid.

16. Roger E. Kasperson and Jeanne X. Kasperson, eds., *Nuclear Risk Analysis in Comparative Perspective: The Impacts of Large-scale Risk Assessment in Five Countries* (Boston: Allen and Unwin, 1987).

17. W. Edwards and D. von Winterfeldt, "Public Disputes About Risky Technologies: Stakeholders and Arenas," in *Risk Evaluation and Management,* V.T. Covello, J. Mumpower, and J. Menkes, eds. (New York: Plenum Press, 1986), pp. 69–92.

18. A. Weinberg, "Science and Trans-science," *Minerva,* vol. 10, no. 2 (Winter 1972), pp. 209–222.

19. See World Commission, *Our Common Future.*

20. Ibid., p. 325.

21. Timothy O'Riordan and Steve Rayner, "Chasing a Spectre: Risk Management for Global Environmental Change," in *Understanding Global Environmental Change: The Contributions of Risk Analysis and Management,* R.E. Kasperson, K. Dow, D. Golding, and J.X. Kasperson, eds. (Worcester, Mass.: Clark University, Earth Transformed Program, 1990), pp. 45–62.

22. Ibid., p. 45.

23. Silvio O. Funtowicz and Jerome R. Ravetz, *Global Environmental Issues and the Emergence of Second Order Science*, EUR 12803 EN (Ispra, Italy: Joint Research Centre of the European Communities, 1990); S.O. Funtowicz and J.R. Ravetz, "Three Types of Risk Assessment and the Emergence of Post-Normal Science," in *Social Theories of Risk*, S. Krimsky and D. Golding, eds. (New York: Praeger, 1992), pp. 251–274.

24. T. Kuhn, *The Structure of Scientific Revolutions* (Chicago: University of Chicago Press, 1962).

25. U.S. National Research Council, *Risk Assessment in the Federal Government: Managing the Process* (Washington, D.C.: National Academy Press, 1983).

26. United Nations, *Agenda 21, Rio Declaration, Forest Principles* (New York: United Nations, 1992).

27. Robert W. Kates, "Managing Technological Hazards: Success, Strain, and Surprise," in *Hazards: Technology and Fairness*, National Academy of Engineering, ed. (Washington, D.C.: National Academy Press, 1985), pp. 206–220.

28. See U.S. Environmental Protection Agency, *Unfinished Business*.

29. See Kasperson, ed., *Equity Issues;* P. Derr, R. Goble, R.E. Kasperson, and R.W. Kates, "Worker/Public Protection: The Double Standard," *Environment*, vol. 25, no. 6 (July–August 1983), pp. 6–11, 35–36; D. MacLean, "Social Values and the Distribution of Risk," in *Values at Risk*, D. MacLean, ed. (Totowa, N.J.: Rowman and Allanheld, 1986), pp. 75–93.

30. Edith Brown Weiss, *In Fairness to Future Generations: International Law, Common Patrimony, and Intergenerational Equity* (New York: Transnational Publishers and the United Nations University, 1989); idem, "In Fairness to Future Generations," *Environment*, vol. 32, no. 3 (1990), pp. 7–11, 30–31; Roger E. Kasperson and Kirstin Dow, "Developmental and Geographical Equity in Global Environmental Change: A Framework for Analysis," *Evaluation Review*, vol. 15, no. 1 (February 1991), pp. 147–169; Anil Agarwal and Sunita Narain, *Global Warming in an Unequal World* (Delhi: Centre for Science and Development, 1991).

31. See Young, *International Cooperation*.

32. Peter Haas, *Saving the Mediterranean: The Politics of International Cooperation* (New York: Columbia University Press, 1990).

33. Harold Jacobson, personal communication, 1992.

34. Paul Stern, Oran Young, and Daniel Druckman, eds., *Global Environmental Change: Understanding the Human Dimensions* (Washington, D.C.: National Academy Press, 1992).

35. See Burton et al., *The Environment as Hazard;* Baird et al., *Towards an Explanation of Disaster Proneness*.

36. U.S. Office of Science and Technology Policy, Committee on Earth and Environmental Sciences, *Reducing the Impacts of Natural Hazards: A Strategy for the Nation* (Washington, D.C.: USGPO, 1992).

37. Margaret B. Davis, "Ecological Systems and Dynamics," in *Toward an Understanding of Global Change*, the National Research Council, Committee on Global Change, ed. (Washington, D.C.: National Academy Press, 1988), pp. 69–106.

38. Robert W. Kates, "The Interaction of Climate and Society," in *Climate Impact Assessment*, R.W. Kates, J.H. Ausubel, and M. Berberian, eds. (Chichester, England: Wiley, 1985), pp. 3–36; Martin L. Parry, "The Impact of Climatic Variations on Agricultural Margins," in *Climate Impact Assessment*, R.W. Kates, J.H. Ausubel, and M. Berberian, eds.

(Chichester, England: Wiley, 1985), pp. 351–368; William Riebsame, *Assessing the Social Implications of Climate Fluctuations: A Guide to Climate Impact Studies* (Nairobi, Kenya: United Nations Environment Programme, World Climate Impacts Programme, 1989).

39. See Liverman, "Vulnerability to Global Environmental Change."

40. See Baird et al., *Towards an Explanation of Disaster Proneness;* Burton et al., *The Environment as Hazard;* and Susman et al., "Global Disasters."

41. C.S. Holling, "The Resilience of Terrestrial Ecosystems: Local Surprise and Global Change," in *Sustainable Development of the Biosphere,* W.C. Clark and R.E. Munn, eds. (Cambridge: Cambridge University Press, 1986), pp. 292–317.

42. R.A. Rappaport, "Toward Postmodern Risk Analysis," *Risk Analysis,* vol. 8, no. 2 (June 1988), pp. 189–191.

43. N.S. Jodha, "The Himalayan Middle Hills," in *Regions at Risk,* J.X. Kasperson, R.E. Kasperson, and B.L. Turner II, eds. (Tokyo: United Nations University, forthcoming 1994).

44. R.E. Kasperson, O. Renn, P. Slovic, H.S. Brown, J. Emel, R. Goble, J.X. Kasperson, and S. Ratick, "The Social Amplification of Risk: A Conceptual Framework," *Risk Analysis,* vol. 8, no. 2 (June 1988), pp. 177–187; Roger E. Kasperson, "The Social Amplification of Risk: Progress in Developing an Integrative Framework of Risk," in *Social Theories of Risk,* S. Krimsky and D. Golding, eds. (New York: Praeger, 1992), pp. 153–178.

45. N. Luhmann, *Ökologische Kommunikation* (Opladen, Germany: Westdeutscher Verlag, 1986), p. 63.

46. B.B. Johnson and V.T. Covello, eds., *The Social and Cultural Construction of Risk* (Dordrecht, Holland: Reidel, 1987).

47. S. Schneider, "The Greenhouse Effect: Science and Policy," *Science,* vol. 243 (February 10, 1989), pp. 771–781.

48. See Kasperson and Kasperson, "Hidden Hazards."

# NINE

## Global Ecopolitics

### PHYLLIS MOFSON

THE GEOPOLITICS of international environmental decision-making are rapidly changing as the implications of environment-related problems exceed local and national concerns. The actors—from governments to activists to the media—are taking on enhanced and more diverse roles, traditional alliances are breaking down, and new partnerships are being forged. Environmental problems are occupying higher priority positions on government agendas worldwide; they have also focused public attention on assessing responsibility for pollution and allocating cleanup costs. The complexity of transnational environmental problems is even changing the role of science in international policy-making.

Diplomats are now working together in international forums to solve common environmental problems and protect common resources. They are being forced to recognize and to move beyond a long list of differences that have traditionally hindered environmental cooperation, including cultural perspectives, economic priorities, and domestic political agendas. In addition, governments have different roles in polluting and regulating non-governmental polluters, and they differ in terms of their commitment to international cooperation. These vast differences make reaching agreement on implementable environmental solutions at the international level a much greater challenge than at the national or local levels.

The creation, impacts, and solutions of a given environmental problem change as the problem involves increasingly larger and more complex ecological and political systems. For example, the widespread use of high-sulfur, brown (or lignite) coal for energy in Eastern Europe has created large strip mines and, in the areas surrounding coal-burning power plants, some of the world's most polluted air. On a regional level, the burning of brown coal contributes to acid rain that damages Europe's forests. The global impact of the many inefficient plants that burn brown coal has been to exacerbate the buildup of greenhouse gases in the atmosphere and contribute to accelerated global climate change. And just as an environmental problem like dependency on brown coal changes as it shifts from the local to the international levels, diverse political systems must be reconciled and coordinated before workable solutions can be found and implemented.

## Ecopolitical Hierarchy

A model of environmental politics can be constructed as an upside-down pyramid with four layers representing local, national, international, and global ecopolitical scales or stages (see Figure 9.1).[1] Each of the pyramid's four sides represents an attribute of a given environmental problem: the complexity of the ecological systems involved, the number of institutional actors, the number of political jurisdictions, and institutional obstacles to forging and implementing solutions. As a problem moves from one level to the next, these variables become more numerous, and their interactions grow more complex. Furthermore, perceived impacts and solutions at one level may contradict those at the next.

Consequently, as a particular problem moves up the ecopolitical hierarchy, resistance to political action also becomes more intransigent. The jump from the national to the international level may be the most challenging of all. Some global issues—for instance, climate change—involve most national governments and non-governmental organizations, in addition to several supranational agencies.

### *Local Level*

The local level, represented by the first layer in the inverted pyramid, embodies its own hierarchy of ecological and political relationships. These move from single neighborhoods up through such first-order administrative units as states and provinces. As the subnational unit increases in size, it inherits the conflicts among the smaller units that compose it. But despite these complexities, the cause-and-effect relationships that pertain to local environmental problems are relatively clear, and the roles of the actors are relatively well defined.

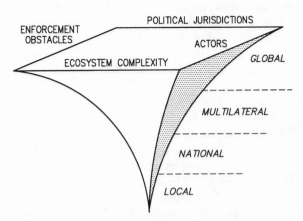

FIGURE 9.1   Ecopolitical hierarchy. SOURCE: Office of the Geographer, U.S. Department of State.

## National Level

At the national level, these relationships become slightly more ambiguous. Here, environmental politics involve the actors from subnational units as well as federal governments, national non-governmental organizations (NGOs), and large industries. Formulating national policy is particularly complicated when the source and impacts of a given environmental problem are not equally shared among the subnational units; a good example of this is the acid rain problem in the United States.

The role of the national government in pollution and cleanup programs is determined largely by the institutional and ideological structures that define the state. The major environmental role of national governments in most industrialized, capitalist countries is to regulate private industry. Although governments do pollute (for example, through defense and energy industry sites), much pollution in these countries is a product of privately owned economic activities. Environmental damage is the result of a variety of inputs, from the by-products of industrial production to the high consumption and accompanying waste generation of residential populations.

In centralized governments, by contrast, most major industries are controlled by ministries, making the state the primary polluter. Since the state is also the regulator of polluting industries, this situation is analogous to the fox guarding the henhouse. In some cases, such as China, the role of the state as polluter and regulator is complicated by the fact that agricultural and other small (often household-level) economic units are major sources of pollution. The ability of a national government to influence individual behavior is limited by often conflicting goals; the goal of reducing agriculture-related pollution, for instance, may conflict with governmental demands to increase agricultural production.

Most environmental problems in the developing world can be traced to rapidly growing, impoverished populations. National governments of poor, agriculture-based economies frequently have less formalized control over subnational units and individuals than those in the industrialized world. They also lack financial and other resources to implement the sometimes rudimentary environmental regulations that may have been legislated. Moreover, even when governments do have the means to regulate polluting activities, they often lack the will to do so. When environmental protection is perceived as detracting from economic development plans, it is often assigned a low priority on political agendas.

The new governments of the countries of Eastern Europe and the former Soviet Union represent a unique combination of inherited and recently acquired characteristics. They carry the legacy of centralized government programs that emphasized large-scale industrial and security-related projects over environmental and other quality-of-life concerns. Recently released data indicate, for example, that industrial air pollution in 103 former Soviet cities has left these municipalities with over five times the acceptable levels of pollutants.[2] The people of Eastern Europe and the former Soviet Union also continue to be subjected to some of the world's most severe water pollution, acid rain damage, and exposure to radiation.

Although these countries have inherited pollution problems that are characteristic of their former totalitarian (state-as-polluter) government structures, their current economies (like those of many Third World countries) are plagued by a lack of financial resources and by competing environmental and developmental priorities. Emerging capitalism in East Germany and the former Soviet Union means that several formerly Communist countries are developing a new set of polluters in the private industrial sector, and their governments are beginning to grapple with Western-style problems of regulating non-government industry while promoting the growth of the private sector.

## International Level

Forging environmental agreements at the international level is complicated by the variety of roles and characters of national governments as well as by the subnational layers of actors and roles below them. Cooperation at this level is made even more complex by almost universal resistance to surrendering any degree of national sovereignty to a supranational authority. International environmental action is further constrained by its high price tag; disagreement over who should pay to rectify damage already done and to prevent further degradation can paralyze negotiations.

## Global Level

Global issues such as climate change, deforestation, loss of biological diversity, and destruction of the ozone layer potentially involve actors at every level, each with its own agenda. Unlike bilateral or regional issues, global programs require the participation of a large number of countries, many of which may consider the issue a low priority or some of which may be tempted to take a free ride, receiving the benefits of the cooperative action without making major changes in their own behavior. The lack of enforcement mechanisms at the international level makes it difficult to prevent or punish such free riders. As was demonstrated by the June 1992 Rio de Janeiro UN Conference on Environment and Development (UNCED), contention between rich and poor countries over what the major problems are, who caused them, and who should pay will continue to dominate multilateral efforts for some time to come.

## The Roads to and from Rio

The participation by over 160 nations in UNCED indicated a general acceptance of the concepts that even local and regional environmental problems often have global implications and that a multilateral governance approach is often necessary to address various types of ecological degradation. UNCED also explicitly acknowledged the inseparability of environmental and development issues and—by addressing the pervasive economic implications of ecological problems—introduced a more intense and high-profile level of politicization into environmental negotiations.

Five major multilateral environmental agreements were reached at UNCED, which will be added to the dozens already in various stages of ratification and implementation. The UNCED agreements are the products of some of the most contentious international negotiations to date in the environmental arena.[3] The negotiation process was characterized by several overall trends: a general north-south debate framework, increasing regionalism, and the growing importance of NGOs.

## The North-South Debate

UNCED's stated aim was to find ways to integrate the dual issues of environment and development. The UNCED secretariat had hoped that negotiations would produce blueprints with which countries, rich and poor, could pursue economic growth without squandering natural resources and reverse environmental damage without derailing development programs.

Although some progress was made, UNCED in general failed to effectively integrate environmental and developmental concerns. Many observers felt that both environment and development issues were perceived and approached very differently by the "northern" industrialized countries and the "southern" developing countries. The north tends to consider such global environmental problems as climate change and deforestation as top global priorities, whereas the south emphasizes the more traditional "development" issues of poverty, access to clean drinking water and sanitation facilities, and programs for financial and technological assistance. These differing approaches made for a painfully slow and disorganized UNCED negotiation process, which sometimes erupted into heated accusations and mutual distrust.

Some NGOs and Third World countries argue that, because the north's own historical industrialization process was unchecked by environmental regulation, that region is thus responsible for most global environmental problems. They charge that the north is now attempting to redefine these problems in order to share the responsibility and cost with the agricultural south. Developing countries argue that if the industrialized world wants them to change their behavior in a way that will benefit the north (perhaps even more than the south), then the north must make available new and additional assistance of all kinds to facilitate the changes.

The north counters that any agreement to limit greenhouse gas or ozone-depleting emissions is meaningless without the participation of such large developing countries as India, China, and Brazil, whose emissions in the next ten years could surpass those of the industrialized countries several times over if unchecked. The north further argues that the south also will benefit from such agreements and from efforts to pursue future economic development plans in an environmentally sound manner. Though willing to offer some financial and technological assistance to developing countries for implementation of global environmental agreements, the industrialized countries feel that the expenses they will incur in changing their own behavior will be so great that they will be simply unable to offer unlimited amounts of aid to others.

In its most antagonistic form, the north-south debate has been characterized by mutual suspicion: a "southern" suspicion that the north is attempting to limit developing countries' sovereignty over their own territories and resources and to sabotage their development plans, and a "northern" suspicion that the south is only engaging in environmental discussions in order to obtain huge amounts of additional financial aid and access to free technology. Clearly, some on both sides do harbor such suspicions, but most participants and observers would find them flawed for several reasons: Many people in developing countries are concerned with global environmental problems; industrialized countries also consider economic development a top priority, not only for the south but also for themselves; and the "north" and the "south" do not actually exist as cohesive, exclusive blocs with common positions.

## *Regionalism*

The categories of "north" and "south" should be understood as loose groupings of countries with widely varying orientations. Some of the most heated debates in the UNCED process took place among the industrialized members of the Organization for Economic Cooperation and Development (OECD). In fact, disagreement between the United States and several European countries over the inclusion of targets and timetables for greenhouse gas reductions in the climate change convention almost derailed pre-UNCED negotiations. Disagreement among developing countries is equally pronounced; Brazil, for example, now favors global forest conservation efforts, but others, like Malaysia, have denounced such programs, viewing them as northern schemes to take control of southern resources.

The fall of the totalitarian governments of the former Soviet Union and several Eastern European countries has also created a new geographic-economic category that is neither north nor south. In UNCED documents, these countries are referred to as "economies in transition" that fall somewhere between the conditions and expectations placed on developed and developing countries.

It may be more accurate to view UNCED negotiations as discussions among several single-issue regional coalitions. The groupings are small, the issues are fluid, and both are based on common geopolitical interests. For example, several South Pacific countries concerned about potential sea-level rise formed the Association of Small Island States (AOSIS) to present a unified call for strict and binding limits on greenhouse gas emissions. Similarly, oil-producing Persian Gulf states acted as a regional bloc in the climate negotiations, lobbying against any calls to limit carbon dioxide emissions. Because small numbers and proximity are more likely to engender real common interests than are large and disparate groupings, future negotiators may find regional cooperation efforts more efficient and effective than global agreements in the UNCED tradition.

## NGOs

Most environmental NGOs are focused at the local and national levels, but international affiliations of these organizations are also becoming more widespread and active as concern for global issues grows. Increasingly, NGOs are organizing in developing countries, participating in international organizations, and proposing and negotiating international agreements. More than 1,000 NGOs participated in the Global Forum, a parallel non-governmental conference held in tandem with UNCED. These groups included human rights and indigenous peoples organizations, in addition to specifically environmental NGOs; their constituencies ranged from single neighborhoods to worldwide memberships.

NGOs played an important role throughout the almost five-year negotiating process leading up to the adoption of the climate change convention at UNCED. In 1990, for example, Greenpeace published a scientific report that was parallel in structure and severely criticized a document issued by the UN-sponsored Intergovernmental Panel on Climate Change. The Greenpeace report generated much media and public attention on the climate change issue and the activities of the UN and national negotiating parties. Though this attention created some pressure upon governments, the final climate change convention ultimately fell far short of Greenpeace's findings and prescriptions.

At UNCED, NGOs discovered new ways to exert influence. They lobbied sympathetic national governments to sponsor positions and to present them as their own in official negotiations. Several of the amendments offered by the Australian, New Zealand, and some European delegations during the UNCED proceedings originated with NGO proposals. In addition, many NGOs prepared comments and alternate texts to official UNCED documents under discussion and made them widely available; some of these texts found their way into official discussions and often into the final products, despite the NGOs' official "observer" status. Numerous press conferences held at or near the UNCED and Global Forum sites increased the NGO-generated pressure on participating governments.

## *Environment and Development*

UNCED's title shows its explicit recognition of the dual nature of environmental and developmental issues. But the relationship between the two functions is multifaceted and complex. Environmental degradation can result both from affluence and from poverty, and countries approach issues of environment and development according to their own levels of industrialization and environmental degradation.

Although poor countries often charge that the industrialized north is the source of most global atmospheric pollution, they cannot deny that much of the world's deforestation and consequent soil erosion, desertification, and flooding—resulting from widespread demand for fuelwood and poor agricultural practices—occurs within their own borders. Because industrial plants in Third World countries are often technologically outdated, they often lack the environmental protection equipment that is readily available to their richer counterparts.

A perceived trade-off between forwarding environmental and developmental agendas is not strictly a phenomenon of the developing world. Developing countries argue that they can ill afford costly environmental protection laws and programs when their first priority is to improve the lives of their people, and industrialized countries often cite similar arguments. Indeed, current economic problems make even rich countries feel they are too poor to implement costly environmental programs at home, let alone to fund other countries' participation in multilateral agreements.

In 1987, the UN-sponsored World Commission on Environment and Development gave wide exposure to the concept of sustainable development in order to debunk the myth that a trade-off between environmental and developmental objectives must exist.[4] It suggests that environmentally sound development can actually enhance economic growth efforts and that, conversely, industrialization without environmental safeguards will be costly in the long run.

The sustainable development concept, though logically sound, has not been widely translated into policy because it is vaguely defined and because it requires policy-makers to take a long-range view that inevitably entails some short-term sacrifice. The latter makes the sustainable development concept ill suited to policy-making processes dictated by annual budget battles. Many political systems make it difficult, if not impossible, for sustainable development policies to be fully implemented; long before anticipated benefits can be reaped, political leaders may have been ousted by challengers offering quick-fix alternatives.

### *"Politicization"*

Recently, the international environmental negotiation process has been widely criticized for becoming increasingly politicized. For example, many participants in the March 1992 conference of the parties to the Conference on International Trade in Endangered Species (CITES) charged that political, rather than scientific, concerns dominated the conference. They claimed the decision to retain the three-year-old ban on international trade in ivory, despite scientific evidence that some elephant herds are not endangered, showed that signatories were influenced more by symbolism and public relations results than by objective scientific evidence.

The charge of politicization implies two assumptions, both false. It first suggests that the process of international environmental negotiation previously took place in a vacuum, unaffected by the political concerns that drive actors in other issue areas. This assumption derives from the naive belief that governments are able to rely solely on "objective" scientific testimony to arrive at universally acceptable prescriptions. But environmental science is a complex body of disciplines, all in their relative infancies, and the scientific community itself is in a state of intense debate over ecological systems and processes. There is no indication that definitive scientific answers will be found in the short run, and this makes the science-policy relationship an extremely complicated one. Although close consideration of current scientific findings is a necessary component of sound environmental policy-making, the assumption that either the findings themselves or the outcomes of the policy process will be shielded from the political milieu in which they exist is wishful thinking.

The second false assumption implied by the politicization criticism is that it is impossible to forge effective agreements within the political context of international relations. The international negotiating process, on any issue, will always be influenced by the political agendas of the participating countries. The domestic-foreign policy interface is a porous membrane in all types of governmental systems; policy-makers in democracies and centralized systems alike are influenced by demands from domestic constituencies for competing foreign policy options. Negotiations would be better served if participants together sought goals and implementation strategies that satisfied both domestic and international agendas. A global emissions-trading program, for example, could give financial incentives to private actors to reduce pollution.

## International Environmental Agreements in Context

A multilateral agreement, once reached, is only the midpoint in a process that begins well before the negotiations start and continues through steps toward implementation, creation of institutional frameworks, monitoring, enforcement, and modification. The latter steps are complicated by several general characteristics of international environmental cooperation efforts: Participation is largely voluntary; implementation is costly for participating governments; there are often no real mechanisms capable of forcing compliance by signatories; and implementation and enforcement take place in the context of underlying political themes, agendas, and controversies.

Though posing strong obstacles to the universal implementation of environmental agreements, these characteristics do not doom such agreements to being only symbolic gestures. It is unlikely that supranational institutions with real enforcement powers will be created in the foreseeable future, but there are, nonetheless, powerful incentives for governments to forge and comply with multilateral environmental cooperation efforts. These incentives include the linkage of environmental cooperation to other types of international relations, such as economic assistance, trade, technological cooperation, and security relationships. The strong presence of NGOs and the media can focus public attention on "environmental outlaws," and the prominent place of environmental issues on most domestic political agendas encourages national leaders to "take the high road" on the international environmental stage. More emphasis will likely be placed on these "carrots" in the negotiation and implementation of future agreements.

## Outlook

Perhaps more than any other single issue in international relations, environmental problems point out the limitations of the nation-state as an international actor. Disputes over natural resource exploitation, transboundary pollution, and energy generation all have, at their bases, a classic collective-action dilemma. Even where there is a universally acknowledged common interest among members of a group, "unless there is coercion or some other special device to make individual [countries] act in their common interest, rational, self-interested individuals will not [usually] act to achieve their common or group interests."[5] The challenges for international environmental policy-makers involve identifying the common interest, devising a widely accepted strategy for advancing that interest, and providing the "special device" that will motivate countries to voluntarily implement that strategy in concert but, ultimately, each within its own unique constraints.

Although global conventions and other multilateral cooperation efforts are essential for providing a level playing field on which to take otherwise unilaterally costly action, the international community may find that post-UNCED achievements can be more easily accomplished at the local, national, and regional levels. Smaller-scale projects are less susceptible to such UNCED-type pitfalls as emphasizing symbolism over substance, succumbing to global ideological debates, and sacrificing commitment to real action for achieving consensus on text.

Unilateral actions, such as the introduction by some European countries of a carbon tax (well ahead of an anticipated but stalled EC-wide tax), are less complicated and often less costly than the implementation of a new global convention would be. Regional and bilateral environmental assistance programs are implemented at a lower level on a more routine basis than global agreements, and they may benefit from a relative lack of public and media scrutiny. Programs involving the participation of only a few actors can be put into practice relatively quickly, rather than being dragged through the signing, ratification, and other entry-into-force requirements that can slow global conventions. Examples include Norway's aid to Russia in cleaning up radioactive waste sites and the U.S. effort to help Mexico to implement an environmental cleanup plan in the border area.

Such projects are generally designed to advance the national interest of the country or countries involved, so the collective-action problem of national interests conflicting with common interests often does not come into play. It is the local and regional environmental problems that, in aggregate, make up most global problems. Consequently, relatively small improvements made at the local level also contribute in aggregate to global solutions. As long as sovereign nation-states are the principal actors in the international system, the forging of global agreements will not be a panacea or a substitute for ongoing unilateral environmental activities; rather it will complement them.

## Notes

1. See William B. Wood, George J. Demko, and Phyllis Mofson, "Ecopolitics in the Global Greenhouse," *Environment,* vol. 31, no. 7 (September 1989), pp. 12–17, 32–34, for a more in-depth discussion of the ecopolitical hierarchy.

2. Murray Feshbach and Alfred Friendly, Jr., *Ecocide in the USSR: Health and Nature Under Siege* (New York: Basic Books, 1992), pp. 2–3.

3. The UNCED agreements are: The Rio Declaration on Environment and Development, The United Nations Framework Convention on Climate Change, The United Nations Framework Convention on Biodiversity, a non–legally binding authoritative statement of principles for a global consensus on the management, conservation, and sustainable use of all types of forests, and Agenda 21.

4. The World Commission on Environment and Development, *Our Common Future* (Oxford: Oxford University Press, 1987), p. 43. The report defines sustainable development as "development that meets the needs of the present without compromising the ability of future generations to meet their own needs."

5. Mancur Olson, *The Logic of Collective Action* (Cambridge, Mass.: Harvard University Press, 1965), p. 2.

# TEN

## Population, Politics, and Geography: A Global Perspective

### GEORGE J. DEMKO

SINCE THE END OF WORLD WAR II, there has been a very rapid growth in awareness of and concern for the global "population problem." This chapter examines the problem by disassembling it into its component parts and assessing these parts from a geographical perspective. At the same time, population growth and distribution issues will be discussed in terms of their impact on international relations. These relations involve, of course, not only sovereign states but also intergovernmental organizations (IGOs) and non-governmental organizations (NGOs).

The population problem all too frequently is viewed as an aggregate global population issue—that is, a population menacingly large and growing at a rate that imperils the global environment, food supply, and resource base. The planet's population in 1993 was estimated to be over 5.5 billion, growing at a rate of 1.6 percent per year, and on average, every woman on earth will give birth to 3.3 children in her lifetime. All this information has the ring of catastrophe about it, and indeed, it has stimulated an increasingly shrill debate among scholars and policymakers. This debate cannot be evaluated, though, without first understanding that there are a number of different population problems, each with its political ramifications.

The population problem has at least five components, each of which is significant. These problems include: (1) population growth or lack of growth, (2) the population distribution problem, (3) the issue of international population flows (migration of all kinds), (4) mortality and morbidity rates of population, and (5) cultural intolerance by populations (racism, gender discrimination, and so forth). Clearly, these components are interrelated and complex; they also vary greatly from place to place and have significant international implications.

The issue of global population growth was identified by the English parson and economist Thomas Malthus. His famous prophecy of population growth outstripping the means of subsistence continues to influence some social scientists and is vehemently rejected by others. Among the most outspoken examples of these demographic extremes are Paul Ehrlich and Julian Simon. Ehrlich argues that population is, indeed, a socioeconomic time bomb threatening the planet, whereas Simon contends that population growth stimulates economic growth. The population argument raises related issues like the maximum carrying capacity of the planet, the rate of global environmental degradation, the role and growth of technology and human ingenuity, and much more.

Obviously, the question of which argument is correct has no immediate, definitive answer. It would appear reasonable to advise the planet's decision-makers to err on the more conservative side and promote efforts to check population growth. But from a geographic perspective, it is more important to consider the issue more specifically from a regional or disaggregated point of view. In short, there are, indeed, some places in the world where population growth is too high and poses a serious problem; conversely, there are other places on the globe where a lack of population growth is a serious concern. The global aggregate view is distorting and must be clarified with a region-specific analysis.

Even at the global level, the rate of population growth has slowed—the total fertility rate dropped from 5.0 in 1950 to 3.3 in 1993.[1] The problem is that the high fertility rates of the 1950s, 1960s, and 1970s are reflected in high population growth rates in the 1990s as the children born twenty to thirty years ago have reached child-bearing age. To overcome this "lag" effect, a fertility rate decline must be sustained for a long period to produce a decline in population growth.

At a disaggregated level, however, it is possible to note remarkable variation in the population growth problem. The data in Table 10.1 present a sample of this variation. Obviously, a number of places are experiencing a severe problem of high growth. These states are predominantly in the Third World, and their problems of poverty and low quality of life are exacerbated by population growth. It is also clear that a number of states have made enormous progress in reducing rates of growth (e.g., China and Singapore), and much can be learned from these examples. And for a growing number of states, low population growth rates compounded by aging populations are of growing concern. The population of Japan, for example, will begin to decline by 2011. Nearly sixty of the world's states have reached or dropped below replacement-level growth rates, a situation with interesting and complex implications for international migration, labor issues, and other processes. And many of the developed states will be faced with aging populations, which will affect labor demand and pension funds and may lead to a renewed round of labor immigration from the Third World. The latter may become a very sensitive issue, given the problems already experienced in Western Europe with guest workers and the growing xenophobia in a number of countries.

The variation in population growth rates just described may clarify the population growth problem, but it only provides a clear focus on those areas that require some type of population aid. In fact, the specter of these populations grow-

TABLE 10.1  *Total Fertility Rates for Selected Regions and Countries, 1993*

|  | Total Fertility Rate |
|---|---|
| MORE DEVELOPED COUNTRIES | 1.8 |
| LESS DEVELOPED COUNTRIES | 3.7 |
| Africa | 6.1 |
| Asia (excluding China) | 4.0 |
| Latin America | 3.2 |
| Europe | 1.6 |
| Niger | 7.4 |
| Malawi | 7.7 |
| Uganda | 7.3 |
| Iraq | 7.0 |
| Syria | 7.1 |
| Yemen | 7.5 |
| Philippines | 4.1 |
| India | 3.9 |
| Iran | 6.6 |
| Singapore | 1.7 |
| China | 1.9 |
| Hong Kong | 1.2 |
| Japan | 1.5 |
| Mexico | 3.4 |
| Honduras | 5.6 |
| Cuba | 1.8 |
| Argentina | 2.9 |
| Italy | 1.3 |
| Germany | 1.7 |
| Russia | 1.7 |
| United States | 2.0 |

SOURCE: Population Reference Bureau, *Population Data Sheet* (Washington, D.C., 1993).

ing at unacceptable rates actually led to a global effort to develop policies and programs to ameliorate the problem. By 1965, many developed states were providing "population aid" in the form of family-planning support to interested developing countries. The U.S. Agency for International Development (USAID), for example, was given a mandate to provide technical assistance for population control to interested states.

In 1971, a World Population Plan of Action was created in which many developing states stressed the "value of people" to emphasize their right to decide on population issues. The Bucharest global population conference in 1974 reached a consensus in recognizing the value of family planning, but with the urging of the Soviet bloc in those Cold War years, it insisted on the need for "socioeconomic transformation"—a euphemism for the need to invoke political reform of a Marxist type. By 1981, the direct external assistance for population programs to developing countries was more than $500 million a year, and the United States provided about 40 percent of this total. In 1984, at the Mexico City Conference on Population, the majority of the world's states insisted on the importance of population aid programs for developing countries, funded by the West. The United States, however, injected a note of restraint regarding the use of abortion and coercion in family-planning programs, and the population issue became remarkably politicized. The U.S. policy ostensibly was aimed at curbing coercive family-planning programs and promoting a "humane system" of options for women. Many specialists and others around the world, however, argued that it was an attempt to impose prevailing American morality on others and resulted in depriving women of their rights.

The impact of U.S. policy was great. Funds were cut off to a number of very important intergovernmental and non-governmental organizations, such as the United Nations Fund for Population Activities (UNFPA) and the International Planned Parenthood Federation (IPPF), and tensions arose between these groups and the United States. China was affected by the UNFPA cuts, which increased the strain in U.S.-Chinese foreign relations. A number of Western European states expressed their disagreement with the U.S. policy, and the Soviet Union stooped to the occasion by making its first-ever donation to UNFPA—in hard currency! This demographic issue remained highly politicized until 1993, when the U.S. government formally rescinded its Mexico City Population Policy.[2]

The current period is marked by a shift toward a concern for population growth and the environment. Threats to the tropical rain forest, biodiversity, and related environmental issues have focused attention on developing countries and their rapidly growing populations that need land and resources. On a per capita basis, greater environmental damage is inflicted by high levels of consumption in developed states than by actions of populations and governments in the Third World. It has been politically sensitive, however, to bring pressure to bear on Third World states over their high population growth rates. This concern was weakly finessed in the Rio Conference on Environment and Development, in Principle 8 of the Draft of Environmental Rules: "To achieve sustainable development and a higher quality of life for all people, states should reduce and eliminate unsustainable patterns of production and consumption and promote appropriate demographic policies."[3]

The planned World Population Conference, to be held in Cairo in 1994, must address population issues in a more realistic way and at least reach some consensus over measures needed to address related problems, including where the resources to pay for amelioration and solution will be found. This conference has the potential to usher in a new era of cooperation in population matters. There is little doubt that population policies, global and national, will increasingly and overtly be directed to environmental concerns. And the role of population in the development and environmental arenas will and must receive more attention.

## Population Distribution

At the end of the 1970s, the United Nations began a regular process of surveying its member states about their various population problems. Many were surprised to find that population distribution problems were identified as significant for the overwhelming number of countries, and for many, population distribution was noted as the most serious problem. In most cases, the problem was defined as a rural-versus-urban maldistribution of population, with the growth of large urban centers (primate cities) ranking first among the issues. Rapid urbanization, though, is often tied to rapid population growth in particular rural regions. Such maldistribution problems are always serious national concerns, and they increasingly impinge on the global stage. Political instability and insurgency and the use and diffusion of drugs spill out of such demographic cauldrons. The global urbanization process also stands out as a major concern. Urban population growth in the Third World exceeds 3.5 percent per year—outstripping the overall population rate. Tied into the global economic system, the megacities that are being created are difficult to manage, filled with poverty and crime, and plagued by infrastructure and housing shortages. Of the ten largest cities in the world, eight are in the developing world, and of the largest thirty cities, twenty-two are in the Third World. By 1990, there were 215 million households in cities without safe water, and 340 million had inadequate sanitation. During the 1970s, Third World cities had to house 30 million people each year; by the 1990s, that figure rose to 60 million a year.

Drugs, crime, pollution, insurgency, and violent ideologies are largely concentrated in today's megacities. Governments are demanding new and more research and policy aid from intergovernmental organizations such as the UN and other international bodies, in efforts to manage congested, impoverished urban populations.

## International Population Flows

Cross-boundary flows of population have recently reached magnitudes not experienced since World War II (see also Chapter 11). These flows are varied and include refugees and asylum seekers, immigrants (legal and illegal), contract laborers (guest workers), and even international circulators (individuals who cross international boundaries for many reasons, with intentions of returning to their home countries). Currently, at least 100 million people around the world live in countries other than those in which they were born.[4] The bulk of this massive flow consists of people moving from the south (developing world) to other parts of the Third World and, to a lesser degree, to the north (developed states). The flows of poor migrants and refugees from developing countries to other Third World states have exacerbated the problems of the developing world, and though the flows to developed states can more reasonably be accommodated, they have been significant and caused much stress. From 1980 to 1985, the three traditional countries of immigration—the United States, Australia, and Canada—took in nearly 4 million people. From 1985 to 1989, they accepted 750,000 individuals from developing countries alone—over 70 percent of their total admissions. And in 1992, the United States accepted 810,635 legal immigrants. Today, there are more than 18 million refugees in the world, and probably an equal number of displaced persons still live within their own countries. Events in the early 1990s produced tens of thousands of emigrants from the former Soviet bloc, and more than 1 million asylum seekers entered Western European states (mainly Germany) from the former Yugoslavia.

These massive spatial flows of people are becoming increasingly politicized, and many governments are altering their policies with regard to such flows. A former head of the U.S. Immigration and Naturalization Service notes that the increase in pressure from migrants "challenges the capacity of governments to uphold basic sovereignty, in this case, the choice of who resides in one's own country."[5] Sadako Ogata, the UN High Commissioner for Refugees, states that "migration must be treated not only as a matter for humanitarian agencies of the UN, but also as a political problem which must be placed in the mainstream of the international agenda as a potential threat to international peace and security."[6]

Many intergovernmental and non-governmental agencies have become deeply involved with these population flows. Agencies ranging from the United Nations High Commission for Refugees to the International Rescue Committee have challenged governments and risked bankruptcy to provide aid and to attempt to bring down boundary barriers. The reactions of governments have varied, with most Western European states raising barriers and tightening asylum and refugee rules. Canada, Australia, and the United States initially relaxed admission requirements, but they are in the throes of reevaluating asylum and immigration policies as flows—legal and illegal—affect domestic economies. The near future appears to hold little relief from such population flows for increased economic development is bound to stimulate migration from developing states. Moreover, the nationalism that has generated much of the recent turmoil and population flight is hardly on the wane. What is clearly needed is a greater effort on the part of all actors—IGOs, NGOs, and states—to coordinate efforts to ameliorate the pain of some flows and perhaps even find solutions for others.

## Mortality and Morbidity

Rates of dying (or, alternatively, longevity) and levels of health (or, alternatively, morbidity) vary remarkably within and among the globe's states. The variation is readily apparent in Table 10.2, where the greatest longevity gap is nearly forty years; similarly, infant mortality rates vary from a high of 170 to a low of 4. Although mortality and morbidity are normally considered the exclusive concerns of sovereign governments, these issues have also spilled over boundaries and have become global and politicized. Conditions of overpopulation and economic deprivation in a number of regions of the globe (Bangladesh, Somalia) have become so persistent or have been so exacerbated by despotic governments on segments of the population (Sudan, Iraq) that international efforts have been mounted to bring a measure of relief or to avert a massive loss of life.

TABLE 10.2   *Life Expectancy at Birth and Infant Mortality for Selected Regions and Countries, 1993*

| | Life Expectancy at Birth | Infant Mortality (infant deaths before age 1 per 1,000 live births) |
|---|---|---|
| DEVELOPED COUNTRIES | 74 | 14 |
| LESS DEVELOPED COUNTRIES | 63 | 77 |
| Africa | 54 | 94 |
| Asia (excluding China) | 61 | 82 |
| Latin America | 68 | 49 |
| Europe | 75 | 10 |
| Guinea | 42 | 149 |
| Kenya | 62 | 75 |
| Uganda | 43 | 106 |
| Israel | 76 | 9 |
| Yemen | 46 | 131 |
| Afghanistan | 42 | 168 |
| Sri Lanka | 71 | 19 |
| Singapore | 74 | 5 |
| China | 70 | 53 |
| Japan | 79 | 4 |
| Costa Rica | 76 | 15 |
| Mexico | 70 | 38 |
| Haiti | 54 | 105 |
| Sweden | 78 | 6 |
| Russia | 69 | 23 |
| Turkmenistan | 66 | 56 |
| United States | 75 | 9 |

SOURCE: Population Reference Bureau, *Population Data Sheet* (Washington, D.C., 1993).

Although health has improved in most places on the globe over the past forty years, there is great unevenness in these gains. Sub-Saharan Africa, for instance, has experienced relatively little improvement. Deaths from AIDS, malaria, and tobacco-related causes result in 2 million deaths a year, and aid for health has dropped from 7 percent of the total official foreign assistance in the 1980s to 6 percent in the 1990s.[7] Hunger and related nutritional diseases affect millions of people around the globe. Indeed, it is estimated that over 500 million of the world's people are undernourished, or 10 percent of the total world population. Contrary to conventional wisdom, most of the malnourished suffer from "silent hunger," or chronic malnourishment, as opposed to the acute effects of famines. And of the eleven major famines since 1960, seven were caused primarily by civil war, war, or government policies, not natural catastrophes or overpopulation. Silent or chronic hunger, which affects more than 95 percent of the hungry, does not necessarily kill.[8] It raises morbidity by increasing susceptibility to other diseases, increasing infant mortality and maiming victims physically and mentally. Closely related to poverty, chronic hunger has a myriad of causes. It is found in places of poor resource endowment, high population growth, severe resource inequality, low or inappropriate agricultural technology, and combinations of all these factors.

Spatially, hunger exists everywhere, but its greatest concentration is, of course, in the Third World. The "hunger belt," focused on Sub-Saharan Africa and South Asia (Bangladesh, Bhutan, India, Nepal, Pakistan, and Sri Lanka), is the most critical set of regions of need. There are, however, other pockets of hunger in East Asia and the Pacific (40 million people), Latin America and the Caribbean (50 million), and the Middle East and North Africa (10 million). Much of the difficulty in resolving the hunger issue is tied not to a global lack of food but rather to myriad barriers to distribution, including economic and political barriers at subnational and international levels. A study by the International Institute for Applied Systems Analysis (IIASA) estimates that if all the hungry were located in one place, it would take about $21 billion to feed them adequately, or only $20 per person.[9]

Although there is enough food in the world to feed all the hungry adequately and although there is an extensive international aid system to feed the hungry, hunger persists. The solution, of course, lies in providing the hungry with the means to feed themselves. But achieving such a noble goal requires complex and place-specific sets of programs. In many cases, it will require a change in government, the infusion of technology, massive infrastructure development, and myriad measures necessary to promote economic development in the poor regions of the world. It may also require lower population growth rates in some areas, so that improvements in agricultural production are not offset by high birth rates.

A large number of international governmental organizations (e.g., FAO, the World Bank, the World Health Organization), a myriad of non-governmental organizations (e.g., Bread for the World, World Hunger Program), and many national governmental programs work diligently to address problems of unnecessary mortality and excessive morbidity. Many operate in conflict with states, and often they have only scarce resources to bring succor to the needy. All too often, these well-meaning efforts fall short because of lack of a cooperation and coordination with local agencies and governments.

## AIDS

One of the most ominous plagues in modern times, of course, is AIDS and its precursor, the HIV infection. The disease raises victims' morbidity level and is, at this point in time, always fatal. By 1993, 14 million people worldwide were infected with the virus (see Table 10.3), and projections for the year 2000 rise to between 30 and 40 million.[10]

The disease continues to have enormous political, geographic, and economic implications. During the Cold War, Soviet propaganda accused the United States of developing and spreading the virus, and the USSR maliciously dispersed this misinformation in badly afflicted Sub-Saharan Africa. A number of foreign governments in the 1980s, seriously frightened by the high rate of AIDS in the United

TABLE 10.3  *Estimated Number of HIV Cases by Continental Areas, 1993*

|  | *Estimated Cumulative Cases* |
|---|---|
| North America | >1,000,000 |
| Latin America and the Caribbean | 1,500,000 |
| Western Europe | 500,000 |
| North Africa and the Middle East | >75,000 |
| Sub-Saharan Africa | >8,000,000 |
| Eastern Europe and Central Asia | >50,000 |
| East Asia and the Pacific | >25,000 |
| South and Southeast Asia | >1,500,000 |
| Australasia | >25,000 |

SOURCE: "Aids Around the Globe," *New York Times International,* June 6, 1993, p. 20.

States, began to demand the right to inspect American military personnel at U.S. bases. A number of countries rapidly altered their immigration rules, demanding special tests and rules for HIV- and AIDS-infected people. More recent concerns focus on the continued rapid rate of growth in AIDS cases and especially the rate and spatial diffusion in certain parts of the world. The incidence of HIV and AIDS among males, especially homosexuals and intravenous drug users, has increased the mortality rates of males aged 18 to 35 in the United States. Clearly, the impact of AIDS and HIV differs greatly from group to group and from region to region, demanding that solutions and even policies be population- and place-specific. In Sub-Saharan Africa, the heterosexual diffusion of the disease has reached enormous levels and threatens large segments of the populations in Uganda, Zambia, and other countries. The estimated number of deaths in Africa from AIDS is an astounding 500,000. In South and Southeast Asia, the incidence of AIDS and HIV has increased remarkably, threatening untold numbers of people in such places as Thailand and India.

Given that the types and methods of diffusion of the disease vary widely from place to place and that there has been a rapid increase in the variety of genotypes, a solution to the problem is unlikely to appear in the near future. The need for an unprecedented and massive international effort is obvious. The totality of issues affecting global and regional rates of morbidity and mortality from HIV and AIDS is serious, and these issues connect the populations of every place on the globe. As we approach the end of the twentieth century, state governments, intergovernmental organizations, and non-governmental organizations have a moral obligation to address hunger and public-health threats like AIDS in a more efficient, coordinated, and cooperative manner.

## Cultural Intolerance by Populations

Most demographic textbooks include a brief section on the demographic characteristics of population. The "acquired" characteristics, such as religion or education, are discussed along with "biological" characteristics, such as age, gender, or race, and they are related to the fundamental demographic processes—fertility, mortality, and mobility. These characteristics are, no doubt, equally important in terms of how certain populations treat or mistreat each other. At this point in time, an enormous explosion in and awareness of the many types of intolerance that affect our planet has occurred. The problems vary widely from country to country and region to region—from gender discrimination in nearly every part of the world to racial, religious, and ethnic hatred and intolerance of many groups in most countries of the world.

These problems have been intensified and magnified by a number of global geographic and political processes. The enormous flows of international migrants over international boundaries—from legal and illegal movers to refugees, tourists, and others—have greatly increased the contact between dissimilar groups. The millions who have fled political repressions are being replaced or supplemented with hundreds of thousands fleeing the upheaval caused by the collapse of the Marxist states. Meanwhile, ancient religious and related hatreds, once controlled by coercive governments, have flared into bloody confrontations over territory and other real and perceived affronts in the former Yugoslavia and USSR. Many flee from violence and economic insecurity to countries where they are confronted with hostile populations concerned with their own welfare.

Examples of cultural intolerance are varied, ranging from the xenophobic hostility toward immigrant populations in Western Europe (especially Germany) in the early 1990s and intraethnic civil war among Croatians, Serbs, and Muslims in the former Yugoslavia to the aborting and infanticide of female fetuses and babies in South and East Asia. Awareness of gender discrimination reached such a level in the early 1990s that one of the principles of the environmental rules developed at the Rio Conference on Environment and Development in 1993 calls for the "full participation (of women) in environmental management and development." And in 1993, the Canadian government extended "asylum" to a Middle Eastern woman whose claim of persecution by her own government was found valid, setting a new and important precedent in asylum practices.

The first international conference on human rights, sponsored by the United Nations and held in Vienna in June 1993, was remarkable for its tumultuousness. Thousands of oppressed groups and human rights NGOs gathered outside the main meeting halls to display evidence of cultural intolerance and resultant persecution in every region and in every state of the world. The conference clearly demonstrated the significance of these issues and the relative impotence of the UN in taking effective measures to alleviate the problems.

## Conclusion

Although population problems are most often debated at the national level, like environmental processes, they are no longer confined within the boundaries of states. Population pressures respect no boundaries, and they impinge on the global community, engaging all global actors. "Overpopulation" in one region of the world impacts on all the world's states in the form of political instability and outflows of migrants—from illegal "economic" migrants to asylum seekers. Such movers impinge on states with aging populations, high levels of economic development, and increasingly exclusive border controls meant to reject foreigners. Burgeoning megacities affect the "global village" in a similar way, in that they are intimately connected to all the world's population via the spatial diffusion of drugs, crime, AIDS, terrorism, and more. Cultural intolerance, whether expressed in terms of gender, race, religion, ethnicity, class, or any other form, only produces more hatred or civil turmoil.

Many of the demographic issues discussed in this chapter are or can be interrelated. For example, falling birth rates can be tied to better public health programs in family-planning centers in rural areas. Similarly, such programs can be bases for educating women and girls, a strategy known to lower fertility and improve health levels. Finally, such programs and centers can distribute condoms and educate populations about AIDS and HIV.

As a New World Order of some type emerges at the onset of the twenty-first century, it will certainly be influenced by how the world manages its population. International instruments and governance will rapidly increase in number and significance. It would seem obvious that in such a spatially interconnected world, states, international IGOs, and NGOs must address demographic issues more collectively. Cooperation and coordination are mandatory, if only to ameliorate the high price of political-demographic problems. These issues are too important to allow the current chaos and unilateral decision-making to continue on issues that determine the death and life of millions of humans. Clearly, such international efforts can address concerns of cost, definitions, aid, policy coordination, and more in a manner worthy of a twenty-first century global community. In a world of 8.5 billion, foreseen by the year 2025, there will be even greater pressure on our resources (especially water), and there will probably be less tolerance and less latitude for political decision-making. Clearly, then, the time to act is upon us.

## Notes

1. The total fertility rate (TFR) is the number of children a woman will have, on average, in her lifetime (measured at current birth rates). The level of population replacement is represented by a TFR of 2.1.

2. "Recession of the US 'Mexico City Policy,'" *Population and Development Review*, vol. 19, no. 1 (March 1993), pp. 215–216.

3. "Draft of Environmental Rules: 'Global Partnership,'" *New York Times*, April 4, 1992.

4. "Migration Report," United Nations Population Fund (New York: United Nations, July 6, 1993).

5. Doris Meissner, "Managing Migrations," *Foreign Policy*, vol. 86 (Spring 1992), p. 68.

6. G. Lyons and M. Mastanduno, *Beyond Westphalia? International Intervention, State Sovereignty, and the Future of International Society* (Hanover, N.H.: Dartmouth College, 1992), p. 20.

7. *World Development Report, 1993* (Washington, D.C.: World Bank, 1993).

8. G. Fisher, K. Frohberg, M.A. Keyzer, K.S. Parikh, and W. Tims, *Hunger: Beyond the Reach of the Invisible Hand* (Laxenburg, Australia: International Institute for Applied Systems Analysis, October 1991).

9. Ibid., p. 37.

10. "At AIDS Talks, Science Confronts Daunting Maze," *New York Times International,* June 6, 1993, p. 20.

# ELEVEN

## Crossing the Line:
## Geopolitics of International Migration

### WILLIAM B. WOOD

*What approach to immigration and refugee issues is appropriate for a new
international order? During the Cold War things were simple as far as
movement of people is concerned. It was a very restrictive regime. People
were not allowed to move around. Those refugees who left the Communist
countries were welcome, because they had left the ideologically repressive
regimes. Things are no longer that simple. With the fall of the Berlin Wall,
the world is heralding a liberal framework. We want free movement of goods
and information; what are we going to do about free movement of people?
This is the issue we will all have to address. How do we put order into a
liberal framework for the movement of people?*

—Sadako Ogata, United Nations High Commissioner for Refugees[1]

OVER THE PAST DECADE, Western governments have been grappling with the dilemmas of controlling immigration and providing support for growing numbers
of refugees. All migrants are influenced by many of the same social, cultural, political, ecological, and economic forces that lead individuals and groups to leave
one area for another. What makes international migration different is that it involves crossing a politically determined, often arbitrarily drawn, sovereign, international boundary line. Such boundaries separate the recognized territories of
sovereign governments, which often administer their countries using different
sets of laws, economic systems, and cultural values.

Historically, international migration—whether forced or voluntary—has
served as a major conduit between countries, often permanently changing their
population compositions, their economies, and even their landscapes. In a
post–Cold War world economy, which is accompanied by a resurgent nationalism and entrenched poverty, international migration poses an unprecedented

challenge to both individuals and governments. Migration from one country to another, for example, might be viewed from two quite different perspectives: For some of the migrants involved, it is a once-in-a-lifetime opportunity to escape harsh living conditions in their home countries and to seek their fortune elsewhere; for some politicians in the receiving country, the same migration flow is a threat to national stability and the cause of a wide range of social problems, from unemployment to crime. As debates over immigration and refugee policies intensify, a political geographic perspective can shed light on a host of issues tied to international migrations.

## Change Agents

Migrants cause change. Their departure from one area and arrival in another generate profound changes in local labor markets and in local resource use and production.[2] In addition, migrants bring with them their traditions, social structures, and political orientations, which can radically transform their new homelands. Migration is also an emotional experience, primarily for the migrants themselves but also for the more sedentary groups whose lives are affected by those moving in or moving out. At an institutional level, governments often have been confused over how to handle the many migrants who move within their international borders as well as those who cross them.

The U.S. Immigration Reform and Control Act of 1986 was aimed, in part, at stemming the flow of several million illegal immigrants in the decades after World War II. These "illegals," mostly from Mexico, place demands on local governmental services, but they also provide low-wage labor for agricultural production in the United States.[3] Debates over the costs and benefits of illegal immigration and on appropriate and fair ways to control the number of "illegal aliens" will continue well into the next century.[4] In Europe, long-standing efforts to form a tightly integrated European Community (EC) are being hampered by fears that a "flood" of Third World and Eastern European asylum seekers will take advantage of weakened border controls between European countries. Nationalistic political parties in Europe have used these fears to advocate much stricter immigration and asylum laws and to postpone the lifting of restrictions on labor mobility within the EC.

The international migrants most often in the news are refugees, be they Kurd, Bosnian, Cambodian, or Somali. They all symbolize societies torn apart by civil war and the tragic human toll of military conflict. Many of those forcibly displaced are members of oppressed nations who are being deliberately removed from their homelands by state-controlled military forces (see Chapter 13). Some of the refugees from such repression cross an international boundary but remain within the traditional territory of their nation—which, for them, may be a more important factor in their forced migration. One example is the Pushtuns who fled into Pakistan after the Soviet invasion of Afghanistan but remained within the Pushtun area in the border zone.

UN-directed efforts to protect and assist these victims are greatly strained by the growing numbers of refugees worldwide, now estimated to be over 18 million. The United Nations High Commissioner for Refugees (UNHCR) currently faces escalating costs and the difficult logistics of providing immediate care and protection, possible third-country resettlement, and, ideally, safe repatriation for all refugees. In addition, the UNHCR is beginning to cope with large numbers of forcibly displaced people—those who flee persecution, war, or other life-threatening situations but remain within their own countries.

Although they have attracted most of the political attention, refugees, asylum seekers, and illegals represent only the tip of a migration iceberg that lies beneath the surface of national aspirations for political stability and economic development. If governments hope to be more effective in managing migration flows within and across their boundaries, they will have to develop strategies that address migration as a loose bundle of issues. The migration bundle involves comparative economic opportunities, political jurisdictions, ethnic tensions, human rights, basic needs, and, perhaps increasingly, environmental stability. In other words, policy-makers will need to understand the political, economic, and cultural geographies that serve as the signposts along current and future migration routes.

International migration entails crossing an international boundary for an extended period of time (tourism is not usually included). As in other types of migration, the time frame is deliberately ambiguous because a migration journey may be of several months duration or permanent. The migrants themselves may have little information on their possible destinations, only a vague plan of how to get there, and little idea of how long they will stay once they arrive.

Over 100 million people might be classified as international migrants today because they reside in a country other than their place of birth. This is only a rough estimate because the measurement of international migration is haphazard at best. Border guards and immigration officials may record a particular crossing for someone who is granted official permission to enter, but once the boundary is crossed, most migrations within and perhaps out of the new country will likely go unrecorded. Illegal migrations are even less well understood or measured. Statistics on interdictions and deportations of illegal aliens reflect only the minority that are caught and depend on the government's efforts to catch them. Before discussing trends in legal and illegal international migration, though, characteristics common to all types of migration must be outlined.

## Migration Theory

Two of the three basic demographic processes—birth and death—are relatively easy to record and are predictable (at least in the short term). The third—migration—is much more frustrating to those who study population change.[5] The reason is simple: Excluding the possible influence of reincarnation and renewed religious commitment, we are born only once, and barring any new medical breakthroughs in cryonics, we will die only once. Between those two rather significant events, we, like many other organisms, move around—and there lies the problem. Individual and family moves are usually only counted in a decennial census if a change of residence is involved and if a political boundary (municipal, county, state, or national) is crossed. Many local moves are thus lost in the census shuffle.

## More Than One Way to Move

There are many forms and patterns of mobility and different ways of classifying migrations. None is completely satisfactory because of the broad range of movements in which people engage: commuting to and from work or school; nomadic herding and shifting cultivation, ancient practices that have allowed small groups to survive harsh environmental conditions; seasonal migration, involving crop planting and harvesting cycles and off-farm employment; and rural-to-urban migration, a shift in population distribution that continues to change the socioeconomic foundation of every country. Of all the varied types of migration during the past few decades, the most profound consequences have come from the transformation of rural peasants into city dwellers, who often reside in crowded, sprawling squatter settlements and are usually resigned to only very low-wage, sporadic employment.[6] These migrants are literally urbanizing the world, most rapidly in the poorer countries; of the world's 5.5 billion people, over 42 percent are already living in urban areas.

## Push and Pull

Since E. G. Ravenstein set down his laws of migration over a century ago, social scientists have pondered the linkages between migration flows and a list of influencing variables, including age, gender, distance, economic conditions, and rural-urban disparities. Migration can be usefully described as a process determined by "push-and-pull" variables that operate at both the origin and destination places.[7] In between these places, intervening obstacles affect the ability of a migrant to complete his or her journey. Not all obstacles are physical, nor is the distance between places the primary deterrent in undertaking a journey (as it probably was when Ravenstein formulated his laws). Anyone who has bought an airline ticket can testify to the poor correlation between distance and travel cost. Thus, the major obstacle to international migration today is more likely to be governmental red tape than vast distances.

From a historical and geographic view, migration may be considered within a broad "mobility transition" model in which evolving patterns of mobility are tied to stages of economic development. Under this model, "advanced" and "superadvanced" societies require much less mobility than "transitional" societies, largely because of improvements in telecommunications.[8] Despite mind-boggling innovations that are enjoyed by some in the "information age" of the 1990s, much of the world's population must continue to move in order to survive.

Over the past two decades, migration research has focused on the selectivity of migration: Why do some people migrate and others stay put? This line of research has involved surveys of migrant decision-making, kinship linkages, communication networks, and perceptions of the pros and cons of moving to a new place. In the early 1970s, the debate on rural-to-urban migration was sharpened with the use of migration decision-making models. Michael Todaro's model was based on estimates of expected future earnings from an urban job, weighed against current incomes and an estimated cost of moving.[9] Many empirical studies have since underscored the importance of perceived economic opportunities in migration decision-making, whether the intended journey is across town or across an ocean.

Geographers studying migration have focused on migration patterns, especially between rural and urban places. They have also looked at how migration affects the hierarchical development of human settlements and how various types of migration flows—from seasonal to circular—are economic survival strategies. Migration and urbanization studies are closely intertwined, particularly in many poor countries where large rural populations provide a steady supply of migrants to rapidly growing cities. Poor job prospects and low incomes in cities and villages force tens of millions of migrants to shuttle back and forth between tiny farms, villages on the urban periphery, and inner-city squatter settlements, blurring the distinction between urban and rural economies. Government policies directed at achieving economic development goals have also often had unanticipated—and frequently undesired—impacts on migration flows.[10]

## International Migrations

Migration decisions are made within the context of an increasingly integrated and interdependent world economic system, but they are also swayed by cultural ties, social institutions, and governmental policies. Despite the powerful worldwide economic forces that push and pull international migrants, the impacts of their moves are felt primarily at the local, community level.

### *International Economic Migrants*

The types of people engaged in cross-border economic migration defy stereotypes: nomads, laborers, merchants, and business executives. They all seek to improve their economic prospects by moving, temporarily or permanently, to another country. Their main problem is usually whether the country they wish to migrate to will let them in and, if they are allowed in, how long that country will permit them to stay. Immigration policies that may change the course of their lives—as well as the demographic composition of the countries involved—may be based not on economic principles but rather on ambiguous and often unstated political agendas.[11]

In a purely economic world, there would be no political boundaries interfering with international labor migration. Indeed, only in the last century have political boundaries become such a commonplace barrier to migration streams.

Until the last few decades, most migrants moved through frontier regions, which were often dangerous zones for travelers because they were on the periphery of areas controlled by adjacent kingdoms. The clearest physical boundaries were the high walls around castles and fortified cities. Drawbridges once served much the same purpose as today's immigration and customs checkpoints at every international airport: They regulated who could enter sovereign territory.

Worldwide economic interdependence, the growing influence of the UN, and new concerns over humanitarian issues, human rights, environmental protection, and weapons of mass destruction are now challenging the concept of unquestioned sovereign space (see Chapter 12). Capital is electronically transferred among world cities, with or without governmental involvement, and foreign investments are sought to help promote economic growth (see Chapter 16). Many potential international migrants are merely trying to follow these capital investments to areas where future returns and incomes are the most promising. Those potential immigrants who are willing to invest large sums in their new homes, such as wealthy émigrés from Hong Kong, usually receive red-carpet treatment. Those without wealth, such as Eastern European Gypsies, are likely to face a cooler reception, particularly when jobs in traditional destination countries are scarce. Those who circumvent immigration laws are branded as illegals and live under the threat of deportation if they are apprehended by the immigration police. And those who hire illegals become implicated themselves in a far-reaching network of illegal migration-related activities.

International migrants often play a vital economic role in the places of origin and destination as well as the places in between. Migrants are usually not the poorest or the richest members of their societies, and typically, they have had more education than their stay-at-home peers. The emigrations of educated young people have been portrayed negatively as a "brain drain" that hinders economic development in their home countries. In labor-surplus economies, however, even college-educated young people often find themselves unemployed or underemployed at jobs well beneath their skill or educational levels. These emigrants would probably argue that their talents would be wasted if they were to stay put and that migration is the only way they know to develop their individual potential. Those that do become immigrants in countries with relatively high wages, however, all too often find themselves working at low-status jobs they would have shunned in their home countries.

The benefits of remittances from overseas migrants in terms of stimulating local economic growth are also debated among social scientists, with some claiming that received funds are primarily used for nonproductive consumption. In lieu of other sources of income, however, remittances become a critical pillar of family and village economies, especially in such labor-export countries as Mexico, the Philippines, Bangladesh, Pakistan, Jordan, and Egypt. When the hundreds of thousands of foreign workers who fled from Iraq and Kuwait in 1990 finally made it back to their home countries, they faced high unemployment rates and families who now had to get by without much-needed remittances.

## Unwelcome Guests

Economic immigrants are often seen as a large, almost bottomless labor pool for national development plans, whether in Europe or the Middle East. When there is a domestic labor shortage in an industrializing or oil-exporting country, migrants (or, more politely, "guest workers") are allowed temporary residence. When the economy contracts during a recession and domestic unemployment rises, these guests become less welcome, regardless of how long they have stayed and how much they have contributed to prior economic growth. Germany, which relied heavily on several million guest workers from the former Yugoslavia and Turkey, is now faced with absorbing a large group of young eastern Germans. Amid growing anti-immigrant sentiment and antiforeigner violence, the government is trying to provide financial incentives for its guest workers to return home. Many of these workers, however, have children who were born and raised in Germany, and they have little desire to return to their impoverished home countries.

## Refugees

UNHCR chief Ogata summarized the predicament of refugee and relief agencies by stating that "the end of the Cold War has not resulted in a new international order, but has created instability in which regional disputes and ethnic confrontations occur over and over again . . . generating more refugees each day than returnees."[12] By the end of 1992, the UNHCR had registered 18.5 million refugees around the world, a jump of several million since the mid-1980s (Figure 11.1). In the past two years, Europe has joined Asia and Africa as a major refugee-generating region, and new refugee flows may dash UNHCR hopes of making the 1990s the "decade of repatriation." Although large numbers of Afghans and Cambodians are finally returning home, their homelands are far from stable, and despite UN peace-keeping efforts, renewed fighting could quickly create new refugee flows in these troubled regions.

UN and non-governmental refugee relief agencies have also become more entangled in political and military issues. The return of several hundred thousand Kurds to their homeland in northern Iraq in 1991 went relatively smoothly, but it required the presence of a defined safe-haven area, a multilateral military force, and a UN guard force. Meanwhile, the likelihood that Kurds will become refugees once again is closely tied to their volatile relations with the regime in Baghdad. And efforts to assist Iraqi Kurds raised difficult institutional problems for UN relief agencies, especially concerning the sovereignty of member states and the obvious need for "humanitarian intervention."

Relief prospects for over 3 million refugees and displaced persons (those who are uprooted by force but remain within their own countries) in the former Yugoslav republics and several million Somalis are dependent on the success of the UN and NGOs, particularly the Red Cross, in negotiating with warring factions over food and relief distribution. Furthermore, brutal "ethnic cleansing" in

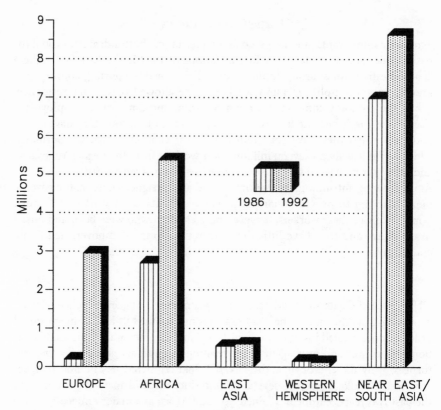

FIGURE 11.1   World refugee population, by region of asylum. SOURCE: U.S. Department of State, *World Refugee Report,* 1987; draft 1993, 2436 8-93 STATE (INR/GE).

numerous towns and cities in the former Yugoslavia may prevent many refugees from ever returning home. The pattern of ethnic cleansing of Bosnian Moslem communities has been especially disturbing because their forced displacement was not a by-product of war but rather a military strategy for controlling territory. Unlike those in many other places experiencing war, the perpetrators of ethnic cleansing never intend to allow the displaced to return home.

In Somalia, the tragedy of civil war has been compounded by a severe drought, resulting in as many as 300,000 deaths and rivaling the Ethiopian famine almost a decade earlier. Many of these Somali famine victims are nomads whose herds have perished and who have moved to towns in Somalia and refugee camps in Kenya in the desperate hope of being fed. Every day in the Horn of Africa during the summer and fall of 1992, several thousands of displaced people, mostly children, starved to death while relief agencies tried to keep food supplies from being stolen by armed gangs. Finally, famine and anarchy compelled the UN to authorize the use of a strong military presence to open up relief delivery corridors and feeding stations. Over 600,000 Somali refugees in neighboring Kenya and Ethiopia—who had fled with literally nothing—as well as many more who remained in Somalia will need several years to rebuild their herds and reestablish their small farms, if that is even possible; many will end up in cities and towns. Thus, chronic political instability and deeply imbedded poverty will remain a powerful generator of refugees in Somalia and much of the rest of Africa for the foreseeable future (see Figure 11.2).

Refugees and other forcibly displaced migrants are barometers of change in geopolitical pressure. A quick tally of newspaper headlines on international issues since the fall of the Berlin Wall would probably show that the most frequent

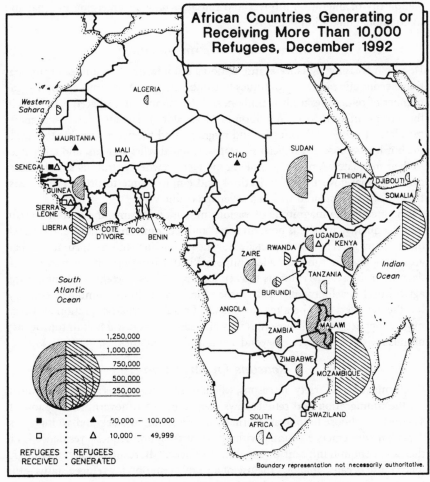

FIGURE 11.2   African countries generating or receiving more than 10,000 refugees, December, 1992. SOURCE: Office of the Geographer, U.S. Department of State.

and prominent stories were those stemming from Iraq's invasion of Kuwait and the breakup of the former Soviet Union and Yugoslavia. These three geopolitical changes have generated several million displaced persons, refugees, and new economic migrants. By the mid-1990s, there were no long-term solutions as to where these migrants will go and who will provide protection and relief assistance for them.

# International Migration and Refugee Trends

Over the next few years, several migration trends will influence international relations: increasing mobility at local, regional, and international levels; growing complexity of migration motives and causal factors; and merging internal and international migration patterns.

## *More People Are on the Move*

Despite increasing vigilance at international boundaries, the number of international economic migrants continues to climb beyond the 100-million mark—the number of refugees exceeds 18 million, and the number of displaced persons is in the tens of millions (over 18 million in Africa alone). The international agencies mandated to cope with refugees and migrants find themselves unable to handle the burden because of financial shortages, strained relief systems, and challenges to their mandates. A pressing issue for the 1990s is whether the UN should disregard national government objections and employ force to protect and assist those violently displaced within a sovereign country.

The greater the magnitude of various migration streams, the more powerful their cumulative impact is both on social and economic institutions and on each other. Many governments especially fear the population shift from rural to urban areas. At the same time, crowded, impoverished urban populations may intimidate urban-based governments to keep food prices low, thereby weakening rural agricultural development.[13] This "urban bias" varies from country to country, but the net effect may be a reinforcement of rural-to-urban migration and even more congested cities. These cities may also serve as a critical link in the journey of those wishing to migrate beyond a country's boundaries.

## *Reasons for Migration*

People move for a variety of reasons, which often overlap. This is a simple truism, yet the immigration and refugee laws created by many governments ignore it. These states choose to look at international migration in black-and-white terms: A person who enters a country without permission and requests residence is either an economic migrant or a political refugee.[14] Bureaucratically, this might make sense because it allows the use of a simple criterion for refugee status—the presence of persecution or civil war in the asylum applicant's home country. For some people, there is clear evidence that justifies asylum claims, such as when a military force clearly targets a group for elimination. For many other asylum seekers, though, such clear evidence is lacking, which results in buck-passing among governmental agencies and tensions between the country where the migrant first applies for asylum and other potential resettlement countries.

The lack of simple and distinct causal factors in migration is forcing refugee and immigration agencies to look more closely at the relationships between places of origin and destination. Forced migrations can be caused by a broad range of factors: invasion by a foreign army or civil war, organized persecution of a minority group (usually by a government), and life-threatening hardship from either economic or environmental crises. Often, these factors are closely intertwined, as they are in the Horn of Africa where militias have uprooted millions of peasants, killed off their herds, burned their crops, and stolen their food. Under such oppressive conditions, a drought can push hundreds of thousands of peasants and nomads over the edge from chronic malnutrition to death by starvation.

### Internal and International Migration

The presence of an international political boundary—an artificial construct that hinders the flow of people much more than it does the flow of capital, ideas, and goods—is the only significant feature that distinguishes international migration from internal migration. Much international migration today is also an extension of several decades of unprecedented urbanization around the world. In fact, many long-distance international migrations are really urban-to-urban migrations. "Global cities," with their closely interconnected business and financial networks, will likely remain the strongest magnets attracting international migrants.

The means that allow people to move—transportation networks, extended kinship connections, and more loosely structured, low-wage employment (the informal sector)—are facilitating both internal and international migration. A world with much more mobility within countries will foster much greater mobility among countries, unless draconian immigration policies are ruthlessly enforced. Efforts to discourage unwanted international migrations have had mixed results, and any success in returning "illegals" is usually only temporary.

## The New World's Disorderly Flows

Many refugee policies in Europe and North America were conceived within a Cold War context, in which "East and West" was divided by an impenetrable iron curtain. Asylum was virtually guaranteed to anyone who survived a crossing over the divide into the "free world." With the iron curtain essentially gone, Western governments are now reevaluating asylum policies, especially in light of increased applications from those fleeing formerly Communist states. Western governments have become tied up in legal and even constitutional conundrums over asylum claims, while trying to ignore much larger numbers of migrants who move because of grim destitution.

The next decade's international migration and refugee flows might be better understood within the context of a reordered world. These new world categories should not be based on ideological principles but on a wide disparity in economic opportunities among poor and rich countries. Within the framework of this world economy, three new types of migration emerge: among poor countries, among rich countries, and among rich and poor countries (see Figure 11.3).

## Migration Among Poor Countries

The vast majority of migrants and refugees move among the low-income countries, which usually have per capita yearly incomes of under $600. Impoverished countries such as Malawi, Sudan, and Pakistan have hosted hundreds of thousands of refugees. Without substantial international support, these groups would pose an intolerable strain on local populations, and even when long-term international support is provided, underlying socioeconomic conditions of chronic regional instability are rarely addressed. Some countries, such as Iraq and the former Yugoslavia (which once had somewhat favorable prospects for economic growth), have been embroiled in tragic wars, nationalist uprisings, and racial-ethnic-tribal conflicts that have destroyed fundamental economic structures. Even if peace is restored and displaced groups are returned home, their economies will take many years to recover, and many young people will want to leave in the interim.

The poorest countries of the world will continue to bear a disproportionate share of the migration and refugee burden. A difficult problem for the UN and NGO relief agencies concerns how the poor countries, which generate and receive most of the world's migrants and refugees, can be assisted without contributing to their permanent dependency on foreign aid. Deeply impoverished populations suffer from ecological degradation (especially soil erosion and inadequate water supplies) and declining per capita agricultural productivity, trends

| Characteristics of Migration | Global Migration Flows Among Countries | | |
|---|---|---|---|
| | Poor ←→ Poor | Rich ←→ Rich | Poor ←→ Rich |
| More Mobility | | | |
| Overlap of Causal Factors | | | |
| International/ Internal Migration Linkages | | | |

FIGURE 11.3   International migration and refugee flows.

that are very difficult to reverse and that help ensure the mass displacement of future populations.

## Migration Among Rich Countries

Given the worldwide economic problems, few countries are willing to admit that they are rich. Nevertheless, among the industrialized or developed countries, migration of highly skilled workers, managers employed by multinationals, and students help to integrate these countries more closely within an interdependent world economy. Migrants and travelers (including businesspeople and tourists) move among the global cities of the world, where identical hotels and fast food restaurants help make the cultural transitions much easier to endure. Excluding tourists, this is a small migration circuit—perhaps even in the tens of thousands—but it is important because it includes the world's key political and economic decision-makers.

## Migration Between Rich and Poor Countries

The movement of people from poor to rich countries is perhaps the most contentious arena of migration policy-making. Like other international migrations, it, too, is complicated and may involve quite distinct rich, poor, and middle-class migration streams and counterstreams. Historically, the migration of Europeans to the far-flung colonies (or from the present-day "rich" to the present-day "poor" countries) established economic, political, and cultural linkages.[15] But even within these historical migration streams, there were divisions between rich and poor, with wealthy migrants becoming major landholders and merchants in the colonies while the poor endured very harsh conditions as laborers. As with migration among rich countries, the migration of wealthy elites from poor or middle-income countries is usually not a problem because these people bring money with them.

The migration of poor migrants from poor to rich countries, in contrast, is now considered a major problem for industrialized nations undergoing economic recessions because poor migrants bring with them only their labor and their aspirations. Much of the antiforeigner backlash in Europe can be traced to the perception that poor people (usually from former colonies) are "flooding" into Europe, where they will take jobs away from locals. When the national economy is growing and unemployment is low (as in Germany in the 1960s), poor migrants are invited in as guest workers (as people from Turkey were); when the jobs are scarce, these same guests and their families are no longer welcome. As unemployment rates climb, immigrants become convenient scapegoats, and immigration and asylum policies become highly charged geopolitical issues.

## Global Disparity

These three generalized migration patterns reflect two global trends that will drive most international migration flows to unprecedented levels: the growing economic and demographic disparities between rich and poor countries. Poor countries generally have low rates of economic growth and high rates of population growth. Few have reasonable prospects of creating enough domestic jobs to keep up with the basic demands of the current and next generation of workers. Frustrated young adults in these poor countries—some with college educations—understand all too well that these global disparities will influence their future as well as their children's future. For many, the answer to this global inequity is simple in theory but difficult in practice: Move to a richer country with a smaller labor surplus.

## Conclusion

International migration has become a major domestic political issue in many countries and a major topic of debate. Thus far, most attention has centered on the plight of refugees or on ways to curb the flow of illegal immigrants. As more and more migrants cross international boundary lines, however, governments are realizing that immigration and asylum problems cannot be separated from broader socioeconomic and political issues, nor can they be resolved by countries acting unilaterally. Even with this understanding, attempts to develop multilateral strategies to ease international tensions arising from uncontrolled migrations will be complicated by economic disparities, regional political tensions, and mounting population and ecological pressures. If they hope to manage increasingly difficult refugee, migration, and humanitarian relief issues, UN agencies and NGOs will have to adopt programs that are designed to meet the needs of local groups affected by regional conflicts; their success will hinge on their ability to integrate geopolitical, economic, cultural, demographic, and ecological dimensions.

### Notes

The views expressed are those of the author and do not necessarily reflect those of the U.S. government.

1. Sadako Ogata, "Refugees and Migrants in the Post–Cold War Era," in *The Annual Meeting of the Trilateral Commission* (New York: The Trilateral Commission, 1992).
2. Lawrence Brown, *Place, Migration, and Development in the Third World* (London and New York: Routledge, 1991).
3. Philip Martin, *Illegal Immigration and the Colonization of the American Labor Market* (New York: Center for Immigration Studies, January 1986).
4. Frank Bean, Georges Vernez, and Charles B. Keely, *Opening and Closing the Doors—Evaluating Immigration Reform and Control* (Washington, D.C.: The Urban Institute Press, 1989).
5. Huw Jones, *A Population Geography* (London: Paul Chapman, 1990).
6. Alan Gilbert and Josef Gugler, *Cities, Poverty and Development: Urbanization in the Third World* (Oxford: Oxford University Press, 1982).
7. Everett Lee, "A Theory of Migration," *Demography,* vol. 3 (1966), pp. 47–57.

8. Wilbur Zelinsky, "The Hypothesis of the Mobility Transition," *Geographical Review,* vol. 61 (1971), pp. 219–249.

9. Michael Todaro, *Internal Migration in Developing Countries: A Review of Theory, Evidence, Methodology and Research Priorities* (Geneva: ILO, 1976).

10. George Demko and Roland Fuchs, eds., *Population Distribution Policies in Development Planning* (New York: UN Population Division, 1981).

11. Mary Kritz, ed., *U.S. Immigration and Refugee Policy* (Lexington, Mass.: Lexington Books, 1983); William R. Brubaker, ed., *Immigration and the Politics of Citizenship in Europe and North America* (Washington, D.C.: University Press of America, 1989).

12. Al Kamen, "Cold War Consensus on Refugee Aid Ebbing Despite Relentless Need," *Washington Post,* July 20, 1992, p. A8.

13. Michael Todaro and Jerry Stilkind, *City Bias and Rural Neglect: The Dilemma of Urban Development* (New York: The Population Council, 1981).

14. Leon Gordenker, *Refugees in International Politics* (New York: Columbia University Press, 1987).

15. Philip Ogden, *Migration and Geographical Change* (London: Cambridge University Press, 1984).

# PART THREE

Changing International Processes
and Relations

# TWELVE

## International Law and the Sovereign State: Challenges to the Status Quo

### ALEXANDER B. MURPHY

INTERNATIONAL LAW is a set of rules or principles that govern the actions and behavior of states. It is understood to encompass such matters as the right of one state to use force against another and the right of states to exercise control over ocean resources. But for all the importance of these kinds of international legal norms, a preoccupation with the role of international law as a simple regulator of state action can obscure a larger reality: that international law is the embodiment of widely accepted views of how territory should be organized and used. Indeed, the idea that the land surface of the earth should be divided up into more or less autonomous sovereign states is, itself, a principle of international law.

Comprehending the spatial organization of societies requires an understanding of the territorial ideas and arrangements expressed in and shaped by international law. How do particular ideas about the use of territory develop? How do they become implemented? And how does the implementation of these territorial concepts affect matters ranging from ethnic group relations to the alteration of the physical environment? This chapter focuses on the nature and significance of changing international legal norms with respect to territorial control. Particular attention is devoted to evolving concepts of state sovereignty and the ways in which international law reflects and shapes territorial organization and human-environment relations.

## The State in Contemporary International Law

The roots of the contemporary system of international governance may be traced to the fourteenth century, when Europe began to move out of an era in which territory was contested space over which feudal lords and kings vied for control. During this time, the declining influence of the church, the rise of mercantilism, and the development of more sophisticated military technology allowed authoritarian rulers in some parts of Europe to claim and enforce relatively exclusive control over substantial domains.[1] In the succeeding centuries, European legal scholars began to elaborate principles to govern relations among these self-proclaimed independent territorial units. Inspired by precedents set in ancient Greece as well as the political realities of the time, scholars such as Francisco de Vitoria (1480–1546) in Spain and Hugo Grotius (1583–1645) in Holland argued for a system of international relations based on the absolute sovereignty of states. From the perspective of these founders of modern international law, any political authority who exercised effective control over a significant territory was entitled to govern that territory free of outside interference.

The principle of territorial sovereignty assumed wider formal status with the signing of the Peace of Westphalia in 1648. Each party to the treaties ending the Thirty Years' War agreed to honor the boundaries of the others and to refrain from interfering in their internal affairs. In so doing, a fundamental principle of the international system was established. Although this principle is often violated, it nonetheless continues to be the legal and intellectual foundation on which societies claim to base their international relations.

## Modern States

The commitment to state territorial sovereignty took on a new form with the spread of the political ideas of the Enlightenment through Europe during the eighteenth and nineteenth centuries. Whereas the right to control territory had previously been viewed as the province of a ruling monarch, political legitimacy increasingly came to be seen as stemming from the rights of "the people." The people were understood to be a culturally cohesive community (a nation) that was entitled to control its own affairs. The Enlightenment worldview thus presupposed an international political order made up of discrete nations, each of which could be given its own autonomous territory, or nation-state. The extraordinary naïveté of this view is taken up elsewhere in this volume (see Chapter 4). The Enlightenment ushered in an era in Europe during which sovereign nation-states were assumed to be the political geographic ideal. Nations were seen as distinct political and cultural communities with the right to control their own affairs in a territory that offered security and freedom from outside oppression. The notion of territorial sovereignty thus acquired a new kind of legitimacy, one premised on the ideological bedrock of "national" rights.

## European Ideals

Europe embraced the nation-state ideal in the aftermath of the French Revolution. During the nineteenth and early twentieth centuries, the nation-state was incorporated into the national iconography of Europe's states, and great rhetorical deference was paid to it as Europe's great empires were carved up into states after World War I. Although there were many violations of national sovereignty during this period and although geopolitics played an extremely important role in the post–World War I negotiations over the fate of Central and Eastern Europe, states consistently acted in the name of a European order based on the principle of national territorial sovereignty. As such, the nation-states principle acquired the status of a fundamental norm of international relations in Europe.

Europe's global economic, political, and military reach meant that the European political order became the model for the emerging international state system. The Europeans did not treat their colonies as sovereign nation-states, considering them too "primitive" to have national communities and hence unable to enjoy the privileges of statehood. But the control that Europe and its North American offshoot exerted in international relations meant that any entity seeking freedom from colonial control and a place in the international order had to join a system that, at least in theory, was made up of sovereign nation-states. Ironically, twentieth-century independence movements to throw off the yoke of European colonialism could only succeed if they claimed a status that itself was a European creation.

## Questionable Sovereignty

The observance of state sovereignty has never been absolute, and more powerful states usually have been able to exert some control over the affairs of less powerful ones. Indeed, the control exerted by the Soviet Union over states in Eastern Europe from the close of World War II until the late 1980s, the assistance provided by the United States to the Nicaraguan contras in the 1980s, and Israel's maintenance of a security zone in southern Lebanon all seem to belie the notion of a world order built on state territorial sovereignty. Similarly, neither Afghanistan during the 1980s nor El Salvador today possesses anything like the same degree of sovereignty as that of the United States, Germany, or Japan.

Despite the many instances in which state sovereignty appears illusory, it remains a clearly articulated precept on which international relations are based. This can be seen in the major international legal instruments of the twentieth century. In 1919, the Covenant of the League of Nations bound all members "to respect and preserve as against external aggression the territorial integrity and existing political independence of all Members." Similarly, Article 2(7) of the Charter of the United Nations, adopted after World War II, holds that "nothing contained in the present Charter shall authorize the United Nations to intervene in matters which are essentially within the domestic jurisdiction of any state or shall require the Members to submit such matters to settlement under the present Charter." Embedded in these and countless other international legal instruments is the notion that state territorial sovereignty cannot be abridged by international law.

## Might Makes Right?

There exists, then, a conundrum. On the one hand, state territorial sovereignty appears to be a deeply rooted assumption of the international legal order. On the other hand, there are so many visible instances in which the sovereignty of one state is violated by another that it is tempting to dismiss that assumption as essentially meaningless. In analyses of international governance, this conundrum is often resolved by downplaying the issue of state sovereignty altogether: Territorial sovereignty is seen simply as a function of a state's economic and political might and therefore unworthy of serious consideration.[2] Yet by adopting this approach, the ramifications of a historically rooted commitment to the principle of state territorial sovereignty are left unexamined. To make such a point is not to deny the variable character of territorial sovereignty or the growing challenges to state autonomy that have accompanied international law in the last few decades. Rather, it is to suggest that there has been no clean break with the historically rooted commitment to the ideal of state territorial sovereignty. International relations continue to be influenced by the assumption that the world is made up of largely autonomous nation-states. And that assumption is an integral part of the international legal order.

## The Commitment to State Territorial Sovereignty

The broadest and most pervasive evidence that the commitment to state territorial sovereignty has some meaning is the fact that most issues and problems around the world tend to be conceptualized in state terms. Despite pervasive evidence of the international nature of issues ranging from poverty to environmental degradation, the individual state is usually seen as the appropriate political-geographic framework for confronting specific instances of these problems. Squatter settlements around Mexico City are thought to be Mexico's problem, the pollution of Lake Baikal is Russia's problem, and the conflict between the Tamils and the Sinhalese is Sri Lanka's problem. Indeed, for every instance in which international involvement occurs or is deemed appropriate, there are thousands in which the state is assumed to be the rightful controller of the situation. What this means in practice is that ecological, social, economic, and ethnic problems are generally confronted within political frameworks that do not bear any resemblance to the spatial-territorial dimensions of the problems themselves.

The norms of international diplomacy also confirm the influence that the concept of state territorial sovereignty has in the contemporary world. One remarkable feature of international relations is the general unwillingness of states to allow any party other than another state to sign an international agreement. This presumably reflects the assumption that states are the sole entities with the power or authority to assume international legal obligations. Even well-organized groups like the Palestine Liberation Organization have generally been able to participate in negotiations over international agreements only as members of another state's delegation. Moreover, international bodies have often refused to recognize claims that do not arise from states. Despite the avowed commitment of the United Nations to national self-determination, it has refused to support the claims for territorial autonomy of such groups as the Kurds and the Biafrans since the territories they seek to control lie within the boundaries of existing states.

Assumptions about the preeminent role of states in international relations are also evident in the foreign policy practices of most states. Typically, such policies are much more likely to be driven by reactions to the positions of other state governments, rather than to non-governmental actors within those states. Thus, during the 1970s and 1980s, U.S. foreign policy toward Iran was far more influenced by the actions of the shah and then the Ayatollah Khomeini than by anything else that was going on in that country. As a result, diplomats focus on the workings of government in foreign capitals, while often ignoring regional issues and problems.

The extent to which notions of state territorial sovereignty govern international relations is revealed in the skepticism that is often expressed about the notion of international law itself. How can there be international law, many ask, when the only real power rests with states? This view improperly equates law with effective, centralized enforcement—although such an approach would disqualify many domestic laws from being regarded as true laws—and it ignores the role of law as a standard against which most parties measure right and wrong. Moreover, it fails to take into consideration the pains to which states go, in most instances, to comply with international legal norms as well as the repercussions that can fall on a state for lack of compliance, ranging from economic sanctions to military intervention.

The strength of the myth that there is no true international law reflects the continuation of the centuries-old doctrine that state political authorities should be the arbiters of what happens within their boundaries. This myth, in turn, greatly complicates the task of garnering support in many countries for international initiatives. Indeed, it is one of the great impediments to the adoption of more sweeping international agreements over the world's oceans and seas.

## Territorial Conflicts

The power that the concept of state sovereignty holds in the modern world is strikingly demonstrated in the role it has played in international territorial conflict. Despite the invocations against attacking the territory of neighboring states found in international legal agreements, more than half of the world's states have been involved in some sort of territorial dispute with a neighbor since the close of World War II.[3] Such disputes may seem to illustrate the meaninglessness of the principle of state territorial sovereignty, but a more careful examination of them actually reveals the important role that the sovereignty principle plays in shaping the location and character of international conflicts.

During the past forty-five years, interstate territorial conflicts have almost always involved territory that one state could claim was wrongfully taken from it at some prior time.[4] In some cases, the claim may be weak, but usually there is some historical period when the territory was either within its domain or within the domain of a political-territorial antecedent of that state (a colony or an administrative territory within an empire). Why should this be? If interstate relations are based solely on political and economic power, why are the territories in dispute not simply those that offer the greatest riches or strategic advantages to states? Valuable territories often *are* in dispute, of course, but why has Japan pursued so aggressively its claim to a few small, sparsely inhabited islands northeast of Hokkaido (the Northern Territories) instead of more economically and militarily valuable islands farther north? And why does Venezuela persist in laying claim to agriculturally unproductive rain forest areas in Guyana instead of the oil-rich area of northern Colombia just across the border? The answers lie in the continuing vitality of state territorial sovereignty as a principle of international relations.

The pursuit by one state of a claim to territory in another requires that some sort of explicit justification be advanced, to rally support for the cause and to avoid international isolation or condemnation. To be successful, the claim must be "fair." Notions of fairness, however, are subjective and constantly changing. Since World War II, the dominant view has been that no state has the right to seize the territory of another. This principle, incorporated in most major international agreements, is a direct reflection of a commitment to territorial sovereignty.

The only generally recognized exception to this rule is that a state whose territory has been wrongfully seized by another may act to retake the "stolen" territory. Thus, if state X marches into state Y and seizes a third of its territory, state Y is generally thought to be justified in mounting an action to recover the territory, even if it takes some time for the necessary forces to be assembled. Without a statute of limitations for territorial "theft," a restitution claim can always be made without directly challenging dominant international understandings of justice.

## Justifying Claims

A variety of economic, political, cultural, and strategic motives are behind most interstate conflicts over territory.[5] Yet with few exceptions, the only *stated* reason for pursuing a territorial claim is to regain wrongfully appropriated land. Government leaders rarely declare, either before their own people or in front of the world community, that they are entitled to territory in a neighboring state because it would expand their domestic oil reserves or allow them to exert more effective control over the surrounding seas. Rather, whether it is Argentina claiming the Falkland Islands, China claiming territory across the Amur River in Russia, or Togo claiming part of eastern Ghana, the leaders argue that they are merely seeking to retake land that historically belonged to their state. Only by raising this type of argument can the state hope to gain national and international support for its cause since other possible arguments would overtly challenge notions of justice rooted in the ideology of state territorial sovereignty.

Articulated justifications for territorial claims, even if little more than hollow rhetoric, are not just meaningless statements; they have a significant impact on the pursuit of such claims and have shaped the geography of interstate territorial conflict. And because historical arguments are normally needed to justify territorial claims, states whose boundaries have not undergone significant changes are unlikely to raise extrastate claims to territory. This has been the case throughout much of Sub-Saharan Africa, which has experienced considerably fewer interstate conflicts over territory in the post–World War II era than has the Middle East, Latin America, or Asia.[6]

On a smaller scale, the reliance on territorial justifications can affect the nature and extent of the territories in dispute. Thus, Ecuador's claim to northern Peru (see Figure 12.1) cannot be understood merely as a quest to control an oil-producing region, as some have claimed. If Ecuador were concerned merely with enhancing its oil supplies, it could claim the oil fields around Talara in Peru or

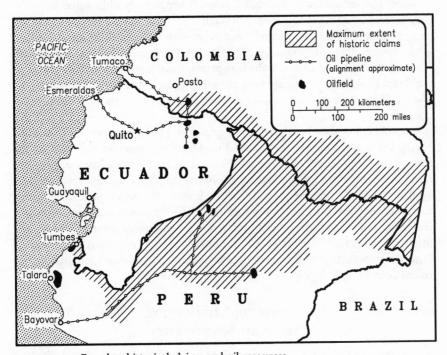

FIGURE 12.1   Ecuador: historical claims and oil resources.

those near Pasto in Colombia. The sole claim that Ecuador can hope to sustain in accordance with modern conceptions of justice is to the territory that was controlled by its colonial antecedent for a time during the Spanish occupation and that was awarded to Peru under questionable circumstances in a 1942 protocol witnessed by four other guarantor states. Since the legitimacy of Ecuador's claim would be compromised if its actions were not consistent with its claim, the state can push for no more and no less than the area that was in dispute at the time of the 1942 protocol.

The influence of the doctrine of state territorial sovereignty arguably extends beyond interstate conflicts over territory to the willingness of states to intervene in distant conflicts. A remarkable feature of the U.S.-led effort to retake Kuwait after Iraq's invasion of that country in 1990 was the large number of nations involved. Many have argued that the U.S. desire to retake Kuwait was motivated mostly by strategic and economic concerns. This may be true, but it does not explain why the United States was able to garner such widespread support from other governments. Nor does it explain why Washington has not sent troops into other places of great economic and strategic significance, such as Egypt after the Suez Canal was closed in 1967 or Yugoslavia after the Serbs attempted to crush the Croatian and Bosnian independence movements. The answer to these puzzles almost certainly lies in the powerful role that the concept of state sovereignty continues to play in the world today.

When Iraq invaded and annexed Kuwait, it temporarily obliterated from the map a recognized sovereign state. Although Iraq advanced a weak historical argument after the fact, the invasion was never widely regarded as an attempt to retake wrongfully appropriated territory. Rather, it was seen as a violation of both Kuwait's sovereignty and one of the core principles of international law. This legal argument provided the primary pretext for justifying military involvement by the United States, and it was essential to orchestrating broad support from other countries.

The concept of state territorial sovereignty thus plays important roles in influencing the ways in which international problems are understood as well as the foreign policy practices of states and the norms that govern international behavior. Consequently, it is misleading to dismiss the ideal of state sovereignty as a total sham simply because it is violated with some frequency. Instead, we must recognize the ideal for what it is: a historically rooted concept of human territorial organization that continues to influence, albeit sometimes in indirect ways, international actions and behavior. Although state sovereignty is still "sacred," however, important developments in international governance have unfolded in recent decades that impinge on significant aspects of it.

## Growing Challenges
## to State Sovereignty

As the interdependencies that characterize our world increase in complexity and visibility, more and more pressure is being brought to bear on sovereignty as an underlying precept of the international order.[7] In fact, it is difficult to think of any significant social problem that does not have some sort of international dimension, be it environmental pollution, civil strife, human rights violations, or government debt. Moreover, supranational aspects of these problems are fueling unprecedented growth in international law. This growth, in turn, is precipitating a subtle shift away from the state as the spatial unit within which problems are assumed to be most appropriately confronted. At the same time, the rise of substate nationalism and regionalism in the post–World War II era is challenging the sanctity of the state. Although traditional understandings of state sovereignty continue to color international relations in fundamental ways, it is an open question whether a shift away from the state signals the beginning of a more fundamental change in the spatial-territorial assumptions that undergird the international system.

Three important international legal developments exemplify the changing position of the state in international relations: the elaboration of a comprehensive set of rules governing ocean use and management, the incorporation of human rights principles into international law, and the rise of the European Community as an international actor. In each case, traditional notions of state sovereignty have been challenged, with implications for the current spatial-territorial order.

## Control and Use of the Seas

Historically, the open seas have not been subject to state jurisdiction. Resources of the open seas were assumed to be inexhaustible, and given their immensity, conflicts over use were minimal. Through the 1950s, states generally exercised exclusive control over the so-called territorial waters within 3 nautical miles of their coastlines.

The traditional treatment of the open ocean as a "commons" did not grow out of an abrogation of the principle of state sovereignty. It merely reflected the lack of any perceived need to exercise control over such a vast and limitless resource. Conflicts developed over various enclosed or semienclosed seas, and some states sought to extend the limits of their territorial waters, but the open seas were of little immediate concern to most states. Portions of the oceans began to change in the twentieth century, however, with the rapid expansion in oceangoing traffic, the discovery of valuable resources in the continental shelves, the overexploitation of certain ocean resources, and the growth of such potentially damaging activities as offshore oil drilling and the dumping of waste materials.

The initial reaction to these developments confirmed the traditional role that state sovereignty played. In 1945, following more than two decades of discussion about the need to codify the rights of individual states to ocean resources, the United States announced that it intended to exercise exclusive control over the resources of the continental shelf and adjacent waters within 200 miles of its coastline. The United States made clear that it did not intend to limit navigation outside its traditional territorial waters, but its actions prompted a spate of similar claims by other states. Some states did not stop with assertions of control over resources; in 1947, for example, Chile and Peru claimed exclusive sovereignty over the 200-mile-wide stretch of ocean extending from their shores.

Despite the adoption of conventions dealing with certain aspects of international control and use of the oceans over the next two decades, efforts to gain widespread support for a single, comprehensive approach to ocean governance were unsuccessful. By the late 1960s, states were making increasingly extravagant claims to ocean resources, and there was growing public concern over pollution, overfishing, and the military use of the seas. In 1967, the United Nations established a committee to explore the peaceful uses of the ocean, and in 1970, the UN General Assembly adopted a resolution calling for the seabed and ocean floor to be treated as a "common heritage of mankind." These events set the stage for a series of important international meetings on the law of the seas between 1973 and 1982, organized under the auspices of the United Nations. The meetings culminated with the adoption, by an overwhelming majority of participants, of the United Nations Convention on the Law of the Sea.

In brief, the convention calls for a uniform 12-mile territorial sea over which states have exclusive authority (with the exception of "innocent passage") and a 200-mile exclusive economic zone (EEZ) in which states can exercise sovereign rights over resources. The remaining seas are treated as commons but not in the sense that they are open to unrestricted use by any state. Rather, they are to be used for peaceful purposes and are subject to rules on resource exploitation and scientific research established by the International Seabed Authority. The convention represents, at least in part, a departure from the traditional idea that individual states have ultimate control over the surface of the earth. Instead of dividing the oceans into national territories, the convention calls for the establishment of a cooperative system with rules articulated not by the individual states but by an international authority.

Many issues were left unresolved, and much in the convention reaffirms the principle of state sovereignty including the nature and extent of the territorial waters and the EEZ. Even though the overwhelming majority of states signed the convention, several influential states—including the United States, the United Kingdom, and West Germany (now Germany)—refused to do so. The United States in particular has objected to the convention's restrictions on deep seabed mining. Yet despite these problems, the convention represents a significant milestone in the management and use of the oceans. Even nonsignators like the United States accept that much of the convention embodies customary international law, and to that extent, they have been willing to abide by it. In 1983, the United States even declared its own EEZ in accordance with the principles set forth in the convention.

From a broader perspective, the convention demonstrates a willingness on the part of the international community to confront a major issue in a manner that transcends traditional concepts of state sovereignty. It provides the frame of reference against which decisions and actions with respect to the oceans are now judged. No longer are the open seas seen as domains of exclusive state sovereignty or as realms within which states can do what they please. Instead, increasing attention has been directed to such issues as the functioning of international regulatory bodies, the need for regional seas cooperation, and future uses of the oceans.

# Human Rights

States have long recognized an international legal obligation to respect the basic rights of visitors from foreign countries. But until quite recently, it was assumed that the treatment of nationals within a state was beyond the purview of international law. Indeed, there is no better example of the status of state territorial sovereignty than the free hand most states had in dealing with their own citizens. The first real challenge to this did not come until World War II, when "the atrocities of the Third Reich brought home that large-scale deprivations of human rights not only decimate individuals or groups but endanger peace and security."[8] As a direct consequence, the protection of human rights became one of the primary stated objectives of the United Nations. The International Commission of Human Rights was convened after the war, and, in 1948, the UN adopted, without dissent, the commission's Universal Declaration of Human Rights (several countries did, however, abstain, including the Soviet Union, Yugoslavia, and Saudi Arabia).

The declaration set forth fundamental principles for the treatment of peoples in all states, and though not legally binding, it has been quite influential. Over the next four decades, many countries adopted statutory and constitutional provisions consistent with it. The declaration also led to the adoption of several important international conventions on human rights in the 1960s and 1970s, and current domestic and international legal instruments pertaining to human rights demonstrate a widespread commitment, at least in theory, to the idea that states have a duty to safeguard the basic human rights of their citizens. States are believed to be obligated to protect their citizens, to guarantee them equal protection of the law, and to grant them fundamental political, social, and economic rights.[9] Willful violations of these obligations may provide sufficient grounds for international condemnation and even sanctions.

The precise international legal status of much of human rights law is disputed. In practice, the commitment to state sovereignty is still sufficiently strong that human rights violations by themselves rarely provide adequate grounds for international intervention. Nonetheless, the international recognition of human rights principles has fundamentally challenged the nineteenth-century view that states have unlimited freedom to treat their citizens in whatever manner they please. Some states have even incorporated international understandings of human rights into their domestic legal codes.

The imposition of economic sanctions against South Africa in the 1980s largely grew out of international reaction to the state-supported system of apartheid. Crude and undiplomatic actions have also been taken in response to reports by governmental and non-governmental organizations on the human rights records of particular governments. One of the stated reasons for deferring Turkey's application to join the European Community, for example, was its weak human rights record.

The extent to which an international commitment to human rights has undermined traditional notions of sovereignty is most clearly seen in the international response to the plight of the Kurds and the Shiite Moslems in Iraq after the Persian Gulf War. The plight of the Kurds in northern Iraq prompted the United Nations Security Council to adopt a resolution in April 1991 stating that a government could be required to accept foreign aid. This, in turn, was used as the legal basis for the U.S., British, and French establishment of a "security zone" in northern Iraq for the returning Kurds. In a further effort to protect the rights of minority groups in Iraq, internationally sanctioned "no-fly" zones were established first in northern Iraq where the Kurds live and then in the Shiite-dominated south. Any Iraqi military plane that flies in these areas was threatened with attack from outside forces. Since these measures followed a major armed conflict, they are, in a sense, extraordinary. But they also signal that there are limits to international tolerance of what a recognized state can do against its citizens.

State sovereignty has not, however, become irrelevant in the human rights realm; most states are still reluctant to become involved in human rights issues within other states without some kind of external or special provocation. Furthermore, human rights principles are now enshrined in the international state system: "As a corollary of its membership in the international community, every state is under a duty to respect the human rights and fundamental freedoms of every human being and to subject itself to legitimate measures of international scrutiny that the international community is entitled to utilize to ensure protection of human rights and fundamental freedoms."[10] Human rights advocacy may not be universally accepted, but it is indicative of a trend toward viewing the protection of such rights as an obligation that transcends the sovereign territorial rights of states.

## The Special Case
## of the European Community

Most efforts at encouraging regional cooperation have had little impact on state sovereignty. The European Community (EC) is a marked exception. From a modest beginning in the late 1950s, the EC has come to represent by far the most ambitious effort at interstate regional cooperation in modern history. The twelve member states (the Netherlands, Belgium, Luxembourg, France, Germany, Italy, Denmark, the United Kingdom, Ireland, Greece, Spain, and Portugal) have vested substantial authority in the central institutions of the European Community on matters ranging from agricultural subsidies to environmental pollution.

The EC is often thought of simply as a common market—an interstate area in which the marketing of goods and services is unaffected by common international boundaries. In fact, a common market was the major thrust of European integration in its early stages, but it soon became clear that closely coordinated economic policies among the member states were required. Such matters as environmental quality standards and regional socioeconomic differences also brought the integration process into sharper focus. As a result, the EC gradually developed more powerful central governmental institutions with authority to promulgate a variety of rules and regulations.

EC-wide laws now deal with the movement of goods and people across boundaries, monetary exchange rates, basic environmental standards, transportation, working conditions, regional development, and much more. Despite the broad reach of EC legislation, the majority of the rules do not directly challenge the sovereignty of member states. Until very recently, most major EC decisions could not be made without the unanimous support of member countries, and significant realms of economic and political decision-making have remained within their purview. To conclude, however, that the EC has few implications for the doctrine of state sovereignty is to ignore some fundamental institutional developments within Europe over the past two decades.

When the central institutions of the EC were established, substantial authority was vested in a bureaucracy located in Brussels. This bureaucracy, which encompasses some 14,000 functionaries who do not act officially on behalf of individual countries, comprises the staff of the Commission of the European Communities. Although lacking the power to adopt legislation in many areas, the commission is the driving force of the EC because it alone makes proposals for rules and regulations. It also is responsible for implementing EC rules and managing the EC's budget.

The commission's proposals can only be adopted by the Council of Ministers, made up of representatives from member states. Traditionally, any proposal involving an essential interest of a member state could only be adopted by a unanimous vote. Although the essential interest doctrine was frequently invoked, many important decisions during the 1970s and 1980s were made simply by majority vote. But with the adoption of the Single European Act, the requirement for unanimous consent has been greatly curtailed. Now, all that is necessary to pass major legislation in such areas as farm subsidies and environmental regulation is a qualified majority (whereby the votes of larger countries are weighted more heavily than those of the smaller countries, allowing two or more large countries to block an affirmative vote).

In practice, EC member states have ceded important aspects of their sovereignty to these centralized institutions. Proposals considered for implementation, for example, emanate from an extrastate bureaucracy, and many are enacted without unanimous consent; nonetheless, they are accepted as law by the member states. The EC may be moving in the direction of even closer economic relations, and it is exploring an expanded political capacity. Denmark's 1992 rejection of the Maastricht Treaty, which calls for closer economic and political union by the end of the 1990s, is a sign of the continued strength of national differences within Europe and the hesitancy of many to cede local powers to a distant bureaucracy. But any significant revocation of the core economic and social powers that have been vested in the institutions of the EC is unlikely.

The implications of European integration for state sovereignty extend beyond the movement of the EC into realms traditionally controlled by states. As barriers between member states continue to weaken, the ability of local governments and businesses to forge links across international boundaries is enhanced. Cross-border regional cooperation schemes are growing, such as those along the Upper Rhine between France and Germany, and significant economic and cultural links are developing among geographically dispersed regions within different states.[11] A striking example of this is the cooperation agreement entered into by Rhône-Alps (France), Baden-Württemberg (Germany), Catalonia (Spain), and Lombardy (Italy) in 1990 (Figure 12.2). These developments expand the range of international activity that is beyond state government control. New EC programs

FIGURE 12.2   Regions participating in the "Four Motors" agreement.

have been developed to encourage even closer cross-border and interregional co-operation. Although most cooperation schemes are still controlled by the state, the importance of state sovereignty will diminish as they expand.

Since the EC itself is a creation of international law and since it, in turn, makes international laws, EC developments have implications beyond Europe. One important indication of this is that the EC has increasingly been treated by other states as an international actor analogous to a sovereign state. During the crisis in Yugoslavia in the early 1990s, it was the EC, as much or more than any individual state, that was looked to as a potential intervener. Precedents established by the EC are also regarded in other parts of the world as bases for interstate cooperation. The newly created Commonwealth of Independent States (most of the Republics of the former Soviet Union), as well as the free trade agreements between Mexico, Canada, and the United States are institutional structures derived, at least in part, from the EC model. The future stability of these regional cooperation schemes may be in doubt, but the institutional structure of the EC will still be viewed as a pioneering, forward-looking response to regional issues and problems. Since the EC structure embodies a departure from the traditional norms of international governance, its acceptance represents a formidable challenge to the notion that a successful international state system must be premised on state territorial sovereignty.

## Conclusion

Despite indications that its ideological power is weakening, state sovereignty remains an important organizing force in the modern world. The preeminent position it holds is revealed most strikingly in the place that the political map occupies in our conceptualizations of the world around us. If people are familiar with any map of the world at all, it is likely to be the map of so-called sovereign states. How many people, when they think of South America, have a mental picture of a continent divided up into different physiographic regions or different ethnic areas or different vegetation zones? All these are interesting and important divisions within South America, yet most people who know anything at all about the continent think of a map showing Brazil, Argentina, Chile, and the like. Moreover, our descriptions of the world are based on the political map; when references are made to the Ganges Plain or the humid subtropical climate zone of South Asia, the states of India, Pakistan, and Bangladesh immediately come to mind.

The habitual use of political maps as frameworks for thinking about the world reflects a tacit assumption: that the units shown on those maps are meaningful spatial compartments for considering most international issues. This assumption, which has its roots in the concept of state sovereignty, has been woven into the norms of international governance over the past few centuries and is likely to be with us for some time to come. But human society and its norms of governance are not static. As the twentieth century draws to a close, the traditional concept of the state is being challenged by several key trends: growing economic interdependencies among states; the development of transportation, communication, and information technologies that facilitate international linkages; the rise of substate nationalism; and the growth of an extrastate corporate culture. As those challenges become more apparent, the conceptual hegemony of state sovereignty is likely to come under more critical scrutiny. Though the legacy of the Peace of Westphalia remains very much with us, its future is increasingly clouded.

## Notes

1. Jean Gottmann, *The Significance of Territory* (Charlottesville: University of Virginia Press, 1973).

2. Peter J. Taylor, "Contra Political Geography," in *Tijdschrift voor Economische en Sociale Geografie* (forthcoming 1994).

3. Alan J. Day, ed., *Border and Territorial Disputes,* 2d ed. (Harlow, England: Longman Group, 1987).

4. Alexander B. Murphy, "Historical Justifications for Territorial Claims," *Annals of the Association of American Geographers,* vol. 80, no. 4 (1990), pp. 531–548.

5. Andrew F. Burghardt, "The Bases of Territorial Claims," *The Geographical Review,* vol. 63, no. 2 (1973), pp. 225–245.

6. Herman Van der Wusten, "The Geography of Conflict Since 1945," in *The Geography of Peace and War,* D. Pepper and A. Jenkins, eds. (Oxford: Basil Blackwell, 1985), pp. 13–18.

7. Stephen D. Krasner, "Sovereignty: An Institutional Perspective," *Comparative Political Studies,* vol. 21, no. 1 (1988), pp. 66–94.

8. Lung-Chu Chen, *An Introduction to Contemporary International Law: A Policy Oriented Approach,* vol. 204 (New Haven: Yale University Press, 1989).

9. Ibid.

10. B.G. Ramcharan, "Strategies for the International Protection of Human Rights in the 1990s," *Human Rights Quarterly,* vol. 13 (1991), pp. 1655–1669.

11. Alexander B. Murphy, "Emerging Regional Linkages Within the European Community: Challenging the Dominance of the State," in *Tijdschrift voor Economische en Sociale Geografie* (forthcoming 1994).

# THIRTEEN

## The Fourth World: Nations Versus States

### BERNARD NIETSCHMANN

IN THE EARLY 1980s, new perspectives and theories emerged to explain persistent global patterns of ethnocide and ecocide that resulted from attempts by 168 international states to occupy, suppress, and exploit more than 5,000 nations. These ideas came to be known as the Fourth World theory or the Fourth World perspective, referring to the 5,000 to 8,000 ancient but internationally unrecognized nations of the Fourth World that predate and continue to resist the spread of the modern state. Fourth World theory was developed by a diverse group of individuals—activists, human rights lawyers, and academics but principally leaders of resisting nations—who shared information, ideas, and resistance strategies in meetings and by photocopy, mail, telephone, fax, computer modem, and computer bulletin boards.

Unlike the traditional geopolitical research and writing of academics, politicians, and journalists, Fourth World analysis cannot be accessed by a library card. This is because: (1) Fourth World theory seeks to change the world, not just describe and publish an article about it; (2) Fourth World advocates rely on the electronic circulation of firsthand information; and (3) it is counterproductive to discuss plans, strategies, and an overall theory that are aimed at resisting and reversing the territorial and political occupation of nations by states.

## Nations and Peoples

The fundamentally different starting point of Fourth World analysis is that it describes and maps geography, history, and politics based on the world's 5,000 nations, instead of focusing on states, regions, blocs, and superpowers as traditional analyses do. This produces a dramatically distinct, "ground-up" portrait of the significance and centrality of people in most world issues, problems, and solutions. Traditional studies interpret the world as enclosed by a fixed, legal network of some 191 international states that relegate people to the nationless status of ethnic groups and minorities. Fourth World analysis, by contrast, examines how colonial empires and modern states invaded and now occupy most of the world's 5,000 legitimate nations and peoples. It also explores how this destructive expansion jeopardizes the world's biological and cultural diversity and ultimately rebounds to break down and break up states.

To understand this different geopolitical perspective, it is necessary to carefully examine the meaning and use of several basic political terms: *nation, state, nation-state, a people,* and *an ethnic group.* The misuse of these and related terms distorts and obscures the identity, geography, and reasons behind most wars, refugee flows, genocide, and human rights violations as well as much of the environmental destruction. In almost every textbook, academic or newspaper article, and TV or radio news program, the terms *state, nation, nation-state, people,* and *ethnic group* are misused without regard to common usage either among the world's distinct peoples or in the world's dictionaries. *Nation, state,* and *nation-state,* for example, are used interchangeably even though their origins, geographies, histories, and structures are very different.

## Nation

The term *nation* refers to the geographically bounded territory of a common people as well as to the people themselves. A nation is a cultural territory made up of communities of individuals who see themselves as "one people" on the basis of common ancestry, history, society, institutions, ideology, language, territory, and, often, religion. A person is born into a specific nation by being born a Kurd, a Basque, or a Tibetan, for instance. An outsider cannot become a Tibetan by moving to Tibet. Nor can an outsider become Basque by learning to speak Basque, by moving to Euzkadi and becoming a citizen of Spain, or by being born in Euzkadi: To be Basque is to be born Basque. Thus, a nation is both the cultural homeland of a people and a people who have a cultural homeland. Furthermore, a nation is self-identifying: If Spain and all the other states in the world did not recognize or even mention Catalonia, it would still exist and persist as it has for hundreds of years. The existence of nations is ancient; they came into existence slowly and usually do not celebrate a date or year when they were created. Having developed in every region and on every continent, there are currently some 5,000 to 8,000 nations, of all shapes and sizes.

A nation, then, is a community of self-identifying people who have a common culture and a historically common territory. And because no group of people has ever voluntarily given up its territory, resources, or identity, a nation is the world's most enduring, persistent, and resistant organization of people and territory. The majority of the territory and resources of continents, islands, and coastal and continental shelf waters have long been claimed and used by nations.

# A People

Like a nation, a people is self-defined. A people considers itself to be distinct from other peoples, adjacent or far, who may, in turn, recognize the difference. A people is characterized by: a common history, a common geographical location and territory, racial or ethnic ties, cultural or linguistic ties, religious or ideological ties, a common economic base, and a sufficient number of individuals to maintain a common identity. Every people is a nation.

## States and Ethnic Groups

The modern state is an outgrowth of European kingdoms, overseas colonialism, and the division of large colonial empires into smaller and smaller neocolonial pieces.

The term *a state* is used to define a centralized political system within international legal boundaries recognized by other states. Further, it uses a civilian-military bureaucracy to establish one government and to enforce one set of institutions and laws. It typically has one language, one economy, one claim over all resources, one currency, one flag, and sometimes one religion. This system is imposed on many preexisting nations and peoples.

A state is a legal creation that comes into existence on a specific date, giving every person and all peoples within the new artificial boundaries a fresh international identity: Soviet, Bangladeshi, Yugoslavian, and so on. (Somehow, the founders of the United States neglected to create an accurate name for the new country: *American* applies to the hemisphere, not to a citizen of the United States. Spanish, not English, has an appropriate term: *estadounidense*, "United-statesian.") Having gone to bed "Nicaraguan" one night in 1960, members of the Miskito nation living north of the Río Coco (Wangki) woke up "Honduran" the next day because the International Court of Justice ruled on a boundary dispute between the two states. Similarly, in a story on the rise and fall of states in Europe, the *New York Times* gave an account of what happened to one man in the Hungarian region of Eastern Europe: "Mr. Csukas's life story encapsulates the shifting fortunes of Hungarians living on the border of what was, before 1918, one of Europe's bigger nations. He has been a citizen of five different countries, but has never left the narrow strip of rural villages along what is now the border between Hungary and Slovakia."[1]

Imposed upon unconsenting nations, states then create a new history and geography to make it appear that their birth and expansion predate, preclude, and prevent all preexisting national claims to territory, people, or resources. The main goal is to create the illusion that the nations are under state authority. Nowhere are states depicted as recent intrusions whose authority derives from force (two-thirds of the world's states use their armies against people they claim as citizens), intimidation (the most widespread and numerous human rights violations are committed by states against nation peoples), and "statespeak" (states train academics, journalists, and government people to think, speak, and write correctly about the state—any state). For example, in the text that accompanies *The Times Atlas of China,* Tibet is not described as being occupied by Han China; instead, the Tibetans are said to "occupy" a region of China. Nor is Tibet described as having been militarily invaded by China in 1950; rather, we are told that Tibet was finally brought under firm Chinese central control after the rebellion of 1959, and in 1965 the Tibet Autonomous Region was set up to administer the area. Similarly, in *A Map History of China,*[2] Brian Catchpole writes the following in a chapter on "The Minority Peoples":

> Scattered across China are millions of people belonging to fifty-one nationalities. Most of them live in the frontier regions which are vital to China's security. China needs to be sure of the loyalty and cooperation of these people and is anxious to integrate them fully into the People's Republic. This is why China fosters the growth of cooperatives and communes among people who until recently were primitive hunters, herdsmen or "slash-and-burn" farmers, and why she strives to make them literate and capable of exploiting to the full the industrial and agricultural potential of their homelands.

A Fourth World translation of this quote might read a bit differently:

> The Han have extended and expanded the state of China to enclose, divide, and fragment more than 150 non-Han peoples and their nations. Many of these nations are in state border regions and have been divided and occupied by China, India, the USSR, Vietnam, Burma, Mongolia, and other states. Han China has sent its army and assimilation experts to force these nations to give allegiance and transfer sovereignty to Beijing. This is why Han China uses cooperatives and communes to replace the economies and communities of non-Han peoples, such as the Kazakh, Kirghiz, Tibetan, Uighur, Tadzhik, Miao, Lisu and Lahu, and to exploit and plunder their homelands.

All states attempt to erase the histories and geographies of the peoples they occupy: New names for new state peoples are invented, new maps are made, and new histories are written. These new "scripts" are then given to the schools and media to re-educate the various groups, teaching them that they are now "one people" living in "one nation."

Though most states assert that they are a single nation with a single common people, some 95 percent of the the world's 191 current states are multinational, that is, composed of the peoples and territories of many nations, sometimes without their consent. These states assert sovereignty over the 5,000 or more nations and peoples on earth as well as all the continents, 40 percent of the oceans, and even the reaches of the atmosphere. Compared to nations, these states are new, and they range in size from Nauru with a population of 10,000 and Belize and the Bahamas with some 200,000 each to Indonesia, which stretches across 3,000 miles, 13,700 islands, and 250 nations and has the world's fourth-largest population.

A nation-state is rare. Only a few—less than 5 percent—of the world's states are nation-states, where well over a majority of the population is a single people. A common people with a common identity, a common territory, and a government that is internationally recognized is a nation-state. Thus, Iceland and Portugal are nation-states. Most states are multinational, such as Nigeria with 450 nations, Ethiopia with 90, and India with 350.

States try to become nations through nation-building programs based on political, cultural, and territorial integration and development and education. They seek to create a common unity through the creation of common symbols, such as a flag, national anthem, history, and school-map geography. To help accomplish this, all states have institutions (schools, universities, and media) that produce histories and school-map geographies to create a sense of common place and destiny for a common people. When Italy was first unified in the mid-nineteenth century, Italian nationalist statesman d'Azaglio remarked, "We have made Italy, now we have to make Italians."

When states themselves speak of nation-building, however, what they actually mean, in most cases, is state-building by destroying nations (see Table 13.1). One of the most common state-building tactics is the creation of terms to describe both new state peoples and preexisting nation peoples. For example, when a state is created (most often by war, expansion, occupation, legacy of colonialism, or the breakup of a larger state), new terms are invented to refer collectively to all the distinct peoples within an internationally recognized territory. These are artificial identities that have to be taught by central government institutions—unlike nation identity, which is learned through culture, family, and language

TABLE 13.1  *Terminology of "Nation-building" and Fourth World Translation*

| Terminology of Nation-building by Nation-destroying States | Fourth World Translation |
| --- | --- |
| an ethnic group | a state-occupied people and homeland |
| an ethnolinguistic group | a nation stripped of all but language |
| a people | a state people instantly created |
| a nation | an ideal of multinational states |
| nation-building | state-building by nation-destroying |
| political integration | invasion |
| state economy | systematic plunder of nations |
| economic development | occupation and resource plunder |
| assimilation | ethnocide |
| nation-building | nation-destroying |
| peasants | unnamed members of an unnamed nation |
| separatists | a nation that never joined a state |
| rebels | a large group of armed nation people |
| terrorists | a small group of armed nation people |
| national liberation | colonialism by non-Europeans |
| national security | state military occupation of nations |
| the national interest | the state interest |

and which may disappear overnight (as happened to Soviet, Czechoslovak, and Yugoslav state identities but not to Russian, Ukranian, Slovak, and Bosnian nation identities).

Almost no nation people in the world calls itself by the terms used by most academics, journalists, and state government and military leaders: *ethnic groups, minorities, peasants, tribes, herders, agriculturalists, lower class,* or, simply, *a group, a population,* or *the poor.* From the Fourth World perspective, all these terms have the common purpose of supporting the state by suppressing the nation. They do not identify any nation people, they do not identify any nation place, and they do not identify any nation activity.

All nation peoples have a name for themselves and their territories, and most seek self-determination and resist incorporation into one or more states. Therefore, states invented a terminology to try to render invisible the independent and autonomous peoples and nations that were being invaded and incorporated as state citizens and state lands. However, totally different histories, geographies, and problems are revealed by using terms like *Karen* instead of *a Thai hill tribe, Tigreans* instead of *Ethiopian peasants, Palestinians* instead of *an Israeli ethnic group, Kurds* instead of *mountain Turks, Yapti Tasba* instead of *eastern Nicaragua,* or *West Papua* instead of *Irian Jaya.*

In the international context, a people has rights to self-determination, sovereignty, and national territory (UN Resolution 1514). But because almost all states are formed over unconsenting peoples and nations, recognition of them *as* a people would jeopardize state territorial claims. Therefore, the world's nation peoples are almost universally referred by generic, faceless, and placeless names.

If nation peoples take up arms against a state invasion and occupation, they will be referred to as *rebels, separatists, extremists, dissidents, insurgents, terrorists, fanatics, mercenaries,* or *Communists* but almost never by their real names and real places. For example, what nation peoples were fighting in the 1980s and early 1990s in southern Sudan, Kashmir, Burma, Iraq, Turkey, Angola, and West Papua?

Fourth World analysis, writings, and maps replace the missing identities, geographies, and histories of the world's peoples and nations that make up the usually hidden "other side" in the invasions and occupations that produce most of the world's wars, refugees, genocide, human rights violations, and environmental destruction.

*Ethnic* originally meant "heathen" or referred to nations that were neither Jewish nor Christian. Today, the word is widely misused to mean any nonwhite people who are not in power. In common usage, *ethnic group* implies a people who are *outside* their original country and are in another people's country, who maintain their identity, and who are a *group* within a state that they do not govern. Tibetans in India or Nepal might be called an ethnic group, but in Tibet they are *a people,* not an ethnic group or a "national minority." Similarly, a people within its homeland is a people, not an ethnic group. An ethnic group within its own nation is a contradiction in terms.

During the 1984 peace negotiations in Bogotá, Colombia, Sandinista commander Luis Carrión asked resistance leader Brooklyn Rivera if the Miskito would accept special status as a Nicaraguan ethnic group. Rivera replied, "Ethnic groups run restaurants. We are a people. We have an army. We want self-determination."[3]

Ethnic groups are placeless minorities within a state. According to the United Nations Human Rights Sub-Commission, a *minority* is defined as a group numerically smaller than the rest of the population of a State, in a nondominant position, whose members—being citizens of the State—possess ethnic, religious, or linguistic characteristics differing from those of others in the population and who show, if only implicitly, a sense of solidarity directed toward preserving their culture, tradition, religion, and livelihood.

Nothing is mentioned in this state-based definition of *a minority* (the state term for a people and its nation) of the people's history of independence, self-government, tradition of nationhood, and desire to preserve control over its own territory, resources, affairs, and freedoms. According to the United Nations and almost all individual states, nation peoples are but minorities (or ethnic groups) that may keep their folklore while the state takes their land, resources, and freedom. This is why almost no nation people living within their homeland, even if it is occupied, accept being called an ethnic group or minority. (See Table 13.2.)

TABLE 13.2   *Some Differences Between States and Nations*

|  | *Nation* | *State* |
|---|---|---|
| DEFINITION | Those of a common culture and homeland who have evolved into a territorially based and self-defined identifying people with shared aspirations | A military and civilian bureau-legal authority to represent a body of diverse people within the borders established by territorial expansion, wars, or treaties |
| LATIN WORD ORIGIN | *Natio, nacio:* born into a place (*Nat*-ive) | *Status Rei Publicae* (Roman Legal Code); later *Stato* (Machiavelli). |
| BOUNDARIES | Cultural | Political-military (legal) |
| COMPOSITION OF POPULATION | A single nation | Multinational |
| ORIGINS | Historical, "evolutionary" | Datable and designed (constitutional) |
| RECOGNITION | Self-identifying, taught within culture | By other states (legal), taught within schools/media |
| MEMBERSHIP | Kinship, culture | Citizenship |
| COHESION | Culture, custom | Ideals, laws, force |
| GROUP MOVEMENTS | Nationalism (the recognition and defense of one's homeland) | Patriotism (loyalty to the state) |

SOURCE: Rich Griggs, "The 130 Nations of Europe," *Research and Exploration,* vol. 10, no. 1 (February 1994).

Oren Lyons is a faithkeeper of the Onondaga Nation, a member nation of the Haudenosaunee (Six Nations) Confederacy. He offers an interesting perspective on these issues: "We are the original people on the land. We are the land keepers. We are not a minority within our own nations, within our own lands. One must understand that terminology is very important. How you address yourself is very important to them. If you try and change your terminology, you will find out how important it is. So we must speak of ourselves as a people. . . . If you fall into the category of 'tribes' or 'bands,' a gaggle of geese, a herd, a group . . . you're more than that. It's important not to call Indians 'bands.'"[4]

## Types of Nations

Political science and political geography focus, in large part, on states: types, differences, systems of governments, spatial dimensions of politics, and geopolitics. Fourth World theory focuses on nations: what they are, where they are, their geopolitics, and their different types. Distinguishing nation types is an important developing area of Fourth World theory. With some 5,000 nations in the world today, there obviously must be a variety of types. To be sure, nations could be studied and understood in terms of their cultural, political, and economic systems (of which there are many hundreds of types, with some having promise of wider application) and in terms of the geopolitical significance of their resources, strategic locations, and emerging "green cartel." However, at this point in analyzing nations, research on the Fourth World has categorized them all in terms relating to the state. (See Table 13.3.)

## State-building:
## The Theory of the Repressive State

The vast majority of all nations existed before all states. This means that thousands of nations and associated peoples and cultures were already distributed over the earth's space before states were invented. Given that almost all territory was already occupied, states could only gain a foothold and eventually expand (state-building) by somehow taking over the territories and populations of nations.

A few of the thousands of existing nations sought to become more powerful and richer by expanding and taking over other nations in order to form empires and satellite colonies and eventually to consolidate the occupied territories and peoples as new states.[5] State-building was based on three strategies: (1) convince nations to voluntarily give up their independence and submit themselves to being ruled by outsiders; (2) invade, occupy, and then acculturate (or deculturate) nations so that they identify with state-manufactured identity and culture; and (3) invade, occupy, and repress resistance by genocide, ethnocide, ecocide, or

TABLE 13.3    *Types of Nations*

| | |
|---|---|
| Autonomous nations | Nations that have endured long-standing state attempts at cultural and territorial assimilation and whose autonomy is recognized by the state, e.g., Catalonia, Kuna Yala |
| Enduring nations | Nations that have endured long-standing state attempts at cultural and territorial assimilation and have achieved a partial or limited autonomy, e.g., Saamiland, Yapti Tasba |
| Renascent nations | Historical nations that are becoming stronger by cultural renaissance and political movements seeking greater political recognition, e.g., Scotland, Wales |
| Remnant nations | Long-dormant nations (low levels of cultural activity) that have weak, incipient national movements, regenerating because of the example of neighboring nations |
| Nation cores of states | Most states have and are run by nation cores that become both the point of expansion and the hegemonic culture of the idealized nation-state, e.g., England/UK, Russia/USSR, Castile/Spain, Java/Indonesia, Han/China |
| Irredenta | Parts of nation cores of states lost to states by treaty or war. In some cases, groups within the "broken piece." Nations see themselves being ruled by the "wrong" state, e.g., Northern Ireland |
| Recognized nations | Nations that endured state occupation and won independence, e.g., Latvia, Estonia, Lithuania, Eritrea |
| Fragmented nations | Many nations are occupied by two or more states, which often hinders political mobilization and territorial reconsolidation, e.g., Kurdistan is occupied by 5 states, Saamiland by 4, and Kawthoolei (in Burma) by 2 |
| Militarily occupied nations | Many nations have all or part of their territories militarily occupied by one or more states, e.g., the northern one-third of the Miskito nation is occupied by Honduras, and the southern two-thirds have partial autonomy |
| Armed resistance nations | Of the world's 120-some wars (as of April 1993), 80 percent involved Fourth World nations resisting state military forces, e.g., Kawthoolei versus Burma, West Papua versus Indonesia, East Timor versus Indonesia, Chittagong Hill Tracts versus Bangladesh, Saharawi Republic versus Morocco |

forced removal or displacement. Historical sociologist Charles Tilly succinctly characterizes state-building when he writes: "War made the state and the state made war."[6]

State-building is part of a worldwide process that appears to follow a progression of chronological and spatial stages. All of these begin at different times and take place at different rates with individual states. Thus, at any given time, the many stages of state-building appear to exist simultaneously.

To help clarify this geographic-historical concept of process, let us first consider coral reefs. Similar to stars, mountains, deserts, and states, the creation of a coral reef is a large-scale historical-geographical process that includes varied stages that can be studied to unravel and explain the sequence of the process itself. For example, aboard the HMS *Beagle* in 1936, Charles Darwin studied coral reefs and proposed in his "Subsidence Theory" (1841) that the presence of different types of shallow-water coral reefs in the deep ocean could be explained by the subsidence of volcanic islands and the upward growth of corals (from reefless volcano to fringing reef to atoll). Darwin reasoned that all of the island-reef types he observed were part of a single, geographic-historical process. Harvard professor Steven Jay Gould writes of Darwin's coral reef study:

> His book is about coral but it is also about historical reasoning. . . . Since large-scale processes begin at different times and proceed at diverse rates, the varied stages of different examples should exist simultaneously in the present. To establish history in such cases, we must construct a theory that will explain a series of present phenomena as stages of a single historical process. The method is quite general. Darwin used it to explain the formation of coral reefs. We invoke it today to infer the history of stars. Darwin also employed it to establish organic evolution itself. Some species are just beginning to split from their ancestors, others are midway through the process, still others are on the verge of completing it.[7]

My own "theory of the repressive state" suggests that "state-building" by nation-destruction—like the formation of stars, deserts, or coral reefs—proceeds through various stages, many of which may exist simultaneously. Most state governments share and replicate state-building strategies. Because the common underpinnings of such strategies are force and tyranny, most are repressive and are reeled out with but minor variations (Table 13.4). The theory postulates that since no nation voluntarily gives up its independence, state-building proceeds through various military and legal mopping-up stages. Thus, if one studies what is happening between states and nations at any one time (e.g., the interactions in 1993 between 191 states and 5,000 or more nations), the series of present phenomena can be understood as stages of a single historical geographic process. This has immense potential for the defense of nations and for an understanding of the buildup and breakup of states. For example, for their 1981–1989 defensive war against the Nicaraguan state, the Miskitos' Misurasata and Yatama armed resistance forces studied several Fourth World wars, including Kawthoolei versus Burma (1948– ), Eritrea versus Ethiopia (1961–1991), West Papua versus Indonesia (1962– ), East Timor versus Indonesia (1975– ), and the Saharawi Republic versus Morocco (1975– ). From these and other similar conflicts, a chronological and spatial model was constructed of common state strategies for invasion, occupation, and justification. Construction and analysis of the model and theory helped the Miskito resistance to anticipate and prepare for Nicaraguan state-building strategies and to accelerate their military and political strategies for autonomy. In 1982, Miskitos were arrested and killed by the Sandinistas for demanding autonomy; by 1987, the Sandinistas were forced to include autonomy

TABLE 13.4  *The Repressive State: A Historical-Geographic Sequence of State-building (abbreviated from a fifty-stage model)*

Stage 1: Establish a geographic-historical reason for the state to expand
- manifest destiny
- the targeted nation is a "natural" part of the state
- the state must have a "pathway to the sea" or "security over its international borders"

Stage 2: Establish the infrastructure for invasion and annexation
- build roads, airfields, and communication lines
- offer and send in technical assistance
- send in missionaries and academics
- offer jobs in exchange for helping develop natural resources (oil fields, mining of minerals, forestry, hydroelectric power)

Stage 3: Create a justification for the invasion
- the people are starving
- terrorists or drug traffickers are operating in the area
- the area is being used as a base for attacks against the state
- the new road, dam, mine, oil field, or forestry project is threatened
- the local people have requested help from the state army
- the local people are but wandering, primitive groups and really have no capacity to efficiently use the resources or to develop themselves

Stage 4: Invade under the mantle of liberation and development
- the underdevelopment will be ended in the region
- the region will be freed from colonial or neighboring-state domination
- the region's impoverished people will be developed, given medical and educational services, and set free from the yoke of misery and poverty

Stage 5: Dismantle and replace the nation's social, economic, political, religious, and educational leadership, institutions, and structures with those of the state

Stage 6: Move in state citizens and international companies and ask international organizations to pay
- occupation by resettlement programs for state peoples
- exploitation of natural resources
- "protection" of natural resources ("national parks")

Stage 7: Condemn the first signs of political resistance
- resistance is due to tribalism, ethnic hatred, racism
- resistance is due to the region having a retarded history, being backward

Stage 8: Denounce the first signs of armed resistance
- instigated by a neighboring enemy state
- caused by mercenaries, bandits, terrorists, Communists
- caused by "the new Communists": drug traffickers or fundamentalist Moslems
- caused by the CIA (the KGB is no longer strong enough to be blamed)

Stage 9: Put nation peoples into the state armies and into the occupation government
- attempt to blur the "we versus them" conflict
- break cultural ties when nation people get shot at by nation people

Stage 10: If armed resistance has any meaningful successes, crack down on the civilians in the occupied nation—the "rice-or-bullets policy"
- burn communities and crops
- create curfews and identity cards

(Continues)

TABLE 13.4 (Continued)

- control access to and distribution of food and medical supplies
- use arbitrary brutality to terrorize people into submission
- arrest and imprison leaders and kill their followers
- force nation people to flee (often backfires because as international refugees, nation peoples may be able to inform the world and to support resistance)

Stage 11: Create a plausible reason for or plausible denial of "the troubles"
- the half-lie: tell the truth about what is known, lie about the rest
- it is the enemy; the state is protecting the people
- the enemy has agents and friends in the international press
- exactly what happened may never be known

Stage 12: Relocate civilians into state camps
- isolate civilians from supporting armed resistance (food, information, shelter, recruits, morale)
- divide nation into state-controlled zones and free-fire zone
- locate state camps away from international borders
- refer to the state camps as economic development and new communities

Stage 13: Develop "talk-and-shoot" strategy
- offer amnesty to resistance leaders and their forces
- create a bogus "we are you" agenda
- admit some "excesses" and promise a new deal
- upgrade military with more helicopters and better communications
- reorganize traditional military forces into smaller "guerrilla-hunter" units that track down and eliminate nation resistance forces—tell the world peace is at hand

Stage 14: Call for a vote to legitimize the occupation
- this is to be done when state has moved a numerical majority into the occupied nation
- could be a vote or a UN-supervised referendum

Stage 15: Settle down for decades of low-intensity resistance
- the state will maintain an expensive military occupation
- the resistance will try to economically bleed the state by three strategies: (1) continue small ambushes and sabotages that force the state to keep a large and expensive military in the field; (2) destroy or disrupt all state economic exploitation of nation resources; and (3) through external political and environmental activism, block state receipt of "development" (occupation) funds from international sources

in the Nicaraguan constitution; and in 1990, the Miskitos elected a Miskito government for the autonomous Región Autónoma del Atlántico Norte (RAAN) area.

## State-Nation Conflicts

States and nations represent two seemingly irrepressible forces in collision: states, with their large armies, expansionist ideologies and economies, and international state-support networks, and nations, with their historical and geographic tenacity anchored by the most indestructible of all human inventions—place-based culture. After many years of geographical conflict, the end of the Cold War and the demise of the Soviet Union have lessened the superpower control that once repressively "stabilized" many world regions. As a result, many nations are now moving to disentangle themselves from state occupation. These efforts form the conflicts of the 1990s and those to come in the first decade of the new millennium. Judging from conflicts in the recent past, the wars for self-determination that will be waged in the next two decades will take millions of lives and produce millions of refugees.

State versus nation conflicts since World War II have produced the most numerous and the longest wars, the greatest number of civilian casualties from state-directed genocide, the greatest number of refugees, and the fewest peaceful solutions (Table 13.5).

Despite the fact that most of the world's wars, refugees, and genocide are the result of conflicts over territory and resources between states and nations, they generally do not come under international laws, rules, instruments, conventions, or agreements. States make international laws. It is no wonder, then, that attempts to protect some nations by amending the Geneva Convention of August 12, 1949 (the "rules of war" that resulted from the atrocities committed against civilians and prisoners of war in World War II), were voted down. From the point of view of the state, only "terrorists" resist state takeover.

Without new international laws and policies regarding nations, much of the world will continue to look on, revolted but paralyzed, as the deaths from state-nation conflicts mount.

TABLE 13.5   *Human Dimensions of the State Wars Against the Fourth World*

| 1993 wars[a] | State versus nation | 97 |
|---|---|---|
| | State versus state | 1 |
| | State versus insurgency | 15 |
| | Nation versus nation | 6 |
| | Nation versus insurgency | 3 |
| | | 122 |
| Average duration of wars, 1945–1993 | State versus state | 2.8 yrs. |
| | State versus nation | 10.2 yrs. |
| 1993 refugees | Nation and state refugees recognized by the UNHCR | 18,000,000 (est.) |
| | Nation and state refugees not recognized by the UNHCR | 18,000,000 (est.) 36,000,000 [b] |
| State-directed genocide against nation peoples, 1945–1993 | 73,500,000 deaths, 81% of all genocide | |

[a]Updated from calculations in Bernard Nietschmann, "The Third World War," *Cultural Survival Quarterly,* vol. 11, no. 3 (1987).
[b]Of which some 20 million are from nations.

## State Breakdown and Breakup

More than 90 percent of all states that have ever existed have broken up. And modern states and their territories are still breaking down and breaking up: In 1945, there were 72 states and colonies; by mid-1993, the total had risen to 191, with the new ones mainly coming from the breakup of European state colonies (in Africa, South and Southeast Asia, the Pacific, and the Caribbean) and the breakup of the Soviet Union, Yugoslavia, Czechoslovakia, and Ethiopia.

Breakdown and breakup are natural parts in the life cycle of a state. As artificial creations, most states are but fragile, centralized, and expansionist empires imposed on unconsenting nations and held together by laws, force, and patriotic symbols. States break down when they become stretched too far, both economically and geographically: The political and economic costs of the occupations exceed the returns, and the empire becomes too expensive to maintain. For example, if one nation resistance person with an AK-47 automatic rifle and 500 rounds of ammunition ($500) shoots off one 30-round clip ($10.00), the occupation state may respond by buying a $1.2-million-dollar Mi-25 helicopter gunship and spending $4,000 to put it in the air for a few hours.

The common strategies of state-building by nation-destroying sows the seeds for the state's eventual breakdown or breakup. As states become overextended militarily or economically, they become even more restrictive, repressive, and environmentally destructive, hastening their demise. Indeed, as Leopold Kohr notes, the sheer size and complexity of many states dooms them to breakdown.[8] Kohr's very simple yet powerful idea—and the theme of his book—is that when something is wrong, chances are it is too big to operate well. Arnold Toynbee has shown that collapse invariably results from "forcible political unification in a universal state," and Lewis Mumford argues that the consolidation of nations under a central government in large cities was accompanied by the creation of empires, classes, slaves, protests, disorder, repression, environmental ruin, and the waging of more and bigger wars. To interrupt this destructive cycle, Kohr recommends small, democratic, autonomous regions. In place of France, Germany, Russia, and Italy, he suggests forty or fifty Venezias, Lombardies, Savoys, Burgundies, and Estonias.

Kohr's vision, more than fifty years old, is coming true as European states break down and break up. In Europe, two simultaneous forces impinge upon the state and the notion of state sovereignty: the creation of the European Community—with no borders or passports and a single currency—and, with the exception of Bosnia, the successes of Europe's 100 nations that, for the most part, are centers of economic booms and political stability.

Indeed, when states are faced with internal disintegration due to political unrest, economic stagnation, and environmental devastation, they usually select solutions that often hasten breakdown. They may expand further (e.g., the USSR's movement into Afghanistan, Argentina's into the Falklands, Morocco's into Saharawi Republic); apply more repression (e.g., Ethiopia, Nicaragua, Guatemala, and Sri Lanka in the 1980s and Burma in the 1980s and 1990s); loosen up economic control but maintain the political and military occupation of nations (e.g., the USSR in the late 1980s); try to decentralize as little as possible within the existing state system (e.g., Canada and Quebec and home rule for indigenous peoples in the north); or develop a new method of international governance based on federations or confederations of nations that run their own affairs domestically and loosely unite to run the affairs of regions (trade, pollution, communications, defense, and illegal drugs).

Russia, China, India, Pakistan, Indonesia, Afghanistan, and South Africa are examples of multinational state empires that may be too large, too environmentally destructive, and too repressive and occupy too many nations to avoid or prevent breakdown and breakup.

## Cultural and Biological Diversity

The diversity of life on the planet consists of both biological diversity—the variety of species, genes, and environments—and cultural diversity—the variety of peoples, knowledge, and landscapes. Cultural and biological diversities are the building blocks of life. And where there is a concentration of nation peoples (cultural diversity), there is typically a concentration of species, genes, and ecosystems (biological diversity). For example, a poster-size map published by the National Geographic Society and entitled "The Coexistence of Indigenous Peoples and Natural Environments in Central America," dramatically shows that this region's remaining tropical forests are almost exclusively in the territories of indigenous nations, which compose some 40 percent of Central America's area and 25 percent of its population.[9] The geographic overlap of nations and biological diversity appears to be a general worldwide pattern. Indeed, the vast majority of the world's 5,000 nations are centers of surviving biological diversity and ecological variety.

Because most nation peoples depend upon local biological resources that occur within their historical, traditional territories, they have evolved lifeways generally adapted to sustaining environments and conserving biological diversity. This is called the theory of Fourth World environments: Where there are nation peoples with an intact, self-governed homeland, there are still biologically rich environments. A physical map of the world aptly demonstrates this, showing that the still-forested areas of the world are areas lived in by nation peoples. The converse is equally striking: State environments—where the non–nation peoples live—are almost always areas of destructive deforestation, desertification, massive freshwater depletion and pollution, and large-scale reduction of genetic-biological diversity.

From the Fourth World perspective, the world's states are but internationally recognized governments that begin without environments or resources; it is the preexisting nations that have the land, freshwater, fertile soils, forests, minerals, fisheries, and wildlife. As such, most states exist only by the invasion and takeover (called nation-building, political integration, or economic development) of unconsenting nations' environments and resources. Following an ideology of centrifugal expansion to fuel unchecked growth, many states commonly use environmental and resource-destroying methods and often military force to extract the biological wealth and suppress the culture of nations.

The history and geography of state expansion versus nation resistance have produced two remarkably different kinds of environments in the world. First, there are *state environments*, dominated by new state cultures and state peoples— usually characterized by large and dense numbers, environmentally unsustainable centrifugal economies, biological impoverishment, and, most often, razed landscapes. Second, there are *nation environments*, historically populated by nation peoples and characterized by ecologically adapted, centripetal cultures and economies, surviving biological richness, and variegated, healthy landscapes.

Seeing that biodiversity is not evenly distributed over the earth's surface but concentrated in certain areas due to geographic factors (range of topography, latitude, and isolation), biologists identified twelve "megadiversity" states where some 60 to 70 percent of the world's biodiversity is found. However, the Fourth World perspective requires that this interpretation be rethought: Biodiversity occurs in the nations claimed by the states, not in the states; if biodiversity were under state control, it would be gone. (See Table 13.6.)

From the First and Third World state perspective, the 2,310 nations—46 percent of the world total—and all the biodiversity within these twelve states' territories are state citizens and state resources, respectively, to be centrally governed and exploited. From the Fourth World perspective, however, states are expansionist and destroy nature and nations, and the central governments in these particular states—from Australia to Zaire—all have track records of destruction. The

TABLE 13.6    *The Coexistence of Biological Diversity and Nations*

| "Megadiversity State" | Number of Occupied Nations |
|---|---|
| Australia | 250 |
| Brazil | 210 |
| China | 150 |
| Colombia | 60 |
| Ecuador | 35 |
| India | 380 |
| Indonesia | 670 |
| Madagascar | 20 |
| Malaysia | 20 |
| Mexico | 240 |
| Peru | 65 |
| Zaire | 210 |
| Total | 2,310 |

SOURCE: Alan Thein Durning, "Guardians of the Land: Indigenous Peoples and the Health of the Earth," *Worldwatch Paper no. 112* (Washington, D.C.: Worldwatch Institute, 1992).

exceptionally high cultural and biological diversity in these and other areas exists in spite of, not because of, state rule.

The Convention on Biological Diversity, signed by about 150 countries at the Earth Summit in Rio de Janeiro in 1992 and by the United States in 1993, promotes plans to manage and protect global biological and environmental resources. To be sure, these are worthy and important goals, but most agreements have been made without consulting any of the nations whose lands and waters contain the vast bulk of surviving biodiversity, whose cultures contain the knowledge and experience to maintain biodiversity, and whose peoples have protected biodiversity. The First and Third World perspective is that the states will decide how best to use and protect biodiversity for development, relegating nations to the status of local communities that may be asked for assistance. In contrast, the Fourth World perspective is that the biodiversity that remains within nation territories should be protected and managed for the benefit of nations, not states: The biodiversity does not belong to the states, who would only destroy it by expansionist consumption.

The new environmentalism recognizes that one of the best ways to protect the world's surviving biodiversity is to support nation rights, territories, and self-determination. The next advances in conservation will be accomplished by ensuring nation self-determination.

## Nation Self-Determination

Because they are occupied parts of states, nations will not be "given" self-determination. Self-determination is something that is taken, not given; it is achieved by economic, political, and military force, not by the goodwill of state governments. A wide array of nation self-determination movements exist globally, and many nations have achieved various measures of self-determination within their territories (Table 13.7).

Though many nations recently have become independent, such as the Ukraine, Latvia, Estonia, and Lithuania, the self-determination goals of most

TABLE 13.7 *Nations Exercising Self-Determination Within Autonomous Areas*

The Inuit in Nunavut (Northwest Territories, Canada)
The Dene and Metis people in northern Canada
The Inuit in Kalaalit Nunaat (Greenland)
The Miskito in Yapti Tasba (RAAN, northeastern Nicaragua)
The Kuna in Kuna Yala (Caribbean coast of Panama)
The Bontoc and other Cordillera nations (North Central Luzon, Philippines)
The Naga in Nagaland (northeast India)
The Catalans in Catalonia (northeast Spain)
The Basques in Euzkadi (northwest Spain)
The Faeroe Islanders, Faeroe Islands (Denmark)
The Corsicans, Corsica (France)

others is to achieve self-rule within their territories and then work out other political arrangements with either the old state or a new state made up of a federation of nations. Meanwhile, these new "nation states" are creating tensions with "nonnatives" who may have resided in them for several generations.

It is apparent, then, that a new political architecture is developing globally, formed from the cultural boundaries of nations. States come and go—nations remain.

## Notes

1. *New York Times,* January 25, 1993.

2. Brian Catchpole, *A Map History of China* (London: Heinemann Educational Books, 1982).

3. Bernard Nietschmann, "The Third World War," *Cultural Survival Quarterly,* vol. 11, no. 3 (1987), p. 4.

4. Oren Lyons, "When You Are Talking About Client Relationships, You Are Talking About the Future of Nations," *Rethinking Indian Law* (New York: National Lawyers' Guild, Committee on Native American Struggles, 1982), p. iv.

5. Also identified as the process of nationalism, this is a complex and long-term endeavor.

6. Charles Tilly, "Reflections on the History of European State Making," in *The Formation of National States in Western Europe,* Charles Tilly, ed. (Princeton: Princeton University Press, 1975), p. 42.

7. Stephen Jay Gould, *Hen's Teeth and Horse's Toes* (New York: Norton, 1983).

8. Kohr stated this in his 1941 essay "Disunion Now: A Plea for a Society Based on Small Autonomous Units," included in the 1957 reprint of *The Breakdown of Nations* (New York: E. P. Dutton).

9. "The Coexistence of Indigenous Peoples and Natural Environments in Central America," map published by *Research and Exploration* (Summer 1992).

# FOURTEEN

## The United Nations and NGOs: Future Roles

### CHRISTINE DRAKE

IN THE RAPIDLY CHANGING WORLD following the end of the Cold War and the demise of the Soviet Union, new states are being created at an unprecedented rate, and old ethnic and economic tensions are erupting into new conflicts. At one level, regional associations are being strengthened as countries agree to give up some of their sovereignty to create larger economic and political groupings. Paradoxically, though, nationalistic feelings are becoming much stronger, and tensions among peoples, ethnic groups, tribes, and even clans are boiling over into open conflict. National boundaries have become more permeable, and national sovereignty less sacrosanct. Some even argue that in today's increasingly interdependent world, the nation-state concept—upon which the present international world order is based—is an anachronism and a hindrance to world peace and to solving many global problems. To progress toward the resolution of conflicts, identity and loyalty to ethnic and national units must increasingly be redirected toward regional and international entities.

Changes are also occurring among country blocs. Throughout most of the history of the United Nations, the growing number of member countries aligned themselves with either the United States and its allies or the Soviet bloc, despite the facade of the Nonaligned Movement (NAM, or Group of 77), which claimed neutrality but included such obviously partisan countries as Cuba, South Yemen, and Vietnam. Since the end of the Cold War, the Soviet bloc has all but disappeared, and increasingly, the world seems to be aligning itself along a north (developed)–south (developing) division. The power and wealth found overwhelmingly on the side of the north have a profound impact on the working of the UN. In the General Assembly, where each country has an equal voice (and vote), the north is completely dominated by the south. But the General Assembly has no direct law-making authority, and its resolutions are nonbinding, taking the form of recommendations and declarations only; thus, they can be ignored by the north. However, the conventions it passes, when ratified by enough states, do become part of international law. Even here, though, nonparticipation by a great power can undermine or weaken the impact of a convention, as can be clearly seen in the U.S. failure to sign many conventions (including that on the Law of the Sea). This situation of numerical domination by the south also exists in the Economic and Social Council (ECOSOC), where approximately 80 percent of the UN budget is allocated. But although developing countries are in the majority in ECOSOC and can pass resolutions favorable to their own interests by majority vote, implementation depends upon financial support from the developed world. As a result, although the fifty-four members of ECOSOC are supposed to rotate on and off the council every three years, in practice, the permanent members of the Security Council are regularly reelected. Despite their lack of power, developing countries see the UN as an important forum for debate, for drawing the world's attention to serious problems, and for tempering the dominance of the rich north (see Figure 14.1).

In such a fast-changing, contentious, and interdependent world, the need for a more effective and stronger United Nations has never been greater in order to accomplish the major goals for which the UN was established: "to maintain international peace and security (and to that end to take effective collective measures for the prevention and removal of threats to the peace . . . ); to develop friendly relations among nations based on respect for the principle of equal rights and self-determination of peoples; and to achieve international cooperation in solving international problems of an economic, social, cultural, or humanitarian character, and in promoting and encouraging respect for human rights and fundamental freedoms for all."[1]

Although the goals of the United Nations, as established in the UN Charter, remain the same, its roles have changed since its founding in 1945. Changes include the decreased emphasis on decolonization now that almost all former colonies have become independent; an increased emphasis on the protection of human rights and on human rights monitoring, even including a greater willingness to intervene in the internal affairs of sovereign countries; more focus on election monitoring; increased responsibility for meeting humanitarian needs in catastrophic situations; and a greater effort to deal with some of the transnational problems that confront the world today—such as environmental deterioration, the growing gap between rich and poor countries, entrenched malnutrition and poverty, the international drug trade, arms proliferation, the spread of weapons of mass destruction, and the AIDS pandemic. In addition to the UN, a whole range of other intergovernmental and non-governmental organizations (IGOs and NGOs), some regional and some issue-specific, are also involved in trying to solve regional global problems, generally working cooperatively but sometimes competitively.

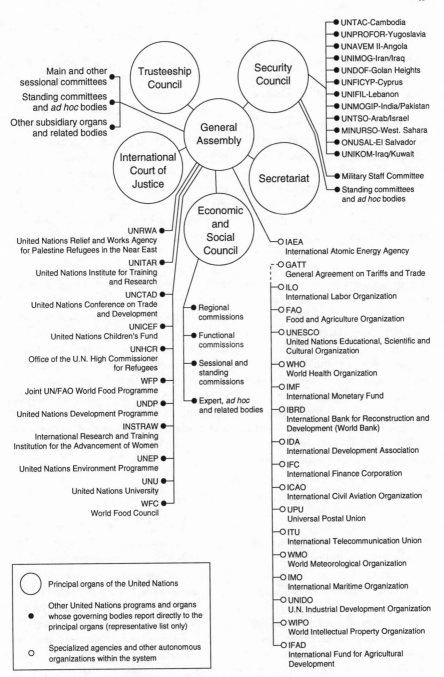

Main and other sessional committees

Standing committees and *ad hoc* bodies

Other subsidiary organs and related bodies

Trusteeship Council

Security Council

● UNTAC-Cambodia
● UNPROFOR-Yugoslavia
● UNAVEM II-Angola
● UNIMOG-Iran/Iraq
● UNDOF-Golan Heights
● UNFICYP-Cyprus
● UNIFIL-Lebanon
● UNMOGIP-India/Pakistan
● UNTSO-Arab/Israel
● MINURSO-West. Sahara
● ONUSAL-El Salvador
● UNIKOM-Iraq/Kuwait

General Assembly

International Court of Justice

Secretariat

● Military Staff Committee
● Standing committees and *ad hoc* bodies

UNRWA ●
United Nations Relief and Works Agency
for Palestine Refugees in the Near East

UNITAR ●
United Nations Institute for Training
and Research

UNCTAD ●
United Nations Conference on Trade
and Development

UNICEF ●
United Nations Children's Fund

UNHCR ●
Office of the U.N. High Commissioner
for Refugees

WFP ●
Joint UN/FAO World Food Programme

UNDP ●
United Nations Development Programme

INSTRAW ●
International Research and Training
Institution for the Advancement of Women

UNEP ●
United Nations Environment Programme

UNU ●
United Nations University

WFC ●
World Food Council

Economic and Social Council

● Regional commissions

● Functional commissions

● Sessional and standing commissions

● Expert, *ad hoc* and related bodies

O IAEA
International Atomic Energy Agency

O GATT
General Agreement on Tariffs and Trade

O ILO
International Labor Organization

O FAO
Food and Agriculture Organization

O UNESCO
United Nations Educational, Scientific and
Cultural Organization

O WHO
World Health Organization

O IMF
International Monetary Fund

O IBRD
International Bank for Reconstruction and
Development (World Bank)

O IDA
International Development Association

O IFC
International Finance Corporation

O ICAO
International Civil Aviation Organization

O UPU
Universal Postal Union

O ITU
International Telecommunication Union

O WMO
World Meteorological Organization

O IMO
International Maritime Organization

O UNIDO
U.N. Industrial Development Organization

O WIPO
World Intellectual Property Organization

O IFAD
International Fund for Agricultural
Development

○ Principal organs of the United Nations

● Other United Nations programs and organs
whose governing bodies report directly to the
principal organs (representative list only)

O Specialized agencies and other autonomous
organizations within the system

FIGURE 14.1   The United Nations system.

## Composition of the United Nations

The UN started in 1945 with 51 member countries. In its first decade, it grew slowly, with the United States and USSR each blocking the admission of states sympathetic to the other. Then, in a compromise, 16 new members were admitted at once, and from 1960 onward, membership increased rapidly as former colonies became independent and joined the world body. After the demise of the Soviet Union in December 1991, the breakup of Yugoslavia and Czechoslovakia, and the admission of other countries, including North and South Korea, Micronesia, the Marshall Islands, and San Marino, the number quickly grew, reaching 181 by early 1993. Membership is now all but universal, with only Switzerland refusing to join because of its intense neutrality. South Africa, whose delegates' credentials have been rejected since 1974 because of its governmental policy of apartheid, is expected to become a full, participating member again in the near future, as soon as majority rule is established.

Nations without states have thus far been excluded from membership. Despite serious attempts by the Arab countries to have Palestine recognized as a member, the United States has blocked its application for membership and, indeed, has threatened to withhold funds and withdraw from any UN-related organization that accepts the State of Palestine or the Palestine Liberation Organization into membership. Other national groups without recognized states, like the Kurds and the Sikhs, are unlikely to be accepted into membership in the UN. However, membership can be expected to grow as more states break up, such as the rest of Yugoslavia and Ethiopia; as microstates like Monaco and Andorra follow Liechtenstein's and San Marino's example in applying for membership; and as the last vestiges of colonialism are eradicated (for example, among the small island groups in the Pacific). It is also possible that more groups may be accepted into observer status, as Palestine has been.

## Changing Views on Sovereignty and International Intervention

The UN Charter, ratified as a multinational treaty in 1945, is based on a number of principles, including democracy, self-determination, parliamentarianism, majoritarianism, the rule of law and justice, and the separation of powers. Other principles are specifically set forth in Article 2 of the charter: the sovereign equality of all members, good-faith fulfillment of charter obligations, peaceful settlement of international disputes, nonuse of force or the threat of force for aggressive purposes, support for UN enforcement action, and nonintervention in matters that are essentially within a state's domestic jurisdiction. Together, these principles constitute the basic rules of international conduct that all member states theoretically are committed to observe, although such principles remain as ideals or guidelines for action rather than practiced laws.

Indeed, some of these principles are increasingly seen as contradictory and inconsistent since the peaceful settlement of disputes, protection of human rights, control of weapons of mass destruction, and protection of the environment may necessitate outside intervention in the form of inspections and other means of external involvement in countries' internal affairs. In 1974, Inis Claude pointed out the inherent dilemma in trying to protect both a nation's sovereignty or "domestic jurisdiction" and the right of the international community to intervene. He commented that the restriction not to intervene in matters under the domestic jurisdiction of member states means "almost nothing" because ratification of the charter by a state puts "practically every conceivable subject . . . into the international domain so that there is precious little domestic jurisdiction left to infringe upon."[2] Alternatively, if the domestic jurisdiction clause is accepted in an absolute way, then most of the charter is vitiated. The issue therefore lies in the interpretation of and the balance between the rights of individual states and those of the international community. This issue is exemplified most clearly in the recent debates over the enforcement of human rights in such countries as Bosnia-Herzegovina, the establishment of order in Somalia, and the relief operations on behalf of the Kurds in Iraq. In our increasingly interdependent world, the sovereignty of states appears to be eroding while the authority of the international community is expanding.

The shift in the understanding and acceptance of sovereignty has been most apparent since the end of the Cold War; until then, the use of the veto in the Security Council prevented almost every attempt at collective UN intervention in countries' internal affairs. The threat of retaliation also severely limited unilateral intervention by the United States or USSR, at least in the internal affairs of a country within the other superpower's sphere of influence. Thus, for example, little was done to assist the Tibetans in preventing the destruction of their culture by the Chinese or to protest human rights violations, famine, or the destruction of the environment in the Soviet Union and its allies. The United Nations was also largely impotent in trying to end wars that were primarily caused by East-West tensions. Only since 1989 have significant changes occurred in the level and intensity of UN involvement in the internal affairs of countries, particularly in Cambodia, Iraq, Somalia, and the former Yugoslavia.

Fundamentally, sovereignty permits independent states to pursue their own interests within their bounded territory only as long as they act to protect their citizens and do not destroy each other or the international system of which they are a part. In other words, sovereignty comes with obligations and responsibilities, which are spelled out in the UN Charter. When a state fails to meet these basic responsibilities, the UN Security Council may intervene (as it did in expelling Iraq from Kuwait and in protecting the Kurds in Iraq). The concept that it is the duty of the international community to intervene for humanitarian reasons or to protect minorities threatened by starvation, repression, or genocide was accepted in principle by the General Assembly in early 1991. A precedent for such intervention was set by Security Council Resolution 688 (passed in April 1991), which requested the secretary general to use all the resources at his disposal to assist and protect Iraqi refugees and displaced persons. The resolution passed despite fears that such intervention constituted an intrusion on the rights of a sovereign nation and despite Russia's and China's fears that such a mandate might be turned against them in the future (for both have significant internal security and minority problems). Since then, the UN has tried to ensure the security of the Kurds living in northern Iraq, although Iraq has repeatedly attempted to block UN personnel and prevent aid deliveries to the Kurds.

The concept of protecting minorities was expressed eloquently by former UN Secretary General Javíer Perez de Cuellar in his 1991 annual report: "There is an irresistible shift in public attitudes towards the belief that the defence of the oppressed in the name of morality should prevail over frontiers and legal documents. It is now increasingly felt that the principle of non-interference in the essential domestic jurisdiction of states cannot be regarded as a protective barrier behind which human rights can be massively or systematically violated with impunity. The Universal Declaration of Human Rights implicitly calls into question the inviolable notion of sovereignty."

The prohibition against involvement in the internal affairs of countries has traditionally extended to other UN agencies as well, such as the UN High Commissioner for Refugees (UNHCR). The UNHCR mandate proscribes intervention to protect displaced persons within their own countries, which has meant, for example, that hundreds of thousands of southern Sudanese displaced by the civil war in the Sudan have no international protection. Some have suggested that the UNHCR's ability to help refugees could be improved by (1) expanding its legal mandate and its legal responsibility for displaced persons to include those who do not fit the current definition of *refugee,* and (2) establishing new human rights enforcement mechanisms, such as a UN human rights court and high commissioner for human rights.

Intervention by the UN has also increased over the years because of the growing number of conventions it has passed that bind countries to certain standards and contain provisions for their enforcement. For example, inspections are carried out by the International Atomic Energy Agency, and more in-depth investigations into human rights violations occur now than in the past. The international community's attempts to influence governments range from persuasion through negotiations to efforts to isolate countries by cutting off diplomatic or economic relations. Unsuccessful sanctions can lead the UN and the NGOs to physically cross borders to accomplish specific goals, such as destroying weapons of mass destruction or delivering humanitarian assistance.

The UN has also become more active in international law enforcement. For example, in January 1992, the Security Council passed a resolution virtually demanding that Libya hand over agents accused of involvement in the 1988 bombing of Pan Am flight 103 over Lockerbie, Scotland, or face the threat of economic sanctions. It also called on Libya to cooperate with the investigation into the 1989 destruction of French airliner UTA 772 over Niger and to renounce terrorism. Because of Libya's refusal to comply, the Security Council voted in April 1992 to impose a travel and trade embargo; this move was hailed as another step forward in the UN's emergence as a strong enforcer of international law.

International intervention is thus becoming increasingly acceptable. The Security Council has begun to function more as its originators intended—providing collective security and acting on behalf of the international community in maintaining international peace and security. In addition, there is a growing recognition that internal unrest can lead to massive refugee streams; hence, internal conflict has become an international concern for practical as well as humanitarian reasons.

However, Gene Lyons and Michael Mastanduno argue that "it is one thing to recognize that there are limitations on sovereignty and that sovereignty carries with it responsibilities. It is quite another to determine whether or not states have met their obligations not only directly under the Charter, but also under the treaties and agreements that derive from the broad aims of the Charter. . . . The important question is who determines that a state has not met its sovereign obligations and that the consequences are such that intervention is justified to force compliance."[4] Moreover, countries often disagree upon the type of intervention needed, as verified by the different attitudes of many states regarding the civil war in the former Yugoslavia.

Although increased UN intervention is generally more accepted now, it still creates apprehension and consternation among members. Developing countries fear interference in their sovereign jurisdiction, and developed countries fear the dangers of a possible UN overextension and an escalation of costs. Even though preventing the growth of local disputes into full-fledged wars is *far* less expensive than having to stop wars in progress, many governments back away from UN peace-keeping missions and their associated costs. In reality, UN peace-keeping absorbs only a tiny fraction of global military expenditures (in 1991–1992, it cost approximately $2.7 billion—less than one-third of 1 percent), but many countries are unwilling to yield any part of their sovereignty to what they fear could become a "world government" or to assist in the buildup of a "UN army."

## The Changing Role of the United States in the UN

The attitude of both superpowers toward the United Nations changed in recent years. Instead of ignoring it or using it for posturing purposes, both countries—first the Soviets under Gorbachev and then the United States—began cooperating and working with the UN. Although the invasion of Kuwait was initiated and led by the United States, for example, the Bush administration took pains to develop a coalition and portray its mission as implementing UN Security Council resolutions. Similarly, when the United States decided to act in Somalia, it did not intervene unilaterally but offered its troops to the UN to work with a combined force in delivering humanitarian aid and restoring order to that war-torn country.

Such behavior contrasts markedly with U.S. attitudes toward the UN during the 1970s and especially the 1980s when U.S. officials undertook unilateral actions (as in Nicaragua, Panama, Libya, and Grenada) and held the UN in low esteem. This earlier attitude resulted from a number of factors; for example, the Group of 77 blamed their economic plight on their former colonizers and sought a fairer international economic order. Their swelling numbers, as more and more former colonial countries joined their ranks through independence, helped to put the United States on the defensive. In addition, sympathy for the Palestinians and the power of certain Arab countries, especially after the 1973 Arab-Israeli War and the oil embargo against the West, led to anti-Israeli and, by extension, anti-American rhetoric in the UN. This culminated in the infamous "zionism is racism" resolution of 1975, which further provoked anti-UN sentiment in the United States. The Cold War itself and the frequent use of the veto in the Security Council (279 times between 1945 and 1989) also led the United States to think more in terms of unilateral or Western-allied action rather than multilateral action through the UN.

With the demise of the Soviet bloc, the UN no longer poses a diplomatic threat to the United States; altering its stance, America now seeks to cooperate more fully with the UN, partly to avoid accusations of neoimperialism and partly because it sees the UN as a more acceptable and less expensive way to promote world peace. More than ever, it is now in the economic, humanitarian, and security interests of the United States to work with the UN in pursuit of its goals: maintaining international peace and security; promoting justice, human rights, and democracy; and achieving social progress and better standards of living for the whole world.

## The Changing Role
## of the Security Council

Although the Security Council is the most important organ of the UN because of its role in maintaining international peace and security, it has been far less successful than was anticipated by its founders because of Cold War animosities and because of its procedures. Resolutions, which carry the force of law, require the approval of nine of the council's fifteen members, including either a yes vote or an abstention from all five permanent members (China, France, Russia, the United Kingdom, and the United States).

Only since the end of the bipolar era has the Security Council begun to act as it was originally intended. As a consequence, its work—in terms of meetings, consultations, resolutions, and peace-keeping operations—has more than doubled. It was also able to undertake collective action for only the second time in its history when it acted in unison against Iraq after Baghdad's invasion of Kuwait in August 1990. Through condemnation, sanctions, and, finally, the authorization of "all means necessary," the Security Council's resolutions directed U.S.-led coalition forces to oust Iraq's troops from Kuwait. In contrast, even though there has been a UN presence in the region since March 1992, the Security Council has been unable to stop the fighting among and within the states of the former Yugo-slavia. Nor has the council been able to defuse wars within a number of countries, many of which spill over into the international arena. Arguments against UN intervention have included appeals to the nonintervention clause of the charter, divergent views on how to handle various crises, the dilemma of whether the peace-keeping forces should maintain strict neutrality or directly oppose an aggressor, and inadequate funding of the UN and its peace-keeping forces.

During the Cold War, the Soviet Union and United States were on opposite sides of almost all issues. Today, it is China that seems most resistant to involving the Security Council in solving disputes. China and other developing countries fear that the West-dominated Security Council may threaten them by slowly increasing UN involvement in the internal affairs of their countries. Hence, China abstained on the vote authorizing "all means necessary" in the resolution on Iraq and on enforcing the no-fly zone over Bosnia. Significantly, however, it did not use its veto power.

Dissatisfaction with the composition of the Security Council has also been expressed by countries such as Germany and Japan, which want permanent representation on the council in line with their large financial contributions to the UN and their growing economic power and international clout. However, both countries' demands have been undercut by their constitutions, which prohibit them from sending troops to serve in combat outside their boundaries. Some even question whether France and the United Kingdom should retain permanent council seats, given their diminished status in the world and their involvement in an increasingly integrated European Community (if the EC were given a seat on the Security Council, there would be no need for separate seats for France, Great Britain, and Germany). There is also a move to expand membership in the Security Council (as was done once before, in 1965, when membership was increased from eleven to the current fifteen) and include as permanent members the larger developing countries, such as India, Brazil, and Nigeria. This would give more influence to developing countries, which make up a large majority in the UN. At present, only eight members of the council come from the developing world (five from Asia and Africa, two from Latin America, and China).

However, since power remains firmly in the hands of the north and since any amendment to the UN Charter must be approved by the five permanent members, radical changes seem unlikely. It is improbable that France and Great Britain would agree to give up their permanent seats, and regional tensions may work against the acceptance of some likely candidates for new seats (e.g., Pakistan would oppose a seat for India). It is also argued that an expanded Security Council would be unwieldy and inefficient. Meanwhile, discussions continue about needed reforms in the Security Council's structure.

## The UN Role in Peace-keeping

Although the UN has been only partially successful in achieving its primary goal—"to maintain international peace and security," its record, given the UN's inherent weaknesses and the limitations imposed by the Cold War, has been surprisingly strong. Of more than 180 disputes considered by the Security Council and the General Assembly since 1945, only about a dozen persist as long-range problems that defy final solution. The vast majority of disputes considered by the United Nations have been resolved or ameliorated through one or another of the UN's principal organs—the Security Council, the secretary general, or the General Assembly through its "uniting-for-peace" capability. In addition, the secretary general has also prevented a number of disputes from being submitted to the Security Council or the General Assembly by arranging for settlement through his good offices. Since much of this behind-the-scenes work takes place in secret, the UN often fails to get the recognition it deserves for preventing or settling many disputes.

Peace-keeping per se was not included in the UN Charter; rather, the goal was collective security. East-West tensions prevented the Security Council from acquiring the military capability Articles 42–47 provided. Instead, members used Article 51 to expand collective self-defense arrangements. The United States, for example, developed a series of complex and extensive alliances and bilateral military pacts to assure regional security and autonomy, including the North Atlantic Treaty Organization (NATO) in 1949, the Australian–New Zealand–United States Treaty (ANZUS) in 1951, the Southeast Asia Treaty Organization (SEATO) in 1954, and the Central Treaty Organization (CENTRO) in 1955.

Only once before the end of the Cold War did the UN come close to using military means for collective security purposes. In 1950, during a Soviet boycott of the Security Council, the council adopted resolutions to counteract North Korean aggression against South Korea and authorized a unified command under the United Nations flag and U.S. leadership. However, since more than 90 percent of the ground and naval personnel and almost all of the air power came from just the United States and South Korea, this was not truly a *collective* security action; such an action would feature multinational participation and unanimity among the great powers (although a substantial number of countries did commit troops to fight in Korea). The only other example of UN collective security enforcement involving massive ground forces occurred in 1990 after Iraq's invasion of Kuwait. But as in 1950, the United States dominated operations and would probably have carried out its policy of expelling Iraq with or without UN support.

In every other instance, the UN has found other ways to deal with international violence. Aside from diplomacy, the most significant and innovative development thus far has been "peace-keeping," in which a UN mission is deployed to help maintain peace in times of high tension.[5] It may perform this function by observing border violations, policing a cease-fire or truce line, serving as a buffer between hostile forces, or even helping to maintain domestic order during a transition period. Traditionally, however, a peace-keeping force can be deployed only with the consent of the sovereign of the territory where it will operate and with the approval of all governments involved; such a force has been effective only where opposing sides have cooperated and respected the UN presence. Most peace-keeping efforts have been designed to prevent local disputes from escalating by separating combatants and bringing order to an area so that settlement of political differences can be negotiated.

The UN has been actively involved in peace-keeping almost since its inception in 1945, although at the beginning, most UN groups were small observer missions rather than true peace-keeping operations. The term *peace-keeping* was first used in 1956 when the General Assembly established the UN Emergency Force (UNEF) to take temporary control of the Suez Canal area and facilitate the withdrawal of British, French, and Israeli forces from Egyptian territory. Altogether, the UN has undertaken some twenty-seven peace-keeping assignments; thirteen of these were still in operation at the beginning of 1993 (see Figure 14.2). Indeed, in the four years after the end of the Cold War (1988–1992), more peace-keeping operations (fourteen) were launched than in the first forty-three years of UN history. The most recent and significant examples—and the ones where the UN's role is changing some of the ground rules—are in Iraq, Cambodia, Somalia, and the former Yugoslavia.

Following Iraq's invasion of Kuwait in August 1990 and the subsequent sequence of sanctions and finally war (Desert Storm) in January and February 1992, the UN Iraq-Kuwait Observation Mission (UNIKOM) was deployed to monitor the demilitarized zone along the Iraq-Kuwaiti border. However, UNIKOM's mandate did not extend to protecting the thousands of refugees in the area. After Iraq rejected proposals to deploy a UN police contingent in the north to protect returning Kurdish refugees, a force of UN guards was substituted. Teams of Scandinavian field officers were dispatched to the Kurdish area by the UNHCR to take over all relief operations from U.S. and other coalition troops. No-fly zones were established by the U.S.-led coalition north of the 36th parallel and south of the 32nd parallel (to protect the Shias), zones considered illegal by Iraq. Attempts by Iraq to contravene the no-fly zones have met with swift U.S. and British reaction.

As part of the cease-fire agreement, Iraq consented to allow UN inspectors into the country to oversee the destruction or removal of Iraq's nuclear, chemical, and biological weapons and facilities. This was an unprecedented assignment for the UN, and it has been marred by continual friction between UN personnel and Iraq over the latter's repeated noncompliance and lack of cooperation.

Another part of the UN cease-fire agreement called for a resolution of the boundary dispute between Iraq and Kuwait. The boundary drawn by the UN Iraq-Kuwait Boundary Demarcation Commission may, however, have only planted seeds for more conflict. Not only does it give Kuwait a larger portion of the prodigious Rumaila oil field, which was one of the flashpoints for Iraq's invasion of Kuwait in the first place, it also denies Iraq control of the deepwater channel to the harbor of Umm Qasr, Iraq's only dry cargo port since Basra was rendered unusable. (Basra's entranceway, the Shatt al-Arab, was blocked by sunken

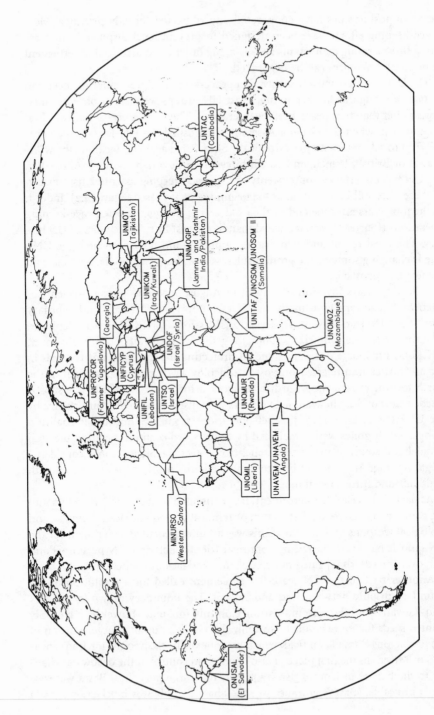

FIGURE 14.2   United Nations peace-keeping forces and observer missions, February 1993.

ships and silt, and it is estimated that it will take years to remove this material. Moreover, removal will only be possible with Iran's consent.) The new boundary also runs just south of Umm Qasr through the naval base that Iraq built during its war with Iran, thus blocking southward expansion of that port. The loss of land at both Umm Qasr and Rumaila and Iraq's fears of denied access to the Persian Gulf will most likely become an irredentist rallying cry by future Iraqi leaders. And Iraqi troops have already tested the new boundary via incursions into the Kuwaiti border area to retrieve war matériel—incursions reported by UN observers who did not have the power to stop them. Such impotence has again raised the question of altering the mandate of the peace-keepers, who heretofore have been only lightly armed and thus basically ineffective.

The UN peace plan in Cambodia has probably been the most ambitious and complex peace-keeping operation the UN has ever attempted. After years of civil war following Vietnam's invasion of Cambodia in 1978, the UN brokered a peace treaty in Paris in October 1991. The three opposition groups accepted the UN proposal that provided for a cease-fire and the demobilization of 70 percent of the existing forces (with the other 30 percent remaining under UN supervision), the return of approximately 360,000 Cambodians from refugee camps in Thailand, and UN administration of the country until it can organize and conduct free and fair elections. Between February 1992 and late 1993, over 22,000 UN military and civilian personnel were deployed to Cambodia. The military part of this effort involves supervising, monitoring, and verifying the cease-fire and overseeing both the withdrawal of foreign troops and the regrouping, cantonment, disarming, and subsequent demobilization of the armed forces of the four Cambodian factions. The civilian part includes such innovative responsibilities as the supervision of administrative structures and police forces as well as measures to promote human rights. In addition, the UN Transitional Authority in Cambodia (UNTAC) is responsible for coordinating rehabilitation assistance. As Boutros Boutros-Ghali said, "The United Nations is faced with the daunting task of nurturing national reconciliation, fostering the democratic process, and building peace and stability in a country ravaged by two decades of war. Such a role for the UN would have been unimaginable a decade ago."[6]

Under the UN peace plan, the Khmer Rouge—who had power in the 1970s and killed over 1 million Cambodians—were included in the four-faction coalition because they were too militarily powerful to be excluded, but their inclusion troubled many UN members. Although the other factions tried, for the most part, to adhere to the UN peace plan, the Khmer Rouge were generally intransigent and noncompliant. They refused to give UNTAC access to the areas they controlled. They did not disband and disarm their troops as required under the Paris accords, and in mid-1992, they again began attacking villages outside their area of control. They even took UN peace-keepers hostage and killed UN personnel on several occasions in early 1993. The UN did, however, successfully oversee the national election in Cambodia in June 1993.

In Somalia, the UN again confronted the need to reconstruct an entire nation that had slid into anarchy; over 350,000 people died from starvation, and most of the basic infrastructure had been destroyed. The deployment of troops under a U.S. initiative in December 1992 and the subsequent agreement to a cease-fire and a conference on national reconciliation brought stability to the hunger situation.

Somalia's tragedy, however, has been labeled "an international embarrassment for the UN" because of the United Nations' ineffectiveness early in the conflict.[7] UN agencies withdrew their personnel from Mogadishu immediately after Somalia's president, Siad Barre, fell from power in January 1991, and they remained disengaged even when full-scale civil war broke out the following November. It was not until January 1992 that a UN team went to Mogadishu to hold talks aimed at bringing about a cessation of hostilities and securing the international relief community's access to civilians. The Security Council urged all parties to end hostilities and placed a general embargo on deliveries of weapons and military equipment to Somalia. But by the time a cease-fire had been negotiated between the two major rival leaders, several hundred thousand refugees had fled to neighboring countries. Hundreds of thousands more were displaced within their own country, partly as a result of famine caused by both the civil war and the drought. Famine and starvation threatened a further 2 million people.

By late 1992, the country had disintegrated into anarchy based not on inter-ethnic rivalries but on interclan feuding. Only when the media began graphically portraying the suffering and death in Somalia in August 1992 did the UN send 500 armed troops to try to guarantee the safe delivery of humanitarian aid supplies, which had often been the target of looting by armed gangs. But because these peace-keepers were not authorized to use the force needed to protect relief shipments from gunmen, they were ineffectual. Conditions continued to deteriorate until December 1992, when the United States took the initiative in offering up to 28,000 troops to the UN to safeguard the delivery of humanitarian assistance and restore order in the country. Within a few weeks, troops from twenty-two other countries had joined the U.S. contingent in a truly multinational effort. The UN did, however, assume full control of the humanitarian, peace-keeping, and peace-making mission after the withdrawal of most U.S. troops by mid-1993.

The situation in the former Yugoslavia provides perhaps the best example of the dilemma currently confronting the United Nations. Yugoslavia, a multinational state consisting of six republics, was once held together by a strong wartime Communist partisan leader, Josef Tito, who successfully balanced each republic against the others. But there were other centripetal forces at play in addition to the centralized, powerful leadership: the country's discernible improvement in living standards until the 1980s, some relatively harmonious ethnic mixing, and the legitimacy inherent in being the only Communist regime not imposed by the USSR. Until the early 1980s, none of the major nationalities felt that its existence was endangered, although each thought it was being exploited by one or more of the others.

However, after Tito's death, centrifugal forces became more powerful: Power dispersed to the republics, the economy declined, and nationalism (especially Serbian nationalism) grew. Fear of Serbian domination and of the diminution of the other five republics' hard-won autonomy weakened the sense of Yugoslav national identity. Slovenia and Croatia held plebiscites on independence in 1990 and, in the face of still-growing national tensions, exercised their right to self-determination as guaranteed by the Yugoslav constitution. In Croatia and later in Bosnia-Herzegovina, independence declarations triggered civil war and the involvement of the Serb-dominated Yugoslav federal army. Intense inter-group fighting, the expulsion of minority populations (especially Moslems) in "ethnic-cleansing" operations, and brutal atrocities soon displaced over 2 million people.

At first, efforts were made to handle the conflict on a regional basis, as provided for in Article 52 of the UN Charter. The European Community brokered a number of cease-fires, issued declarations calling for peaceful solutions, sent monitors to the scene, and convened a peace conference among the leaders. But even recognition of the independence of three republics by both the European Community and the United Nations failed to dampen the fighting. After repeated but unsuccessful efforts to stop the fighting, the EC turned to the UN in September 1991. At first, some members of the Security Council objected to UN involvement, citing the principle of noninterference in the internal affairs of states, but these arguments became moot once the Serb-dominated government in Belgrade asked the UN to act and the secretary general decided the conflict posed a threat to international peace and security.

The Security Council established an arms embargo and, later, a trade embargo against Yugoslavia and sent an envoy to try to defuse the situation. In April 1992, the council sent peace-keeping troops to Croatia (UNPROFOR) to monitor the cease-fire there, to protect Serbian enclaves, to disarm local Serb militias, and to enable humanitarian assistance to reach civilians. Next came a series of partially successful, UN-led efforts to bring urgently needed supplies to Serbian-besieged cities in Bosnia-Herzegovina. But attempts to work out a permanent cease-fire, to relieve the suffering of the displaced, and to find a political solution under the combined auspices of the UN and the EC had not reached fruition by late 1993. Meanwhile, the international community remained increasingly split about what the UN should do, with some calling for much more decisive military action and others favoring additional UN-sponsored peace negotiations.

As of early 1993, UN peace-keepers were in increasingly dangerous and untenable situations within both Croatia and Bosnia-Herzegovina. In an attempt to prevent Serbian expansion of the war into Kosovo (an autonomous province within Serbia, populated overwhelmingly by Albanians but of great historical significance to Serbia) and into Macedonia, UN forces were deployed on the borders of these areas. But again, they were inadequately armed and insufficient in number to repel any full-fledged Serbian aggression.

# Future UN Trends in Peace-keeping, Peace-making, and Preventive Diplomacy

Since the end of the Cold War, there has been not only an explosive growth of UN peace-keeping but also a significant movement to place greater emphasis on preventive diplomacy (a change from crisis management to crisis prevention). The UN is now enhancing traditional UN "peace-keeping" with more active "peace-making" and "peace-building." Despite the domestic jurisdiction clause in the charter, member states recognize that it is increasingly difficult to regard any conflict as only domestic. More and more threats to international peace are rooted in internal conflict, as outsiders are dragged in on the side of one belligerent or another, thereby increasing internal instability. Frequently, too, domestic conflicts lead to the forced displacement of people, who then cross international boundaries to become refugees in other countries, creating instability there as well.

The hostilities in the Persian Gulf in the early 1990s—which brought the devastation of two states, enormous loss of innocent lives, great damage to the environment, and immense suffering by millions of people—represent an unacceptable failure of collective diplomacy. With the gulf crisis in mind, UN members are now showing a new willingness to expand the UN's traditional role of peace-keeping into peace-making and even peace-enforcement, which does not require the consent of the parties involved. Although it appears to be succeeding in Somalia, the UN has thus far backed away from similar assertive action in Croatia and Bosnia-Herzegovina.

Increased involvement in countries' internal affairs is also prompted by the need to impose some kind of order so that humanitarian aid can be delivered and some form of government reestablished in places where social norms have broken down, as in Cambodia and Somalia. If successful, the UN's plan to impose a peace in Cambodia, which has long been torn by civil war, could become a model for similar missions in the future. And Nelson Mandela and the African National Congress have already appealed to the Security Council for assistance in stopping the violence in South Africa.

Another area where a greater UN presence may be required in countries' internal affairs is in monitoring elections. To date, the UN has overseen elections in Namibia, El Salvador, Haiti, Nicaragua, Angola, and Cambodia. In 1991, the General Assembly passed a resolution calling on the secretary general to designate a senior official as coordinator of election-monitoring and verification activities, and it also called for the establishment of a voluntary fund to help pay for a UN electoral mission. In 1992, the UN provided technical assistance for elections in Albania, El Salvador, and ten African states; it was also assisting in preparations for referenda planned for Eritrea and Western Sahara.

The scope of peace-making was enlarged further at a January 1992 Security Council summit meeting, the first ever called involving the heads of state or government of the fifteen members. The summit recognized that "the absence of war and military conflicts among states does not in itself ensure international peace and security but that the non-military sources of instability in the economic, social, humanitarian, and ecological fields have become threats to peace and security." Boutros Boutros-Ghali argues that the United Nations has a crucial responsibility to address the deepest causes of conflict—economic despair, social injustice, and political oppression—and to monitor economic and social trends that may become sources of political tensions, violence, and repression.[8] His proposals include a more muscular UN: a world body that works harder—through fact-finding, better intelligence, and diplomacy—to prevent conflicts from erupting. He also believes the UN must be keenly aware that efforts to build peace and security must reach beyond military threats to embrace economic and human rights concerns. He urges efforts "to enhance respect for human rights and fundamental freedoms, to promote sustainable economic and social development for wider prosperity, to alleviate distress, and to curtail the existence and use of massively destructive weapons."

In places where tensions could lead to an outbreak of conflict, the UN should supplement these peace-building efforts with *preventive diplomacy*. It should avert possible violence by using such tools as confidence-building measures, fact-finding missions, early-warning mechanisms, the deployment of a UN presence in a threatened country, and the establishment of demilitarized zones.

Where conflict erupts, the UN's role is to engage in *peace-making* to help hostile parties resolve their differences: Mechanisms include the World Court, mediation, and the provision of positive incentives. *Peace-enforcement* is also part of the Security Council's option "to take military action to maintain or restore international peace and security" after peaceful means have failed. In the secretary general's view, swifter, more effective military action against aggression and to deter crises and enhance UN credibility requires the creation of a permanent UN rapid-deployment force, which would be ready to move quickly into unstable situations and stop warring factions from escalating conflicts. Member states would negotiate agreements with the Security Council to provide standby forces on a permanent basis. Proponents of this approach argue that such a force could act much more quickly and aggressively than the traditional UN peace-keeping missions, reduce loss of life and destruction of property, and act as a deterrent to potential conflict-makers. Opponents fear that there is too much instability in the world for the UN to meet all requests for help and that such a force might be used to uphold an unpopular and possibly corrupt regime that should be overthrown. France, Russia, and the United States have already gone on record as favoring such a force.

In addition to these forces, Boutros-Ghali has proposed the creation of "peace-enforcement units," which would be more heavily armed than peace-keeping troops, to restore and maintain cease-fires that unravel. He has also suggested the physical insertion of UN personnel inside a state when clashes occur, which would not require a request by the government or by all parties affected. Such a precedent was set with Security Council Resolution 688, which created a safe haven for the Kurds in northern Iraq, and in other actions authorizing the delivery of relief supplies in the former Yugoslavia and Somalia.

Successful peace-making and peace-keeping operations, however, also require comprehensive efforts to identify and support structures and actions that will consolidate peace and advance a sense of confidence and well-being among people. As Boutros-Ghali states in *An Agenda for Peace:* "Through agreements ending civil strife, these [efforts] may include disarming the previously warring parties and the restoration of order, the custody and possible destruction of weapons, de-mining areas, repatriating refugees, advisory and training support for security personnel, monitoring elections, advancing efforts to protect human rights, reforming or strengthening governmental institutions, and promoting formal and informal processes of political participation."[9] Postconflict peace-building—through cooperative and mutually beneficial projects, joint programs, cultural exchanges, and other confidence-building measures—are all essential to prevent a recurrence of hostilities, as are the reconstruction and rehabilitation of basic social and economic infrastructures.

## The UN Role
## in Non-Peace-keeping Activities

In addition to its very important role in peace-keeping, the UN has other critical purposes defined in the charter. These include seeking "to achieve international cooperation in solving international problems . . . and in promoting and encouraging respect for human rights and fundamental freedoms." The UN has done much to promote international cooperation in addressing a great variety of transnational problems, among them: environmental issues (such as desertification, ozone protection, and climate change), social issues (such as population, sanitation and drinking water, and illiteracy), cultural issues (such as the preservation of historical sites and cultural treasures and the protection of indigenous peoples), and economic concerns (such as trade, technology transfer, and debt relief). The various agencies of the UN system make great contributions in dealing with these and many other issues. Each one, often in collaboration with others, assists governments by providing guidance, technical cooperation, project planning, and program execution.

The UN also focuses on specific issues through its international conferences on topics like trade and development, population, and women. These conferences often lead to agreements on strategies and cooperation among governments. They marshal political commitment and direct governments' attention to critical issues. They open paths for cooperation between governmental and nongovernmental organizations and increase public awareness and political support. For example, the World Summit for Children in 1990 led to the Declaration and Convention on the Rights of the Child, which was signed by 140 heads of government. This convention set goals, such as saving the lives of 50 million children by the end of the decade and improving the lives of millions more, and stimulated more than 130 countries to prepare national strategies to achieve these goals. It mobilized greater cooperation among a wide range of UN organizations, including those dealing with health, basic education, nutrition, water and sanitation, and the rights of women and children, and it encouraged the active involvement of many NGOs.

Similarly, the 1992 Rio Conference on Environment and Development emphasized the interrelationships of the environmental, social, political, and economic dimensions of development and their connection to peace. As Boutros-Ghali has said:

> There has never been a more evident need for an integrated approach to the objectives of peace, democracy and human rights, and the requirements of development; the needs of development and the protection of the environment; the economic as well as the social dimensions of development; the interrelationships among trade, finance, investment and technology; [and] the meeting of immediate needs for emergency and humanitarian assistance and setting the conditions for long term development. The UN is the only institution capable of comprehensively addressing global problems in their political, humanitarian and socio-economic dimensions.[10]

The Rio Conference focused the world's attention on the problems of environmental degradation and produced a comprehensive and far-reaching program for sustainable development (see Chapter 9).

The UN will continue to play an important role in all aspects of development, including impartial data-gathering and analysis and the review of global economic trends and policies. Both its research and technical cooperation activities are expected to continue to increase and expand. Similarly, UN regional commissions are anticipated to assume a greater role in promoting regional cooperation on a wide range of issues. The UN's current emphasis on "humanizing" development (focusing on people and improvement of the human condition) is expected to become the basis for future international socioeconomic development programs.

The UN is in the unique position of being able to forge a new partnership for development among countries at all stages of development, based on the recognition of sovereign equality, mutual interest, and shared responsibilities. As Boutros-Ghali expresses it, "Only through such a partnership [can] the global community erase the scourge of poverty and deprivation, provide international support for national reform programs, encourage efficient use of precious global resources, and address economic and social problems through coherent and mutually reinforcing policies."[11]

One of the UN's greatest successes has been its role in overseeing and encouraging decolonization. By 1993, very few areas in the world remained colonized. Apart from Hong Kong, which will revert to China in 1997, and Macao, which reverts to China later, just eighteen colonies remain. Most are very small and isolated, such as Pitcairn Island where forty-eight descendants of the mutineers from the H.M.S. *Bounty* live under the light hand of a British governor based several thousand miles away in New Zealand. The eighteen colonies contain fewer than 1.5 million colonized people, some of whom flatly reject the idea of independence. Questions remain about the futures of Guam, Palau, Gibraltar, and the U.S. Virgin Islands for the advantages of independence do not always outweigh the disadvantages. The futures of East Timor, which was annexed by Indonesia in 1976 but whose independence is still championed by some East Timorese and Portuguese, and New Caledonia, where the French have pledged to hold a referendum on independence in 1998, are also unclear.

The UN is also thoroughly committed to integrating human rights and social and economic development. The designation of 1993 as the International Year of the World's Indigenous People is but one attempt to promote respect for the minority rights of vulnerable groups. But the UN is concerned with the involvement of other vulnerable groups, including the elderly, the disabled, and women, in the development process. Human rights are perceived as an essential component of sustainable development. Yet despite the Universal Declaration of Human Rights and the two international Human Rights Covenants, massive violations continue that the United Nations seems unable to end. Clearly, the UN role in preventing violations as well as stopping them needs to be strengthened. Suggestions range from further empowering the Security Council to act more decisively on human rights issues to establishing a human rights court. The UN Human Rights Conference in Vienna in June 1993 was a step in the appropriate direction. Boutros-Ghali argues that an integrated, comprehensive approach to the diverse development and human rights issues can best be promoted through a stronger UN.

## International Organizations

International organizations seek to secure the cooperation of governments, private agencies, and individuals in attaining their objectives, which can range in seriousness from the abolition of war to the promotion of yoga. They include both intergovernmental organizations (IGOs), whose memberships consist solely of national governments and occasionally regional groupings of states, and non-governmental organizations (NGOs), whose members are private organizations and individuals (see Table 14.1). Many NGOs are affiliated with IGOs; others work independently. The number, type, activities, and importance of IGOs and NGOs have increased enormously during the twentieth century: There are at least ten times as many IGOs and sixty-seven times as many NGOs now as in 1900. An average state may have membership in about forty-five IGOs. These trends are the result of the world's growing international contact, brought about by revolutions in communications and transportation, as well as increased global interdependence and the ever-mounting number of transnational issues requiring an international response.

TABLE 14.1    *Types of International Organizations*

| | General Purpose | | Specialized Purpose | |
| --- | --- | --- | --- | --- |
| | IGO | NGO | IGO | NGO |
| NON-REGIONAL | United Nations | Roman Catholic Church | World Health Organization | Amnesty International |
| | Commonwealth | International Criminal Police Organization (INTERPOL) | OPEC | World Wildlife Fund |
| REGIONAL | European Union (EU) | Union of European Feminists | North Atlantic Treaty Organization (NATO) | Scientific Association of the Pacific |
| | Organization of American States (OAS) | Conference of European Churches | Economic Community of West African States (ECOWAS) | Movement Against Apartheid |

# International Intergovernmental Organizations

No other international organization has such universal representation as the United Nations. Only Switzerland and some microstates and colonial remnants remain outside its inclusive umbrella. Its specialized agencies, such as the World Health Organization and the International Labour Organization, and its other organs, such as the United Nations High Commission for Refugees and the United Nations Population Fund, are examples of universal IGOs. The oldest surviving global IGO is the International Telegraphic (now Telecommunications) Union, founded in 1865.

An example of a nonregionally restricted IGO that exists outside the UN network is the Commonwealth of Nations. The Commonwealth is a free association of fifty diverse, self-governing countries bonded together by their common historical experience as part of the British Empire, their present recognition of the British sovereign as head of the Commonwealth, their use of the English language and legal system, and their belief that Commonwealth membership brings them important benefits. Founded in 1926, the Commonwealth evolved from a hierarchical structure to an organization in which all members are equal; it grew from an organization with no constitution and secretariat to a strong consultative group with a permanent secretariat that meets regularly to discuss a broad range of issues. Despite disagreements and conflicts among members and between members and other states, the Commonwealth has thrived: Only three countries have withdrawn from membership—Ireland in 1949, South Africa in 1961, and Pakistan in 1972.

At the end of World War II, the Organization of European Economic Cooperation (OEEC) was established to administer U.S. economic assistance in the European Recovery Program, more commonly known as the Marshall Plan. Eighteen European countries (all except those under Communist rule) joined to rebuild Europe's shattered economy. By 1961, the OEEC was so successful that its scope was enlarged, and it was converted into the Organization for Economic Cooperation and Development (OECD). It ceased being a strictly European IGO, admitting the United States and Canada to (charter) membership and later adding Japan, Finland, Turkey, Australia, and New Zealand. It changed its emphasis from recovery to development, the expansion of world trade, and efforts to help developing countries. With its headquarters in Paris, the OECD has developed an elaborate structure, and it now deals with a broad list of issues affecting trade and economic development.

Among the key IGOs are the small but very powerful G-7 (a group of the world's top industrialized countries), the Group of 77 (which consists of approximately 130 developing countries), and the Organization of Petroleum Exporting Countries (OPEC). The Nonaligned Movement, founded in 1955, has attempted to act as a mouthpiece for the poorer and weaker countries of the world; despite the group's name, its members have always included countries that were clearly aligned with one or another of the two superpowers. OPEC was constituted in 1960 to unify and coordinate members' petroleum policies and to safeguard their interests in trade and development dealings with industrialized oil-consuming nations. OPEC showed its clout in 1973 when it embargoed oil sales to Israel and its allies and quadrupled prices; it raised prices again in 1979. Since then, however, internal squabbles and wars, differences over policies to restrict output, and an increase in non-OPEC countries exporting oil have undermined its power.

In addition to global organizations, there are many groups working within specific regions. Some focus more narrowly on limited functions, such as defense and economic, social, or cultural cooperation; others are more multipurpose. NATO and the Economic Community of West African States (ECOWAS) are examples of specialized regional IGOs that concentrate on defense and economic cooperation. More encompassing regional IGOs include the increasingly important European Community, the Organization of African Unity (OAU), and the Organization of American States (OAS).

## Non-Governmental Organizations (NGOs)

By 1993, there were over 11,100 international organizations in existence. All are international in scope, membership, or interest, concerned with almost every conceivable field of human activity. Over 6,000 of these are multinational and binational nonprofit membership associations, and a further 5,000 are national nonprofit membership associations headquartered in over 180 countries around the world. More than 1,300 of these have a consultative role with the United Nations, mostly through ECOSOC or the UN Department of Public Information (DPI). NGOs accredited by ECOSOC (those with consultative status) have the right to make statements before its committees.

From its inception, the UN has recognized that NGOs have an important and constructive role to play in furthering the purposes and principles of the United Nations Charter. NGOs have made significant contributions to the work of the UN by drawing attention to issues, by suggesting ideas, programs, and solutions to problems, and by disseminating information and mobilizing public opinion about specific issues and the UN's aims and activities. Some NGOs do a number of traditional UN tasks more efficiently and effectively than UN agencies themselves, such as responding to disasters, providing humanitarian aid, and meeting many social and developmental needs. In recognition of their value, the main organs of the UN and their subsidiary agencies increasingly call upon NGOs to participate in and contribute to their programs and activities.

NGOs associated with the UN have not only increased in number from 270 in 1972 to over 1,300 in 1993, they have also become increasingly effective in making statements, promoting their views with delegates, and presenting their positions before international conferences. They also have an important watchdog function, keeping the United Nations focused on issues and on the implementation of decisions made by UN and national bodies.

NGOs in industrial countries have become more and more important in international development assistance. They, too, have grown in number, and they are used by governments to channel aid to developing countries. However, even with their capabilities and success, NGOs still need coordination to avoid redundancy and competition and to ensure wise use of donated resources. Such a coordinating role may best be played by the UN through a reformed and better-run ECOSOC.

## Conclusion

In today's increasingly interdependent but explosive world, the roles of both IGOs and NGOs are of growing significance and can be expected to expand. The UN will, however, remain paramount: To achieve its goals, it must encourage member states to replace reliance on unilateral force with collective security, capable of protecting the weak against the strong and of responding quickly to major breaches of international peace. But to do this, the United Nations clearly needs more authority and power. The UN is currently overextended, with inadequate support and funding. Despite the huge increase in its work load, the size of its personnel has not grown, and it remains understaffed and inadequately managed.[12] In addition, the willingness of countries to work together after the end of the Cold War is beginning to be strained for many complex problems remain unresolved. Moreover, greater clarity is needed on whether the UN should maintain its traditional neutral role in peace-keeping or engage in outright military action to oppose aggression and impose peace.

The previous reluctance to use UN channels resulted, in part, from deeply ingrained feelings of nationalism and the concern for sovereign rights, which discouraged the use of international approaches in conflict resolution. But increasingly, clashes are being brought before either the UN or regional organizations. The secretary general has advocated greater use of regional organizations, but such groups may be manipulated by regional powers, and, in any case, they need to work in cooperation with the UN in implementing its mandate. To be effective, the UN must get involved earlier in future conflicts and be more active and persistent in implementing its mandate.

In terms of Security Council decisions, the Cold War tensions of the past will likely be replaced by more divergence between China and the West and between north and south—a polarization that could boil over in the UN in any number of ways. As the world shrinks and the global village becomes more of a reality, there will be a greater acceptance of the UN's right to intervene more forcefully and quickly in countries' internal affairs when people are being persecuted and killed, threatened with weapons of mass destruction, or deprived of the basic necessities of food and shelter.

Increased ethnic tensions and conflict can be expected in many parts of the world—in Africa and Asia and perhaps especially in Eastern Europe and the former Soviet Union, where fierce new assertions of nationalism and sovereignty have already begun to occur. Yet even with a greater international willingness to allow more UN involvement in countries' internal affairs, the UN is limited in what it can accomplish. It is obviously incapable of resolving all the world's tensions and conflicts. Consequently, many violations of human rights will probably continue to go unheeded, brutal civil wars will be overlooked, and the proliferation of weapons of mass destruction will continue. Tragically, delayed responses to incipient conflicts can result in far greater costs as well as more intense suffering.

Overall, the UN will continue to play very important roles in peace-keeping and conflict resolution, in focusing global attention on major international issues and problems, and in providing a neutral forum for countries to discuss critical issues. The UN could undoubtedly do a better job: It could do more to accomplish the goals established in its charter, and its bureaucracy and structure clearly need reform. But the United Nations will only be as good and effective as its member states allow it to be. Frequently, national leaders have blamed the UN for failure when they are the ones who have limited the power and ability of that organization to respond to crises and other needs. As Boutros-Ghali expresses it: "The United Nations is a gathering of sovereign states and what it can do depends on the common ground between them."[13] Only when countries understand that it is in their own self-interest to work together and to intervene in certain situations that do not directly affect them will the UN be more effective in solving the world's many problems.

## Notes

1. Charter of the United Nations, Chapter 1, Article 1.

2. Inis Claude, *Swords into Plowshares,* 4th ed. (New York: Random House, 1974), pp. 183–184.

3. "The Limits of Sovereignty," *United Nations Focus: Human Rights* (New York: United Nations Dept. of Public Information DPI/1178, February 1992), p. 1.

4. Gene M. Lyons and Michael Mastanduno, *Beyond Westphalia? International Intervention, State Sovereignty, and the Future of International Society,* summary of a conference held at Dartmouth College, May 18–20, 1992 (Hanover, N.H.: Dartmouth College, 1992), p. 9.

5. An interesting exception occurred in Somalia in 1993 when the UN forces attacked a warlord stronghold. This action bears a stronger resemblance to "peace-making" and may be a notable precedent.

6. Boutros Boutros-Ghali, *An Agenda for Peace: Preventive Diplomacy, Peacemaking, and Peace-Keeping,* Report of the Secretary-General Pursuant to the Statement Adopted by the Summit Meeting of the Security Council on 31 January 1992 (New York: United Nations, June 1992), p. 53.

7. *Current History,* vol. 91, no. 565 (September 1992), pp. 230–234.

8. Boutros-Ghali, *An Agenda for Peace,* p. 8.

9. Ibid., p. 32.

10. Boutros Boutros-Ghali, *Report on the Work of the Organization from the Forty-sixth to the Forty-seventh Session of the General Assembly* (New York: United Nations, September 1992), p. 27.

11. Ibid, p. 29.

12. A major report by former UN Deputy Secretary General Richard Thornburgh lists the plethora of internal problems and inefficiencies of the UN. See Richard Thornburgh, "Report to the Secretary-General of the United Nations," mimeo (March 1, 1993).

13. Boutros Boutros-Ghali, *An Agenda for Peace,* p. 1.

# FIFTEEN

## Global Hegemony
## Versus National Economy:
## The United States
## in the New World Order

JOHN AGNEW

"SUPERPOWER RETAKES GUTTED SECOND CITY": This front-page headline in the London *Observer* of May 3, 1992, described the U.S. National Guard's reestablishment of public authority in the aftermath of the Los Angeles riots between April 29 and May 1, 1992. It also captured the paradoxical position of the United States in the contemporary world. Although it is acquiring an apparent military and cultural hegemony at the global scale, its national economy is suffering from stagnation, increased income inequality between regions and within metropolitan areas, and growing social polarization.

The Cold War is won, positive images of American and Western European market capitalism sweep Eastern Europe and the former Soviet Union, the world's largest McDonald's has opened in Beijing, and Mickey Mouse has a home in France. At this historical moment of cultural and economic dominance, however, a wave of self-doubt sweeps across the United States. Opinion polls suggest that two-thirds of Americans believe their country is "on the wrong track." For the first time in a generation, parents do not believe that their children will have a better life than they themselves have had. In Los Angeles, a city that has long represented the possibility of a better life for all, some of the country's worst riots in a century erupted among the city's poor.

The Los Angeles riots were something new in American history, the country's first multiethnic urban riots. They involved mutual hostility and the looting of several different ethnic groups—Mexican, African-American, white, Asian, and Central American. What emerges beyond the statistics of the riots—58 deaths, 2,383 injuries, 5,383 fires, 16,291 arrests, $785 million in damages—is a picture of a rigidly segregated and socioeconomically divided city. Its residents share little of the faith in the future that characterized immigrants and the poor in the American past.

The districts most affected by the riots have been in a state of protracted economic crisis. Higher-paying manufacturing jobs have all but disappeared as the city's economy has been "restructured" in the face of increased foreign competition, the relocation of American firms abroad, and the decline of major defense industries in southern California. The outbreak of rioting was caused by more than a set of economic problems: Los Angeles city politics, bias in the judicial system, and a militant police system all contributed. Today, the best new jobs, requiring many years of schooling and high skill levels, are in the suburbs or downtown office buildings. Jobs that are more prevalent in the neighborhoods affected by the riots are low-paying ones in retailing and other consumer services. Yet the American dream of high consumption is still shared by all. It is the failure of "the Establishment" or "the system" to deliver on the promise that generates pessimism and despair among looters and victims alike.

In this chapter, I will argue that U.S. global hegemony has imposed costs upon the American national economy, produced local economic problems, and generated the national mood of pessimism. My central claim is that the New World Order being made under American auspices is a "transnational liberal economic order" that now detracts from, rather than augments, the material conditions of life for both the "average" and the poorest people within the territorial boundaries of the United States.[1] The economic impacts of America's global hegemony also vary from place to place in the United States. The first section of this chapter surveys the evidence for this claim. The second section lays out a suggested explanation for why U.S. global hegemony has produced a "globalized" world economic order. The third section attempts to identify the specific economic processes producing the negative consequences within the U.S. "territorial economy." A fourth and final section states the main conclusions.

## Postprosperity in the United States

### Income Divergence

The boom years for the post–World War II American economy ended in 1973. In that year, the median earnings for males peaked, then entered a twenty-year period of decline and stagnation. Median household incomes have also stagnated and have only held their own because of increases in paid employment for women. During the same period, *average* family income did inch upward—a rate of increase of 0.04 percent per year, compared to the 2.72 average of the fifteen years prior to 1973—but this masks a significant redistribution of income within the population. If the distribution of family incomes is divided in tenths (deciles) and if 1977 is compared to 1988, it can be shown that real (after-inflation) incomes declined for every tenth except the highest two. In the lowest tenth, family incomes (which averaged an amazingly low $3,504 in 1988) were 14.8 percent lower in 1988 than in 1977 in constant dollars. In the middle-income groups—the fifth, sixth, and seventh tenths—average family incomes were lower by 5 percent. Even the eighth tenth saw a shrinkage in incomes, off 1.8 percent in constant dollars. The ninth decile had a minor increase of 1.0 percent; the biggest increase, 16.5 percent, occurred in the wealthiest tenth decile, which captured most of the increase in gross national product (GNP) over the ten-year period.[2]

These data suggest a decline in prosperity for the mass of the U.S. population after a period in which improvement had become an almost universal expectation for Americans. Perhaps more significant, the income distribution has also become more polarized. More Americans are rich now, and more are poor. Fewer have stayed in the middle-income groups. In the 1980s, the "middle class," which has given the United States its reputation for high mass consumption and political stability, shrank by about 10 percent. One study estimates that in the 1980s, 2 percent of those in the $18,500–$55,000 (1987 dollars) income group (75 percent of the population in 1980) rose into the upper income brackets and that 30 percent slid downward.[3] With fewer people moving into the middle range from either end of the distribution, the net result is the politically controversial phenomenon of the "shrinking" middle class.

The most proximate cause of the upward redistribution of income and the erosion of the middle class is the changing structure of the job market. High-skilled workers are earning more and lower-skilled workers are earning less as the American economy uses fewer highly paid, unskilled laborers than it did during the "glory days" after World War II. The earnings gap between the rich and poor began to widen in the late 1960s but increased even faster in the 1970s and 1980s. To be sure, income polarization is occurring in other industrial economies, but elsewhere, especially in Europe, family earnings have been more protected by government benefits, and fewer people have fallen into the low-income groups.

Behind the change in the job market lies a fundamental restructuring of the American economy in the face of increased exposure and vulnerability to the world economy. More simply put, the increase in U.S. trade over the past twenty years bears much of the blame for the surge in income inequality and the shrinking size of the American middle class. From 1979 until 1989, as the sum of exported and imported goods rose from 55 percent to 82 percent of U.S. manufacturing output, the average pay and benefits of American factory workers fell 6 percent after inflation, even as plant productivity rose 42 percent.[4] At the same time, job growth in the American economy has been concentrated in the services sector, which is strongly polarized between low-earning and high-earning jobs. It is manufacturing jobs that traditionally provided America's middle incomes. In 1975, 45 percent of manufacturing jobs had incomes that clustered close to the national median. In contrast, the incomes of service-sector jobs are skewed downward or are distributed bimodally; for example, those in the retail sector (a major growth area in the 1980s) are skewed downward, and the producer-services sector is bimodal.

If world trade in services is liberalized (i.e., if tariff barriers are reduced or eliminated) as the U.S. government intends under the Uruguay Round of the General Agreement on Tariffs and Trade (GATT), then many service jobs (excepting those in banking and finance) may also be in jeopardy from foreign competition.[5]

## Regional Divergence

New low-wage service jobs do not compensate adequately for the lost manufacturing jobs and lower incomes in manufacturing brought about by the U.S. economy's increased involvement in world trade. The widening inequality of incomes this creates poses major challenges to the country. As poverty among people in the peak years of employment increases, the costs of welfare and unemployment will mount, and resentment of the wealthy may well grow. One new trend is that, after thirty years of convergence, average regional per capita incomes began to *diverge* in the 1980s.[6] This reverses the nation-building trend of the postwar period and opens the long-term possibility for regional fragmentation like that experienced in the aftermath of the Cold War in Eastern Europe and the former Soviet Union. Much of the rural U.S. South remains poor, with inadequate school systems and high rates of illiteracy, and all regional and metropolitan economies show startling variations in incomes and prosperity. Regions with large minority populations display particular signs of decline in these areas.

Not all of this geographical variation is due to the direct effects of trade upon manufacturing industry. Fluctuations in defense spending, cutbacks in government welfare programs, and the concentration of the most dynamic high-technology manufacturing (especially computers) and high-growth service (especially finance) industries have all played their part. Cutbacks in defense spending will particularly affect those regions, such as New England and southern California, that had become especially dependent on the militarization of the U.S. economy during the Cold War.[7] The impact is clear: As U.S. manufacturing trade grew by 60 percent in the 1972–1985 period, the average annual income of 17 million professionals was 9 percent higher than it would have been otherwise, and the average annual income of 90 million other workers was 3 percent lower than it would have been without the growth in trade.[8]

What happened? From one point of view, the period after World War II was exceptional. The U.S. economy reigned supreme in a world not yet recovered from the mass destruction of war. After the depression and war, there was an unprecedented potential for capital investment (at home and abroad) and for domestic consumer spending. Federal government activism in the form of the interstate highway system and civil rights legislation integrated the South, previously a backwater region, into the national economy. National housing legislation and highway development allowed the massive suburbanization that stimulated a large number of industries. Meanwhile, industrial production was largely organized around national markets with limited foreign competition. The *Pax Americana* of the postwar years gave the U.S. economy significant leverage over the world's financial and trading systems, even though the United States itself was only modestly exposed to the vagaries of either. But after 1973, this exceptional political economy ran out of steam.

Two events of 1972–1973—the U.S. government's abrogation of the Bretton Woods agreement that had stabilized the world monetary system after World War II and the OPEC oil price increases—jointly symbolize the emergence of a world economy to which the U.S. national economy was increasingly exposed and vulnerable. If the world economy seemed a benign or beneficent influence upon the American economy before 1973, everything changed thereafter. Eurocurrency markets (U.S. dollars in circulation outside the United States) became more important, and international banks began to privatize and globalize the international financial system, thereby effectively reducing U.S. government control over capital. The growth of producer cartels, especially OPEC, and of the European Community in the 1960s limited U.S. control of vital raw materials and foreign markets. And mounting trade deficits signaled the arrival of a more internationalized production, from which the United States could not be sheltered without imposing costs upon its own businesses. At the same time, military-political reverses in Vietnam (and, later, in Iran) challenged American preeminence within its various alliances and undermined the political consensus in the United States that sustained both the U.S. military presence overseas and the growing welfare state at home.[9]

## The United States and Globalization

To portray the U.S. territorial economy as a "victim" of the worldwide growth in trade would be misleading in two respects. First, some Americans and specific American localities have benefited from trade. Second and more fundamentally, the contemporary world economy is largely a product of U.S. design and ideology. Since the late nineteenth century, American business and political leaders have been major sponsors of an integrated and interdependent world economy. The U.S. economy was the first industrial economy to abandon a territorial mode of operation for what can be called an *interactional mode of operation*. After the U.S. continental·frontier closed in the 1890s, American businessmen focused on commerce and trade largely independent of the territorial entanglements that constrained and drained their counterparts in Europe and Japan. Paralleling this was a progressive expansion in the geographical scope of U.S. economic interests—from continental and hemispheric scales of emphasis in the early 1900s to a global scale after World War II.

At the root of the American rise to hegemony and the creation of the world economy as we know it today lay two features of the U.S. historical experience. First, America's own colonial past made territorial colonialism an ideologically difficult enterprise; U.S. institutions claimed their origins in colonial revolt rather than dynastic or national continuity. Second, after the Civil War, an integrated national economy emerged that was increasingly dominated by large firms, and as they developed overseas interests, these firms were able to shape the American international agenda. For many years, the division of the world into trading blocs and territorial empires limited U.S. influence. Powerful strains of public opinion were also opposed to American involvement in foreign economic and political affairs. After World War II, however, an intensely internationalist American agenda, sponsoring free trade, currency convertibility, and international investment, was advanced in explicit counterpoint to the autarkic dogmas of Soviet Communism and as a response to the competitive trading blocs that were seen as partly responsible for the depression of the 1930s. The effort to design a "free world" order in the immediate postwar years laid the groundwork for the internationalization of economic activities in the 1960s that brought tremendous expansion in U.S. firms' investment overseas and the increased importance of trade for the U.S. territorial economy.

Between 1960 and 1970, new American corporate investments abroad expanded from 21 percent to 40 percent of total investments. Much of this reflected the desire to augment markets by avoiding trade barriers, such as tariffs and quotas. But some of it involved a search for lower wage costs on the part of labor-intensive industries. For example, Motorola now has only 44 percent of its 100,000 employees in the United States versus nearly 100 percent in 1960. At the same time, the products of Motorola and of other firms, both American and foreign, were building markets in the United States as imports. A "global shift," or internationalization of production, was under way.[10]

The new transnational economic order has three important features that set it apart from those of earlier periods. First, foreign direct investment among major industrial countries has increased at a faster rate than has the growth of exports among them. The ties that bind industrialized economies together are those of investment more than trade. In the 1980s, the rate of growth of foreign direct investments in the world economy was three times that of the growth of world exports of goods and services.[11]

Second, national trade accounts can be misleading guides to the complex patterns of trade and investment that characterize the new global economy. Perhaps 40 percent of total world trade between countries as of 1990 was trade within firms.[12] Further, more than half of all trade between the major industrial countries is trade between firms and their foreign affiliates. A third of U.S. exports go to American-owned firms abroad; another third goes from foreign firms in America to their home countries. And because the new global trading networks involve the exchange of services as much as the movement of components and finished goods, many products no longer have distinctive national identities. The U.S. 1986 trade deficit of $144 billion thus becomes a trade surplus of $77 billion if the activities of U.S.-owned firms outside the United States and foreign-owned firms in the United States are included in the calculations.[13]

Third, as the U.S. territorial economy loses manufacturing jobs and shares of world production to other places, the global shares of its firms are maintained or enhanced. As the U.S. share of world manufactured exports went from 17.5 percent in 1966 to 14.0 percent in 1984, American firms and their affiliates increased their shares from 17.7 percent to 18.1 percent.[14] This leads to the question, "Who is US?" in relation to government policies that can favor U.S. firms rather than the U.S. economy.[15] From this point of view, helping "foreign" firms locate in the United States benefits the U.S. territorial economy more than helping "American" firms, which may be owned by Americans or headquartered in the United States but have most of their facilities and employees located overseas.[16]

## The Economic Mechanisms Producing Negative Consequences for the U.S. Economy

How has the "globalization" of the U.S. economy produced the redistribution of incomes and the shrinking middle class described in the first section of this chapter? Three interlocking mechanisms have been particularly important in producing these negative consequences. First, U.S. government macroeconomic policies and the activities of American firms have increased the exposure and vulnerability of the U.S. economy to international competition. The GATT and bilateral agreements on limiting impediments to trade began to open up the U.S. economy in the 1960s, while American firms began globalizing their operations. The net effect has been a reduction in the U.S. share of total world production (though the United States remains the single largest producer) and an increasing American involvement in world trade (as measured by U.S. exports as a share of total world exports). Consequently, as goods have been traded more freely, prices and production costs have been set globally. Labor-intensive goods are more cheaply produced in low-wage countries, so low-skilled work formerly done by American labor (sometimes under generous contracts negotiated by trade unions) has flowed overseas. Competitive trading has also led to declines in the incomes of low-skilled U.S. workers. In addition, the recent political weakness of labor unions in the United States has meant that American firms have found it relatively easy to adjust to changed conditions at the expense of low-skilled workers.

Second, the U.S. economy suffers from a low rate of fixed investment in manufacturing plants, research and development, and employee training. The consequences of this are lower productivity increases relative to many other countries, a drop in national economic competitiveness (particularly relative to Japan and Germany), and a frantic search for quick fixes to counter declines in profitability. (Much-publicized fixes have included payoffs, employee "paybacks," moving to states or municipalities that offer fiscal "sweeteners" such as tax breaks, moving offshore, stripping assets from established operations, and moving into new sectors.)

Many factors have been at work in "hollowing out" the American economy. One is the increasingly fragmented and transient nature of firm ownership in the United States.[17] Institutional investors, such as pension funds, have increased their share of total firm equity from 8 percent in 1950 to 60 percent in 1990. This gives managers considerable autonomy but at the expense of long-term investment. For example, in the 1980s, many managers and "corporate raiders" preferred the short-term results coming from mergers and acquisitions to such long-term strategies as investment in new products and worker training. Of course, one effect of this in the 1980s was to increase employment and incomes in the financial services industry.

Another factor accounting for low investment is America's low savings rate. Funding personal consumption has increasingly taken priority over saving and investment, which has affected both business fixed investment and public investment in infrastructure. The lack of investment in physical infrastructure (roads, sewers, and so on) may have had a particularly negative impact on productivity since the late 1960s.[18] Although capital markets are increasingly globalized and American firms can draw on foreign sources, there is still a fairly high positive correlation between domestic savings and domestic investment across a range of countries, including the United States.[19] By 1990, 58 percent of national savings were absorbed in paying the U.S. federal budget deficit, compared to the 2-percent average of the 1960s. Thus, the federal deficit now operates as a drag on the national economy by absorbing domestic savings and by diverting potentially productive foreign portfolio investment into debt service.

A large portion of the U.S. current account deficit (the gap between what the U.S. territorial economy "earns" outside and the total amount that comes into the United States) is attributable to foreign borrowing to cover the federal budget deficit ($400 billion alone in 1992, or 6.7 percent of GNP). This cuts into American living standards by sending abroad payments that could be invested in the productive capacity of the U.S. territorial economy. The debt's effect upon interest rates and the value of the U.S. dollar against other currencies also constrains the U.S. government's use of fiscal and monetary policy to manage the economy. Since the late 1970s, the American economy has become trapped in a vortex of currency and interest-rate volatility as successive governments have tried, through accords with foreign governments and shifts in interest rates, to create a better national economic climate.[20] The dollar, as the major standard for global exchange, remains a major weapon in the hands of U.S. policy-makers now that the federal deficit has reduced the possibility of government spending being used as an economic catalyst. American leverage over the world economy and domestic investment has faded as a result of increased openness in that world economy and low levels of private investment; it has also been squandered by successive national governments that increased military and entitlement (e.g., social security) spending without raising taxes.[21]

The third "mechanism" that is squeezing the middle class is the decline in American technological leadership. The relative competitiveness of industries depends, in part, upon their ability to identify and exploit new products and production technologies. In the aftermath of World War II, the United States had no peer in this regard. Since the 1970s, however, the U.S. patent balance (a measure of the flow of innovative technologies) with Japan and Germany has turned increasingly negative. Although U.S. firms now find themselves faced with entire markets dominated by foreign producers (such as that for semiconductors), they apparently continue to give relatively low priority to investment in research and development (R&D). More importantly, perhaps, the huge U.S. government investment in science and technology over the past few decades has largely been in areas connected to military applications rather than market-oriented research. With U.S. R&D dominated by the defense sector, foreign competitors have been able to go "straight to market" with innovations; meanwhile, the American technology policy required slow and costly justifications in terms of national security.

The end of the Cold War may allow the U.S. government to reorder its technological priorities. Even so, technologies and new innovations are the property of the firms that bought or created them, rather than the territories in which they may have been developed. With economic globalization, technologies are no longer tied to particular national economic spaces or to increasing the productivity of a national or local economy. The incomes of those who invent and develop technologies can increase without a "filtering down" of benefits to workers and communities. And even high-end activities, such as research and development, can also move abroad, as has happened with IBM and Motorola.

Increased openness places a premium on the ability of a territorial economy to generate the investment and technologies that can meet the challenge of foreign competition. Failure to do so in a "free trade" world exacts a heavy price for a national economy. But American firms regard the world as their oyster; they are not necessarily constrained by loyalty to the U.S. territorial economy if they can be more successful elsewhere. As one businessman declared, "The United States does not have an automatic call on our resources. There is no mindset that puts the country first."[22] This is at the heart of the seeming paradox between American global hegemony and the changed condition of the U.S. territorial economy.

## Conclusion

There is nothing "natural" or inevitable about a world divided into national or territorial economies. Under American influence, the growth in trade and financial flows has produced a world economy in which even U.S. hegemony cannot guarantee a perpetual dividend for America's national economy. For many Americans, there is a divorce rather than an identity of interest between the U.S. and world economies. The "free world" that the Cold War was fought to sustain no longer seems so unambiguously a good thing.

After the Cold War, not only Americans are asking the "who is us?" question. The consequences of increased trade and capital mobility for all national economies and the incomes of relatively immobile populations everywhere are beginning to excite tremendous popular interest all over the world. Yet discussions about geopolitics and economic development continue to be cast largely in terms of the national territories and "national interests" of conventional theories of international relations. It is as if the world economy did not exist.

Superficially, the United States now stands in the position it occupied in 1945. It was the world's only military superpower then, and so it is now. It was the world's largest economy then, and so it is now. And if anything, its cultural influence is greater now than then. But America is no longer confident of its position. Like "ordinary" countries, it now feels the pressure of the outside world on its economy, and many Americans fear internal social fragmentation will result. The new world economy has no natural sympathies, even in the homeland of those who did the most to create it.

## Notes

Earlier versions of this chapter were presented as lectures at the University of Macerata, Italy (June 10, 1991), and at Cambridge University, England (February 9, 1992). The interesting questions and suggestions that I received in both places have helped me in rewriting the chapter for this volume.

1. S. Gill, *American Hegemony and the Trilateral Commission* (Cambridge: Cambridge University Press, 1990).

2. W. Peterson, "The Silent Depression," *Challenge* (July-August 1991), pp. 30–31; K. Phillips, *The Politics of Rich and Poor* (New York: Random House, 1991).

3. G.J. Duncan, T.M. Smeeding, and W. Rodgers, *W(h)ither the Middle Class? A Dynamic View*, Income Security Policy Studies Series, no. 1 (Syracuse, N.Y.: Metropolitan Studies Program, Maxwell School, Syracuse University, 1992).

4. M.H. Kosters, *Workers and Their Wages* (Washington, D.C.: American Enterprise Institute, 1992).

5. R. Erzan and A.J. Yeats, "Implications of Current Factor Proportions Indices for the Competitive Position of the U.S. Manufacturing and Service Industries in the Year 2000," *Journal of Business*, vol. 64 (1991), pp. 229–254.

6. See Phillips, *The Politics of Rich and Poor.*

7. Office of Technology Assessment (OTA), *After the Cold War: Living with Lower Defense Spending* (Washington D.C.: OTA, 1992).

8. E.E. Leamer, *Wage Effects of a U.S.-Mexican Free Trade Agreement,* Working Paper 3991 (Cambridge, Mass.: National Bureau of Economic Research, 1992).

9. J.A. Agnew, *The United States in the World Economy: A Regional Geography* (Cambridge: Cambridge University Press, 1987).

10. P. Dicken, *Global Shift: The Internationalization of Economic Activity* (New York: Guilford Press, 1992).

11. "Globetrotting," *Economist,* July 27, 1991, p. 58.

12. R.B. Reich, *The Work of Nations: Preparing Ourselves for 21st Century Capitalism* (New York: Knopf, 1991).

13. D. Julius, *Global Companies and Public Policy: The Growing Challenge of Foreign Direct Investment* (New York: Council on Foreign Relations, 1990).

14. R. Lipsey and I. Kravis, "The Competitiveness and Comparative Advantage of U.S. Multinationals, 1957–1984," *Banca Nazionale del Lavoro Quarterly Review*, vol. 161 (1987), pp. 81–96.

15. R.B. Reich, "Who Is Us?" *Harvard Business Review* (January-February 1990), pp. 53–64.

16. L.D. Tyson, "They Are Not Us: Why American Ownership Still Matters," *The American Prospect* (Winter 1991), pp. 37–49; R.B. Reich, "Who Do We Think They Are?" *The American Prospect* (Winter 1991), pp. 49–53.

17. M. Porter, *Capital Choices: Changing the Way America Invests in Industry* (Cambridge, Mass.: Harvard Business School, 1992).

18. A.H. Munnell, "Why Has Productivity Growth Declined? Productivity and Public Investment," *New England Economic Review* (January-February 1990), pp. 3–22.

19. T. Bayoumi, *Saving-Investment Correlations,* Working Paper 89/66 (Washington, D.C.: IMF, 1989).

20. R. McCulloch, "Macroeconomic Policy, Trade, and the Dollar," in *The Economics of the Dollar Cycle,* S. Gerlach and P.A. Petri, eds. (Cambridge, Mass.: MIT Press, 1990).

21. B.M. Friedman, *Day of Reckoning: The Consequences of American Economic Policy* (New York: Random House, 1989); D.P. Calleo, *The Bankrupting of America: How the Federal Budget Is Impoverishing the Nation* (New York: Morrow, 1992).

22. L. Uchitelle, "U.S. Businesses Loosen Link to Mother Country," *New York Times,* May 21, 1989.

# SIXTEEN

## Maximizing Entropy?
## New Geopolitical Orders and
## the Internationalization of Business

### STUART CORBRIDGE

THE CONDUCT AND WRITING of geopolitics has changed greatly over the past twenty years. At one level, this reflects the end of the Cold War and the demise of the Soviet Union. The breakup of the state Socialist economies of Eastern Europe signaled further unease with the concept and practice of Socialism, and some commentators have prematurely proclaimed the end of history.[1] In geopolitical theory, the end of the Cold War has coincided with an upsurge in writings about geopolitics and the ability of the United States to manage the geopolitical world order.[2] At this level, political geographers are moving "inside" the surviving superpower to interrogate its governing myths and the words and practices by which it defines its external relations.[3]

Political geographers are also studying the growing transnationalization of economic and political relations. This approach to geopolitics moves away from an analysis of "the impact of *fixed* geographical conditions (heartlands/rimlands, lifelines, choke-points, critical strategic zones, domino effects) upon the activities of the 'Great Powers.'"[4] It focuses on industrial and financial capital flows that are redefining international relations and blurring national boundaries. Notwithstanding its military power, the United States is far from hegemonic in international economic and financial circles. In fact, the contemporary geopolitical economy has three centers of economic and political power—the United States, the European Community (EC), and Japan—that are defined by an emerging worldwide hierarchy of city-systems and by flows of capital, institutions, and agents. This new world of quasi-states and uncertain sovereignties presents opportunities for both stable international relationships and the creation of new instabilities.[5]

This chapter's focus is on the prospects for hegemonic stability and stable international relations in the face of rapidly internationalizing relations of economic production and exchange. Must this age of "late modernity"—a post–Cold War era of "deepening time-space compression"[6]—return us to a state of anarchy (or even entropy) in international political relations?

The second section of this chapter examines the internationalization and globalization of business (including the business of money and information) since 1945, briefly noting its changing geographies and raisons d'être. The third section discusses whether the recent internationalization of economic relations is linked to a period of hegemonic instability in which internationalist rules and regulations cannot easily be applied. Particular attention is paid to international trading relationships and the international debt crisis. An opposing hypothesis is considered in the fourth section: that the multilateralization of economic relationships and the creation of a decentralized global division of labor can support new and stable international relationships. This section also challenges the idea that nation-states must be at the heart of geopolitical analysis. Finally, in the fifth section, the contradictions between contemporary geopolitics and a changing global geopolitical economy are highlighted. Caution is urged for those who would proclaim the end of history and the end of geography and those who claim to already detect the outlines of a New World Order. Few such signs are clearly visible. Ours is still an uncertain world.

## Toward Globalization:
## The World Economy Since 1944–1945

The economic context for international political relations has changed dramatically over the past fifty years. This chapter provides a stylized and chronological account of the development of a global political economy since 1944–1945, paying particular attention to the differences between internationalization and globalization and to the geographical consequences and implications of these "global shifts."[7]

Although the world economy was never a collection of isolated regional and national economies, the first great era of economic internationalism coincided with Britain's rise to power as a global hegemony in the mid-to-late nineteenth century. Under the classical gold standard system that operated from 1870 to 1914, individual countries were required to run their economies in accordance with the economic imperatives of free trade and free capital movements.[8] At this time, too, large amounts of British capital were exported around the world, particularly to the United States, Canada, South Africa, and Argentina. The colonized countries were also expected to run their economies in line with the economic orthodoxies advanced in the colonial capitals, though a tendency to imperial zones of preference and creeping protectionism was already apparent by the turn of the century.

In the interwar years (1919–1939), this internationalized world economy fell apart. World War I had all but bankrupted Britain, and the United States was becoming the world's leading creditor country. Although the gold standard was reinvented in the 1920s, it could not survive past 1928, not least of all because Great Britain lacked the power to enforce the old rules of the game.[9] Following the crash of 1929 and the depression of 1929–1933, many countries—including Germany and Japan—sought to rebuild their economies by means of protectionism, competitive devaluations, and territorial expansionism. The world economy was now wracked by predatory economic and political mercantilism and the absence of international economic cooperation.

As World War II drew toward a close in 1944–1945, it became apparent that the United States would emerge as an unrivaled economic and financial superpower (although the Soviet Union would shortly match its military capabilities). It also became clear to the internationalists within the U.S. government that the United States could not prosper after the war without also laying the foundations for economic growth and recovery in Europe (and possibly in Japan, although that became more obvious at the time of the Korean War). This, in turn, meant that the United States would have to establish and then police a system of international relations that encouraged economic integration and provided for stable financial conditions. This system was duly mapped out at the United Nations Monetary and Financial Conference, held at Bretton Woods in July 1944. At this conference, U.S. negotiators closed the door on that version of U.S. isolationism that called for the ruralization of Germany and the rebuilding of "fortress America";[10] instead, they adapted John Maynard Keynes's vision of a postwar economic order based upon free trade between independent countries, with currency convertibility tied to a fixed-peg exchange rate system. Propping up the Bretton Woods system would be the might of the U.S. economy (perhaps half of the world economy in 1950), reflected in the U.S. dollar. The U.S. dollar would serve as the main unit of international account currency, and other currencies would price themselves in relation to this currency. The U.S. government agreed to fix the value of the U.S. dollar against gold and thus not to print excessive greenbacks.[11]

The Bretton Woods monetary system set the stage for the golden age of capitalism, which cushioned the advanced industrial world from 1945 to 1970.[12] With Bretton Woods establishing the new rules of the game in 1944—and with them, the International Bank for Reconstruction and Development (IBRD, or World Bank) and the International Monetary Fund (IMF)—the U.S. government moved to rebuild the economies of Western Europe and Japan by several means: IBRD transfers ($700 million between 1947 and 1952); the Marshall Plan for European Recovery (transfers of $13 billion between 1948 and 1952); increased spending on arms during both the Korean War and the Cold War (dwarfing official economic transfers); creating the world's first large-scale program of official development assistance (mainly to Latin America, Israel, and Southeast Asia); and encouraging investment overseas by private U.S. firms.

In the 1950s, U.S. firms—including Ford, General Motors, IBM, ITT, and Exxon—massively expanded their production facilities in Western Europe amid an estimated net private capital flow from the United States to Western Europe of $80 billion between 1950 and 1960. American corporations were attracted to countries across the Atlantic by the relatively low cost of labor in many European nations and by the access to burgeoning local markets (which had been rebuilt with U.S. dollars and given further impetus by the founding of the European Economic Community [EC] in 1957). This first wave of postwar foreign investment by U.S.-based multinational corporations was also made possible by new communications technologies, by new systems of corporate management and accounting, and by the emergence in Europe of currency markets that accepted dollar deposits beyond the regulatory reach of U.S. authorities. As Richard O'Brien points out: "In the earliest days the demand for eurocurrency loans came as a result of an increase in activities in Europe by U.S. multinationals. One of the first borrowers of eurodollars was IBM Europe. Although this was in the days of fixed exchange rates and thus limited foreign exchange risk, lending dollars to a company in Europe might have been considered problematic if that company had no clear stream of dollar earnings or access to dollars for repayment. IBM Europe, however, was seen as ultimately having access to dollars through its parent, and thus did not pose any 'geographical mismatch problem.'"[13]

The formation of the Euromarkets did not signal a truly global market in currencies, at least not in the 1950s and 1960s. The early Eurocurrency markets were primarily offshore markets trading currencies that could clearly be linked back to one dominant country, the United States. This was also the case with the multinationalization of production. Although multinational corporations (MNCs) became more important in the 1960s and 1970s—with U.S. corporations moving beyond Western Europe and with European and Japanese firms making their own presences felt worldwide—their production facilities were primarily meant to serve national markets, and the headquarters of most MNCs continued to have strong national affiliations. At this stage, few multinationals had become transnational or global corporations; rather, they were vehicles for the further internationalization of trade and private capital flows, particularly between Europe, Japan, and the United States. The blurring of discrete national economies was further encouraged in the mid-1960s by U.S. government attempts to place restrictions on the domestic activities of U.S. banks, which prompted them (led by the Bank of America and Citibank) to expand their offshore operations away from the eyes of U.S. regulators.[14] In the 1960s, the rate of growth of net Eurocurrency transactions exceeded that of official reserves by a factor of five. Table 16.1 charts the increasing proportion of total assets of resident banking institutions, in different countries from 1960 to 1985, that can be accounted for by foreign-owned institutions.

In August 1971, the U.S. president abandoned America's commitment to maintain a fixed exchange rate between the U.S. dollar and gold. Henceforth, the United States was free to print dollars to the extent that non-U.S. agents and countries were prepared to hold them as IOUs and as a means of international payment. The United States, for its part, sought to restore the competitiveness of

TABLE 16.1    *Relative Importance of Assets of Foreign-owned Banking Institutions Operating in Selected Host Countries, 1960–1985 (in percentages)*[a]

| Host Country | December 1960 | December 1970 | December 1980 | June 1985 |
|---|---|---|---|---|
| Belgium | 8.2[b] | 22.5 | 41.5 | 51.0 |
| Canada | – | – | – | 6.3 |
| France | 7.2 | 12.3 | 15.0 | 18.2[c] |
| Italy | n.a. | n.a. | 0.9 | 2.4 |
| Japan | n.a. | 1.3 | 3.4 | 3.6 |
| Luxembourg[d] | 8.0 | 57.8 | 85.4 | 85.4 |
| Netherlands[e] | n.a. | n.a. | 17.4[f] | 23.6 |
| Switzerland | n.a. | 10.3 | 11.1 | 12.2 |
| United Kingdom | 6.7 | 37.5 | 55.6 | 62.6 |
| United States[g] | n.a. | 5.8[h] | 8.7 | 12.0 |
| West Germany[i] | 0.5 | 1.4 | 1.9 | 2.4 |

[a]Percent of total assets refers to all banking institutions (domestic and foreign-owned) at end of month.
[b]December 1958.
[c]December 1984.
[d]Banks owned by Belgian residents are not considered foreign-owned banking institutions.
[e]Only universal branches of foreign-owned banking institutions.
[f]December 1983.
[g]Only agencies and branches of foreign-owned banking institutions.
[h]December 1976.
[i]Only branches of foreign-owned banking institutions.

SOURCE: Bank for International Settlements, *Recent Innovations in International Banking* (1986, p. 152); after R. Bryant, *International Financial Intermediation* (Washington, D.C.: Brookings Institution, 1987), Table 3–4.

its domestic economy, vis-à-vis a resurgent Germany and Japan, by driving down the value of the U.S. dollar and by printing dollars to finance a growing balance-of-payments deficit.[15]

In the medium-term, this strategy triggered a rising rate of inflation on a global scale. In the early-to-mid-1970s, however, the monetization of the U.S. deficit fueled only a further massive expansion of the privatized Eurocurrency markets. The economic powers of nation-states were slowly being ceded to the financial markets and their major players. The Eurocurrency markets were also boosted by the petrodollar deposits made in them by members of the Organization of Petroleum Exporting Countries (OPEC) following the third Arab-Israeli War of 1973 and the consequent threefold hike in oil prices. This war more or less coincided with the formal ending of the Bretton Woods system of fixed exchange rates. Currencies would now be allowed to float, and financial institutions making loans— not least of all from the Euromarkets to those newly industrialized and most industrialized countries (NICs and MICs) anxious to chase growth or to finance their balance-of-payments deficits—were forced to devise new financial instruments to protect themselves against the resulting foreign exchange risk.

The 1970s became the decade of the syndicated bank loan, with networks of commercial banks joining together under a lead bank to lend moneys to developing countries at floating rates of interest.[16] Once again, MNCs followed these flows of money into many poor countries, and for a short time, it became fashionable to speak about the "end of the Third World."[17] In the early 1960s, President Kennedy promised an "alliance for growth" in Latin America and ushered in the United Nation's "development decade." Both projects "failed," in part, because of a lack of official development assistance and private direct investment. In the 1970s, development would be different. Between 1970 and 1982, about nine money-center banks from the United States alone lent more than $80 billion to the non-oil-developing countries[18] (see Figure 16.1). At this time, too, a revitalized Mexican Border Industrialization Program (first introduced in 1965) brought rapid economic growth to northern Mexico, and parts of southern Brazil and Argentina seemed to emerge as ex–Third World regions. Astonishment was voiced at the phenomenal rates of growth in gross domestic product

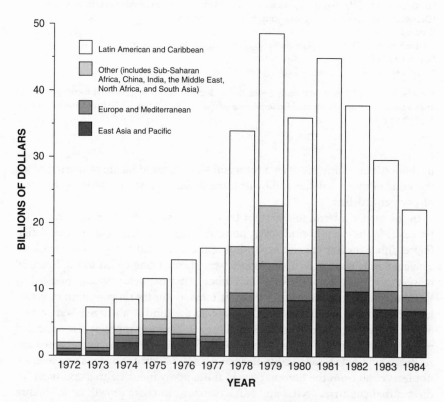

FIGURE 16.1  Syndicated Eurocurrency lending to developing countries, by region, 1972–1984. SOURCE: S. Corbridge, *Debt and Development* (Oxford: Blackwell, 1992), p. 30, using OECD Financial Market Trends data.

(GDP) and exports recorded in South Korea, Taiwan, Singapore, and Hong Kong. As the Ford Motor Corporation laid its plans for a truly global car, the Escort, the time did, indeed, seem ripe to abandon the Three Worlds idea that neatly divided a First World from a Second World and a Third World. In its *World Development Report* of 1980, the World Bank preferred to speak of "centrally planned economies," "capital-surplus oil exporters," "industrialized countries," "middle-income countries," and "low-income countries." The internationalization of business seemed set to herald the dawn of a world economy in which "the greatest challenge [would be] coming to terms with the inexorable spread of economic development over the next hundred years."[19]

The 1980s were not destined to bear out this vision. By 1978, it was apparent to President Carter that the U.S. dollar could not be allowed to fall further and that inflation had reached an unforeseen and threatening level at 14 percent. (It was worse still in the United Kingdom and in many parts of the developing world.) In 1979, the chairman of the Federal Reserve Bank moved swiftly to tighten the money supply in the United States (and, indirectly, in much of the rest of the world). Prime interest rates in the United States climbed from an average of 9.5 percent in 1978 to an average of 15.1 percent in 1982,[20] and the deepest postwar recession (prior to that of the early 1990s) followed. The indebted developing countries suddenly found that moneys they had borrowed at negative real rates of interest now had to be repaid at historically high postwar real rates of interest (see Figure 16.2) and amid a recession marked, above all, by declining nonoil commodity prices. Caught in this bind, most of Latin America followed Mexico's August 1982 slide into debt defaults and a consequent crisis of debt and development. A similar crisis of official debt was apparent in much of low-income Africa. For these countries, the 1980s became a "lost decade of development." By 1990, the combined GDPs of 41 World Bank "low-income countries" (excluding India and China) amounted to less than 1.5 percent of the total combined GDPs of 125 reporting countries. In low-income Africa, the "average" household was worse off in real terms in 1990 than it was in 1960.

In such dire circumstances, talk of globalization seems premature. The 1970s notion that the Third World is no more has been belied by the tragedies of maldevelopment that continue to haunt large parts of Africa, Asia, and Latin America. Although a rush of net inward investment did occur over parts of the Third World in the 1960s and 1970s, capital flows in the 1980s were outward. "To service its foreign debt, Latin America sent to the banks in the industrialized countries, in net terms, $159.1 billion from the end of 1981 to the end of 1986."[21]

The international debt crisis has clearly dented an earlier tendency to construct a global economy. At the same time, though, it has also perversely encouraged a global economy in which the Japanese economy and a globalization of new financial markets and information technologies figure much more prominently.

When Mexico defaulted on its debts in August 1982, it soon became apparent to U.S. authorities that private U.S. banks could fail if Mexico was not provided with the funds to roll over its debt repayments. In the short term, this meant that

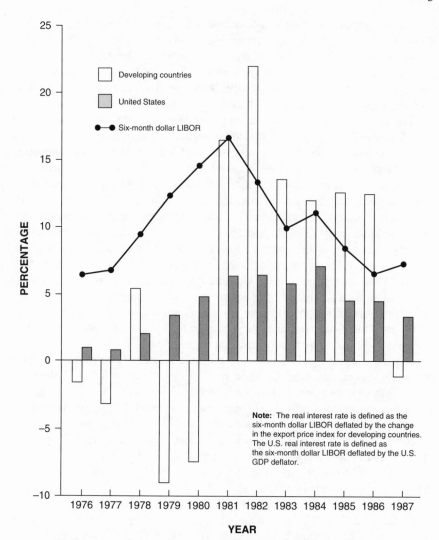

FIGURE 16.2    Real interest rates and the London Inter-Bank Offered Rate (LIBOR).
SOURCE: S. Corbridge, *Debt and Development* (Oxford: Blackwell, 1992), p. 39, using
World Bank data.

U.S. banks had to make further, involuntary loans to Mexico (and other default-
ing countries), under pressure from a newly empowered IMF. The indebted
countries, in turn, would have to engage in structural adjustment programs. In
the medium term, however, it was equally apparent that the indebted countries
could only service their debts by first earning the necessary foreign exchange re-

serves.[22] Given the historical pattern of Latin America's trade, this implied that the U.S. economy would have to be reinvigorated, even at the cost of increased borrowing from abroad. Thus began the second stage of the economic program known as Reaganomics. In 1982, following a period of tight fiscal and monetary policies in 1981 and 1982, Reagan moved to a loose fiscal policy at home, coupled with massively expanded foreign borrowings.[23] A historical buildup of U.S. net assets abroad worth $141 billion by 1982 was turned into a net foreign debt of $112 billion by 1986.[24] By 1990, the United States owed close to 1 trillion U.S. dollars to the rest of the world.

Pumped up by this massive foreign borrowing, the U.S. domestic economy boomed from 1982 to 1989, even though the U.S. current account worsened on the back of a strong U.S. dollar and mounting deindustrialization at home. By 1988, however, it was apparent that the U.S. territorial economy was in long-term decline, even though U.S. firms performed as well as ever on the global stage[25] (see Table 16.2). It was further apparent that Japan had become a major economic

TABLE 16.2    *World's Top Twenty-five Corporations, 1992 (by market value)*

| Rank | | | Market Value |
|------|------|------|------|
| *1992* | *1991* | *Name of Corporation* | *(in billions of U.S. dollars)* |
| 1 | 2 | Royal Dutch/Shell Group (Netherlands/UK) | $77.82 |
| 2 | 1 | Nippon Telegraph & Telephone (Japan) | 77.52 |
| 3 | 2 | Exxon (U.S.) | 75.30 |
| 4 | 6 | Philip Morris (U.S.) | 71.29 |
| 5 | 4 | General Electric (U.S.) | 66.00 |
| 6 | 14 | Wal-Mart Stores | 60.82 |
| 7 | 20 | Coca-Cola (U.S.) | 58.47 |
| 8 | 15 | Merck (U.S.) | 58.41 |
| 9 | 18 | AT&T (U.S.) | 55.85 |
| 10 | 7 | IBM (U.S.) | 51.82 |
| 11 | 16 | Toyota Motor (Japan) | 43.97 |
| 12 | 26 | Glaxo Holdings (UK) | 42.64 |
| 13 | 19 | British Telecom (UK) | 40.45 |
| 14 | 9 | Mitsubishi Bank (Japan) | 39.84 |
| 15 | 17 | Bristol-Myers Squibb (U.S.) | 37.60 |
| 16 | 11 | Sumitomo Bank (Japan) | 37.12 |
| 17 | 22 | du Pont (U.S.) | 35.41 |
| 18 | 28 | Procter & Gamble (U.S.) | 34.74 |
| 19 | 10 | Dai-Ichi Kangyo Bank (Japan) | 34.68 |
| 20 | 5 | Industrial Bank of Japan (Japan) | 34.04 |
| 21 | 8 | Fuji Bank (Japan) | 33.99 |
| 22 | 25 | Johnson & Johnson (U.S.) | 32.28 |
| 23 | 12 | Sanwa Bank (Japan) | 30.41 |
| 24 | 39 | Unilever (Netherlands/UK) | 29.77 |
| 25 | 21 | Tokyo Electric Power (Japan) | 29.25 |

SOURCE: *Business Week,* July 13, 1992.

power, along with a newly united Germany. Although the U.S. economy is still larger than the economies of Germany and Japan combined, the rates of growth of the two latter countries suggest a changing balance of global economic power.[26] Japan signaled its newfound might by acting as the chief underwriter of U.S. external debt in the 1980s while its corporations and citizens bought into American real estate and corporations. By the late 1980s, America's growing dependence on Japan and on financial decisions made in Tokyo were well known.[27]

The emergence of a tripolar world economy is not the only manifestation of the globalization in business affairs. The 1980s also witnessed a concerted attempt by various firms in the service sector to establish bases overseas and on a global stage. This was true not only of the traditional banking sector but also of finance, advertising, accountancy, and insurance companies. This internationalization of services, in turn, represented a still deeper globalization of financial markets and instruments. International trade commonly involves the physical movement of one commodity from one country to another, but the fundability of money in a deregulated world economy means that even customs posts and national identities are often of little significance. The foreign exchange market is international in the sense that "all exchange rates involve different countries,"[28] but it is also globalized. All currencies are exchanged in one way or another. Indeed, there are few entry barriers to the market for it is a twenty-four-hour-a-day market with no special "home," played out on computer screens and telephones all over the world.

The significance of these changes in the global money market should not be underestimated. We have not yet reached "the end of history or geography," nor have we reached the "one world" prophesied by utopian thinkers. The differences between rich and poor places and peoples continue to widen.[29] Nevertheless, we do now live in a global economy in which production is widely internationalized and in which close to 40 percent of international trade is in the form of intrafirm commerce. We also live in a world in which "the markets" can defeat even the most concerted efforts by governments—and groups of governments—to defend particular exchange and interest rates. The withdrawal of the United Kingdom from the European Exchange Rate Mechanism in September 1992 is testimony to the insufficiency of country reserves in the face of massive currency trading on open markets. Today, more than ever, money is a type of information that is traded on computer screens and ignores national identities. The removal of exchange controls and financial deregulation in the early 1980s means that a global capital market now exists more clearly than ever before (see Table 16.3). Even powerful countries like the United States, Germany, and Japan must adapt their economic political ambitions to an internationalized world economy. In this new world, power is rapidly being devolved to the markets and to the IMF and the World Bank (in the case of many developing and ex-Socialist economies). True economic globalization may be in its infancy, but it is apparent nonetheless.

TABLE 16.3    Number of Companies Listed on Various Stock Exchanges at the End of 1990

| Stock Exchange/ Location | Domestic Stocks | Foreign Stocks | Foreign Stocks as Percent of Total | Total |
|---|---|---|---|---|
| Amsterdam | 260 | 238 | 47.8% | 498 |
| London | 2,006 | 553 | 21.6 | 2,559 |
| Frankfurt | 389 | 354 | 47.6 | 743 |
| Paris | 443 | 226 | 33.8 | 669 |
| Zurich | 182 | 240 | 35.9 | 422 |
| Australia | 1,162 | 33 | 2.8 | 1,195 |
| Hong Kong | 284 | 15 | 5.0 | 299 |
| NASDAQ | 3,875 | 256 | 6.2 | 4,131 |
| NYSE | 1,678 | 96 | 5.4 | 1,774 |
| Tokyo | 1,627 | 125 | 7.1 | 1,752 |
| Toronto | 1,127 | 66 | 5.5 | 1,193 |

SOURCE: *Quality of Markets Quarterly Review,* London Stock Exchange, January–March 1991; after R. O'Brien, *Global Financial Integration: The End of Geography* (London: Pinter/RIIA, 1992), Table 1.

## Uncertainty, Instability, and Rivalry in a Posthegemonic World Economy

If an internationalized world economy has emerged forcefully since 1970, what implications might this hold for contemporary geopolitics? The theory of hegemonic stability states that international relations will stabilize when those relationships are defined, regulated, and policed by an unrivaled hegemonic power. Such was the situation when Great Britain was the hegemonic power at the end of the nineteenth century and when free—if often unequal—trade flourished under its tutelage. Such was also the case in the 1950s and 1960s when the United States set the rules of the economic and financial worlds and policed them through its own domestic policies and through the World Bank, the IMF, and the General Agreement on Tariffs and Trade (GATT). At such times, the world economy grew rapidly (if again unequally), and major economic actors were assured a high degree of certainty when they entered into diverse economic transactions.[30] In the period of U.S. hegemony, a complicating factor was the role and position of the Soviet Union as a rival military superpower. Even then, though, the Cold War and an associated balance in spheres of influence ensured that the world system was relatively stable.

According to the theory of hegemonic stability, international relations become fractious and unstable when the accepted hegemony comes under threat and is unable or unwilling to enforce rules that favor multilateral cooperation. This happened in the 1970s, and we continue to live with its consequences. The internationalization of economic relations in the 1950s and 1960s, together with a massive increase in global capital movements, ensured that the economy of the

United States would enter a period of relative decline when compared with the EC and Japan and that the Bretton Woods system of fixed-peg exchange rates, limited capital flows, and balanced regional rates of growth would decay from within.[31] By the mid-1970s, the United States was pursuing an economic policy designed to boost the domestic economy in the short run, with little regard for the medium-term consequences for the world economy.[32] If, in the 1950s and early 1960s, the United States had acted as a benevolent despot, by the 1970s, it was prepared to live with OPEC oil-price rises in the expectation that such rises would hurt Germany and Japan more than the United States. America seemed prepared to stoke the fires of global inflation (by printing excess amounts of U.S. dollars).

The EC and Japan retaliated against the U.S. policies with competitive devaluations and tight money policies of their own. By 1980, new monetary policies were being adopted throughout Western Europe and the United States, and a world recession and international debt crisis followed. The United States, as a declining hegemonic power, was ceding some of its international authority in order to pursue its particular national ambitions.

Hegemonic instability will affect geopolitical-economic relationships of the 1990s in three particular areas: international trade, international capital flows and indebtedness, and the continuing mismatch between U.S. military and economic capabilities.

As of October 1992, the Uruguay Round of the GATT talks continued to founder amid mutual recriminations between the United States and the EC. The range of issues that could not be resolved (international property rights and patents, agricultural policies and subsidies, First World protectionism, high-technology transfers, and so on) suggested a deeper disunity in the modern world economy. International trading relations have never been straightforward, but the GATT impasse suggested a degree of uncertainty and dislocation not apparent at the height of U.S. hegemony. Many developing countries are now openly challenging the doctrine of free trade, even though many of them are being forced to export more primary commodities as part of their agreements with the IMF and the World Bank. The developing countries are also facing new economic rivals from the ex-Socialist world and creeping protectionism in the advanced industrial world. In 1985, the World Bank suggested that "an increase in protectionism [in industrial countries] big enough to produce a 10 percent deterioration in the terms of trade of Latin America would cost the region as much as the real interest cost of their entire debt."[33] For their part, some of the advanced industrial countries are striving to establish semiprotected trading "zones of influence," for example, the North American Free Trade Agreement.

As the world economy moves into its deepest recession since the 1930s, a new form of mercantilism is slowly taking hold, perhaps with a trading bloc in the Americas emerging in parallel to a yen zone in East Asia and Australasia.[34] Against such a backdrop and given the devastation of many of Africa's economies, Western Europe will consolidate its single market by the end of the 1990s while looking eastward to an expanded European Community that might even include former Soviet bloc countries and Turkey. The international trading economy may now resemble the world economy of the 1930s more than the benign trading environment of the 1960s. The present recession may itself reflect a greater volatility in international economic relations. In the 1930s, Keynes suggested that private business investment would only expand when the "animal instincts" of the world's entrepreneurs were undergirded by a general feeling of economic confidence. Confidence, in turn, was boosted to the extent that economic agents could predict a stable future. But in the mid-1980s, such expectations were regularly belied; the value of the pound against the U.S. dollar between 1980 and 1986 fluctuated from close to 1 dollar to 1 pound to 2.4 dollars to 1 pound. Thus, while the world economy was internationalizing, the conditions for stable and expanded international trade were eroded because there was no hegemonic power to enforce order.

The international debt crisis further illustrates hegemonic instability. The origins of the developing countries' debt crisis lie firmly with the actions of OPEC in the 1970s and, more especially, with the unwillingness of the United States and the Bretton Woods institutions to provide official bilateral or multilateral development assistance to oil-importing developing countries that face balance-of-payment difficulties. By the mid-1970s, the United States could not pay for such a program of assistance. In the 1970s, it ceded a good deal of its economic power to the markets and encouraged the private banks to recycle OPEC's petrodollars through the private Eurocurrency markets. The risks associated with international money recycling fell on the indebted countries, which were then hit by the West's tight money policies of the early 1980s. Again, unilateral actions by a declining economic superpower hurt the indebted world very badly. The United States itself then fell into debt, and by the end of the 1980s, the world economy mapped out at Bretton Woods had been turned on its head: Capital now flowed from the poor countries to the rich countries, and the world's most powerful economy was also the most indebted. Debt servicing was dictating a new geography of international trade. Fears grew in Europe and Japan that the United States would service its debt by driving down the U.S. dollar (the currency in which its debt to Japan and other creditors would be made), while aggressively seeking out new markets for its tradable goods and services.

Finally, there is the matter of America's post–Cold War military might. The collapse of the Soviet Union might be read in two ways. It might seem that the world is now a safer place and that rapid steps can be made to rebuild civilian economies—the peace dividend. The United States might also seem to be in a position to lead a multilateral force against those countries, such as Iraq, that transgress international rules of behavior. On the other hand, the war in Iraq also demonstrated a certain weakness in the position of the United States. Although U.S. military might was unrivaled, the mounting costs of modern warfare forced the United States to seek financial assistance from its allies.[35] Against a background of nuclear proliferation and humanitarian crises, America may again be provoked into military actions that it can ill afford. The economic difficulties of the United States—and the relative military weakness of Germany and Japan—will caution America against becoming involved even when it is invited. Either way, the connections between the geopolitical world of military strategy and the economic world of greater complexity and decentralization will become increasingly clear and close.

## Reasons to Be Cheerful
## . . . or Hegemony Revisited

Despite the preceding arguments, the consequences of a decline in U.S. hegemony and an associated internationalization of the circuits of capital may not be all negative. Economic deterritorialization, decentralization, and multilateralism might create bold new opportunities for global political relationships, particularly the possible emergence of "dispersed power principles."[36]

The internationalization of business implies a measure of deterritorialization. The process is clearly evident in the United States where the territorial economy continues to suffer from relative decline even as U.S. firms acquit themselves with distinction on the international stage (see Chapter 15). Deterritorialization can easily provoke a climate of economic protectionism that slides into a cultural xenophobia, such as the popular denunciation of the Japanese in America.[37]

The emergence of a transnational business class means that many economic and political power brokers in the major industrial countries are responsible for substantial assets in countries other than those in which they reside.[38] These multilateral, financial ties belie the notion that Germany, Japan, or the United States might ever go to war with one another to defend their domestic economies. In a very real sense, the "U.S. economy" no longer exists; the same can be said for Japan and Germany, both of which have substantial capital stakes offshore.

Statistics on international trade continue to be collected and published, but their meaning is increasingly open to question. When a customer in Toronto, for example, buys a Chevrolet Spectrum, is it an American car? Ostensibly, it is, but in reality, it is little more than a Japanese Isuzu in disguise, built under license in the United States. When the car is shipped to Canada, can trade statistics accurately express the different geographical origins of value-added in this case? Similarly, how are cross-border, illicit financial transactions accounted for? The cityscapes of New York and Miami are powered, in large part, by massive flows of legal and illegal moneys, which bring together David Harvey's "fictitious capital" (or credit moneys) with an emerging network of "fictitious spaces."[39] The extraordinary scale of these transfers and of the illegal drug and arms trade to which they are sometimes linked illustrates the ever-greater fluidity of the modern world economy. Accountancy firms may be internationalizing, but international accountancy and accounting continue to lag behind the complexity and magnitude of current transactions. Today's geopolitical economy is dominated less by conventional economic centers, such as firms, plants, and industrial regions, than by the flows of money, information, business, and labor that link these centers. These vital economic flows make the defense of space and place, in a conventional geopolitical sense, more difficult than it once was. "Whose space?" and "whose place?" are pertinent questions. Where *do* today's "national" economies begin and end, and who commands or regulates them?

Deterritorialization is also linked to economic decentralization. When so-called geopoliticians and political scientists refer to the "end of history" and the prospects for a decentralized world polity based on democratic, market-based economies, they forget that the Third World, unlike the First World, is not free from immediate military threat. It might even be argued that the construction of today's New World Order is taking place on the backs of the Third World countries, turning an earlier East-West conflict into a North-South battle.[40]

At another level, the notion of decentralization does highlight a real redistribution and reconstruction of the postwar world economy. This is apparent in the emergence of the newly industrialized and newly industrializing countries in parts of Latin America and Eastern Europe. It is also apparent in the emergence of highly developed city-sectors, cities and city regions within even the low- and middle-income countries.

It would be easy to exaggerate the significance of these developments. Such changes matter very little to the lives of most men and women in India, for example, although they are symbols of a wider economic liberalization that does have far-reaching effects.[41] In terms of the contemporary geopolitical economy, the implication surely is that a hierarchy of nation-states is not the only means by which we might conceptualize, order, and classify the world around us. Such systems of classification are given in the annual reports of the World Bank, the IMF, and the UN (which might list countries in an economic hierarchy, ascending from Mozambique to Switzerland). But the modern world economy also resembles a gigantic central-place system, in which significant power and wealth is concentrated in just a few global cities (London, New York, and Tokyo at a minimum—one for each of the major "eight-hour" time zones), with second-order cities like Paris, Frankfurt, Los Angeles, Sydney, and Hong Kong linking on to cities of the third, fourth, and fifth orders (which might include parts of Bombay and New Delhi, Sao Paulo, Lagos, and Manila).

As with the deterritorialized economy, these decentered spaces or places highlight the differences that beset the modern world economy while also emphasizing the similarities and linkages that bind today's geopolitical economy.[42] In theory, at least, the decentering of economic life should be associated with a similar, if perhaps slower, decentering of political power. For the favored inhabitants of this favored central-place system, the defense of "national space" again becomes problematic. Leaders of indebted Latin America—who allowed capital earned in their countries to take flight to Miami and New York, even as they voiced anti-American rhetoric—proved unwilling to challenge the rules of an international financial system in which many had a large stake. The decentering of economic life (at least away from the old industrial heartlands) goes hand in hand with the further consolidation of an international business class and a parallel internationalization of "domestic" politics.

Finally, there is the matter of multilateralization. In the eyes of some commentators, the war against Iraq was evidence of the enhanced role played by the United Nations in international strategic affairs. The United States was able to prosecute a war against Iraq only after first gaining the support of its economic allies and the General Assembly of the UN. Others disagree, pointing out that the United States (like the EC and Japan) is still as likely to ignore international laws and institutions (e.g., in supporting the contras in Nicaragua) as it is to obey them. The UN has never been a powerful multilateral institution, especially in comparison with the growing powers of bodies working within the global political *economy:* from the World Bank and the IMF to the markets themselves.

For many years now, the World Bank has been the single largest source of official development assistance, but in the 1980s, its role and significance were greatly expanded in response to the global recession and the developing countries' debt crisis.[43] The World Bank began to intervene more directly in the economic management of indebted member countries but not in the economies of First World countries, which also had large balance-of-payment deficits. The bank—and the IMF—pressed economic reforms on poor countries designed to integrate them further into an open international economy. The World Bank also offered funds to countries facing the social unrest over IMF-mandated structural adjustment programs and provided some funds to compensate for unexpected changes in exchange rates and commodity prices.[44]

The IMF assumed a more visible role in international economic affairs, prompting many in Africa to berate the institution and its structural adjustment policies for "imposing misery and famine."[45] In the 1970s, the World Bank and the IMF had seen their power decline in tandem with a decline in their real resources, as compared to official country reserves and private Eurocurrency markets. In the 1980s, their coffers filled again as the United States and some other member countries looked to the two Bretton Woods institutions to repair the damage done by certain commercial banks. By 1990, some countries in low-income Africa (including Mozambique and Tanzania) relied upon official development assistance from multilateral institutions for more than 45 percent of their gross national products. The Bretton Woods institutions also began to play key roles in the reconstruction of Eastern Europe and the former Soviet Union. In all these, governmental decision-making has been compromised by dependence on multilateral financial agencies.

In the advanced industrial world, the capacity of what might be called "multilateralization" is still more limited. As in large parts of the developing world, the multilateralism that matters most is linked to economic and financial markets and the internationalization of business. Throughout the European Community, business interests now look with hope toward a European economic union that will deliver a single European currency by about the year 2000. Businesses are much less concerned about progress toward political unification. National cultural identities can be allowed to survive, but they should not interfere with economic transactions free of national customs posts. Businesses want a stable framework for international investment, which should be provided by a greater use of a common unit of currency such as the European Currency Unit (ECU). The power to regulate this currency will most likely fall upon Germany's Bundesbank. This might seem to suggest that the German national economy plays a leading role, but the Bundesbank, like the U.S. Federal Reserve (and unlike the Bank of England), is free from direct political interference. Interest and exchange rate policies will be set by the Bundesbank and perhaps prompted by financial authorities in Japan and the United States and, much more importantly, by the financial markets themselves.

If developments in Europe are matched by similar developments elsewhere, the geopolitical economic (geopolinomic) world order of the early twenty-first century will be quite unlike the order of the mid-twentieth century. Geopolitics in the advanced industrial world, based on an internationalized community of capital, will have less regard for military might and far more regard for the disciplining of labor and resurgent nationalism. Geopolitics will not only be funded by a world economy, it will increasingly be obliged to serve it.

Cleavage in this New World Order will not be between East and West, nor between Europe, Japan, and the United States. In a deterritorializing, decentering, and multilateralizing world system, hegemony might reside not with a single country but with the markets themselves. Capital transactions will be even more abstract, with power exercised, unequally, through various nodal pressure points and networks in an expanding global central-place system. Within this decentralized system, the markets and various supranational institutions—linked by new lines of communication—might pressure the EC, the United States, and Japan to reach agreements on potentially divisive economic and political issues. Slowly, perhaps, but not unsurely, power might seep away from a set of fixed geographical regions and toward a less visible network of economic and political actors, institutions, and transactions.

## Conclusion

This chapter is a thumbnail sketch of some of the contradictory geopolitical implications that are associated with a growing internationalization of business. The path to a New World Order is unclear; signs point in different directions—to both an entropic disorder and a decentered orderliness. The future will remain uncertain because the internationalization of capital and information will continue to destabilize and even dissolve those fixed territorial units that conventionally have been at the heart of geopolitical theory and practice. We must now live with an uncertain world, in part because of a nascent decentering of production and exchange and an associated explosion in new information technologies. As the balance of power in our late-modern world shifts in country-location terms from the United States, Germany, and Japan, it is also changing in form and structure.

The advanced industrial world will slowly expand and will enjoy a period of relative, internal, geopolitical stability (at least in military terms). The south (or those Third World areas within the First World, like the Bronx and south-central Los Angeles) will not fare nearly so well. To the extent that these communities and even countries are only the "clients" of the markets and the multilateral institutions, their disempowerment will surely deny them the fruits of any new system of decentered hegemony that might emerge. For such peoples and places, physical violence will remain intrinsic. Only within the newly hegemonic center of decentered power will geopolitics be written in the language of economic costs and benefits. A geopolitical economy framework is a method of thinking about the modern world system; it will include not only economic warfare but also military warfare and extended use of physical force. Economic inequity continues to reinforce belligerence, but increasingly, it will do so away from the key nodes of a decentered network of hegemonic power.

## Notes

1. F. Fukuyama, "The End of History?" *The National Interest,* vol. 16 (1989), pp. 3–18; idem, *The End of History and the Last Man* (London: Hamish Hamilton, 1991).

2. P. Taylor, *Britain and the Cold War: 1945 as Geopolitical Transition* (London: Pinter, 1990).

3. S. Dalby, *Creating the Second World War: The Discourse of Politics* (London: Pinter, 1990).

4. J. Agnew and S. Corbridge, "The New Geopolitics: The Dynamics of Geopolitical Disorder," in *A World in Crisis? Geographical Perspectives,* 2d ed., R. Johnston and P. Taylor, eds. (Oxford: Blackwell, 1989), p. 267.

5. R. Jackson, *Quasi-States: Sovereignty, International Relations and the Third World* (Cambridge: Cambridge University Press, 1990).

6. D. Harvey, *The Condition of Postmodernity* (Oxford: Blackwell, 1989).

7. P. Dicken, *Global Shift: Industrial Change in a Turbulent World,* 2d ed. (London: Harper and Row, 1991).

8. M. de Cecco, *Money and Empire: The International Gold Standard, 1890–1914* (London: Blackwell, 1974).

9. G. Ingham, *Capitalism Divided? The City and Industry in British Social Development* (London: Macmillan, 1984).

10. H. Wachtel, *The Money Mandarins: The Making of a Supranational Economic Order* (New York: Pantheon Books, 1986).

11. R. Gilpin, *The Political Economy of International Relations* (Princeton: Princeton University Press, 1987).

12. S. Marglin and J. Schor, eds., *The Golden Age of Capitalism: Re-Interpreting the Post-War Experience* (Oxford: Clarendon, 1990).

13. R. O'Brien, *Global Financial Integration: The End of Geography* (London: Pinter/ RIIA, 1992), p. 30.

14. W. Greider, *Secrets of the Temple: How the Federal Reserve Runs the Country* (New York: Simon and Schuster, 1987).

15. R. Parboni, "The Dollar Weapon: From Nixon to Reagan," *New Left Review*, vol. 158 (1986), pp. 3–19.

16. K. Lissakers, *Banks, Borrowers and the Establishment: A Revisionist Account of the International Debt Crisis* (New York: Basic Books, 1991).

17. N. Harris, *The End of the Third World: Newly Industrializing Countries and the End of an Ideology* (Harmondsworth, England: Penguin, 1986).

18. S. Corbridge, *Debt and Development* (Oxford: Blackwell, 1992).

19. M. Beenstock, *The World Economy in Transition* (London: Allen and Unwin, 1983), p. 236.

20. T. Congdon, *The Debt Threat* (Oxford: Blackwell, 1988).

21. S. Branford and B. Kucinski, *The Debt Squads: The US, the Banks and Latin America* (London: Zed, 1988), p. 1.

22. C. Diaz-Alejandro, "Latin American Debt: I Don't Think We Are in Kansas Anymore," *Brookings Papers on Economic Activity*, vol. 2 (Washington, D.C.: Zed, 1984), pp. 335–389.

23. S. Corbridge and J. Agnew, "The US Trade and Budget Deficits in Global Perspective: An Essay in Geopolitical-Economy," *Society and Space*, vol. 9 (1991), pp. 71–90.

24. B. Friedman, "Long-run Costs of US Fiscal Policy: The International Dimension," mimeo, 1987.

25. S. Cohen and J. Zysman, *Manufacturing Matters: The Myth of the Post-Industrial Economy* (New York: Basic Books, 1987).

26. L. Thurow, *Head to Head: The Coming Economic Battle Among Japan, Europe, and America* (New York: William Morrow, 1992).

27. M. Tolchin and S. Tolchin, *Buying into America* (New York: Times Books, 1988).

28. O'Brien, *Global Financial Integration*, p. 34.

29. G. Arrighi, "World Income Inequalities and the Future of Socialism," *New Left Review*, vol. 189 (1991), pp. 39–66.

30. J. Ruggie, "International Regimes, Transactions and Change: Embedded Liberalism in the Postwar Economic Order," *International Organization*, vol. 36 (1982), pp. 379–415.

31. E. Brett, *The World Economy Since the War: The Politics of Uneven Development* (London: Macmillan, 1985).

32. K. Cox, *Production, Power and World Order: Social Forces in the Making of History* (New York: Columbia University Press, 1987).

33. World Bank, *World Development Report: International Capital and Economic Development* (Oxford: Oxford University Press/World Bank, 1985), p. 38.

34. J. Frankel, "Is a Yen Bloc Forming in Pacific Asia?" in *Finance and the International Economy*, vol. 5, R. O'Brien, ed. (Oxford: Oxford University Press, 1991); see also M. Daly and M. Logan, *The Brittle Rim: France, Business and the Pacific Region* (Harmondsworth, England: Penguin, 1989).

35. G. Treverton, ed., *The Shape of the New Europe* (Washington, D.C.: Council on Foreign Relations, 1992).

36. Agnew and Corbridge, "The New Geopolitics," p. 284.

37. *Deterritorialization* refers to the increasingly rapid process of capital and technology flowing across boundaries with ease and rendering "national" space less important in economic location decisions.

38. D. Becker, "Development, Democracy and Dependency in Latin America: A Post-Imperialist View," *Third World Quarterly*, vol. 6 (1984), pp. 411–431.

39. S. Roberts, "Fictitious Capital, Fictitious Spaces? The Geography of Offshore Financial Flows," in *Money, Power and Space*, S. Corbridge, R. Martin, and N. Thrift, eds. (Oxford: Blackwell, forthcoming 1994).

40. N. Chomsky, *Deterring Democracy* (New York: Hill and Wang, 1992); S. George, *A Fate Worse than Debt* (Harmondsworth, England: Penguin, 1989).

41. S. Corbridge, "The Poverty of Planning or Planning for Poverty? An Eye to Economic Liberalization in India," *Progress in Human Geography*, vol. 15 (1991), pp. 467–476; World Bank, *India: An Industrializing Economy in Transition* (Washington, D.C.: World Bank, 1989).

42. A. King, *Global Cities: Post-Imperialism and the Internationalization of London* (London: Routledge, 1990).

43. William Wood, *From Marshall Plan to Debt Crisis: The Making of a Supranational Economic Order* (New York: Pantheon, 1986).

44. P. Mosley, J. Harrigan, and J. Toye, *Aid and Power: The World Bank and Policy-based Lending*, vol. 1 (London: Routledge, 1991).

45. C. Edwards, "The Debt Crisis and Development: A Comparison of Major Competing Theories," *Geoforum*, vol. 18 (1988), pp. 3–28.

# SEVENTEEN

## Geopolitical Information and Communication in Shrinking and Expanding Worlds: 1900–2100

STANLEY D. BRUNN & JEFFERY A. JONES

INFORMATION TECHNOLOGIES and communication form an often overlooked or unquestioned foundation for political geography. With most geopolitics centered on the unit of the state, the definitions of *state* and *nation* are being questioned by some geopoliticians in international relations and political geography.[1] The context of political geography is the product of certain voices in a particular society that use a variety of media to define an issue and the resulting landscape according to the aims and perspective of a specific group or the state. Thus, some immediate questions for political geographers examining the role of communication are key components in exploring information flows and how these flows have changed over time in different societies and economies. Today's political geographer must address profound questions about who uses these information flows and what type of landscape is constructed as "reality" and "truth." Questions arise as to how the political landscape is constructed and maintained by the use of certain information and the suppression of other voices. This chapter sketches an exploratory model for examining these issues and considers the role of information and communication in contemporary and future political geographical analysis.[2]

### The Role of Information

Consider the influence of photographs and film footage on public opinion and resulting political actions and policies, such as:

- Magazine covers and TV newsreels of starving children in Somalia in 1992;
- Images of the fall of the Berlin Wall in 1989 and their impact on people in both Eastern Europe and the West;

- Live coverage of China's ill-fated democratic movement and the resulting 1989 Tiananmen Square massacre;

- Photos and televised images of maimed children, crying women, and burned corpses in Bosnia-Herzegovina;

- Local U.S. coverage of prochoice and prolife parades at the local, national, and international level;

- Photographs taken from space showing earth as a single world in the inky darkness of space; and

- The future impact of the first image of the entire solar system, with the sun and planets just a tiny star and its faint companions.

People usually gauge their reactions to a significant event—the assassination of John F. Kennedy, the fall of the Berlin Wall, the explosion of the space shuttle *Challenger*—not by the time of the event but by the time and place where they themselves were when they first learned of it. We were all there figuratively, but the time and place of our interactions are defined by information. Whether this "being there" is a newsreel of the Kennedy assassination made before one's birth or the mere seconds of delay in live, televised reports, the medium and content of information define these places.

Especially now, with the promises of virtual reality technology, the effects of communication on our construction of reality raise a very important question: How do we interpret events via an electronic medium? Infodramas and docudramas portray historical figures and social analogies according to certain slants to impress on the viewer a certain political message or to enhance entertainment appeal. But just how "real" or objective are these characters and situations to viewers? Is the Columbus who was celebrated in 1892 as a hero any less historically correct than the Columbus of 1992 who is reviewed in society and the media as a purveyor of genocide and environmental destruction? Do viewers of Oliver Stone's movie *JFK* reflect upon this work as only one assassination theory among several, or do they incorporate this dramatization as historical fact? How does this message compare to the state's investigation of the assassination? Future geographic inquiry will likely focus on how people incorporate these images of events, people, and places as "real" versus entertainment, as one possible interpretation versus "the truth." The state will be one of the voices heard and seen, but it will vie with other producers, including other politically motivated groups, to provide facts, interpretations, and truth.

Whatever their conceptualization of reality, news and images have had direct connections to subsequent political policy in all types of countries and at all levels, local to global. It is this interconnectivity across scales and between information and policy that geographers often take for granted. Political geographers have contributed concepts, models, and theories relating to many other disciplines—history, political science, and economics—but not to communications. Although they have worked in transportation, urban, housing, cultural, agricultural, and resource geography, they have not dealt with information economies and the impact of telecommunications on political and social development.[3] As with contributions from other disciplines, the addition of elements from the field of communications can offer geographers insights into the quaternary sector landscapes generated by new information technologies,[4] as well as the concerns of traditional political geography.[5]

## Information in a Geopolitical World

The progress or failure of any political unit is dependent on a series of information-related questions. A useful phrase in describing information geography is David Smith's definition of welfare geography: "Who gets what where?"[6] For the political geographer studying information, the question might be: "Who gets what from whom and where?" The *who* is usually the state, the *what* is all varieties of information, the *from whom* is the source or producer of the information, and the *where* is the location of what is produced, consumed, and exchanged.

Information is a commodity that can be used for beneficial or harmful purposes. The information produced often represents a symbol of power, be it a state, a corporation, or a special interest group. Information "goods," such as a textbook, a map, a television or radio program, a law, or an official photograph of an event, merit scrutiny for their impact on peoples and places.

Recent political geographic studies have included elections, conflict over the siting of noxious facilities, and public service delivery (health, education, and welfare goods); all have information at their base. Likewise, power, ideology, legislation, and constitutions are all information topics. Whoever has the power has the information and vice versa. The topics of elections, laws, and political representation (gerrymandering or apportionment) are based on what information is available, how it is used or misused, and how it affects a people or area. What are the "model" states used in drafting a new constitution, the rights of women and minorities, or the freedom of press, religion, and assembly?

Many wars are also fought over information, and disputes and resolutions are also information-based. Examples in this century include conflicts among European powers during World Wars I and II. Disputed claims often surfaced when subsequent leaders communicated nationalist or irredentist feelings to a population.

The identification of problems and solutions within states are also information-based. Whether the problems are unemployment, foreign investment, ecological crises, or child health care, all have at their root information that is available about populations and areas. To "resolve" a problem means that information is made available (or will be collected) to administer a policy.

## The State as Text and Discourse

Geographers have begun to look at landscapes as text: products "written" by certain "authors" to reflect a specific representation and voice.[7] Indeed, the state can be seen as a text produced to reflect a certain national image drawn and redrawn through the political process. Tied to this dynamic process, however, is the concept of the "discourse." French philosopher Michel Foucault has defined a *discourse* as an interplay of power relationships in which knowledge is constructed within a certain set of rules that both give legitimacy and delimit potential socio-political arrangements.[8] Language, concepts of science and society, and political goals are components of a discourse. For example, since the Enlightenment at least, Western science has fostered a dominant discourse based on intersubjective and repeatable observations in line with the scientific method. This discourse places experiences seen or felt only by a single person and processes not readily repeatable outside of scholarly legitimacy. Extrasensory perception (ESP), religious experiences, and other ways of knowing accepted by some non-Western cultures are not normally included in the Western scientific discourse.

Language is one element defined within a discourse. Rather than being a neutral element of political dialogue, individual language is embedded with nuances and values. The political geographer must examine issues of mistranslation and miscommunication.

With regard to political geography, American history reveals the dynamic changes in the discourse producing the political landscape. Tied to this changing discourse are questions of who speaks in the discourse and what structures are maintained by it. Designed and implemented largely by wealthy colonial men of European heritage, the American system of government legitimizes and creates a formal discourse of elections and representative democracy. The U.S. Constitution scripts a political landscape that removes the potential for monarchies, anarchies, direct democracy, and other government systems, and the electoral political process thus created provides the set of rules for what constitutes a legitimate political voice in the United States. In essence, this single document establishes who may define the political geographies in the United States, how they may be defined, and something of the nature of these geographies.

Until this century, the majority of Americans were not legally allowed to express political concerns through the discourse initiated by the Founding Fathers. Consequently, the legitimized political landscape historically has been defined by the voice of a minority made up of white, adult males. Alternative voices had to be expressed in other ways, for example, through fiction, art, music, and the popular press. Denied political expression, Harriet Beecher Stowe influenced the politics of her day via her novel *Uncle Tom's Cabin.* Similarly, African-Americans and others used music and the popular press to sway voters. Eventually, all these groups have attained a legitimized voice in the political process. Yet the discourse is still dominant: Legitimacy and enfranchisement are only granted by those already holding power, and the system itself is thereby maintained. The changes in the political landscape can thus be viewed as the result of pressure by various groups outside the legitimized discourse to influence the dominant speakers, via alternative information channels, into granting an electoral voice in the political discourse.

Similar to the state's organization of almost all political dialogue toward gaining rights from the state and thus further bolstering the state's existence, a sense of nationhood is also a social construction with an often vague rationale. Benedict Anderson has called nations "imagined communities" because they rely on a common sense of unity that often defies differences.[9] Most Americans will never meet most other Americans. Some New Englanders share more culturally with Canadians than with people in Hawaii or rural Georgia, and many Texans have a history and language more linked to Mexico than to the United States. Yet most people in New England, Hawaii, Georgia, and Texas view themselves as "Americans" through a national system of disseminating "American" cultural values. How has this shared communality of American nationality come into being? A political geographer would examine the state as a partner in the creation of a sense of nationhood: States definitely benefit from the unity imparted by a nationhood shared among its populace.

Anderson also points to the role of what he calls the creole class in developing nations in the Americas. Creoles, or people of European parentage born in the colonies, were historically the dominant class in colonial social hierarchies. Raised in the colonies, creole youth being educated in the home country often found a common identity with other creoles, who were familiar with the foods and customs of home. Politically, creoles sometimes found that the colonial policies dictated by the imperial government (on the treatment of aboriginal populations, slaves, and trade, for example) were unfavorable to maintaining their power base, privilege, and self-interests. What was good for the home country and its standards of morality was not necessarily good for creole colonials. Anderson thus maintains that in the Americas, colonial revolutions for independence were often portrayed by the resulting states as populist revolts. Yet for many of the lower socioeconomic classes, such as slaves and native populations, colonial policies may actually have been more lenient or protective than the laws of the new countries. Therefore, Anderson sees the landed creole gentry as the driving force behind colonial revolutions and the subsequent scripting of popular opinion and history by the state to foster a sense of populist revolution and national commonality.[10]

## Symbols of the State

The state's messages are contained in such symbols as stamps, currency, flags, and logos. What scenes are shown on the first stamps issued by a former colony after winning independence? What emblems and institutions are shown on national currencies, and how are these images chosen? Certain countries may use these symbols to express their social ills; twelve countries, for example, have already produced an AIDS awareness stamp, and the United States has just chosen such a design. How does a government depict national emblems such as Uncle Sam or the American eagle, the British lion, the Russian bear, or Sweden's Mother Svea? In a country that emphasizes the separation of church and state as the

United States does, what is the legality of Christmas stamps? And are other religions' holidays also commemorated by stamps? Just as official government maps portray a certain view of the legal, political, and social makeup of an area as sanctioned by government policy, so do various symbols of the state reveal messages and ideals upheld by a government.

## Key Components in Geopolitical Information Worlds

Four components are important in a study of the role played by the state in information and communication: producers, filters, silenced voices, and consumers. The main elements in the communication cycle are the producers and the consumers of information (Figure 17.1).

Although this discussion focuses on the state and information, nongovernmental organizations (NGOs)—whether scientific, educational, religious, or environmentally based—are also active players in the geopolitical information worlds.

### *The Producers*

The state, often seen as the key player in the information world, defines itself in words, symbols, documents, and advertisements as well as through maps. It designates the official language or languages, what is taught in the schools, what is used in broadcasting and the print media, and the discourse employed in establishing laws, ratifying treaties, and conducting scientific exchanges of information. The introduction of a standardized grammar, speech, and alphabet also affects the standardization of regional dialects. The state decides what information will be collected about individuals and households in censuses. Some information is produced by the state for the state; some is for other consumers. The same applies to atlases and maps as well as photos and news releases. Some of the information may concern how the state has solved a social problem or how it wants others inside or outside the state to see how a problem is being solved. In the

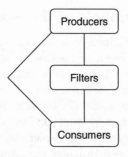

FIGURE 17.1   The communication cycle.

political and military arena, the state defines its friends and adversaries not only on maps but also by words and phrases. Laws, regulations, standards, and qualifications are all defined by the state. All levels of government produce information because it is demanded but also because the state seeks to justify its own existence by what it produces.

## The Filters

Gatekeepers are those who are responsible for what information is produced. The state may be considered a gatekeeper, but within the state, there are individuals and institutions that have the final say about what is said and how it is said or presented; editors and television station executives, for example, are gatekeepers.[11] The biases of the gatekeepers are reflected in what information is produced under their aegis. There are also ministries of information and culture, whose information may also be slanted. Information may be deliberately distorted in numerous ways—through biased views about an ethnic or racial minority, through underreporting of a major disease, through withholding information on an environmental disaster, and so forth. The maps produced by a government reflect how the state looks at the world. Official government newspapers, broadcasts, and telecasts reveal what the state wants to say to its own citizenry and to foreigners.[12] The state also influences what children study in schools via textbooks, and it funds museum exhibits, television programs, and government publications. It can provide fair or biased information.

The state is composed of many sources, avenues, conduits, and channels of information. These send information to other government units within the state and to other states and non-governmental organizations. The state also will have "damage control" operators to correct wrong or misleading news reports from journalists and other sources. All these items reflect something about how the state looks at itself and what it wishes to convey to others about itself.[13] The levels of gatekeeping can vary widely, as Figure 17.2 shows.

States not only produce much information of a cartographical nature, they also construct maps to reflect government policy. The depiction of territorial claims, adversaries, and minorities can be shown using certain colors, map projections, images, and symbols, thereby making a statement graphically. Germany used maps that showed a country cramped by hostile neighbors to rationalize its expansion during two world wars. During the Cold War, the U.S. government and American media produced a number of maps using projections and images to enhance the portrayal of an expansionist Soviet Union and of countries around the rim of Eurasia as dominoes to be protected from Communism.[14]

Finally, who are the cartographers? Are they from military or civilian branches? Does the cartography reflect the ideology in the state promoting itself on television and billboards, in newspapers and textbooks? With the increased use of geographic information systems (GIS), the state is concerned about what information is, can be, and might be available and mapped and for what purposes. A related question focuses on the cost of the geographic information about the

FIGURE 17.2 Censorship in South America, 1986. SOURCE: Charles Humana, *Human Rights Guide* (London: *The Economist*, 1985).

state that is available to the corporate sector, individual consumers, and spy networks. Geographical information thus passes through a number of filters tied to censorship, government policy, cost, and technology.

## Silenced Voices

Examining the nature of information, the basic question is: "Who speaks for the world today?" In the First World, the dominant speakers have been white, wealthy males, those who control by ownership and censorship (of radio, television, advertisements, school texts, and art exhibits), and influential lobbying groups with specific religious, ideological, constitutional, and corporate agendas. We are now witnessing a growing micropress and microcommunications industry for special interest groups that were formerly marginalized. As a result, advances in narrow (TV) casting, video production, desktop publishing, and computer networking are giving voice to groups once silenced—women, African-Americans, Hispanics, gays, the elderly, and the disabled, among others.

The rise of these specialty presses and publications also reveals a growing unification of political groups formed around identity politics. Special interest magazines like *Maturity* (for the elderly), *The Advocate* (for lesbians and gays), *Signs* (for feminists), and *Charisma* (for conservative Christians) represent not just sources of entertainment but also vehicles for the dissemination of information and political strategies. Notices of important pending legislation or news items chosen and phrased to enhance a group's solidarity and viewpoint relate to a state's political geography. Indeed, an examination of where these magazines' subscribers reside would reveal much about a region's political geography.

These specialty publications also provide information on consumer services, such as videos, tapes, and book clubs, and on businesses that provide support via advertisements. This information can give such companies a boost by increasing sales among the growing ranks of politically minded consumers; conversely, it can make these companies targets for boycotts by opposing groups. Thus, Remy Martin cognac, which advertises in leading gay publications, is the fifth most popular cognac in the United States but number one among gay consumers, according to surveys by Overlooked Opinions, a market surveying company in Chicago. Overlooked Opinions, itself a child of this pluralistic information diversification, seeks to identify specialty markets among marginalized groups.

Recent media history has focused on boycotts lobbied against certain television programs and their advertisers by groups opposing the content of these shows. And though theaters in conservative communities may refuse to show a controversial movie like *The Last Temptation of Christ*, this same movie can now be seen on video in many of these same communities. This raises an intriguing question: Does such a movie have less of an impact when it is viewed privately rather than publicly? MTV, the highly popular youth music channel, has also been the subject of debate concerning its inclusion in cable packages. Controversies over groups like Two Live Crew, a rap group judged obscene in Florida, highlight variations in prevailing social climates in different areas. Local Public

Broadcasting Service (PBS) affiliates also differ in terms of which controversial programs they will air, such as a recent program dealing with AIDS, depictions of gay relationships, or subjects touching on religion. Issues of public and private spaces and community debate still await scholarly study by political geographers.

Recent controversies over certain books point out both the political ramifications of media in different parts of the world and the interconnectivity of cultures. The diverse political reactions to Salman Rushdie's *Satanic Verses* by Moslem and Western powers, for example, reflect a contrast in political and cultural perspectives. And interestingly, though the British government condemned the bounty put on Rushdie's head by the Iranian government, the United Kingdom banned the book *Spycatcher* for its revelations of sensitive aspects of British espionage. *Spycatcher* also links into spying as an aspect of information collection and dissemination with strong geographic elements of barriers, degrees of overtness, and covert networks. Thus, whether it is television, shock radio, or a book, even entertainment information is an appropriate field for geopolitical discourse.

In the Second World of the former Soviet bloc, dominant voices are still those of males, members of the leading ethnic groups, and government-sponsored media. The emergence of democracy has lessened government reporting as the major and official voice, but communication bureaucracies still remain powerful. However, women's networks, once institutionalized as aspects of the ideal of Socialist equality, are now demanding increased representation in Eastern and Central Europe's changing societies. Meanwhile, minority ethnic and nationalist movements face difficulties in publishing in their native tongues. Language changes also extend to Central Asia, where non-Cyrillic script is being reintroduced with the decline of Soviet political power. We can expect more voices to emerge in the coming decades, such as those of dissident groups and returning émigrés (many of whom have money as well as knowledge of First World telecommunications technology).

In the Third World, the voices speaking today are those of the wealthy ruling elites, the multinational corporations, and the imported press, videos, and television programming. The power of the voices in the Third World is still strongly tied to First World communications. Distinctions need to be made between indigenous voices and voices linked to the elites, corporations, and importers. This layered "web" of voices is characteristic of Third World communication.

In all parts of the world, the state response to technological innovation is a mixture of policies, often with unintended results. Thus, regulations of the exploding networks of "cyberspace" created by electronic mail are loose. And only in the last year have U.S. politicians begun to recognize the potential of electronic town meetings and E-mail links to the White House.

Similarly, mainland China's entrance into the international business arena has introduced the FAX machine to many Chinese universities and businesses. During the Tiananmen Square massacre, overseas contacts relayed foreign news reports to the mainland via FAX, effectively by-passing the official Chinese news blackout. These same FAX machines were used to get information out of China. Clearly, Chinese censors and officials did not foresee the potential political use of these business tools. Today, the Chinese government and many governments in traditional societies are weighing the impact of new technologies, foreign entertainment, and news media networks on the culture, values, and political structure of their countries. After "plugging into" First World technologies and programming, such countries are finding that social influences from the Western media can influence everything from dietary preferences of the young to morality.

Despite the advances in telecommunications and the ongoing discussions about "global villages" and "instant" communications and news, some groups will still not be heard. In the First World, the silent voices often are the victims of discrimination and inaction. They lack power because they cannot acquire the information needed to be a part of the worlds around them. These silent voices may exist in isolated and inaccessible rural areas or inner cities.

The former Soviet bloc states also have silent voices, many of whom have been silent for decades. Threats, censorship, and imprisonment were among the strategies used to silence individuals and groups. The contents of libraries in Eastern Europe emphasize this point: Although such countries as Romania officially list rather high ratios of library books to population, these "official" books (particularly those with foreign titles) were often unavailable. The silent groups still include dissenters (scientists, poets, philosophers, housewives, and so on), foreign voices (émigrés), ethnic minorities, those supporting religion, the aged, war veterans, AIDS victims, the poor and uneducated, and exploited women.

The list of silent voices includes censored foreign voices and the voices of unorganized and unempowered groups. Based on Charles Humana's 1986 study of human rights for *The Economist*,[15] the United Nations Development Programme concluded that there is a strong correlation between a high number of liberties and economic development.[16] And many of these freedom variables are linked to an unrestricted media and the free expression of an individual's identity. Variations are often sharp, even within a region (see Figure 17.3 for Asia). Thus, communication appears to be a foundation not only for political stability but also for economic stability.

Politics can be viewed as the struggle of multiple voices to be heard, with dominant voices at times suppressing others. For the political geographer, research into the silenced voices of the political landscape is important and insightful. For instance, what percentage of the U.S. population has legally been eligible to vote throughout American history, and how has that varied regionally according to state laws? In college textbooks and respected historical atlases of the United States, how are Native Americans represented? A survey of several leading textbooks and atlases finds that Native American–controlled areas of the eventual United States are almost never depicted as coexisting with European settlements: Instead, European territorial claims are shown. More unsettling, maps in several sources routinely show "settled areas" of the United States over time when, in

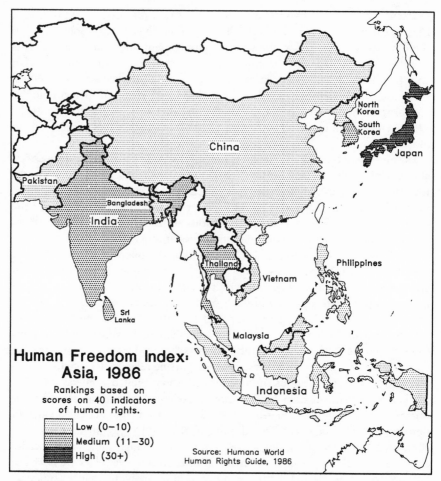

FIGURE 17.3   Human freedom index: Asia, 1986. SOURCE: Charles Humana, *Human Rights Guide* (London: *The Economist,* 1985).

actuality, they are only showing areas settled by European or African populations. Thus, Native Americans have been effectively silenced and erased from cartographic representation in many historical maps.[17]

## The Consumers

We are all consumers who receive information from various technologies, including telephones, radios, and televisions. Within Europe, the number of phones per capita varies widely, especially when comparing the former Eastern Europe with the West (Figure 17.4). Consumers receive information about political events from the state and other information organs on a daily basis. Those who have access only to single sources or irregular amounts of information will

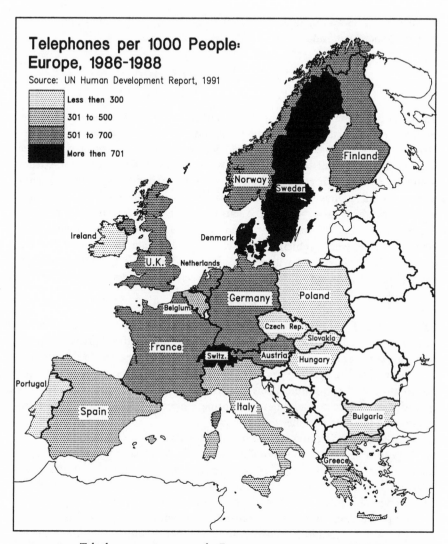

FIGURE 17.4   Telephones per 1,000 people: Europe, 1986–1988. SOURCE: UN Human Development Report, 1991.

have different worldviews than those who receive input from multiple information sources. The media have no political boundaries, and radio and television broadcasts opposed to governments can transcend state borders. Voice of America and Radio Free Europe, for instance, provided residents of Eastern Europe with "official" news about Western Europe and about events within their own states.

Consumers are also identified by their occupation, education, income, and life-style. Some information sources are geared for specific groups, and others are for specific places and regions. Governments also target publications, public service announcements, and programs for specific clienteles.

## Geopolitical Information
## in 1900, 2000, and 2100

The mix of information of a geopolitical nature varies over time as well as space: Information important for the state would not be the same in 1900 as in 2000. Here, we explore the geopolitical information worlds in 1900, 2000, and 2100. We selected three centennials so that the mixes would be different; over time, technological advances in communication and information processing influence what is produced, how it is communicated, who the consumers are, and who the gatekeepers are. By 2100, perhaps the state itself will be replaced by another political structure,[18] but information will continue to play a major role in what decisions are made, what problems are solved, and what data are mapped.[19] In the discussion that follows, we will refer to the matrix in Table 17.1, which displays geopolitical information worlds at these three centennial years.

### *The Worlds in 1900*

For purposes of this discussion, the world at the start of the twentieth century can be considered as a rich world–poor world and one with a European–North Atlantic "core" and a colonized periphery. We define the core as Europe and North America; the periphery is everywhere else. In an information context, the information and communications worlds of the core and the periphery were quite distinct. The core had different information technologies and ways of communicating than the periphery.

The core communicated via the infant communication systems, while much of the poor world still used the oral tradition. The information networks in 1900 included limited phone usage, weak international connections, slow mail, and intermittent wire services. The few major geopolitical centers were located in the core. Geographic information produced in 1900 concerned land use, rivers, agricultural production, minerals, transportation networks, and new industries. Key geopolitical information included that on colonial holdings, European power shifts, and the rise and fall of leaders. Information of this sort was presented in official pronouncements, documents, reports, statistics, and maps. The key gatekeepers of geopolitical information were the major powers and the information "houses" of the major industrial centers. The gatekeepers were the elite, rich, powerful, white males who resided in the centers of political and economic power.

### *The Worlds in 2000*

The worlds at the end of the twentieth century will reflect more geographic variation than at the turn of the previous century. To describe this setting, we have used labels such as First, Second, Third, and Fourth Worlds and cores, semi-peripheries, and peripheries. Though the First World has computers, FAXs, satellite imagery, multiple television channels, and multiple newspapers and radios, these sources and services are less available elsewhere. In the periphery, there is still a reliance on radios, newspapers, limited television, and an irregular postal and telephone system. The widespread usage of advanced communications technologies in the core and the lesser rates in the semiperipheries make up one of the realities of the late twentieth century, mainly a result of economic conditions.

Information at the end of the 1900s will be conveyed via satellite, videocassette recorders (VCRs), and electronic bulletin boards, with multiple centers producing and generating information. Geographical information sought at 2000 will focus on environmental damage, movements of capital, UN voting, and the activities of NGOs. Geopolitical information will be sought regarding global famine forecasting, global grain and oil production and prices, elections in new democracies, satellite coverage, and transborder data sets. The gatekeepers as we approach the twenty-first century will be the state and groups that are interested in what goes on within and beyond the state. These include satellite and computer producers, media and public opinion corporations, research and development labs, and libraries. Key concerns will include what information will be admitted by the gatekeepers, how it will be disseminated, and how it will relate to the goals of states, the NGOs, and the formerly silent voices.

## The Worlds in 2100

Information demands some 100 years from now may be less about First, Second, and other worlds and more about the earth, satellites, and planets. In what we might call the "expanding universe," earth will have launched and established permanent satellites as well as colonies and settlements elsewhere in the universe. Information may encompass fourth- and perhaps fifth-dimensional worlds, not the two used in 1900 and the three used now. We will see further advances in video phones, virtual reality, and portable, *instantaneous* global communication. Extrasensory perception may be feasible, replacing the intuition, mysticism, and astrology of previous centuries. Populations are likely to be connected by transglobal phone directories, postal and money systems, and instant on-line services among major decision centers scattered across the planet and beyond. Examples of geopolitical information might include the growing political power of the periphery, planetary environmental changes, and the distribution of planetary resources and reserves. We may also see further research on manipulating public opinion, determining the psychological behavior of leaders, and parapsychology. More gatekeepers will be non-European, and they will include more international organizations and regional political councils. In addition, there will be many more kinds of spatial data collected, organized, and disseminated in 2100 for investigating planetary problems.

TABLE 17.1   Elements of the Geopolitics of Information and Communication: 1900–2100

| Forms of Communication (technological innovations) | Who Speaks and Has Power (gatekeepers and producers) | Silent Voices (the powerless) | What Is Important/Mapped (information regions) |
|---|---|---|---|
| | **1900: RICH WORLD** | | |
| printed word | Eurocentric world | women | two-dimensional world |
| infant telephone and cinema | the rich and powerful | exploited laborers | agricultural productivity |
| limited wire service | white, Protestant, wealthy | new immigrants | terrain and land uses |
| photography | males | nonunionized labor | transport networks |
| newspapers | colonial powers | illiterates (including | European power shifts |
| infant radio | large companies | women) | resources sites |
| postal service (nodal) | unstandardized national | racial/other minorities | military targets |
| world of mouth | presses | | colonial holdings |
| art | political elites | | time zones |
| currency | few correspondents/wire services | | |
| | **1900: POOR WORLD** | | |
| word of mouth | white colonists | indigenous masses | resources, tribal areas, and |
| oral tradition | white missionaries | exploited masses | transport networks involved |
| art, dance, painting | white commercial elites | native voices/cultures | with colonial administration/ |
| postal service (nodal and usually colonial) | some assimilated native speakers | suppressed | extraction |
| pulpit: missionaries | | women | |
| intuition: astrology, mysticism, tarot, | | | |
| personal couriers | | | |

## 2000: FIRST WORLD

| | | | |
|---|---|---|---|
| printed word | editors | the poor and uneducated | environmental inventories |
| radio | writers in major languages | unorganized minorities | biological diversity |
| television and VCR | radio/TV producers | minority language groups | resource reserves |
| postal service (home delivery) | large NGO leaders | victims of bigotry without access to info networks | standardized regions: (ISBN, bar codes) |
| credit reporting | wealthy white males | computer illiterate | minority group spaces |
| dominance of books/TV | neocolonial powers | rural areas | votes |
| computers | televangelists | | political and legal cultures |
| standardization | major universities | | influence of NGOs |
| desktop publishing | map producers | | TV reception areas |
| FAX | software producers | | newspaper circulation areas |
| electronic mail (instant nodal) | special interest groups | | creditor/debtor relations |
| newspaper | entrance of more women and minority voices | | distribution of electronic networks |
| psychological testing | state leaders | | distribution of banking and ATM networks |
| statistical forecasting | token minority voices | | cultural refuge areas |
| telephones/cellular phones | media | | |
| | large banks, creditors | | |
| | economists | | |

## 2000: (FORMER) SECOND WORLD

| | | | |
|---|---|---|---|
| radio | dominant ethnic groups | dissidents | government controlled areas |
| television | males | ethnic minorities | rebel areas |
| selected/restricted FAX and electronic mail | controlled government media | foreigners | "flash points": politically, culturally, ecologically |
| telephone | censors | religious minorities | satellite coverage |
| newspapers | selective dissidents | women and other victims of bigotry | weather forecasting |

(continues)

TABLE 17.1 (continued)

**2000: THIRD WORLD**

| | | | |
|---|---|---|---|
| radio | neocolonial powers | rural areas | religious influence on politics |
| imported media | First World companies | women | intellectual property rights |
| pulpit | selected elites | classless masses | refugee movements |
| oral traditions | state-dominated media | rebels | sexual slavery/illicit drug trade |
| selected postal and telephone networks | imported media | the poor | human rights abuses |
| | | ethnic minorities | |

**2000: FOURTH WORLD**

| | | | |
|---|---|---|---|
| oral traditions | neocolonial powers | middle classes | |
| intuition | few rich elite | landless/classless | |
| popular leaders/pulpit | elderly and males | illiterates | |
| sparse phone/mail | traditional tribal voices | majority poor | |

**2100: EARTH**

| | | | |
|---|---|---|---|
| telecommuting | multivoiced world | uneducated | areas dominated by special interests |
| electronic meetings | special interests | the poor | corporate states |
| instant video access | NGOs | computer illiterate | global/personal libraries |
| hypermedia | human welfare and environmental groups | the inaccessible and isolated | information resources |
| HDTV | technocrats | | psychological profiles of world leaders |
| electronic mail (home) | | | world court decisions |
| portable phones | | | circumpolar regions |
| enhanced intuition and psychology in marketing/media | | | oceans |
| plastic currency | | | sea floors |

uniform postal service
cyberspace
multisensory imaging and
tactile systems replace
drugs and prostitution
(video addicts)
on-line democracy via
electronic mail
fiber optics

no long-distance charges
global reach
24-hour stock exchanges via
global electronic networks
and orbit
standardization

laser-coded messaging
interplanetary signal booster
satellites

advanced bioengineering systems
carry human gene banks
beyond solar space

rich and powerful
intellectual elites
corporations and states

nations in space

**2100: SATELLITES AND SPACE STATIONS**

poor and marginalized

**2100: PLANETS**

poor countries without space
programs or connections

**2100: BEYOND . . .**

intellectual property rights
trading blocs
on-line global phone directories
political parapsychology
global ecological forecasting
cultural refuges
genetic resources

planetary surfaces
satellite environments
communication grids, solar
winds, and their interactions

terraforming sites
adaptions to new worlds

galactic space

# Information Problems

With the increased production and consumption of information by the state and individuals, there will be a host of new problems. Some key questions will be raised:

1. Can the state satisfy the information demands of its citizens and ensure equity in the information? This question will be relevant for both small, homogeneous cultural states and multiethnic ones. What are the vehicles used to ensure equity in the information? This involves the question of who gets what information from whom and where.

2. What will the role of NGOs be in providing information? To what extent will multiple producers create a new political order?

3. Who will be the producers and gatekeepers of vital information? What will their intentions and biases be?

4. Are the emerging information worlds reducing the gaps between rich and poor, powerful and powerless, cities and countries, democracies and tyrannies? Will there be a "technology information gap" between those who have access to computer-based information systems and those who do not?

5. How will the states and other information producers use maps and spatial data sets to solve political problems? With greater demands for information on environmental, economic, electoral, health, and military trends, the presentation and representation of such data will become more important at all scales.

6. Where will this blizzard of information lead the state and the individual? (The term *blizzard* may apply to the production of information, but *information glut* might more aptly describe the consumer's perception of this.) There is really no end to the amounts and kinds of information demanded by the human population. Important questions include: Who will decide what will and will not be published and disseminated? Who will decide where the information will be available and at what cost? And who will decide what will be discarded? The information consumer will need to know how to sort out the important information and make prudent decisions. One could anticipate information blackouts or brownouts or even information revolutions and conflicts. Clearly, the role of information will become increasingly important in future geopolitics.

7. What rights will a citizen have in a government that collects more and more information about individuals? Information about employment, life history, lifestyle, consumer purchases, and religious preferences is already incorporated into data bases. Who will have access to such data and for what purposes?

8. Will the silent voices be given an opportunity to be heard? What responsibility will the state assume in permitting these disenfranchised voices to produce their own information and to influence decisions made by the state? Women and racial and ethnic minorities are among those rapidly acquiring the skills to influence state policies.

9. To what extent will Americanization be a major global information process? The diffusion of American news, entertainment, and governmental policies via satellite networks is one example of U.S. domination of information.

10. Finally, will the world move toward more uniformity or more diversity in the information that is produced and consumed? With a few major international newspapers, television companies, and information suppliers, global markets are becoming more similar. On the other hand, easier access to information sources and production by many new sources, including former silent voices, may lead to greater diversity.

## Summary: Looking Ahead

We have sketched some promising linkages between political geography and the nascent geographies of information and communication. These concepts challenge our thinking about the role of the state and international organizations. The state has traditionally dominated the "information business," but with the growth of information industries and the introduction and rapid proliferation of new information and communications technologies, the role of the state may be redefined. Political geographic research examining the role of the state and information in a historical, contemporary, or futuristic context may contribute much to the debate about the place of communication in societal transformation.

### Notes

1. J. Der Derian and M.J. Shapiro, eds., *International/Intertextual Relations: Postmodern Readings on World Politics* (Lexington, Mass.: Lexington Books, 1989); R. Ashley, "Living on Border Lines: Man, Poststructuralism and War," in *International/Intertextual Relations: Postmodern Readings on World Politics*, J. Der Derian and M.J. Shapiro, eds. (Lexington, Mass.: Lexington Books, 1989); Simon Dalby, "Critical Geopolitics: Discourse, Difference, and Dissent," *Environment and Planning D: Society and Space*, vol. 9 (1991), pp. 261–283; Benedict Anderson, *Imagined Communities* (New York: Verso, 1989).

2. Ronald F. Abler et al., *Human Geography in a Shrinking World* (North Scituate, Mass.: Duxbury Press, 1975).

3. Stanley D. Brunn and Thomas R. Leinbach, eds., *Collapsing Space and Time: Geographic Aspects of Information and Communication* (New York: Harper/Collins and Routledge, 1991).

4. The quaternary sector refers to economic activities related primarily to information and information flows.

5. Anthony Smith, *The Geopolitics of Information: Non-Western Culture Dominates the World* (New York: Oxford University Press, 1980); Howard Frederick, *Global Communications and International Relations* (Pacific Grove, Calif.: Brooks-Cole, 1992).

6. David A. Smith, *Human Geography: A Welfare Approach* (New York and London: St. Martin's Press, 1977).

7. Trevor J. Barnes and James S. Duncan, eds., *Writing Worlds: Discourse, Text and Metaphor in the Representation of Landscape* (New York: Routledge, 1992).

8. Michel Foucault, *The Archaeology of Knowledge*, trans. A. Sheridan Smith (New York: Pantheon Books, 1972).

9. Anderson, *Imagined Communities*.

10. Ibid.

11. Susan R. Brooker-Gross, "The Changing Concept of Place in the News," in *Geography: The Media and Popular Culture*, J. Burgess and J. R. Gold, eds. (New York: St. Martin's Press, 1985), pp. 63–85.

12. K. Bruce Ryan, "The 'Official' Image of Australia," in *Place Images in the Media: Portrayal, Experience, and Meaning*, Leo Zonn, ed. (Savage, Md.: Rowman and Littlefield, 1991), pp. 135–158.

13. Geroid Ó Tuathil, "Foreign Policy and the Hyperreal: The Reagan Administration and the Scripting of 'South Africa,'" in *Writing Worlds: Discourse, Text and Metaphor in the Representation of Landscape*, Trevor J. Barnes and James S. Duncan, eds. (New York: Routledge, 1992), pp. 176–192; Geroid Ó Tuathil and John Agnew, "Geopolitics and Discourse: Practical Geopolitical Reasoning in American Foreign Policy," *Political Geography*, vol. 11 (1992), pp. 190–204; Alan Jenkins, "A View of Contemporary China: A Production Study of a Documentary Film," in *Place Images in the Media: Portrayal, Experience, and Meaning*, Leo Zonn, ed. (Savage, Md.: Rowman and Littlefield, 1991), pp. 207–229.

14. Derek Hall, "A Geographical Approach to Propaganda," in *Political Studies from Spatial Perspectives: Anglo-American Essays in Political Geography*, Alan D. Burnett and Peter J. Taylor, eds. (Chicester, England, and New York: John Wiley, 1981), pp. 313–339; John Pickles, "Texts, Hermeneutics and Propaganda Maps," in *Writing Worlds: Discourse, Text and Metaphor in the Representation of Landscape*, Trevor J. Barnes and James S. Duncan, eds. (New York: Routledge, 1992), pp. 192–230.

15. Charles Humana, *Human Rights Guide* (London: The Economist, 1985).

16. United Nations Development Programme (UNDP), *Human Development Report* (New York: Oxford University Press, 1991).

17. Jeff Jones, "The Erased Peoples: The Communication of Space and the Representation of Native Americans in Maps" (manuscript, Department of Geography, University of Kentucky, 1993).

18. Stanley D. Brunn, "Future of the Nation-State System," in *Political Geography: Recent Advances and Future Directions*, Peter Taylor and John House, eds. (London: Croom Helm, 1984), pp. 149–167.

19. S.D. Brunn, "Geopolitics in a Shrinking World: A Political Geography of the Twenty-First Century," in *Political Studies from Spatial Perspectives: Anglo-American Essays in Political Geography*, Alan D. Burnett and Peter J. Taylor, eds. (Chicester, England, and New York: John Wiley, 1981), pp. 131–156.

# Selected References

## Chapter 1

Bowman, Isaiah. "Geography vs. Geopolitics." *The Geographical Review,* vol. 32 (1942), pp. 646–658.

Fukayama, Francis. *The End of History and the Last Man.* New York: Free Press, 1992.

Greenfield, Liah. *Nationalism: Five Roads to Modernity.* Cambridge, Mass.: Harvard University Press, 1992.

Kennedy, Paul. *The Rise and Fall of the Great Powers.* New York: Random House, 1987.

Mackinder, Sir Halford. "The Geographical Pivot of History," in *Democratic Ideals and Reality,* Sir Halford Mackinder. New York: W.W. Norton, 1962 (1904).

———. "The Round World and the Winning of the Peace." *Foreign Affairs,* vol. 21 (1943), pp. 595–606.

Spykman, Nicholas. *The Geography of the Peace.* New York: Harcourt, Brace, 1944.

## Chapter 2

Cohen, S. "Global Geopolitical Change in the Post–Cold War Era." *Annals of the Association of American Geographers,* vol. 81, no. 4 (1991), pp. 551–580.

———. "The World Geopolitical System, in Retrospect and Prospect." *Journal of Geography,* vol. 1 (January–February 1990), pp. 1–12.

Hoffman, G.W. "Political Geography and International Relations," in *Earth '88: Changing Geographic Perspective,* Harm de Blij, ed. Washington, D.C.: National Geographic Society, 1988.

Mackinder, Sir Halford. "The Geographical Pivot of History," in *Democratic Ideals and Reality,* Sir Halford Mackinder. New York: W.W. Norton, 1962 (1904).

O'Loughlin, J., and H. van der Wusten. "Political Geography of Panregions." *Geographical Review,* vol. 80 (1990), pp. 1–19.

## Chapter 3

Brown, Lloyd A. *The Story of Maps.* New York: Dover Publications, 1977.

Henrikson, Alan. "Mental Maps," in *Explaining the History of American Foreign Relations.* Cambridge: Cambridge University Press, 1991, pp. 177–178.

*Images of the World: An Atlas of Satellite Imagery and Maps.* Chicago: Rand McNally, 1983.

Momonier, M. *How to Lie with Maps.* Chicago: University of Chicago Press, 1991.

Schwartz, S.I., and R.E. Ehrenberg. *The Mapping of America.* New York: Harry Abrams, 1980.

# Chapter 4

Day, A.J., ed. *Border and Territorial Disputes.* 2d ed. London: Longman, 1987.

Gottman, J. *The Significance of Territory.* Charlottesville: University of Virginia Press, 1973.

Johnston, R.J., David Knight, and Eleonore Kofman. *Nationalism, Self-Determination, and Political Geography.* London: Croom-Helm, 1988.

Knight, D.B. "Statehood: A Politico-Geographic and Legal Perspective." *Geojournal,* vol. 28, no. 3 (1992), pp. 311–318.

Mikesell, M.W., and A. Murphy. "Framework for Comparative Study of Minority-Group Aspirations." *Annals of the Association of American Geographers,* vol. 81 (1991), pp. 581–604.

Murphy, A.B. "Historical Justification of Territorial Claims." *Annals of the Association of American Geographers,* vol. 80 (1990), pp. 531–548.

Sack, R.D. *Conceptions of Space in Social Thought: A Geographic Perspective.* Minneapolis: University of Minnesota Press, 1980.


# Chapter 5

Hartshorne, Richard. "Suggestions on the Terminology of Political Boundaries." *Annals of the Association of American Geographers,* vol. 26 (1936), pp. 56–57.

Jones, S.B. *Boundary-Making: A Handbook for Statesmen, Treaty Editors and Boundary Commissioners.* Washington, D.C.: Carnegie Endowment for International Peace, 1945.

Pearcy, G. Etzel. "Boundary Functions." *Journal of Geography,* vol. 64, no. 8 (1965), pp. 346–349.

———. "Boundary Types." *Journal of Geography,* vol. 64, no. 7 (1965), pp. 300–303.

———. "Dynamic Aspects of Boundaries." *Journal of Geography,* vol. 64, no. 9 (1965), pp. 388–394.


# Chapter 6

Baker, G. "Judicial Determination of Political Gerrymandering: A Totality of Circumstances Approach." *Journal of Law and Politics,* vol. 3 (1986), pp. 1–19.

Cain, B. "Assessing the Partisan Effect of Redistricting." *American Political Science Review,* vol. 79 (1985), pp. 320–333.

Garfinkel, R., and D. Nemhauser. "Political Districting by Implicit Enumeration Techniques." *Management Science,* vol. 16 (1970), pp. B405–B508.

Goodchild, M., and B. Massam. "Some Least-Cost Models of Spatial Administrative Systems." *Geografiska Annaler,* vol. 52B (1969), pp. 86–94.

Grofman, B. "Criteria for Redistricting: A Social Science Perspective." *UCLA Law Review,* vol. 3, 1986, pp. 77–184.

Grofman, B., ed. *Political Gerrymandering and the Courts.* New York: Agathon, 1990.

Gudjin, G., and P. Taylor. *Seats, Votes and the Spatial Organization of Elections.* London: Pion, 1978.

Hardy, L. *The Gerrymander: Origin, Concepts and Reemergence.* Claremont, Calif.: Rose Institute of State and Local Government, 1990.

Hess, S. "Nonpartisan Political Redistricting by Computer." *Operations Research,* vol. 14 (1965), pp. 998–1006.

Selected References 325

Johnston, R. *Politics, Elections and Spatial Systems*. New York: Oxford University Press, 1979.
Morrill, Richard. "Political Redistricting and Geographic Theory." *Resource Publication in Geography*. Washington, D.C.: AAG, 1981.
———. "Redistricting, Region and Representation." *Political Geography Quarterly*, vol. 6 (1987), pp. 241–260.
Niemi, R., and J. Deegan. "A Theory of Political Districting." *American Political Science Review*, vol. 72 (1978), pp. 1304–1323.
O'Loughlin, J., and A.M. Taylor. "Choices in Redistricting and Electoral Outcomes: The Case of Mobile." *Political Geography Quarterly*, vol. 1 (1982), pp. 317–340.
Schwartzberg, J. "Reapportionment, Gerrymandering and the Notion of Compactness." *Minnesota Law Review*, vol. 50 (1966), pp. 443–457.
Shelly, F. "A Constitutional Choice Approach to Electoral Boundary Delineation." *Political Geography Quarterly*, vol. 1 (1982), pp. 341–350.

## Chapter 7

Cutter, S.L., et al. *Exploitation, Conservation, Preservation: A Geographic Perspective on Natural Resource Use*. New York: John Wiley & Sons, 1991.
McKibben, B. *The End of Nature*. New York: Random House, 1989.
Porter, G., and J.W. Brown. *Global Environmental Politics*. Boulder: Westview Press, 1991.
World Resources Institute. *World Resources 1992–93*. New York: Oxford University Press, 1992.

## Chapter 8

Burton, I., R. Kates, and G. White. *The Environment as Hazard*. New York: Oxford University Press, 1978.
Freudenburg, W.R. "Perceived Risk, Real Risk: Social Science and the Art of Probabilistic Risk Assessment." *Science*, vol. 242 (1988), pp. 44–49.
Kasperson, R.E., et al. "The Social Amplification of Risk: A Conceptual Framework." *Risk Analysis*, vol. 8, no. 2 (1988), pp. 177–187.
Kasperson, R.E., K. Dow, D. Golding, and J.X. Kasperson, eds. *Understanding Global Environmental Change: The Contributions of Risk Analysis and Management*. Worcester, Mass.: Clark University, 1990.
Krimsky, S., and D. Golding, eds. *Social Theories of Risk*. New York: Praeger, 1992.
Slovic, P. "Perception of Risk." *Science*, vol. 236 (1987), pp. 280–285.
Smith, R.R. "The Risk Transition." *International Environmental Affairs*, vol. 2, no. 3 (1990), pp. 227–251.

## Chapter 9

Boardman, Robert. *International Organization and the Conservation of Nature*. Bloomington: Indiana University Press, 1981.
Cairncross, Frances. *Costing the Earth*. Boston: Harvard Business School Press, 1992.
Carroll, John E., ed. *International Environmental Diplomacy*. Cambridge: Cambridge University Press, 1988.

*Convention on Biological Diversity.* United Nations Document UNEP/Bio.Div/Conf/L.2, 1992.

Feshbach, Murray, and Alfred Friendly, Jr. *Ecocide in the USSR: Health and Nature Under Siege.* New York: Basic Books, 1992.

*Framework Convention on Climate Change.* United Nations Document A/AC237/18, 1992.

Haas, Peter M., Marc A. Levy, and Edward A. Parson. "How Should We Judge UNCED's Success?" *Environment,* vol. 34, no. 8 (October 1992).

*Non-legally Binding Authoritative Statement of Principles for a Global Consensus on the Management, Conservation, and Sustainable Development of All Types of Forests.* United Nations Document A/CONF.151/6/Rev.1, 1992.

Olson, Mancur. *The Logic of Collective Action.* Cambridge, Mass.: Harvard University Press, 1965.

Parson, Edward A., Peter M. Haas, and Marc A. Levy. "A Summary of the Major Documents Signed at the Earth Summit and the Global Forum." *Environment,* vol. 34, no. 8 (October 1992), pp. 12–15, 34.

Pirages, Dennis. *Global Technopolitics: The International Politics of Technology and Resources.* Pacific Grove, Calif.: Brooks/Cole Publishing, 1989.

*Rio Declaration on Environment and Development.* UN Document A/CONF.151/PC/ WG.III/L.33/Rev.1, 1992.

UNCED. *Agenda 21.* United Nations Document, 1992.

Wood, William B., George J. Demko, and Phyllis Mofson. "Ecopolitics in the Global Greenhouse." *Environment,* vol. 31, no. 7 (September 1989), pp. 12–17, 32–34.

World Commission on Environment and Development. *Our Common Future.* Oxford: Oxford University Press, 1987.

Young, Oran. *International Cooperation: Building Regimes for Natural Resources and the Environment.* Ithaca: Cornell University Press, 1989.

## Chapter 10

Demko, G.J., and R.J. Fuchs, "Population Redistribution: Problems and Policies." *Populi,* vol. 7, no. 4 (December 1981), pp. 26–35.

Ehrlich, P., and A. Ehrlich. *The Population Explosion.* New York: Simon and Schuster, 1990.

Gobalet, Jeanne G. *World Mortality Trends Since 1870.* New York: Garland Publishers, 1989.

Keyfitz, N. "Population and Development Within the Ecosphere: One View of the Literature." *Population Index,* vol. 57, no. 1 (Spring 1991), pp. 5–22.

Malthus, Thomas R. *First Essay on Population—1798,* reprint in facsimile. London: Macmillan, 1966.

National Research Council, Committee on Population, Working Group on Population Growth and Economic Development. *Population Growth and Economic Development Policy Questions.* Washington, D.C.: National Academy Press, 1986.

OECD/SOPEMI. *Trends in International Migration: Continuous Reporting System on Migration.* Paris: OECD, 1992.

Simon, Julian. "A Scheme to Promote World Economic Development with Migration," in *Research in Population Economics,* Julian Simon and P.H. Lindert, eds. Greenwich, Conn.: JAI Press, 1982.

————. *The Ultimate Resource*. Princeton: Princeton University Press, 1981.

United Nations Population Fund. *Population and the Environment: The Challenges Ahead*. New York: UNFPA, 1991.

————. *State of the World's Population*. New York: UNFPA, 1992.

World Health Organization. *Our Planet, Our Health: Report of the WHO Commission on Health and Environment*. Geneva: WHO, 1992.

## Chapter 11

On migration research and theories:

Castles, Stephen, and Mark Miller. *The Age of Migration: International Population Movements in the Modern World*. New York: Guilford Publications, 1993.

Clarke, John, ed. *Geography and Population: Approaches and Applications*. Elmsford, N.Y.: Pergamon Press, 1984.

On refugees:

Black, Richard, and Vaughan Robinson, eds. *Geography and Refugees, Patterns and Processes of Change*. London and New York: Belhaven Press, 1993.

Rogge, John, ed. *Refugees: A Third World Dilemma*. Totowa, N.J.: Rowman and Littlefield, 1987.

U.S. Committee for Refugees. *World Refugee Survey, 1993*.

International migration essays:

Numerous articles in the journal *International Migration Review*, published by the Center for Migration Studies.

Appleyard, Reginald, ed. *International Migration Today, Volume 1: Trends and Prospects*. Paris and Nedlands, Western Australia: UNESCO and University of Western Australia Centre for Migration and Development Studies, 1988.

Stahl, Charles, ed. *International Migration Today, Volume 2: Emerging Issues*. Belgium: UNESCO and University of Western Australia Centre for Migration and Development Studies, 1988.

## Chapter 12

Alexander, Lewis M. "Geography and the Law of the Sea." *Annals of the Association of American Geographers*, vol. 58, no. 1 (1968), pp. 177–197.

Glassner, Martin I., and Harm J. de Blij. *Systematic Political Geography*. 4th ed. New York: John Wiley & Sons, 1989.

Karatochwil, Friedrich, Paul Rohrlich, and Harpeet Mahajan. *Peace and Disputed Sovereignty: Reflections on Conflict over Territory*. Lanham, Md.: University Press of America, 1985.

Williams, Allan M. *The European Community: The Contradictions of Integration*. Oxford: Basil Blackwell, 1991.

## Chapter 13

Barsh, Russell. "The Ethnocidal Character of the State and International Law." *Journal of Ethnic Studies,* vol. 16, no. 4 (1989), pp. 1–30.

Blaut, James. *The National Question: Decolonizing the Theory of Nationalism.* London: Zed Books, 1987.

Bodley, John H. *Victims of Progress.* 3d ed. Mountain View, Calif.: Mayfield Publishing, 1990.

Bodley, John H., ed. *Tribal Peoples and Development Issues: A Global Overview.* Mountain View, Calif.: Mayfield Publishing, 1988.

Bugajski, Janusz. *Fourth World Conflict: Communism and Rural Societies.* Boulder: Westview Press, 1991.

Burger, Julian. *The Gaia Atlas of First Peoples.* New York: Anchor Books, Doubleday, 1990.

———. *Report from the Frontier: The State of the World's Indigenous Peoples.* London: Zed Books, 1987.

Cabral, Amilcar. "National Liberation and Culture," in *Return to the Source,* Amilcar Cabral. New York: Monthly Review Press, 1973.

Chaliand, Gérard, ed. *Minority Peoples in the Age of Nation-States.* London: Pluto Press, 1989.

Chisholm, Michael. "Cultural Diversity Breaks the Mold." *Geographical Magazine* (November 1990), pp. 12–16.

Clay, Jason. "What's a Nation?" *Mother Jones* (November–December 1990), pp. 28, 30.

Connor, Walker. "Nation-Building or Nation-Destroying?" *World Politics,* vol. 24 (1972), pp. 319–355.

d'Encausse, Carrere. *The End of the Soviet Empire: The Triumph of Nations.* New York: Basic Books, 1993.

Grundy-Warr, Carl, and Richard N. Schofield. "Man-Made Lines That Divide the World." *Geographical Magazine* (June 1990), pp. 10–15.

Gurr, Ted Robert, and James R. Scarritt. "Ethnic Warfare and the Changing Priorities of Global Security." *Mediterranean Quarterly,* vol. 1, no. 1 (1989), pp. 82–98.

Johnston, R.J., D.B. Knight, and E. Kofman, eds. *Nationalism, Self-Determination and Political Geography.* London and New York: Croom-Helm, 1998.

Knight, D.B. "The Dilemma of Nations in a Rigid State-structured World," in *Pluralism and Political Geography: People, Territory and State,* Nurit Kliot and Stanley Waterman, eds.. New York: St. Martin's Press, 1983.

———. "Self-Determination as a Geopolitical Force," *Journal of Geography* (July–August 1983).

Kohr, Leopold. *The Breakdown of Nations.* New York: Dutton, 1957.

Mandelbaum, Michael. *The Rise of Nations in the Soviet Union: American Foreign Policy and the Disintegration of the Soviet Union.* New York: Council on Foreign Relations Press, 1991.

Manuel, George, and Michael Posluns. *The Fourth World: An Indian Reality.* New York: Free Press, 1974.

McLaughlin, Jim. "The Political Geography of Nation-Building and Nationalism in Social Sciences." *Political Geography Quarterly,* vol. 5, no. 4 (1986), pp. 299–329.

Nietschmann, Bernard. "The Miskito Nation and the Geopolitics of Self-Determination." *Journal of Political Science,* vol. 19 (1991), pp. 18–40.

————. *The Unknown War: The Miskito Nation, Nicaragua and the United States.* New York: Freedom House Press, 1989.

Schechterman, Bernard, and Martin Slann. "The Ethnic Nationalist Dimension in International Relations." *Journal of Political Science,* vol. 19 (1991).

Shah, Sonia. "The Roots of Ethnic Conflict." *Nuclear Times* (Spring 1992), pp. 9–15.

Weyler, Rex. *Blood on the Land.* New York: Vintage Books, 1984.


## Chapter 14

Bennett, A. Leroy. International Organizations: *Principles and Issues.* 4th ed. Englewood Cliffs, N.J.: Prentice-Hall, 1988.

Boutros-Ghali, Boutros. *Report on the Work of the Organization from the Forty-sixth to the Forty-seventh Session of the General Assembly.* New York: United Nations, 1992.

Falk, Richard A., Samuel S. Kim, and Saul H. Mendlovitz, eds. *The United Nations and a Just World Order.* Boulder: Westview Press, 1991.

*The Interdependent.* New York: United Nations Association of the USA, published quarterly.

Irvin, Linda, ed. *Encyclopedia of Associations and International Organizations.* Detroit: Gale Research, 1992.

Renner, Michael. *Critical Juncture: The Future of Peacekeeping.* Worldwatch Paper 114. Washington, D.C.: Worldwatch Institute, May 1993.

Riggs, Robert E., and Jack C. Plano. *The United Nations: International Organization and World Politics.* Chicago: Dorsey Press, 1988.

Rosenau, James N. *The United Nations in a Turbulent World.* Boulder: Lynne Rienner, 1992.

United Nations. *The Blue Helmets: A Review of United Nations Peace-keeping.* New York: United Nations Department of Public Information, 1990.

*UN Observer and International Report.* New York: Tres Publications, published monthly.


## Chapter 15

Bergsten, C.F. "The United States and the World Economy." *Annals of the American Academy of Political and Social Science,* vol. 460 (1982), pp. 11–20.

National Science Foundation. *Division of Science Resources Studies Report NSF 92–306.* Washington, D.C.: NSF, March 20, 1992.


## Chapter 16

Berman, K. *All That Is Solid Melts into Air.* London: Verso, 1982.

Bryant, R. *International Financial Intermediation.* Washington, D.C.: Brookings Institution, 1987.

Castells, M. *The Information City.* Oxford: Blackwell, 1989.

Claasen, E-M., ed. *International and European Monetary Systems.* London: Heinemann, 1990.

Corbridge, S., R. Martin, and N. Thrift, eds. *Money, Power and Space.* Oxford: Blackwell, forthcoming 1994.

Feldstein, M., and C. Horioka. "Domestic Savings and International Capital Flows." *Economic Journal*, vol. 90 (1980).

Keohane, R. *After Hegemony: Cooperation and Discord in the World Political Economy.* Princeton: Princeton University Press, 1984.

## Chapter 17

*Constitution of the United States: Connecticut General Election Statutes Annotated,* vol. 1. St. Paul, Minn.: West Publishing, 1958.

Oswalt, Wendell. *This Land Was Theirs: A Study of North American Indians.* 4th ed. Mountain View, Calif.: Mayfield Publishing, 1988.

Rheingold, Howard. *They Have a World for It.* Los Angeles: Jeremy P. Tarcher, 1992.

# About the Book and Editors

USING AN INTEGRATIVE APPROACH to international relations, this text returns the "geo" to geopolitical analysis of current global issues. The contributors examine such dilemmas as boundary disputes, refugee flows, ecological degradation, and UN intervention in civil wars. They also assess the redefinition of international relations by instantaneous, world-wide financial and telecommunication linkages and explore the struggles of new multi-national and non-governmental organizations to define their roles as fundamental con-cepts such as the nation-state are challenged. Using current real-world examples, this eminent group of geographers challenges the reader to rethink international relations and reorder the world political map.

**George J. Demko** is director of the Rockefeller Center for the Social Sciences and profes-sor of geography at Dartmouth College. **William B. Wood** is director of the Office of the Geographer, U.S. Department of State.

# About the Contributors

*John Agnew* is professor of geography at Syracuse University.

*Stanley D. Brunn* is professor of geography at the University of Kentucky.

*Saul B. Cohen* is University Professor of Geography at Hunter College, City University of New York.

*Stuart Corbridge* is a member of the geography faculty at the University of Cambridge in England.

*Susan L. Cutter* is chair of the Department of Geography at the University of South Carolina.

*George J. Demko* is director of the Rockefeller Center for the Social Sciences and professor of geography at Dartmouth College.

*Christine Drake* is professor of geography at Old Dominion University.

*Alan K. Henrikson* is professor of history and director of the Fletcher Roundtable on a New World Order at the Fletcher School of Law and Diplomacy at Tufts University.

*Jeffery A. Jones* is a doctoral student at the University of Kentucky.

*Roger E. Kasperson* is professor of geography and provost at Clark University.

*David B. Knight* is dean of the College of Social Science, University of Guelph, Canada.

*Phyllis Mofson* is a former analyst at the U.S. Department of State and is currently a faculty member at Florida Keys Community College.

*Richard Morrill* is professor of geography at the University of Washington.

*Alexander B. Murphy* is professor of geography at the University of Oregon.

*Bernard Nietschmann* is professor of geography at the University of California at Berkeley.

*Bradford L. Thomas* is chief of the Cartography Division, Office of the Geographer, U.S. Department of State.

*William B. Wood* is director of the Office of the Geographer, U.S. Department of State.

# Index

Acid rain, 167, 169
Acquired immunodeficiency syndrome
  (AIDS), 12, 98, 186–187, 189, 244
Afghanistan, 16, 39, 197, 211, 239
  Soviet invasion of, 19, 192, 238
Africa, 30, 87, 91, 92, 186–187, 266
  economy in, 287, 292, 296
  natural resources of, 124–125, 137
  refugees from, 197, 200
  states in, 87, 91, 92
  Sub-Saharan, 18, 25, 28, 30–32, 185–187,
    215
  *See also individual countries*
African-Americans, 304
African National Congress, 258
Afrikaaners, 44
*Agenda for Peace* (Boutros-Ghali), 260
Agriculture, 25, 124–125, 135
  grain merchants in, 135
AIDS. *See* Acquired immunodeficiency
  syndrome
Airspace, boundaries of, 98
Akhromeyev, Sergei, 57
Aland Islanders, 79
Alaska, 37, 43
Albania, 22, 23, 25, 258
Allende, Salvador, 135
Anderson, Benedict, 305
Andorra, 38, 246
Anglo-American region, 28, 30, 37
Anglo-Iranian Oil, 135
Angola, 32, 258
Antarctica, 12, 129
ANZUS. *See* Australian-New Zealand-
  United States Treaty
AOSIS. *See* Association of Small Island
  States
Arab-Israeli War of 1973, 250, 285

Archipelagic waters, 96
Arctic Mediterranean space, in maps, 62
Argentina, 30, 31, 135, 282, 286
  and Falkland Islands, 137, 214–215, 238
Armenia, 80, 90, 91
Arnheim, Rudolf, 58
ASEAN. *See* Association of Southeast
  Asian Nations
Asia, 25, 102, 124, 197, 266, 310
  East, 28, 31, 34, 46, 186, 188, 292
  Offshore, 25, 28, 30–31, 34, 36, 37
  South, 28, 30–32, 34, 36, 137, 186–188
  Southeast, 32, 34, 37, 187
  territory in, 90–92, 215
  *See also individual countries*
Association of Small Island States (AOSIS),
  172
Association of Southeast Asian Nations
  (ASEAN), 21
Ataturk Dam (Turkey), 129
Atmosphere, as natural resource, 129–130
Australasia, 292
Australia, 37, 81, 101, 135, 173, 264
  geopolitical alignment of, 30–31
  immigration to, 183, 184
  mineral resources in, 125, 133
Australian-New Zealand-United States
  Treaty (ANZUS), 252
Austria, 43
Azerbaijan, 20, 80, 90, 91

Baden-Württemberg, 222
*Badham* v. *Eu*, 105
Bahamas, 228
Bahrain, 38
*Baker* v. *Carr*, 104
Balkans, 81
Baltic Republics, 41, 45

Baluchi people, 44
*Bandemer* v. *Davis,* 105
Bangladesh, 22, 80, 162, 184
Bank of America, 284
Bank of England, 297
Banks, international, 284–286, 287–289
Barre, Siad, 256
Basque people, 43
Belarus, 36, 41
Belgium, 43
Belize, 228
Bermuda, 20
Bertalanffy, Ludwig von, 22
Bhutan, 22
Biafrans, 213
Biological diversity, 239–241
Boggs, S. W., 66(n6)
Bonaparte, Napoleon, 49
Border, as term, 94. *See also* Boundaries
Bosnia and Herzegovina, 7, 12, 41, 91, 258
  and human rights, 197, 198, 247, 257
Boundaries, 12, 39, 73, 94–96, 98–99
  in Cold War era, 20, 90
  and colonialism, 7, 87, 90, 92
  in Europe, 87, 90
  fluidity of, 10, 90, 91, 98–99
  in maps, 51, 63
  maritime, 95–98
  and migration, 195–196, 201
  and natural resource access, 125, 129,
    136–137
  of state territory, 72–73, 76, 90, 92
Boutros-Ghali, Boutros, 255, 259–260, 261,
  263, 266
Brazil, 27, 30, 31, 171, 172, 251, 286
Bread for the World, 186
Bretton Woods agreements, 273, 283, 285,
  292, 293
British Labour party, 102
British Petroleum, 135, 136
Brunei, 7
Brzezinski, Zbigniew, 17
Bundesbank, 297
Burma, 34, 44, 234, 238
Bush, George, 57, 61, 116, 249

California, 105, 107, 111, 112, 117, 129

Cambodia, 16, 27, 197, 255
  and United Nations, 247, 253, 255, 258
Canada, 81–83, 125, 135, 239, 264, 282
  electoral districting in, 103, 107
  immigration to, 183, 184, 188
Cape of Good Hope, 31
Carbon dioxide, 143
Carbon tax, 176
Caribbean region, 25, 28, 30, 32, 45, 186
Carrión, Luis, 231
Carter, Jimmy, 287
Cartography, 50–54, 56–59, 66(n4). *See also*
  Maps
Catalan people, 43
Catalonia, 222, 226
Catchpole, Brian, 228
Censorship, 310, 311
Central America, 45, 138, 239. *See also*
  *individual countries*
Central Treaty Organization (CENTRO),
  252
CENTRO. *See* Central Treaty Organization
Chad, 91
Chernobyl, 10, 133
Chile, 30, 31, 125, 135, 218
China, 22, 38, 78, 239, 310–311
  environment of, 125, 133, 169, 171
  and population control, 180, 182
  as power center, 26–29, 31, 32, 34, 36–37,
    46
  territorial claims of, 215, 247, 261
  and United Nations, 248, 251, 266
CIS. *See* Commonwealth of Independent
  States
CITES. *See* Conference on the
  International Trade in Endangered
  Species
Citibank, 284
Clark, William, 144
Claude, Inis, 247
Climate Change Treaty, 129
Coal, 133, 167
"Coexistence of Indigenous Peoples and
  Natural Environments in Central
  America" (map), 239
Cold War era, 4, 90, 237, 283, 291, 307
  geopolitics in, 5, 17–20, 281–282

*Colgrove* v. *Green,* 103
Colombia, 30, 45
Colonialism, 282
 and boundaries, 7, 87, 90, 92
 and state creation, 79, 80, 81, 211, 261–
  262
Commission of the European
  Communities, 221
Common Market Europe, 22
Commonwealth of Independent States
  (CIS), 29, 223
Commonwealth of Nations, 263–264
Communication, 301–302, 309–311, 321
 development of, 314–319
Conference on Security and Cooperation
  in Europe (CSCE), 90
Conference on the International Trade in
  Endangered Species (CITES), 129, 130,
  174
Congo, 32
Containment theory, 5, 18
Continental shelf, 96, 98
Convention on Biological Diversity, 241
Copper, 135
Cores, geopolitical, 35–37
Costa Rica, 27
Council of Europe, 4
Creoles, 305
Croatia, 41, 43, 91, 188, 257, 258
*Crush zone. See* Shatterbelts
CSCE. *See* Conference on Security and
  Cooperation in Europe
Cuba, 22, 27, 32, 125, 243
Cultural diversity, 239–241
Currency, exchanges in, 283–285, 287, 290,
  292, 293, 297
Cyprus, 38
Czechoslovakia, 20, 80, 90

Darwin, Charles, 5, 234
Debt, international, 281, 287–289, 292, 293
Declaration and Convention on the Rights
  of the Child, 260–261
Democratic party (United States), 102, 104,
  105, 111, 115, 117
Denmark, 37, 221

Desert Storm. *See* Persian Gulf War
De Seversky, Alexander, 3
Deterritorialization, 294–295, 297, 299(n36)
Developing countries, 292, 296
 and environment, 169–172
 population of, 180–181, 182
 and United Nations, 243–244, 249, 251,
  261
 *See also* Third World
Domino theory, 18
DPI. *See* United Nations, Department of
  Public Information
Drug trade, 12, 45
Dulles, John Foster, 22
Du Pont Corporation, 134

Earth Summit (1992), 138–139, 141, 148, 241
Eastern Europe, 8, 25, 32, 192, 266
 boundaries in, 90, 91
 economy in, 172, 296
 environment of, 132, 167, 169–170
 as gateway region, 28, 44–45
 information in, 310, 311, 312–313
 and Soviet Union, 19, 211
East Timor, 44, 78, 262
 and Indonesia, 73, 80, 83, 234
EC. *See* European Community
Ecocentrism, 132
Economic Community of West African
  States (ECOWAS), 264
Economic development, 45, 311
 and environment, 144–146, 155, 173–174
 and population changes, 180, 195, 197
Economics, 9, 10. *See also* Geopolinomics
Economy, 84, 282, 292–298
 and decentralization, 294, 295–298
 and deterritorialization, 294–295, 297,
  299(n36)
 and European Community, 296–297
 geopolitical centers of, 281, 290, 295
 geopolitics in, 297–298
 inflation in, 285, 287, 292
 markets in. *See* Markets
 multinational corporations in, 284, 285,
  289, 290
 and trade. *See* Trade

transnationalization of, 281–282, 290–
    295, 297
United States in, 283–285, 287–294
ECOSOC. *See* United Nations, Economic
    and Social Council of
ECOWAS. *See* Economic Community of
    West African States
ECU. *See* European Currency Unit
Ecuador, 27, 137–138, 215–216
EEZs. *See* Exclusive economic zones
Egypt, 8, 21, 27, 34, 216
    and United Nations, 253
Ehrlich, Paul, 180
Electoral districts, 9, 101, 106, 119
    accounting-graphics models in, 113–115
    criteria for, 106–110, 112–113
    and proportional representation, 102,
        103, 109
    redistricting of, 103, 104, 107–117. *See also*
        Gerrymandering
Electoral systems, 101–102
El Salvador, 211, 258
Energy, as natural resource, 125, 133, 134,
    135
England, 37, 102, 103. *See also* United
    Kingdom
Enterprise for the Americas Initiative, 61
Entropy, in world system, 23, 25, 46
Environment
    and agriculture, 124
    change in. *See* Environmental change
    degradation of, 12, 123, 133, 138–139, 173–
        174, 239–241. *See also* Pollution
    and nation peoples, 239–241
    politics of, 168–177
    and population growth, 182
    protection of. *See* Environmental
        protection
    and sovereignty, 12, 84
    *See also* Natural resources
Environmental change, 141–148, 150–163,
    168–173
    assessment of, 142–143, 144, 146, 147–148,
        152
    in climate, 129, 167–168, 170–173
    cumulative, 141–142, 161–162
    and equity issues, 160–163

global, 141–144, 150, 153, 156, 163, 167,
    170–171, 176
regional impact of, 154–155, 157, 160, 161,
    168–170
and risk, 144–148, 152–159
scientific study of, 148–149
societal response model to, 150–153, 157–
    159
systemic, 141–142, 146
warning systems for, 143, 156–157
Environmental protection, 132, 241
    international agreements in, 129–130,
        137–138, 175–176
    and national parks, 137–138
    and sustainable development, 138–139,
        174, 177(n4)
Environmental Protection Agency (EPA)
    (United States), 143, 148
EPA. *See* Environmental Protection Agency
Equilibrium, geopolitical, 15, 19–21, 25, 46
Eritrea, 39, 80, 234, 258
Estonia, 7, 41, 241
Ethiopia, 32, 44, 91, 229, 234, 238
Ethnic cleansing, 197–198, 257
Ethnic groups, 6, 226, 229, 230–231. *See also*
    Minority groups; Nations, and group
    identities
Eurasian continental realm, 28, 29, 31, 32,
    44, 46
Eurocurrency markets, 284, 285, 293, 296
Europe, 6, 22, 37, 102, 312–313
    Central, 8, 28, 32, 44–45, 132, 133, 310
    environment in, 124, 167, 176
    and international law, 209–211
    nations in, 238
    and refugees, 197, 201, 203
    stability of, 87, 90, 91, 238
    states in, 87, 90, 238
    Western, 81, 83, 84, 133, 184, 188, 292–293,
        312–313
    *See also* Eastern Europe; *individual*
        *countries*
European Community (EC), 4, 43, 98, 129,
    264, 293
    Commission of, 221
    Council of Ministers of, 221
    creation of, 6, 284

and economy, 281, 292–293, 296–297
and international law, 217, 220–223, 296
and migration, 192
as model, 223
as power center, 25, 29, 31, 34–37, 46, 281, 297
and regional identities, 83
relations in, 21, 25, 222
and sovereignty, 83–84, 220–221, 223, 238
and Turkey, 219, 293
and United Nations, 251
and United States, 273, 292
and Yugoslavia, 257
European Currency Unit (ECU), 297
European Exchange Rate Mechanism, 290
European Recovery Program. *See* Marshall Plan
Exchange rates. *See* Currency, exchanges in
Exclusive economic zones (EEZs), 95, 96, 137, 218

Fairgrieve, James, 32
Falkland Islands, 137, 215, 238
Family planning, international programs in, 181–182, 189
Famine, causes of, 185
Famine Early-Warning System (FEWS), 143, 157
FAO. *See* Food and Agriculture Organization
Federalism, 19
Federalists, 82–83
Federal Republic of Germany, 6, 218. *See also* Germany
Federal Reserve Bank, 287, 297
Fellowes, Lucy, 58
Fertility rate, 179, 180, 181, 189, 189(n1)
FEWS. *See* Famine Early-Warning System
Fiji, 78
Finland, 38, 79, 264
First World, 240–241, 309–311, 315, 317
Fishing zones, 96
Food and Agriculture Organization (FAO), 149, 186
Ford Motor Corporation, 283, 287

Foreign policy, 72, 138
and maps, 49–50, 57, 60–63, 64(n1), 69(n47)
Foucault, Michel, 304
Fourth World, 225, 228–230, 234, 315, 318
nations in, 225–226, 230, 232, 233, 239–241
France, 37, 101, 129, 135, 136, 220, 222
and United Nations, 251, 259
Freitilin people, 44
Frontier regions, 94, 196
Fuel resources. *See* Energy, as natural resource
Funtowicz, Silvio, 147, 148

Garver, John, 64
Gateways, 28, 38–46
GATT. *See* General Agreement on Tariffs and Trade
Gaza-West Bank, 39
GDP. *See* Gross domestic product
Gender discrimination, 188
General Agreement on Tariffs and Trade (GATT), 272, 275, 291, 292
Geneva Convention, 237
Geographic information systems (GIS), 50, 63, 307
"Geographic Pivot of History" (Mackinder), 5
Geography, 17, 49, 52, 69(n47)
Geopolinomics, 10, 11, 13, 297–298
Geopolitics, 15–20, 21–23, 25
and Cold War era, 5, 17–20, 281–282
as German term, 4, 5, 11, 13, 17
information in, 314–321
and migration flows, 199–200
Nazi use of, 3, 4, 5–7, 17, 57, 58
power centers in, 23, 26–27, 35–37, 41
regions in, 28–32, 34, 38–39, 41, 44, 46
and world economy, 297–298
*See also* Political geography
Geopolitik, 17. *See also* Geopolitics, as German term
Georgia (republic), 20
German Democratic Republic, 6, 27, 170. *See also* Germany

Germany, 37, 45, 102, 129, 137, 222, 277, 307
  economic growth of, 283, 285, 290, 292–
    294, 297
  immigration issues in, 184, 188, 197, 203
  nationalism in, 6, 83
  unification of, 6, 10
  and United Nations, 218, 251
  *See also* Federal Republic of Germany;
    German Democratic Republic
Gerrymandering, 9, 102–119
  partisan, 105–106, 108, 109–113, 115, 116,
    119
  racial, 104, 106, 107, 108, 110–111, 115, 117,
    119
  *See also* Electoral districts, redistricting
    of
Ghana, 27, 215
Gibraltar, 262
GIS. *See* Geographic information systems
Global Forum, 173
Global Risk Assessment Programme, 146–
  147
Global warming, 141, 144, 154–155, 161, 162.
  *See also* Environmental change
Globes, 52, 64
Goa (India), 80
Gold standard, 282, 283, 284
Goodchild, Michael, 115
Gorbachev, Mikhail, 7, 57, 249
Gore, Al, 139
Gottmann, Jean, 77
Gould, Stephen Jay, 234
Government, as criteria, 72, 76, 78, 108,
  112–113
Greece, 37, 39, 45
Greenhouse effect. *See* Global warming
Greenhouse gases, 129–130, 133, 167, 171, 172
Greenpeace, 132, 173
Grenada, 250
Gross domestic product (GDP), world
  changes in, 286–287
Gross national products, in developing
  countries, 296
Grotius, Hugo, 210
Group of Seven nations, 138, 264
Group of 77. *See* Nonaligned Movement
G-7 nations. *See* Group of Seven nations

Guam, 262
Guatemala, 23, 78, 238
Guinea, 32
Guinier, Lani, 117
Guyana, 214
Guyot, Arnold, 17
Gypsies, 196

Haas, Peter, 149
Haiti, 258
Hanseatic League, 38
Harley, Brian, 58, 59
Harrison, Richard Edes, 56, 62–63, 67(n23)
Hartshorne, Richard, 32
Harvey, David, 294
Haudenosaunee Confederacy, 232
Haushofer, Karl von, 5–6, 17
Hawaii, 43
Heartland region, 25–26, 29, 36
Heartland theory, of Mackinder, 5
Helsinki Final Act, 74, 90, 98
Herzegovina. *See* Bosnia and Herzegovina
History, cyclical theories of, 21
Hitler, Adolf, 19
Hokkaido, 37
Hondius, Jodocus, 51
Hong Kong, 20, 37, 261, 287
Humana, Charles, 311
Human rights, 84, 217, 262
  abuses of, 10, 196–198, 219–220, 237, 247–
    248, 253, 257
  and international organizations, 74, 187–
    188, 219
Human Rights Covenants, 262
Hungary, 27, 43, 90, 227
Hunger, as global issue, 185–186
Hurricane Andrew, 155
Hussein, Saddam, 7
Hydro-Quebec, 125

Iberia, 37
IBM Corporation, 277, 283, 284
Iceland, 81, 229
IGBP. *See* International Geosphere-
  Biosphere Program
IGOs. *See* Intergovernmental organizations

IIASA. *See* International Institute for Applied Systems Analysis
IMF. *See* International Monetary Fund
Immigration. *See* Migration
India, 8, 44, 80, 171, 187, 251, 295
    as regional power, 22, 27, 30, 31, 32
    as state, 229, 239
Indochina, 22, 31, 34
Indonesia, 34, 96, 228, 239
    and East Timor, 73, 80, 83, 234
Infant mortality rate, 184, 185
Inflation, world, 285, 287, 292
Information, 301–318, 321(n4)
    access to, 312–313, 320, 321
    development of, 314–319
    gatekeepers in, 307–308, 314, 315, 320
    and minority groups, 304, 309, 311, 320, 321
    politics of, 303, 309–310, 320–321
    state role in, 302, 304–309, 310–311, 320, 321
    technology in, 302, 303, 309–311, 314, 315, 320
Inner Mongolia, 37
Intergovernmental organizations (IGOs), 186, 187, 244
    and population issues, 179, 182–184, 189
    rise of, 4, 7–8, 10, 12, 23, 262, 265
    types of, 263–264
Intergovernmental Panel on Climate Change, 149, 173
Internal waters, 96
International Atomic Energy Agency, 248
International Commission of Human Rights, 219
International Decade for Natural Disaster Reduction, 154, 162
International Geosphere-Biosphere Program (IGBP), 149, 150
International Institute for Applied Systems Analysis (IIASA), 186
International Labour Organization, 263
International law, 209–210, 237
    and European Community, 217, 220–223
    human rights principles in, 217, 219–220
    and sovereignty, 209–213, 216–217, 223–224

and territorial conflicts, 213–219
    and United Nations, 248–249
International Monetary Fund (IMF), 283, 288, 290–292, 295, 296
International Planned Parenthood Federation (IPPF), 182
International Rescue Committee, 184
International Seabed Authority, 218
International Telecommunications Union, 263
International Whaling Commission, 129
International Year of the World's Indigenous People, 262
IPPF. *See* International Planned Parenthood Federation
Iran, 27, 34, 91, 135, 310
    and United States, 213, 273
Iraq, 7, 34, 129, 184, 202
    Kurds in, 196, 197, 220
    Kuwait invasion by, 90–92. *See also* Persian Gulf War
    Shiites in, 220
    and United Nations, 247–255, 258–260
    and United States, 220, 249, 252, 293, 296
Ireland, 37, 102, 264
Israel, 21, 27, 34, 73, 78, 102, 211
    and United Nations, 250
Italy, 37, 38, 43, 222, 229
Ivory, ban on, 174
Ivory Coast, 27

Jacobson, Harold, 150
Japan, 180, 251, 264, 293, 296
    as economic center, 281, 287, 289–290, 294, 297
    electoral system in, 101, 102
    expansionism of, 137, 214
    natural resources in, 135–136
    as regional power, 22, 29, 30–31, 34–38, 46
    rise of, 277, 283, 285, 292
    and United States, 294
Jefferson, Thomas, 59
Johnson, Lyndon B., 64(n1)

Kaliningrad, 41
Kanak people, 43

Kant, Immanuel, 19
Katangese people, 44
Kates, Robert, 148
Kawthoolei nation, 234
Kelly, Philip, 32
Kennan, George, 5, 17
Kennedy, John F., 286
Kennedy, Paul, 6
Keynes, John Maynard, 283, 293
Khmer Rouge, 22, 27, 255
Khomeini, Ayatollah, 213
Kissinger, Henry, 17
Kjellen, Rudolf, 3
Klaipeda, 41
Kohr, Leopold, 238
Korea, 19, 31, 32, 37, 39, 283. *See also* North Korea; South Korea
Korean War, 19, 283
Kurds, 12, 44, 197, 213, 246
    human rights abuses of, 10, 220, 247–248, 253
Kuwait, 28, 196
    Iraqi invasion of, 90–92. *See also* Persian Gulf War
    and United States, 216, 249, 252

Land, arable, 124
Latin America, 87, 90, 102, 186, 215, 286
    debt crisis in, 287, 292, 295
    *See also individual countries*
Latvia, 7, 41, 241
Law, international. *See* International law
League of Nations, 19, 79, 211
Lebanon, 38, 76, 211
Lebensraum, 5, 7, 10
Lenin, Vladimir, 7
Liberia, 22
Libya, 27, 91, 98
    and United Nations, 248–250
Liechtenstein, 246
Life expectancy, 185
Lippman, Walter, 49
Lithuania, 7, 41, 83, 241
Liverman, Diana, 144, 155
Lombard city-states, 38
Lombardy, 222
Los Angeles, riots in, 269–270

LOS Convention. *See* United Nations, Convention on the Law of the Sea
Luxembourg, 20
Lyde, Lionel, 39
Lynch, Kevin, 51–52
Lyons, Gene, 249
Lyons, Oren, 232

Maastricht Treaty, 37, 221
Macao, 261
McKibben, Bill, 138
Mackinder, Sir Halford, 3, 4–6, 7, 10, 17, 29, 45
Maghreb, 25, 28, 30
Mahan, Alfred Thayer, 3, 32
Malawi, 202
Malaysia, 27, 34, 172
Mali, 32
Malta, 38
Malthus, Thomas, 179
Manchuria, 36, 37
Mandela, Nelson, 258
*Map History of China* (Catchpole), 228
*Mappemonde*, 60
Maps, 44, 49–54, 56–64
    azimuthal, 53, 62–63
    emblematic quality of, 50–51, 63
    equal-area, 54, 63, 69(n56)
    hemispheric division in, 60–61, 68(n42)
    hypnotic quality of, 50, 56, 66(n6)
    mental, 51–52
    and New World Order, 15, 18, 19
    orientation of, 54, 56–57, 67(n21)
    politics of, 49–50, 57–63, 64(n1), 67(n32), 307, 309, 320
    projections onto, 52–54, 56, 63
    propaganda, 58
    and psychology, 50–51, 54, 56–57, 58–64, 67(n28)
    symbolization in, 57–58, 63
    synoptic quality of, 50, 63
    in United States politics, 17, 311–312. *See also* United States, and maps
Maritime Europe, as geopolitical region, 28, 29, 30, 35
Maritime realm, 28–30, 32, 34, 44, 46

Markets, 8, 290–293, 296–298
and natural resources, 131–132, 134–135, 138
Marsh, George Perkins, 141
Marshall Islands, 246
Marshall Plan, 264, 283
Massam, Bryan, 115
Mastanduno, Michael, 249
Mauna Loa Station, 143
Media, politics of, 301–302, 309–313
Mercator, Gerardus, 51, 54
Mercator projection, 54, 56, 62, 63
Mexican Border Industrialization Program, 286
Mexico, 23, 37, 43, 45, 212
economy of, 286, 287
and United States, 129, 176, 182, 192, 287–288
*Zona Fronteriza* of, 94
Mexico City Conference on Population (1984), 181
Micronesia, 246
MICs. *See* Most industrialized countries
Middle East, 8, 21, 25, 37, 186, 215
natural resources in, 125, 134, 137
as shatterbelt, 28, 32, 34–35
*See also individual countries*
Migration, 8, 191–195, 199–204
and boundaries, 98–99, 195–196, 201
and cultural intolerance, 179, 187–188, 189
economic, 195–197, 200
effects of, 192, 195–197, 200, 203
illegal, 192, 193, 196, 201, 204
policies toward, 187, 192, 193, 195, 200–201, 203, 204
and population distribution, 179, 183–184
of refugees, 192–193, 197–202, 204
rural-to-urban, 194, 195, 200
Military development, 3, 5, 45, 293–294
Military strategy, in geopolitics, 18–19
Minerals, as natural resource, 125, 126, 129, 134, 135–136
Minority groups, 74, 78, 79, 81
and information politics, 304, 309, 311, 320, 321
political representation of, 104, 107, 110, 117
and United Nations, 231, 248
*See also* Ethnic groups; Nations, and group identities
Miskito nation, 234, 237
Mitchell, John, 66(n10)
Mitchell, S. Augustus, 60
MNCs. *See* Multinational corporations
Modelski, George, 21
Modernization, 81
Moldova, 20
Monaco, 38, 246
Monmonier, Mark, 57, 67(n28)
Monroe Doctrine, 60
Montreal Protocol on Substances That Deplete the Ozone Layer (1987), 63
Morbidity rate, 179, 184–186
Morocco, 27, 28, 91, 234, 238
Mortality rate, 179, 184–186
Most industrialized countries (MICs), 285
Motorola Corporation, 274, 277
Mozambique, 32, 295, 296
Multilateralism, 294, 296
Multinational corporations (MNCs), 13, 23
and natural resources, 131, 132, 134–135
in world economy, 284, 285, 289, 290
Mumford, Lewis, 238
Muslims, in Yugoslavia, 188, 198, 257
Myanmar, 34. *See also* Burma

Nabatea, 38
NAFTA. *See* North American Free Trade Agreement
Nagas people, 44
Nagorno-Karabakh, 91
NAM. *See* Nonaligned Movement
Namibia, 32, 258
Nasser, Gamal Abdel, 27
National Geographic Society, 64, 239
Nationalism, 16, 71, 74, 82–83, 184, 257
rise of, 6–7, 214, 224, 243, 266
and state territory, 74, 78–83, 92
Nations, 233, 238, 305
as cultural homelands, 226, 230, 242
in Fourth World analysis, 225–226, 230, 232, 233, 239–241

and group identities, 74–75, 77–83. *See also* Ethnic groups; Minority groups
and self-determination, 230–231, 237, 241–242
state-less, 246
state relation to, 75, 78, 227–240
as term, 82, 226–227, 229
Nation-state, 176–177, 282, 285, 295
as concept, 75, 81, 210–211, 226, 229, 243
evolution of, 92, 210–211, 242
as geopolitical category, 28, 38, 43
Native Americans, and maps, 311–312
NATO. *See* North Atlantic Treaty Organization
Natural resources, 123–126, 129–139
consumption of, 131–132, 135–136, 138–139
and development, 132–133, 138–139
distribution of, 123–126, 133–137
and ideology, 123, 124, 131–132, 138–139
management of, 123, 129–131, 134–135, 137–138
and markets, 131–132, 134–135, 138
and multinational corporations, 131, 132, 134–135
rights to, 125, 129–130, 135
*See also* Environment
Nauru, 228
Nepal, 22, 27
Netherlands, 102, 129
New Caledonia, 43, 262
*New General Atlas* (Mitchell), 60
New World Order, 12, 282, 295
geopolinomics in, 297–298
and geopolitical equilibrium, 15, 19–21, 46
maps in, 15, 18, 19, 62–63
United States in, 269, 270, 278
*See also* World, order of
New York City, 110
Newly industrialized countries (NICs), 285
New Zealand, 173, 261, 264
NGOs. *See* Nongovernmental organizations
Nicaragua, 23, 27, 227, 258
national resistance in, 234, 237, 238

peace negotiations of, 230–231
and United States, 211, 250
NICs. *See* Newly industrialized countries
Nigeria, 22, 30, 136, 229, 251
Nigerian Civil War, 136
Nixon, Richard, 29
Nonaligned Movement (NAM), 77, 243, 250, 264
Non-governmental organizations (NGOs), 4, 10, 12, 244, 248, 261–265
and the environment, 129, 130, 132, 163, 169, 171, 173, 175
and human rights, 187–188, 219
and information politics, 306, 315, 320
and population issues, 179, 182, 184, 189
refugee aid of, 197, 202, 204
North American Free Trade Agreement (NAFTA), 21, 61, 223, 292
North Atlantic Treaty Organization (NATO), 29, 45, 252, 264
Northern Territories, 214
North Korea, 27, 246, 252. *See also* Korea
North-south, as world division, 171–172, 243, 295
North-West Frontier Province, 94
Norway, 176
Nuclear power, 133

OAS. *See* Organization of American States
OAU. *See* Organization of African Unity
O'Brien, Richard, 284
Oceans, 12, 129
sovereignty over, 94–98, 217–219
OECD. *See* Organization for Economic Cooperation and Development
OEEC. *See* Organization of European Economic Cooperation
Ogata, Sadako, 184, 197
Oil, geopolitics of, 134, 136, 137
Okinawa, 37
Onondaga Nation, 232
Ontario, 37
OPEC. *See* Organization of Petroleum Exporting Countries
Oppenheim, Robert, 73
Organization for Economic Cooperation and Development (OECD), 172

Organization of African Unity (OAU), 80, 90, 264
Organization of American States (OAS), 264
Organization of European Economic Cooperation (OEEC), 264
Organization of Petroleum Exporting Countries (OPEC), 134, 264, 273, 285, 292, 293
*Origin of The Species* (Darwin), 5
O'Riordan, Timothy, 147
Oromo people, 44
Ortelius, Abraham, 51
Ottoman Empire, division of, 7, 90, 92
Overlooked Opinions, 309
Ozone layer, 12, 63, 138, 141, 171

Pacific region, 186
Pacific Rim, 37
Pakistan, 8, 22, 44, 94, 239, 264
migration to, 192, 202
Palau, 262
Palestine, 73, 246
Palestine Liberation Organization, 213, 246
Palestinians, as stateless nation, 12
Panama, and United States, 250
Panama Canal, 31
Papuans, 44
Patents, 25, 276–277
PBS. *See* Public Broadcasting Service
Peace of Westphalia, 210, 224
PEMEX Company, 125
People, as term, 9, 74, 226–227, 229, 230
People's Republic of China, 35–36. *See also* China
Perez de Cuellar, Javíer, 249
Persian Gulf, 8, 21, 28, 172, 258
Persian Gulf War, 7–8, 21, 34, 35, 91, 92, 200, 216, 296
and oil, 8, 10, 137
and United Nations, 7, 247–250, 252–255, 258
Peru, 28, 215–216, 218
Peters, Arno, 54, 63
Peters projection, 54, 63–64, 67(n18), 69(n56), 70(n57)
Philippines, 8, 28, 44, 96

Pitcairn Island, 261
Political geography, 3–6, 8–13, 304
information in, 301–303, 310, 311, 321, 321(n4)
*See also* Geopolitics
Political parties, 102, 192
and gerrymandering, 105–106, 108–113, 115, 116, 119
Political representation, 102–104, 107–110, 117
urban versus rural, 103, 104, 107, 113, 119
Political science, term misuse in, 226
*Politische Geographie* (Ratzel), 5
Pollution, 125, 129–130, 133, 138, 169–171. *See also* Environment, degradation of
Polyocracy, 23
Population
as criteria, 72–75, 78–81, 84, 107, 108, 116
and developing countries, 180–181, 182
distribution of, 179, 180, 182–183, 188–189, 194
and environment, 135, 182, 186
growth problem of, 179–182, 188–189, 189(n1)
and morbidity, 184–186
Portugal, 81, 229
Ptolemy, Claudius, 56
Public Broadcasting Service (PBS), 309–310
Puerto Rico, 45
Pushtans, migration of, 192

Quartersphere of strategic marginality, 31–32
Quebec, 37, 43, 81, 239

RAAN. *See* Región Autónoma del Atlántico Norte
Race, and gerrymandering, 104, 106–108, 110–111, 115, 117, 119
Radiation, exposure to, 170
Radio Free Europe, 313
Rain forests, 138
Rapport, Richard, 156
Ratzel, Friedrich, 3, 4–6, 7, 10, 90, 136
Ravenstein, E. G., 194
Ravetz, Jerome, 147, 148
Rayner, Steve, 147

Reagan, Ronald, 61, 289
Realms, as spatial category, 28–30, 32, 34, 38, 39, 46
Red Cross, 197
Refugees, 75
    United Nations aid to, 193, 197, 200, 202, 204, 248, 249, 253
Regionalism, rise of, 217
Región Autónoma del Atlántico Norte (RAAN), 236
Regions
    development of, 21–23, 25
    geopolitical, 28–32, 34, 38–39, 41, 44, 46
Reich, Robert, 10
Republican party (United States), 102, 104, 105, 111, 115
*Reynolds* v. *Sims,* 104
Rhine, 129
Rhône-Alps, 222
Rio Conference on Environment and Development, 182, 188, 261
Rio Declaration on Environment and Development, 177(n3)
*Rise and Fall of Great Powers* (Kennedy), 6
Rivera, Brooklyn, 231
Robinson, Arthur, 54, 64, 67(n18)
Robinson projection, 64, 70(n58)
Romania, 27, 90, 311
Rosecrance, Richard, 38
Rushdie, Salman, 310
Russia, 16, 20, 38, 215, 239
    People's Congress of Deputies of, 102
    pollution in, 176, 212
    as power center, 29, 31, 32, 34, 36, 41, 44–45, 46
    and United Nations, 248, 259

Saharawi Republic, 234, 238
Salt-water theory, 79–80
Sandinistas, 234, 237
San Marino, 7, 246
*Satanic Verses* (Rushdie), 310
Saudi Arabia, 21, 27, 92, 94, 219
Scandinavia, 102. *See also individual countries*
Scotland, 37, 82
Seas. *See* Oceans

SEATO. *See* Southeast Asia Treaty Organization
Secession, from states, 79–80, 81, 82
Second World, communication in, 310, 311, 315, 317
Self-determination, 81, 230–231, 237, 241–242, 246
    and territorial claims, 79–80, 82, 83, 213
Serbia, 43
Serbs, 91, 188, 257
Shafer, Boyd C., 71, 78
Shan people, 44
Shatterbelts, 28, 32, 34, 39
*Shaw* v. *Reno,* 117
Sheba, 38
Shell Corporation, 134, 136
Shiites, Iraqi abuses of, 220
Sikhs, 246
Simon, Julian, 180
Singapore, 20, 25, 34, 180, 287
Single European Act, 221
Sinkiang, 37
Six Nations Confederacy. *See* Haudenosaunee Confederacy
SLCMs. *See* Submarine-launched cruise missiles
Slovenia, 41, 43, 45, 80, 83, 257
Smith, Adam, 20
Smith, David, 303
Smith, Robert, 144
Somalia, 10, 91, 157, 184, 197–199
    United Nations in, 247, 249, 253, 255–256, 258, 260, 267(n5)
South Africa, 30, 31, 44, 125, 264, 282
    sanctions against, 219
    state of, 27, 78, 239
    and United Nations, 246, 258
South America, 18–19, 25, 28, 30–32. *See also individual countries*
Southeast Asia Treaty Organization (SEATO), 252
South Korea, 27, 37, 246, 252, 287. *See also* Korea
Sovereignty, 10–12, 84, 92, 219–221
    and international law, 209–217, 223–224
    over oceans, 95–98, 217–219
    and self-determination, 79–80

as state criteria, 72, 75–76, 82, 83–84
and United Nations intervention, 84, 246–249, 266
Soviet Russian heartland, as geopolitical region, 28, 31, 34, 46
Soviet Union, 8, 22, 25, 186, 219, 247, 266
and Afghanistan, 19, 192, 238
boundaries in, 90, 91, 98
breakup of, 6–7, 10, 20, 29, 80, 87, 90, 91, 200, 296
communication in, 310, 311
economy of, 172, 296
emigration from, 184, 188
environment in, 33, 125, 132, 133, 138, 169–170
intervention in, 182, 247
map of, 57, 58
nations in, 239
as super power, 22, 211, 283, 291
and United Nations, 243, 246, 249–252
and United States 5, 18, 57, 293
Space, in political geography, 11
Spain, 136, 222
Spatial analysis, 4, 5
Spatial determinism, 16
Spencer, Herbert, 22
*Spycatcher,* 310
Spykman, Nicholas John, 3, 29
Sri Lanka, 8, 22, 212, 238
Stalin, Joseph, 22
START II agreement, 5
State, 6, 9, 11–12, 90, 92
breakdown of, 238–239
and colonialism, 211
criteria for, 72–76, 78–85
development of, 72, 79–81, 83, 87, 211, 238
in Fourth World analysis, 228, 230
geopolitical orders of, 26–27
group identities in, 74–75, 78–83, 231, 232
ideology in, 76, 77, 78
information role of, 302, 304–309, 310–311, 320, 321
in international relations, 211–213, 214, 216–217, 223–224
language of, 229–232
and nations, 12, 74–75, 78–83, 227–240

as polluter, 169–170, 239–241
reach of, 25–27
recognition of, 72, 75–76, 82
secession from, 79–80, 81, 82
sovereignty of. *See* Sovereignty
as term, 85(n2), 226, 227
territory of, 72–73, 76–80, 84
as text, 303–306
Stowe, Harriet Beecher, 304
Strauz-Hupe, Robert, 17
Streit, Clarence, 19
Submarine-launched cruise missiles (SLCMs), 57
Sudan, 27, 184, 202, 248
Suez Canal, 31, 253
Sulu people, 44
Sustainable development, 138–139, 174, 177(n4), 182
Switzerland, 129, 295
and United Nations, 246, 263
Symbols, political use of, 57–58, 63, 305–306
Syria, 21, 34, 129

Taiwan, 27, 37, 287
Tamil Eelam, 39
Tanzania, 27, 32, 296
Taylor, Peter, 44
Technology, 3, 5, 13, 132–133
and information, 302, 303, 309–311, 314, 315, 320
Territory, 20, 77, 80, 84, 136–137
and group identities, 77–83
in international law, 213–216
sea limit to, 95–98
sovereignty over. *See* Sovereignty
and state development, 38, 39, 43, 72–73, 76–80, 84
*See also* Deterritorialization
Terrorism, 12, 84
Texas, 37
Thailand, 27, 34, 187
Third World, 16, 31, 63, 186, 192, 240–241
communication in, 310, 315, 318
development in, 72, 79, 286–287, 295, 297
and environmental issues, 171, 174

population growth in, 180, 183
*See also* Developing countries
Thirty Years' War, 210
Three Worlds idea, 287
Tiananmen Square massacre, 310
Tibet, 37, 228, 247
Tilly, Charles, 233
*Times Atlas of China,* 228
Tito, Josef, 23, 256, 257
Togo, 215
Toynbee, Arnold, 238
Trade, 281–284, 290–294
   illicit, 294, 295
   and United States economy, 271, 272,
      273–275, 277
Transnational corporations. *See*
   Multinational corporations
Transnationalism, 16
Treaty on the Final Settlement with
   Respect to Germany, 6
Trieste, 38
Tunisia, 27
Turkey, 27, 34, 219, 264, 293
Tyre, 38

Uganda, 187
Ukraine, 36, 37, 83, 241
UN. *See* United Nations
UNCED. *See* United Nations, Conference
   on Environment and Development
UNEF. *See* United Nations, Emergency
   Force
UNEP. *See* United Nations, Environmental
   Programme
UNFPA. *See* United Nations, Fund for
   Population Activities
UNHCR. *See* United Nations, High
   Commission for Refugees
UNIKOM. *See* United Nations, Iraq-
   Kuwait Observation Mission
United Kingdom, 37, 107, 136–137, 220, 287,
   310
   as global hegemony, 282–283, 290
   and United Nations, 218, 251
   *See also* England
United Nations (UN), 4, 12, 19, 63, 196, 295
   alignment in, 243–244, 266

bureacracy of, 245
Charter of, 74, 211, 244, 246–247, 249,
   251–252, 257, 260, 265
and colonialism, 261–262
Conference on Environment and
   Development (UNCED), 170–173, 176,
   177(n3)
conferences of, 260–261. *See also*
   *individual conferences*
Convention on the Law of the Sea (LOS
   Convention), 95, 96, 98, 218, 244
Covenant of Civil and Political Rights,
   74
Covenant of Economic, Social and
   Cultural Rights, 74
Department of Public Information
   (DPI), 265
and developing countries, 243–244, 249,
   251, 261, 286
Development Programme of, 311
Economic and Social Council
   (ECOSOC) of, 244, 265
Emergency Force (UNEF), 253
Environmental Programme (UNEP),
   143, 149
and environmental treaties, 130
Framework Convention on Biodiversity,
   177(n3)
Framework Convention on Climate
   Change, 177(n3)
Fund for Population Activities
   (UNFPA), 182
future of, 244, 265–266
General Assembly of, 243–244, 252, 253,
   258
High Commission for Refugees
   (UNHCR), 184, 193, 197, 248, 253, 263
and human rights, 188, 219, 231, 247–248,
   262
Human Rights Conference (Vienna,
   1993), 262
Human Rights Sub-Commission, 231
and international law, 248–249
intervention by, 7–8, 258, 260–262, 296
Iraq-Kuwait Boundary Demarcation
   Commission, 253, 255

Iraq-Kuwait Observation Mission
(UNIKOM), 253
membership in, 246, 263
and minorities, 231, 248
Monetary and Financial Conference. *See*
Bretton Woods agreements
and non-governmental organizations,
264
peace-building role of, 258–260, 266,
267(n5)
peace-keeping missions of, 249, 251–258
Population Fund, 263
and population issues, 182, 184
refugee aid of, 193, 197, 200, 202, 204,
248, 249, 253
Security Council of, 19, 244, 247–252,
256–260, 266
Security Council Resolution 688, 220,
247, 259–260
and self-determination, 80, 213, 230, 246
and state sovereignty, 84, 246–249, 266
Transitional Authority in Cambodia
(UNTAC), 255
*See also individual countries,* and United
Nations
United States, 19, 90, 135, 264, 272, 320
acquired immunodeficiency syndrome
in, 186–187
Agency for International Development
(USAID), 181
census of, 103, 114–116
in Cold War era, 5, 17–18, 307
Constitution of, 103, 107
deficit of, 276, 289–290, 293
as economic center, 273–278, 281–285,
287–294, 297
economic decline of, 287–290, 292, 293,
294
economy of, 269, 270–278
electoral system in, 101–104, 104, 110–112,
115–116, 119
and environment, 125, 129, 133, 135–136,
139, 169, 172, 176
expansionism of, 59, 217
and foreign trade, 271–275, 277, 283–284
as geopolitical center, 22, 25, 28, 31, 32,
34–37, 45, 46

global hegemony of, 269, 270, 277–278,
281, 283, 291, 292, 294
gross national product of, 271, 276
Immigration Reform and Control Act of
1986, 192
immigration to, 183–184, 192
income in, 269, 270–272, 275
and maps, 59–62, 66(n10), 68(n39),
69(n47), 307, 311–312
military of, 272, 277, 293–294
and multilateralism, 247, 250, 252, 293,
294, 296
and New World Order, 269, 270, 278, 281
in political discourse, 304–305
population aid of, 181–182
redistricting in, 103, 104, 107–117
and United Nations, 218, 243, 244, 246,
249–250, 259
*See also individual countries,* and United
States
Universal Declaration of Human Rights,
219, 262
UNPROFOR, 257
UNTAC. *See* United Nations, Transitional
Authority in Cambodia
Uranium, 133
USAID. *See* United States, Agency for
International Development

Van der Grinten projection, 64
Venezuela, 23, 30, 45, 46, 214
Venice, 38
Vietnam, 22, 34, 39, 243, 273
and Cambodia, 27, 255
Vietnam War, 18, 19
Virgin Islands, 262
Vitoria, Francisco de, 210
Voice of America, 313
Voting, and districting, 106, 109. *See also*
Electoral districts
Voting Rights Act (VRA), 104, 107, 117
VRA. *See* Voting Rights Act

Waldseemüller, Martin, 51
Wallerstein, Immanuel, 21
Waloonia, 43

Wars, 84, 237, 303
  over natural resources, 123, 125, 135–138
  territorial, 77, 80, 84, 213–219
Warsaw Pact, breakup of, 45
Washington, George, 59
Water, as natural resource, 125, 129, 137
Wells, H. G., 19
Werner, Heinz, 22
Western Sahara, 91, 258
West European Union, 45
West Irian, 44, 80
West Papuan nation, 234
Wilkes, Charles, 59
Wood, Denis, 58
Wood, William, 144
*Work of Nations* (Reich), 10
World
  economy of. *See* Economy
  integration trend in, 21, 28, 44, 46
  north-south alignment of, 243
  order of, 281, 297–298. *See also* New
    World Order
  political map of, 44, 87, 98, 223
  as system, 16, 20–23, 25, 31, 35–46
World Bank, 186, 283, 287, 290–292, 295,
  296
World Commission on Environment and
  Development, 141, 146, 174, 177(n4)
World Court, 259

*World Development Report* (World Bank),
  287
World Health Organization, 186, 263
World Hunger Program, 186
World Population Conference (1994), 182
World Population Plan of Action, 181
World Summit for Children, 260
World War I, 136–137, 282–283, 303
  and states, 72, 79, 136–137, 211
World War II era, 136–137, 303
  economy during, 272–273, 274, 283–284
  states in, 72, 79, 81, 90, 136–137, 238

Yemen, 10, 94, 243
Young, Oran, 149
Yugoslavia, 6, 7, 27, 36, 219
  boundaries of, 90
  breakup of, 20, 80, 188, 200, 256–257
  emigration from, 184, 188, 197, 202
  human rights abuses in, 10, 197–198
  intervention in, 216, 223, 256–258
  Muslims in, 188, 198, 257
  and United Nations, 247, 249, 251, 253,
    256–258, 260

Zaire, 27, 44
Zambia, 187
Zanzibar, 38
Zimbabwe, 27